Published by Vision Sports Publishing in 2012
Vision Sports Publishing
19-23 High Street
Kingston upon Thames
Surrey
KT1 1LL

www.visionsp.co.uk

© Clive Batty

ISBN: 978-1907637-80-3

Editor: Jim Drewett
Copy editor: Alex Morton
Design: Neal Cobourne
Kit images: David Moor, www.historicalkits.co.uk
All pictures: Getty Images

gettyimages®

Printed and bound in Slovakia by Neografia
A CIP catalogue record for this book is available from the British Library

All statistics in the *Vision Book of Football Records 2013* are correct up until the start of the 2012/13 season

INTRODUCTION

Welcome to the 2013 edition of the Vision Book of Football Records. Now, we all know that the world of football is a fast-moving one both on and off the pitch, but some of the changes that have taken place in the 12 months since the previous edition of this book appeared on the shelves have been truly jaw-dropping. Who, for instance, would have imagined back then that Harry Redknapp, the overwhelming favourite to succeed Fabio Capello as England manager, would not only be overlooked for that plum job but would also be unceremoniously booted out of his White Hart Lane office soon afterwards? Or, to take another striking example, how many fans would have predicted that Chelsea, while stumbling along to their worst ever finish in the Premier League since Roman Abramovich bought the Blues in 2003, would go on to win the Champions League for the first time in the club's history in a dramatic final in Munich? And surely not even Nostradamus himself could have foreseen the incredible, and really rather sad, decline of once-mighty Rangers: the most decorated club in world football and SPL champions as recently as 2011, the Gers kicked off the 2012/13 season

in the fourth tier of Scottish football alongside the likes of Annan Athletic, East Stirling and Elgin City. Minnows? Those teams aren't even krill! Crazy stuff or, as rapper and Crystal Palace fan Dizzee Rascal might put it, 'Bonkers'!

All these, and the many other changes that have taken place on Planet Football over the last year, are reflected in the pages that follow. As well as updating all the facts, figures, stats and records, loads of new entries have been added for the players, managers and clubs who came to the fore during the course of the last season. Meanwhile, a handful of older players who, quite frankly, have seen much better days have been given the chop to make way for the new generation. At this point, I can imagine beads of cold sweat appearing on the foreheads of some well-known Premier League names as they wonder 'Am I still in? Please, please, let me still be in!' Well, lads, here's a handy hint: all the entries are in alphabetical order, so it shouldn't take you long to find out whether or not you've made the cut.

In addition to mini-profiles of the top Premier League stars, this book also contains key stats and facts about

all 92 English league clubs, the 12 SPL clubs (plus Queen's Park, a dominant force in the early years of the game in Scotland and, of course, poor old Rangers), and the most noteworthy clubs in continental Europe. Then there are entries for the leading current world superstars such as Lionel Messi, Cristiano Ronaldo and Neymar, and the great icons of yesteryear, including the likes of Maradona, Matthews and Moore.

You'll also find loads of info on the top football nations, the main domestic and international competitions and 'wild card' entries on a range of different subjects such as 'Age' (did you know that the youngest player ever to appear in a World Cup qualifier was just 13?), 'Ballboys' (get the lowdown on the Brazilian ballgirl who became an overnight celebrity after helping her team score a goal), 'Chants' (find out which Premier League club's fans are the loudest) and 'Numbers' (discover what is the highest number ever worn in a professional football match).

All in all, there should be enough here to keep you occupied during those rare moments when there's no football on the telly or, if you're Harry Redknapp, until the phone rings and another lucrative Premier League job offer comes your way.

CLIVE BATTY

ABANDONED MATCHES

Only three England internationals have been abandoned. The first, against Argentina in Buenos Aires on 17th May 1953, was called off after 21 minutes when torrential rain made the pitch unplayable. The second, against Czechoslovakia in Bratislava on 29th October 1975, was abandoned after 16 minutes due to fog but was played in full the following evening with the home side winning 2-1. Then, on 15th March 1995, crowd trouble brought England's match against Ireland in Dublin to a premature halt after 27 minutes.

• The shortest-ever English game took place in 1894, when a raging blizzard caused the match between Stoke and Wolves at the Victoria Ground to be called off after just three minutes. Only 400 hardy fans had braved the elements, and even they must have been secretly relieved when referee Mr Helme decided the atrocious conditions made any further play impossible.

• A First Division match between Mexican sides Santos Laguna and Monarcas Morelia on 21th August 2011 had to be called off five minutes before half time when a fierce gun battle broke out in the street outside the stadium, the sound of shots being fired sending players running to their dressing rooms and fans diving for cover. One policeman was injured in the incident, which began when armed men travelling in a convoy of vehicles started shooting at a security checkpoint.

• Bulgarian sides Balkan Belogradchik and Gigant Belene played the shortest match ever on 28th March 2010. Gigant started four players short, but when one of their number limped off after a minute the ref had to abandon the match, as the rules state that teams must field at least seven players.

ABERDEEN

Year founded: 1903
Ground: Pittodrie Stadium (22,199)
Nickname: The Dons
Biggest win: 13-0 v Peterhead (1923)
Heaviest defeat: 0-9 v Celtic (2010)

Aberdeen were founded in 1903, following the amalgamation of three city clubs, Aberdeen, Orion and Victoria United. The following year the club joined the Scottish Second Division, and in 1905 the Dons were elected to an expanded First Division. Aberdeen have remained in the top flight ever since, a record shared with just Rangers and Celtic.

• The club was originally known as the Whites and later as the Wasps or the Black and Golds after their early strips, but in 1913 became known as the Dons. This nickname is sometimes said to derive from the involvement of professors at Aberdeen University in the foundation of the club, but is more likely to be a contraction of the word 'Aberdonians', the term used to describe people from Aberdeen.

• Aberdeen first won the Scottish title in 1955, before enjoying a trio of championship successes in the 1980s under manager Alex Ferguson. Before he moved on to even greater triumphs at Old Trafford, Fergie also led the Dons to four victories in five years in the Scottish Cup, which included a record run of 20 cup games without defeat between 1982-85.

• The club's finest hour, though, came in 1983 when the Dons became only the second Scottish club (after Rangers in 1972) to win the European Cup Winners' Cup, beating Real Madrid 2-1 in the final. Later that year Aberdeen defeated Hamburg over two legs to claim the European Super Cup and remain the only Scottish side to win two European trophies.

• In 1984 Aberdeen became the first club outside the Old Firm to win the Double, after finishing seven points clear at the top of the league and beating Celtic 2-1 in the Scottish Cup final.

• Since those glory days, however, the club's fortunes have nosedived. Trophyless since the 1995/96 season, Aberdeen's fortunes reached an all-time low in November 2010 when they were hammered 9-0 by Celtic, the worst result in their history and the heaviest defeat in the SPL since the foundation of the league in 1998.

• Scottish international defender Willie Miller has made more appearances for the club than any other player, an impressive 556 games between 1973 and 1990. Hotshot striker Joe Harper is the Dons' record goalscorer, with 205 during two spells at Pittodrie (1969-72 and 1976-81).

• Aberdeen's most-capped player is Miller's long-time defensive partner and former Aston Villa boss Alex McLeish, who made 77 appearances for Scotland between 1977 and 1990.

• Famed as one of the coldest grounds in Britain, Pittodrie Stadium can claim two historic 'firsts'. In the 1920s it became the first ground to have dug-outs installed, following a request by innovative team coach Donald Coleman. Then, in 1978, Pittodrie became Britain's first-ever all-seater stadium.

HONOURS
Division 1 champions *1955*
Premier Division champions *1980, 1984, 1985*
Scottish Cup *1947, 1970, 1982, 1983, 1984, 1986, 1990*
League Cup *1956, 1977, 1986, 1990, 1996*
European Cup Winners' Cup *1983*
European Super Cup *1983*

ROMAN ABRAMOVICH

Born: Saratov, Russia, 24th October 1966

Chelsea owner Roman Abramovich has a fortune estimated at £8 billion and, since buying the Blues from previous owner Ken Bates in July 2003, he has invested hundreds of millions in the club in an attempt to establish the west Londoners as a dominant force in the English and European game. In January 2011 he provided the funds that allowed Chelsea

---

IS THAT A FACT?
The FA Cup quarter-final tie between Tottenham Hotspur and Bolton at White Hart Lane on 17th March 2012 was abandoned in the first half when Trotters midfielder Fabrice Muamba collapsed after suffering a cardiac arrest. Despite his heart stopping for 78 minutes during the incident, Muamba made a remarkable recovery and was able to leave hospital a month later.

Roman Abramovich: £8 billion fortune, £9.99 shirt

to break the British transfer record, when the Blues splashed out £50 million on Liverpool striker Fernando Torres.

• Abramovich's massive spending spree has been rewarded with three league titles and six domestic cups, including the Double in 2010. For many years his burning ambition to see Chelsea win the Champions League

Robinho prays that AC Milan can add to their 18 Serie A titles

was frustrated – a failure which led Abramovich to sack a number of his managers – but the Blues finally managed to lift the biggest prize of all in 2012 following a dramatic penalty shoot-out against Bayern Munich.

• After starting out selling retread car tyres, Abramovich's business career took off when he began trading oil products out of Russia's largest refinery in western Siberia. He gradually acquired a controlling interest in Sibneft, the country's main oil company, before selling his share to the Russian government-controlled Gazprom for an eye-watering £7.4 billion in 2005.

• Abramovich enjoys a lifestyle befitting his billionaire status, owning a number of luxury homes, three yachts and a private Boeing 737 jet.

AC MILAN

Year founded: 1899
Ground: San Siro (80,018)
Nickname: Rossoneri
League titles: 18
Domestic cups: 5
European cups: 14
International cups: 4

One of the giants of European football, the club was founded by British expatriates as the Milan Cricket and Football Club in 1899. Apart from a period during the fascist dictatorship of Benito Mussolini, the club has always been known as 'Milan' rather than the Italian 'Milano'.

• **Milan were the first Italian side to win the European Cup, beating Benfica in the final at Wembley in 1963, and have gone on to win the trophy seven times – a record surpassed only by Real Madrid, with nine victories.**

• In 1986 the club was acquired by the businessman and future Italian President Silvio Berlusconi, who invested in star players like Marco van Basten, Ruud Gullit and

Frank Rijkaard. Milan went on to enjoy a golden era under coaches Arrigo Sacchi and Fabio Capello, winning three European Cups and four Serie A titles between 1988 and 1994. Incredibly, the club were undefeated for 58 games between 1991 and 1993, the third-longest such run in top-flight European football history behind Celtic (62 games) and Steaua Bucharest (104 games).

• Milan's San Siro stadium, which they share with city rivals Inter, is the largest in Italy, with a capacity of over 80,000. As well as football, the stadium has hosted many pop concerts and in November 2009 was the venue for a rugby international between Italy and the All Blacks which attracted a crowd of 81,018 – a record for Italian rugby.

• Milan's links with Britain have continued into the modern era with a number of stars from these shores, including Jimmy Greaves, Ray Wilkins and David Beckham, having spells with the Italian titans.

HONOURS
Serie A champions 1901, 1906, 1907, 1951, 1955, 1957, 1959, 1962, 1968, 1979, 1988, 1992, 1993, 1994, 1996, 1999, 2004, 2011
Italian Cup 1967, 1972, 1973, 1977, 2003
European Cup/Champions League 1963, 1969, 1989, 1990, 1994, 2003, 2007
European Cup Winners' Cup 1968, 1973
European Super Cup 1989, 1990, 1994, 2003, 2007
Intercontinental Cup 1969, 1989, 1990
Club World Cup 2007

ACCRINGTON STANLEY

Year founded: 1968
Ground: Crown Ground (5,057)
Nickname: The Stans
Biggest win: 10-1 v Lincoln United (1999)
Heaviest defeat: 2-8 v Peterborough (2008)

Accrington Stanley were founded at a meeting in a working men's club in Accrington in 1968, as a successor to the former Football League club of the same name which had folded two years earlier.

• Conference champions in 2006, Stanley were promoted to the Football League in place of relegated Oxford United. Ironically, when a financial crisis forced the old Accrington Stanley to resign from the League in March 1962 the club that replaced them the following season was Oxford!

• In 2010 Stanley reached the fourth round of the FA Cup for only the fourth time in their history. However, their hopes of making a first-ever appearance in the fifth round were dashed by Fulham, who won the tie 3-1.

• The original town club, Accrington, were one of the 12 founder members of the Football League in 1888 but resigned from the League after just five years.

• With a capacity of just 5,057, the club's Crown Ground is the third smallest in the Football League.

> HONOURS
> *Conference champions 2006*

IS THAT A FACT?
For the first time since 1965 the Africa Cup of Nations will be held in an odd year in 2013 in South Africa. The switch from even years was made to prevent the tournament being played in a World Cup year.

Zambia celebrate their surprise triumph in the Africa Cup of Nations in 2012

AFC WIMBLEDON

Year founded: 2002
Ground: The Fans' Stadium, Kingsmeadow (4,850)
Nickname: The Dons
Biggest win: 9-0 v Chessington United (2004) and v Slough Town (2007)
Heaviest defeat: 0-5 v York City (2010)

AFC Wimbledon were founded in 2002 by supporters of the former Premiership club Wimbledon, who opposed the decision of the FA to sanction the 'franchising' of their club when they allowed it to move 56 miles north from their south London base to Milton Keynes in Buckinghamshire (the club later becoming the MK Dons).

• In October 2006 an agreement was reached with the MK Dons that the honours won by the old Wimbledon would return to the London Borough of Merton. This was an important victory for the fans of AFC, who view their club as the true successors to Wimbledon FC.

• In their former incarnation, Wimbledon won the FA Cup in 1988, beating hot favourites Liverpool 1-0 at Wembley. Incredibly, the Dons had only been elected to the Football League just 12 years earlier, but enjoyed a remarkable rise through the divisions, winning promotion to the top flight in 1986. Dubbed the 'Crazy Gang' for their physical approach on the pitch and madcap antics off it, Wimbledon remained in the Premiership until 2000.

• After rising through the non-league pyramid, AFC beat Luton Town on penalties in the 2011 Conference play-off final at Eastlands, securing a place in the Football League just nine years after their formation.

• With a capacity of just 4,850, the club's tiny Kingsmeadow stadium is the smallest in the Football League.

> HONOURS
> *Division 4 champions 1983 (As Wimbledon FC)*
> *FA Cup 1988 (As Wimbledon FC)*
> *FA Amateur Cup 1963 (As Wimbledon FC)*

AFRICA CUP OF NATIONS

The Africa Cup of Nations was founded in 1957. The first tournament was a decidedly small affair consisting of just three competing teams (Egypt, Ethiopia

and hosts Sudan) after South Africa's invitation was withdrawn when they refused to send a multi-racial squad to the finals. Egypt were the first winners, beating Ethiopia 4-0 in the final in Khartoum.

• With seven victories, Egypt are the most successful side in the history of the competition. After triumphing in Angola in 2010 following a 1-0 victory over Ghana in the final, the north Africans claimed a record three consecutive trophies. However, Ghana were the first country to win the tournament three times and, following their third success in 1978, were allowed to keep the original Abdel Abdullah Salem Trophy, named after the first president of the Confederation of African Football.

• The final has been decided on penalties on seven occasions, with Ivory Coast winning the longest shoot-out 11-10 against Ghana in 1992.

• The top scorer in the history of the competition is Cameroon striker Samuel Eto'o, who has hit a total of 18 goals in the tournament to date. Mulamba Ndaye of Zaire holds the record for the most goals in a single tournament, with nine in 1974.

• Egypt and Ghana have each hosted the tournament on a record four occasions.

AFRICAN FOOTBALLER OF THE YEAR

The African Footballer of the Year award was established by the Confederation of African Football in 1992, Nigerian striker Rashidi Yekini topping the first poll the following year.

• Cameroon legend Samuel Eto'o has won the award a record four times, including an unprecedented hat-trick between 2003 and 2005. Three other players have won the award twice: Kanu (1996 and 1999), El Hadji Diouf (2001 and 2002) and Didier Drogba (2006 and 2009).

• The first Premier League-based player to win the award was Arsenal striker Kanu in 1999. Since then the poll has been topped five more times by a player from these shores, with Manchester City midfielder Yaya Toure heading the list in 2011.

• Players from eight different African countries have won the award, with Nigeria and Cameroon (five wins each) enjoying the most success.

AGE

Legendary winger Sir Stanley Matthews is the oldest player to appear in the top flight of English football. 'The Ageless Wonder' had celebrated his 50th birthday five days before playing his last match for Stoke against Fulham in February 1965.

• Matthews, though, was something of a spring chicken compared to Neil McBain, the New Brighton manager, who had to go in goal for his side's Division Three (North) match against Hartlepool during an injury crisis in 1947. He was 51 and 120 days at the time, the oldest player in the history of English football.

• Manchester City goalkeeper John Burridge became the oldest player in the Premiership when he came off the bench at half-time in City's match against Newcastle in April 1995, aged 43. The youngest player is Fulham's Matthew Briggs, who was aged 16 years and 65 days when he made his debut for the Cottagers against Middlesbrough in May 2007.

• The oldest international in British football was Wales's Billy Meredith, who played against England in 1920 at the age of 45. England's youngest international is Arsenal winger Theo Walcott, who was 17 years and 75 days when he played as a sub in the 3-1 victory over Hungary at Old Trafford in May 2006.

TOP 10

YOUNGEST ENGLAND PLAYERS

1. Theo Walcott (2006) 17 years and 75 days
2. Wayne Rooney (2003) 17 years and 111 days
3. James Prinsep (1879) 17 years and 252 days
4. Thurston Rostron (1881) 17 years and 311 days
5. Clement Mitchell (1880) 18 years and 23 days
6. Michael Owen (1998) 18 years and 60 days
7. Micah Richards (2006) 18 years and 144 days
8. Duncan Edwards (1955) 18 years and 183 days
9. James Brown (1881) 18 years and 210 days
10. Jack Wilshere (2010) 18 years and 223 days

Source: www.englandfootballonline.com

• The youngest goalscorer in the history of the Football League is Bristol Rovers' Ronnie Dix who was aged just 15 years and 180 days when he netted in a 3-0 win against Norwich City in 1928.

• According to official FIFA records, Souleymane Maman of Togo became the youngest player ever to appear in a World Cup qualifier when he came on as a sub against Zambia on 6th May 2001, aged 13 years and 310 days. Other sources, however, suggest that he was nearly 16 at the time.

• The youngest player to appear for a professional team anywhere in the world is Mauricio Baldivieso, who was three days short of his 13th birthday when he came on as a substitute in the Bolivian First Division for Aurora FC on 19th July 2009. "I am the happiest man in the world," he said after his nine-minute cameo against La Paz FC.

• In April 2011 18-month-old Baerke van der Meij became the youngest ever child to be signed by a professional club when he was given a 10-year 'symbolic contract' with Dutch outfit VVV Venlo. The club were impressed by young Baerke's potential after watching an impressive short video posted by his father on YouTube, showing the toddler expertly chipping three balls into a toy box, one after another.

SERGIO AGUERO

Born: Quilmes, Argentina, 2nd June 1988
Position: Striker
Club career:
2003-06 Independiente 54 (23)
2006-11 Atletico Madrid 175 (74)
2011- Manchester City 34 (23)
International record:
2006- Argentina 37 (15)

Sergio Aguero, Manchester City's record signing

The second most-expensive player in British football history, Sergio Aguero joined Manchester City from Atletico Madrid for £38 million in July 2011. The fee proved to be a bargain as Aguero banged in 23 Premier League goals in his first season at the club – a total only surpassed by Robin van Persie and Wayne Rooney – including a dramatic last-minute winner against QPR which clinched City's first title since 1968.

• Known as 'El Kun' because of his resemblance to a Japanese cartoon character, Kum Kum, Aguero became the youngest-ever player to appear in Argentina's top flight when he made his debut for Independiente in 2003 aged just 15 years and 35 days. The previous record was set by the legendary Diego Maradona, who is now Aguero's father-in-law.

• In 2006, when still only aged 17, Aguero moved to Atletico where he formed prolific partnerships with Fernando Torres and, later, Diego Forlan. His best moment with the club came in 2010 when he helped Atletico win the inaugural Europa League, following a 2-1 defeat of Fulham in the final.

• A quicksilver striker with superb close control, Aguero made his international debut for Argentina in 2006 against Brazil at Arsenal's Emirates Stadium. He had previously won the FIFA Under-20 World Cup with his country in 2005, a feat he repeated in 2007 when he also collected the competition's Golden Boot. The following year he was a key figure in the Argentina side that won Gold at the Beijing Olympics.

AIR CRASHES

On 6th February 1958 eight members of the Manchester United 'Busby Babes' team, including England internationals Roger Byrne, Duncan Edwards and Tommy Taylor, were killed in the Munich Air Crash. Their plane crashed while attempting to take off in a snowstorm at Munich Airport, where it had stopped to refuel after a European Cup tie in Belgrade. In total, 23 people died in the crash, although manager Matt Busby and Bobby Charlton were among the survivors. Amazingly, United still managed to reach the FA Cup final that year, but lost at Wembley to Bolton Wanderers.

• The entire first team of Torino, the strongest Italian club at the time, were wiped out in an air disaster on 4th May 1949. Returning from a testimonial match in Portugal, the team's plane crashed into the Basilica of Superga outside Turin. Among the 31 dead were 10 members of the Italian national side and the club's English manager, Leslie Lievesley. Torino fielded their youth team in their four remaining fixtures and, with their opponents doing the same as a mark of respect, won a fifth consecutive league title at the end of the season.

• On 28th April 1993 a plane crash off the coast of Gabon claimed the lives of 18 members of the Zambia team. The squad was on its way to Senegal to play a World Cup qualifier.

AJAX

Year founded: 1900
Ground: Ajax ArenA (52,342)
Nickname: The Jews
League titles: 31
Domestic cups: 18
European cups: 8
International cups: 2

Founded in 1900 in Amsterdam, Ajax are named after the Greek mythological hero. The club is the most successful in Holland, having won the league a record 31 times, most recently in 2012, and the Dutch Cup a record 18 times.

• Ajax's white shirts with a broad vertical red stripe are among the most iconic in world football. However, the club's original kit was very different – an all-black outfit with a red sash tied around the players' waists.

• The Dutch side's most glorious decade was in the 1970s when, with a team

Ajax have been Dutch champions a record 31 times, most recently in 2012

TOP 10

GREATEST AJAX PLAYERS

1. Johan Cruyff (1964-73 & 1981-83)
2. Marco van Basten (1982-87)
3. Dennis Bergkamp (1986-93)
4. Frank Rijkaard (1980-87 & 1993-95)
5. Edwin Van der Sar (1990-99)
6. Michael Laudrup (1997-98)
7. Johnny Rep (1971-75)
8. Jari Litmanen (1992-99 & 2002-04)
9. Johan Neeskens (1970-74)
10. Wesley Sneijder (2002-07)

Poll on www.rankopedia.com

featuring legends like Johan Cruyff, Johan Neeskens and Johnny Rep, Ajax won the European Cup three times on the trot, playing a fluid system known as 'Total Football'. In 1995 a young Ajax team won the trophy for a fourth time, Patrick Kluivert scoring the winner in the final against AC Milan.

• **When Ajax beat Torino in the final of the UEFA Cup in 1992 they became only the second team, after Juventus, to win all three major European trophies.**

• Ajax moved into a brand new all-seater stadium, the Amsterdam ArenA, in 1996.

With a capacity in excess of 50,000, it is the largest football stadium in Holland.

HONOURS

Dutch League champions *1918, 1919, 1931, 1932, 1934, 1937, 1939, 1947, 1957, 1960, 1966, 1967, 1968, 1970, 1972, 1973, 1977, 1979, 1980, 1982, 1983, 1985, 1990, 1994, 1995, 1996, 1998, 2002, 2004, 2011, 2012*
Dutch Cup *1917, 1943, 1961, 1967, 1970, 1971, 1972, 1979, 1983, 1986, 1987, 1993, 1998, 1999, 2002, 2006, 2007, 2010*
European Cup/Champions League *1971, 1972, 1973, 1995*
European Cup Winners' Cup *1987*
UEFA Cup *1992*
European Super Cup *1973, 1995*
Intercontinental Cup *1972, 1995*

ALDERSHOT TOWN

Year founded: 1992
Ground: The Recreation Ground (7,100)
Nickname: The Shots
Biggest win: 6-0 v Grays (2000)
Heaviest defeat: 1-6 v Burton Albion (2009)

Aldershot Town were founded in the spring of 1992 as successors to Aldershot FC, who had been forced to resign from the Football League for financial reasons just weeks earlier. The newly formed Shots began life in the Isthmian League Division Three, five tiers below the Football League.

• **Remarkably, the club rose through the divisions to finally clinch a place in League Two in 2008 by winning the Conference with a then record tally of 101 points.**

• Although most of their short existence has been as a non-league club, a number of famous names have turned out for the Shots, including former Manchester United and England midfielder Neil Webb and Marcus Gayle, previously a battling striker with Wimbledon during the Dons' Premiership heyday.

• **The club enjoyed their best ever cup run in the 2011/12 season, losing 3-0 at home to Manchester United in the last 16 of the Carling Cup.**

• Defender Jason Chewins is the club's record appearance maker, turning out 489 times between 1994 and 2004. Stuart Udal, brother of former England cricketer Shaun, is fourth on the club's list with 236 appearances in the 1990s.

HONOURS
Conference champions 2008

Sam Allardyce got the bubbles blowing again at West Ham by getting them back into the Premier League in 2012

SAM ALLARDYCE

Born: Dudley, 19th October 1954
Managerial career:
1991-92 Limerick
1992 Preston North End (caretaker)
1994-96 Blackpool
1997-99 Notts County
1999-2007 Bolton Wanderers
2007-08 Newcastle United
2008-10 Blackburn Rovers
2011- West Ham United

Along with Mark Hughes, West Ham supremo Sam Allardyce is one of just two current Premier League bosses to have managed four top-flight clubs. Prior to landing the Upton Park job in June 2011, 'Big Sam', as he is known in football circles, was in charge at Bolton Wanderers, Newcastle United and Blackburn Rovers.

• It was at Bolton that Allardyce first came to the fore, leading the Trotters back into the Premier League in 2001, taking them to the Carling Cup final in 2004 and into the UEFA Cup for the first time in the club's history the following year.

• His spells at Newcastle and Blackburn were less successful, although he was unfortunate to be sacked by Rovers'

new owners in December 2010 with the club lying safely in mid-table – a decision described by Sir Alex Ferguson as "absolutely ridiculous".

• **Allardyce bounced back, though, by taking West Ham into the Premier League in his first season in East London, the Hammers clinching their place in the top flight with a 2-1 play-off final victory over Blackpool at Wembley.**

ANIMALS

In a 1985 Staffordshire Sunday Cup match a dog scored a goal for Knave of Clubs against Newcastle Town. A shot from a Knave striker was heading harmlessly wide until the pooch ran onto the pitch and bundled the ball over the line. The referee awarded the goal, although the dog's effort couldn't prevent Knave going down to a 3-2 defeat.

• **During a match between Brazilian sides Botafogo and Gremio in 2002, a giant lapwing bird swooped from the sky and deflected a goalbound shot from Botafogo striker Fabio away from the line. Gremio fans celebrated their team's lucky escape by chanting**

'lapwing, lapwing' and the game ended in a draw.

• On the final day of the 1986/87 season a police dog inadvertently played a part in saving Torquay from relegation from the Football League. With minutes to go, the Gulls were losing 2-1 at home to Crewe when the dog, named Bryn, ran onto the pitch and bit Torquay player Jim McNichol. In the time added on for treatment to his injury, Torquay launched a desperate last attack and scored an equaliser. As a show of gratitude to the dog, chairman Lew Pope gave him a juicy steak.

• **The most famous dog in football, Pickles, never appeared on the pitch but, to the relief of fans around the globe, discovered the World Cup trophy which was stolen while on display at an exhibition in Central Hall, Westminster, on 20th March 1966. A black and white mongrel, Pickles found the trophy under a bush while out for a walk on Beulah Hill in south London with his owner. He was hailed as a national hero but, sadly, later that same year he was strangled by his lead while chasing after a cat.**

• The World Cup also made an international celebrity of Paul, an octopus based at the Sea Life Aquarium in Oberhausen, Germany. During the 2010 finals in South Africa, the two-year-old cephalopod correctly predicted the result of all seven of Germany's games by choosing his favourite food, mussels, from one of two boxes marked with the national flag of the competing teams. Before the final between Holland and Spain, Paul's choice of breakfast snack suggested that the trophy would be heading to Madrid rather than Amsterdam... and, yet again, the amazing 'psychic' octopus was spot on!

IS THAT A FACT?

The Premier League match between Blackburn and Wigan on 8th May 2012 was briefly interrupted when a chicken draped in Rovers' colours appeared on the pitch, released by a fan protesting at Rovers' owners Venky's, an Indian poultry company. After a dull first 45 minutes Radio Five Live commentator John Murray quipped, "In many ways the highlight of the first half has been the chicken."

A

ALLARDYCE

APPEARANCES

Goalkeeping legend Peter Shilton holds the record for the most League appearances, playing in 1,005 games between 1966 and 1997. His total was made up as follows: Leicester City (286 games), Stoke City (110), Nottingham Forest (202), Southampton (188), Derby County (175), Plymouth (34), Bolton (1) and Orient (9). Shilton is followed in the all-time list by Tony Ford (938 appearances, 1975-2001) and former England international Terry Paine (824, 1957-77).

• Manchester United midfielder Ryan Giggs holds the Premier League appearance record, making 598 appearances since making his bow in 1992, in the inaugural season of the new league. Brad Friedel holds the consecutive games record with 314 for Blackburn, Aston Villa and Tottenham.

• The record for most League games with one club is held by Swindon Town's stalwart defender John Trollope, who appeared 770 times for the Robins between 1960 and 1980.

• Between 1989 and 2011 Linfield defender Noel Bailie played an incredible 1,013 games for the Northern Irish club. No other player in the world has made as many competitive appearances for the same team.

• Legendary Spanish striker Raul holds the record for the most appearances in the Champions League, having played in 144 games in the competition since 1995 with Real Madrid and Stuttgart.

ARGENTINA

First international: Uruguay 2 Argentina 3, 1901
Most capped player: Javier Zanetti, 145 caps (1994-)
Leading goalscorer: Gabriel Batistuta, 56 goals (1991-2002)
First World Cup appearance: Argentina 1 France 0, 1930
Biggest win: 12-0 v Ecuador, 1942
Heaviest defeat: 1-6 v Czechoslovakia (1958) and v Bolivia (2009)

Outside Britain, Argentina is the oldest football nation on the planet. The roots of the game in this football-obsessed country go back to 1865, when the Buenos Aires Football Club was founded by British residents in the Argentine capital. Six clubs formed the first league in 1891, making it the oldest anywhere in the world outside Britain.

• **Losing finalists in the first World Cup final in 1930, Argentina had to wait until 1978 before winning the competition for the first time, defeating Holland 3-1 on home soil. Another success, inspired by brilliant captain Diego Maradona, followed in 1986 and Argentina came close to retaining their trophy four years later, losing in the final to West Germany. Argentina have also won the Copa America 14 times, a record only bettered by Uruguay.**

• Argentina's oldest rivals are neighbours Uruguay. The two countries first met in 1901, in the first official international to be played outside Britain, with Argentina winning 3-2 in Montevideo. In the ensuing years the two sides have played each other 177 times, making the Argentina-Uruguay fixture the most played in the history of international football.

• **With an impressive 56 goals in 78 matches, former Fiorentina striker Gabriel Batistuta is Argentina's highest-ever goalscorer. 'Batigol' is followed by another pair of legendary South Americans, Hernan Crespo (35 goals) and Diego Maradona (34 goals).**

HONOURS
World Cup 1978, 1986
Copa America 1921, 1925, 1927, 1929, 1937, 1941, 1945, 1946, 1947, 1955, 1957, 1959, 1991, 1993
World Cup record
1930 Runners-up
1934 Round 1
1938 Did not enter
1950 Did not enter
1954 Did not enter
1958 Round 1
1962 Round 1
1966 Quarter-finals
1970 Did not qualify
1974 Round 2
1978 Winners
1982 Round 2
1986 Winners
1990 Runners-up
1994 Round 2
1998 Quarter-finals
2002 Round 1
2006 Quarter-finals
2010 Quarter-finals

'Wow!' Lionel Messi may be a football superstar but he still loves his bubbles!

ARSENAL

Year founded: 1886
Ground: Emirates Stadium (60,361)
Previous name: Dial Square, Royal Arsenal, Woolwich Arsenal
Nickname: The Gunners
Biggest win: 12-0 v Ashford United (1893) and v Loughborough Town (1900)
Heaviest defeat: 0-8 v Loughborough Town (1896)

Founded as Dial Square in 1886 by workers at the Royal Arsenal in Woolwich, the club was renamed Royal Arsenal soon afterwards. Another name change, to Woolwich Arsenal, followed in 1891 when the club turned professional. Then, a year after moving north of the river to the Arsenal Stadium in 1913, the club became simply 'Arsenal'.

• One of the most successful clubs in the history of English football, Arsenal enjoyed a first golden period in the 1930s under innovative manager Herbert Chapman. The Gunners won the FA Cup for the first time in 1930 and later in the decade became only the second club to win three league titles on the trot. The first was the club Chapman managed in the 1920s, Huddersfield Town.

• Arsenal were the first club from London to win the league, topping the table in 1931 after scoring an incredible 60 goals in 21 away matches — an all-time record for the Football League.

• More recently, Arsenal have experienced enormous success under French manager Arsène Wenger. In 1998, just two years after Wenger arrived in England, the Gunners won the Double, a feat they repeated in 2002 while winning a top-flight record 14 consecutive league games. The club had previously won the league and FA Cup in the same season for the first time in 1971, and their total of three Doubles is only matched by Manchester United.

• Wenger's greatest triumph, though, came in the 2003/04 season when his team were crowned Premier League champions after going through the entire campaign undefeated. Only Preston North End had previously matched this feat, way back in 1888/89, but they had only played 22 league games compared to the 38 of Wenger's 'Invincibles'.

Arsenal hold the record for the longest unbroken run in the top flight — 93 years

- The following season Arsenal extended their unbeaten run to 49 matches – setting an English league record in the process – before crashing to a bad-tempered 2-0 defeat against Manchester United at Old Trafford on 24th October 2004.
- One of the stars of that great Arsenal side was striker Thierry Henry, who is the Gunners' all-time leading scorer with 228 goals in all competitions in two spells at the club between 1999 and 2012. The former fans' favourite is also the most-capped Arsenal player, appearing 81 times for France during his time with the club.
- **In 1989 Arsenal won the closest-ever title race by beating Liverpool 2-0 at Anfield in the final match of the season to pip the Reds to the championship on goals scored (the two sides had the same goal difference). But for a last-minute goal by Gunners midfielder Michael Thomas the title would have stayed on Merseyside.**
- Irish international defender David O'Leary made a club record 722 first-team appearances for Arsenal between 1975 and 1993.
- **Arsenal endured a nightmare season in 1912/13, finishing bottom of Division One and winning just one home game during the campaign – an all-time record. However, the Gunners returned to the top flight in 1919 and have stayed there ever since – the longest unbroken run in the top tier.**
- Arsenal tube station on the Piccadilly Line is the only train station in Britain to be named after a football club. It used to be called Gillespie Road, until Herbert Chapman successfully lobbied for the name change in 1932.
- **Three years later, on 14th December 1935, Arsenal thrashed Aston Villa 7-1 at Villa Park. Incredibly, centre forward Ted Drake grabbed all seven of the Gunners' goals to set a top-flight record that still stands to this day.**
- Arsenal spent 93 years at their old ground, Highbury, before moving to the state-of-the-art Emirates Stadium in 2006. With a capacity of 60,361, the Emirates is the second-biggest club

stadium in England after Old Trafford.
- **When Arsenal won the FA Cup in 1950, beating Liverpool 2-0 in the final, they had the oldest team of any cup winners with an average age of 31 years and seven months.**
- Previously famed for being a rather dull team who specialised in 1-0 victories, Arsenal have become the great entertainers in the Wenger era. Proof of the Gunners' attacking prowess came when they established an English league record by scoring in 55 consecutive matches between 2001-02.
- **Arsenal's most expensive signing is Spanish playmaker Santi Cazorla who cost the Gunners £16 million when he joined them from Malaga in August 2012. The club's record sale is Cesc Fabregas, who boosted the Gunners' coffers by £25.4 million when he signed for Barcelona in 2011.**
- The Gunners have a host of celebrity supporters, including athletics star Mo Farah, novelist Nick Hornby and actor Alan Davies. Prince Harry is also a fan as, apparently, is his grandmother. In 2007 a Buckingham Palace spokesman surprised the football world by revealing that, "Her Majesty has been fond of Arsenal for over 50 years."

HONOURS
Division 1 champions 1931, 1933, 1934, 1935, 1948, 1953, 1971, 1989, 1991
Premier League champions 1998, 2002, 2004
FA Cup 1930, 1936, 1950, 1971, 1979, 1993, 1998, 2002, 2003, 2005
League Cup 1987, 1993
Double 1971, 1998, 2002
Fairs Cup 1970
European Cup Winners' Cup 1994

IS THAT A FACT?
Arsenal provided a record seven members of England's starting line up against Italy at Highbury on 14th November 1934: Cliff Bastin, Ray Bowden, Wilf Copping, Ted Drake, Eddie Hapgood, George Male and goalkeeper Frank Moss. England won a brutal match, dubbed 'The Battle of Highbury', 3-2.

ASTON VILLA

Year founded: 1874
Ground: Villa Park (42,788)
Nickname: The Villans
Biggest win: 13-0 v Wednesbury Old Athletic (1886)
Heaviest defeat: 1-8 v Blackburn Rovers (1889)

One of England's most famous and distinguished clubs, Aston Villa were founded in 1874 by members of the Villa Cross Wesleyan Chapel in Aston, Birmingham. The club were founder members of the Football League in 1888, winning their first title six years later.
- **The most successful team of the Victorian era, Villa became only the second club to win the league and FA Cup Double in 1897 (Preston North End were the first in 1889). Villa's manager at the time was the legendary George Ramsay, who went on to guide the Villans to six league titles and six FA Cups – a trophy haul which has only been surpassed by Liverpool's Bob Paisley and, more recently, Manchester United boss Sir Alex Ferguson.**
- Ramsay is also the second longest-serving manager in the history of English football, taking charge of the Villans for an incredible 42 years between 1884 and 1926. Only West Brom's Fred Everiss has managed a club for longer, racking up 46 years' service at the Hawthorns.
- **Although they slipped as low as the old Third Division in the early 1970s, Villa have spent more time in the top flight than any other club apart from Everton (102 seasons compared to the Toffees' 110). The two clubs have played each other 194 times to date, making Aston Villa v Everton the most played fixture in the history of league football.**
- Villa won the last of their seven league titles in 1980/81, when manager Ron Saunders used just 14 players throughout the whole campaign – equalling Liverpool's record set in 1965/66. The following season Villa became only the fourth English club to win the European Cup when they beat Bayern Munich 1-0 in the final in Rotterdam.

• In 1961 Villa won the League Cup in the competition's inaugural season, beating Rotherham 3-2 in a two-legged final. The Villans are the second most successful side in the tournament behind Liverpool with five triumphs, and have won more games (129) and scored more goals (437) in the competition than any other club.

• Aston Villa have provided a record 72 internationals for England, including current players Gabriel Agbonlahor and Darren Bent.

• Stalwart defender Charlie Aitken made more appearances for the club than any other player, turning out in 657 games between 1959 and 1976. Villa's all-time top goalscorer is Billy Walker, who found the back of the net an incredible 244 times between 1919 and 1933.

• Walker helped Villa bang in 128 league goals in the 1930/31 season, a record for the top flight which is unlikely ever to be broken. In the same campaign Tom 'Pongo' Waring scored a club record 49 league goals.

• Before FA Cup semi-finals moved to Wembley, Villa Park staged a record 55 of these fixtures. The stadium has also hosted 16 England internationals and was the first venue to be used by the national team in three different centuries.

• Villa's biggest league win came back in 1892 when they thrashed Accrington Stanley 12-2 in Division One – no side has scored more goals in a top flight fixture. Six years earlier, though, the club recorded their biggest ever victory in the FA Cup, humiliating Wednesbury Old Athletic 13-0. In total Villa have scored 828 goals in the cup, a record unmatched by any other club.

• More recently, in 1990, Villa became the first top-flight club to appoint a foreign manager when Jozef Venglos took over from new England boss Graham Taylor. However, the Czech failed to make much of an impression, leaving Villa Park after a single season in charge.

• Famous Villa fans include punk violinist Nigel Kennedy, Prince William and David Cameron, who is a nephew of former club chairman Sir William Dugdale.

> **HONOURS**
> *Division 1 champions 1894, 1896, 1897, 1899, 1900, 1910, 1981*
> *Division 2 champions 1938, 1960*
> *Division 3 champions 1972*
> *FA Cup 1887, 1895, 1897, 1905, 1913, 1920, 1957*
> *Double 1897*
> *League Cup 1961, 1975, 1977, 1994, 1996*
> *European Cup 1982*
> *European Super Cup 1982*

ATTENDANCES

The Maracana stadium in Rio de Janeiro holds the world record for a football match attendance, 199,589 spectators having watched the final match of the 1950 World Cup between Brazil and Uruguay. Most of the fans, though, went home in tears after Uruguay came from behind to win 2-1 and claim the trophy for a second time.

• The biggest crowd at a match in Britain was for the first-ever FA Cup final at Wembley in 1923. The official attendance for the match between Bolton and West Ham was 126,047 although, with thousands more fans gaining entry without paying, the actual crowd was estimated at 150,000-200,000. The record official attendance for a match in Britain is 149,547, set in 1937 for Scotland's 3-1 victory over England in the Home International Championship at Hampden Park.

• In 1948 a crowd of 83,260 watched Manchester United entertain Arsenal at Maine Road (United's temporary home in the post-war years after Old Trafford suffered bomb damage), a record for the Football League. The following year, on 27th December 1949, the 44 Football League games played that day were watched by a record aggregate of 1,272,815 fans – an average of 28,913 per match.

• The highest attendance at a Premier League match is 76,097 for the game between Manchester United and Blackburn Rovers on 31st March 2007. At the other end of the scale, just 3,039 fans turned out for Wimbledon's home game against Everton at Selhurst Park on 26th January 1993.

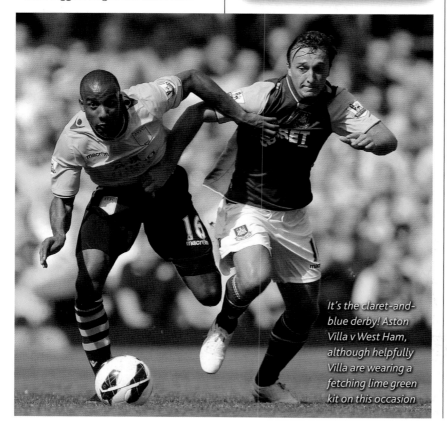

It's the claret-and-blue derby! Aston Villa v West Ham, although helpfully Villa are wearing a fetching lime green kit on this occasion

TOP 10

AVERAGE PREMIER LEAGUE ATTENDANCE 2011/12

1.	Manchester United	75,387
2.	Arsenal	60,000
3.	Newcastle United	49,935
4.	Manchester City	47,044
5.	Liverpool	44,253
6.	Chelsea	41,478
7.	Sunderland	39,095
8.	Tottenham Hotspur	36,026
9.	Aston Villa	33,873
10.	Everton	33,228

GARETH BALE

Born: Cardiff, 16th July 1989
Position: Midfielder
Club career:
2006-07 Southampton 40 (5)
2007- Tottenham Hotspur 113 (21)
International record:
2006- Wales 34 (6)

Tottenham's fleet-footed left-sided midfielder Gareth Bale is the youngest player to appear for Wales, making his debut against Trinidad and Tobago on 27th May 2006 when he was aged 16 years and 315 days. Later that year he scored his first international goal, in a 5-1 home defeat by Slovakia, to become his country's youngest-ever scorer.

• Bale began his career at Southampton, where he was the second-youngest player to debut for the club (behind Theo Walcott) when he appeared in a 2-0 win against Millwall in April 2006. The following season his outstanding displays for the Saints earned him the Football League Young Player of the Year award.

• In the summer of 2007 Bale joined Tottenham for an initial fee of £5 million. Incredibly, he failed to feature on the winning side for Spurs in his first 24 league games – a Premier League record – but once he had buried that jinx his form rapidly improved, and he was soon being hailed as one of the most exciting talents in the game.

• Bale enjoyed an outstanding season with Spurs in 2010/11 and at the end of the campaign he was named PFA Player of the Year – only the fourth Welshman to receive this honour. He was also the only Premier League player to be voted into the UEFA Team of the Year for 2011.

BALL BOYS

Ball boys developed from a gimmick employed by Chelsea in the 1905/06 season. To emphasise the

Amazingly, it took Gareth Bale a record 24 Premier League games to play in a winning Spurs team

IS THAT A FACT?

In a lower league game in Brazil in 2012 a ball boy came to the aid of the home team, Guarany, when he kicked a shot off the line, depriving the away side, Sergipe, of a certain goal. The incident sparked a brawl between both sets of players when the referee blew for full time rather than awarding a goal.

extraordinary bulk of the team's 23-stone goalkeeper, William 'Fatty' Foulke, two young boys would stand behind his goal. They soon proved themselves useful in retrieving the ball when it went out of play, and so the concept of the ball boy was born.

• Amazingly, a ball boy scored a goal in a match between Santacruzense and Atletico Sorocaba in Brazil in 2006. Santacruzense were trailing 1-0 when one of their players fired wide in the last minute. Instead of handing the ball back to the Atletico goalkeeper, the ball boy kicked it into the net and the goal was awarded by the female referee despite the angry protests of the Atletico players.

• Almost as bizarrely, a ball girl was credited with an 'assist' during a Brazilian state championship match between Botafogo and Vasco de Gama in 2012. After the ball went out of play, 22-year-old Fernanda Maia quickly threw the ball she was carrying to a Botafogo player whose equally rapid throw-in was crossed for striker Maicosuel to score. Helped by her good looks, Maia became an instant celebrity in Brazil and cashed in on her newfound fame by baring all for *Playboy* magazine.

• Sion's Serey Die hit the headlines in 2012 after slapping a ball boy in the face after his team's 1-0 defeat away to Laussane. The Ivory Coast midfielder was reported to be angry with the ball boy's time-wasting tactics during the match.

The game was a bit dull, so Mario Balotelli decided to entertain the fans by performing a striptease routine

BALLS

The laws of football specify that the ball must be an air-filled sphere with a circumference of 68-70cm and a weight before the start of the game of 410-450g. Before the first plastic footballs appeared in the 1950s, balls were made from leather and in wet conditions would become progressively heavier, sometimes actually doubling in weight.

• Most modern footballs are made in Pakistan, especially in the city of Sialkot, and are usually stitched from 32 panels of waterproofed leather or plastic. In the past child labour was often used in the production of the balls but, following pressure from UNICEF and the International Labour Organisation, manufacturers agreed in 1997 not to employ underage workers.

• Adidas have supplied the official ball for the World Cup since 1970. The ball for the 2010 tournament in South Africa, the Jabulani, was widely considered to be the worst in the competition's history, its unpredictable trajectory attracting much criticism from players, managers and fans. FIFA, though, refused to bow to demands for the ball to be changed, although it later admitted that the Jabulani's ability to pick up 'incredible speed' may have been a factor in the numerous goalkeeping errors at the finals.

• Nike are the official supplier of balls for the Premier League, taking over the role from Mitre in 2000. A winter 'Hi-Vis' yellow ball has been used in the league since the 2004/05 season.

• The record for juggling a football in the air without the use of hands ('keepy uppy') is held by England's Dan Magness, who clocked up 24 hours (an estimated 250,000 touches) in Covent Garden on 1st May 2009. The following year Magness set another record when he juggled a ball 30 miles across London, visiting every Premier League ground in the capital along the way.

• Remarkably, the ball burst during both the 1946 and 1947 FA Cup finals at Wembley – an unlikely coincidence which was probably caused by the poor quality of leather available after World War II.

MARIO BALOTELLI

Born: Palermo, Italy, 12th August 1990
Position: Striker
Club career:
2005-06 Lumezzane 2 (0)
2007-10 Inter Milan 59 (20)
2010- Manchester City 40 (19)
International record:
2010- Italy 14 (4)

One of the most unpredictable players in the Premier League, Manchester City striker Mario Balotelli has played a big part in his club's recent successes. He was Man of the Match when City beat Stoke in the 2011 FA Cup final, and the following year he helped the club win a first league title since 1968.

• Arguably, though, Balotelli is more famous for his madcap antics off the pitch than for anything he has done on the field of play. These include setting off fireworks in his bathroom, throwing darts at a youth team player and turning his garden into a quad bike course. If anything, however, his quirky behaviour has only endeared him even more to City's fans.

• The son of Ghanaian immigrants to Sicily who was cared for by foster parents as a child, Balotelli rose to prominence with Inter Milan. In November 2008 he became the club's youngest-ever scorer in the Champions League when, aged 18 years and 85 days, he netted in a 3-3 draw against Cypriot outfit Anorthosis Famagusta. He helped Inter win consecutive Serie A titles between 2008 and 2010, but his lax attitude to training and volatile personality did not impress then Inter boss Jose Mourinho and he was sold to City for £23.5 million in the summer of 2010.

• In the same year Balotelli became the first black player to represent Italy at full international level when he played in a 1-0 friendly defeat against Ivory Coast. Two years later he starred for the Azzurri at Euro 2012, scoring both Italy's goals in their 2-1 semi-final defeat of Germany.

GORDON BANKS

Born: Sheffield, 30th December 1937
Position: Goalkeeper
Club career:
1955-59 Chesterfield 23
1959-67 Leicester City 293
1967-72 Stoke City 194
1977 St Patrick's 1
1977-78 Fort Lauderdale Strikers 39
International record:
1963-72 England 73

One of the finest goalkeepers ever, Gordon Banks will always be remembered for his part in England's 1966 World Cup success. Dubbed 'Banks of England' (because he had "the safest hands in the country"), he lived up to his nickname by keeping four straight clean sheets at the start of the tournament – part of an England record run of 718 minutes without conceding a goal.

• **His greatest single moment, though, came at the 1970 World Cup in Mexico when he produced a save which is widely considered to be the best in the history of the game. A powerful downward header by the legendary Brazilian striker Pele seemed destined for the bottom corner of the goal, but somehow Banks managed to rush across his line before diving slightly backwards to turn the ball over the bar.**

• The tournament ended badly for Banks, though, as a stomach upset kept him out of England's quarter-final defeat by West Germany. England manager Sir Alf Ramsey believed that the result might have been very different if Banks had played, wistfully saying, "Of all the players to lose, we had to lose him."

• **In club football, Banks won the League Cup with Leicester in 1964 and Stoke in 1972 and was a beaten FA Cup finalist with the Foxes in 1961 and 1969. He was awarded the OBE in 1970 and was Footballer of the Year in 1972.**

• Aged 34, Banks's career in England was ended in 1972 when he lost the sight in his right eye in a car crash, although he later played for Irish club St Patrick's and in the North American Soccer League with Fort Lauderdale Strikers.

BARCELONA

Year founded: 1899
Ground: Nou Camp (99,354)
Nickname: Barça
League titles: 21
Domestic cups: 26
European cups: 15
International cups: 2

One of the most famous and popular clubs in the world, Barcelona were founded in 1899 by bank worker Joan Gamper, a former captain of Swiss club Basel. The club were founder members and first winners of the Spanish championship, La Liga, in 1928 and have remained in the top flight of Spanish football ever since.

• **For the people of Catalonia, Barcelona is more like a national team than a mere club. As former manager Bobby Robson once succinctly put it, "Catalonia is a country and FC Barcelona is their army."**

• Along with Ajax, Juventus and Bayern Munich, Barcelona are one of just four clubs to have won three different European trophies: the European Cup/Champions League, the European Cup Winners' Cup (a record four times) and the Fairs Cup (Barça being the first winners of the competition in 1958).

• **With a capacity of 99,354, Barcelona's Nou Camp stadium is the largest in Europe. Among the stadium's many facilities are a museum which attracts over one million visitors a year, mini training pitches and a chapel for the players.**

• For many years Barcelona played second fiddle to bitter rivals Real Madrid. Finally, in the 1990s, under former player turned coach Johan Cruyff, Barça turned the tables on the team from the Spanish capital, winning four La Liga titles on the trot between 1991 and 1994. Cruyff also led the Catalans to a first taste of glory in the European Cup, Barcelona beating Sampdoria at

Wembley in 1992. The club have since won the Champions League on three more occasions, beating Arsenal 2-1 in the 2006 final and, under former manager Pep Guardiola, Manchester United 2-0 and 3-1 in 2009 and 2011 respectively.

• **With 26 victories to their name, Barcelona have won the Copa del Rey (the Spanish version of the FA Cup) more times than any other club.**

HONOURS
Spanish League *1929, 1945, 1948, 1949, 1952, 1953, 1959, 1960, 1974, 1985, 1991, 1992, 1993, 1994, 1998, 1999, 2005, 2006, 2009, 2010, 2011*
Spanish Cup *1910, 1912, 1913, 1920, 1922, 1925, 1926, 1928, 1942, 1951, 1952, 1953, 1957, 1959, 1963, 1968, 1971, 1978, 1981, 1983, 1988, 1990, 1997, 1998, 2009, 2012*
European Cup/Champions League *1992, 2006, 2009, 2011*
European Cup Winners' Cup *1979, 1982, 1989, 1997*
Fairs Cup *1958, 1960, 1961*
European Super Cup *1992, 1997, 2009, 2011*
Club World Cup *2009, 2011*

Barcelona captain Carlos Puyol

BARNET

Year founded: 1888
Ground: Underhill Stadium (6,023)
Previous name: Barnet Alston FC
Nickname: The Bees
Biggest win: 7-0 v Blackpool (2000)
Heaviest defeat: 1-9 v Peterborough United (1998)

Founded in 1888, Barnet spent more than a hundred years in non-league football before finally gaining promotion from the Conference to the Fourth Division in 1991. In recent seasons the Bees (the nickname derives from their distinctive amber-and-black-striped shirts) have gained a reputation as last-ditch survival specialists, narrowly avoiding relegation back to the Conference in 2010, 2011 and 2012.

• Barnet may be London's smallest league club, but some famous names have been associated with the Bees over the years. Legendary England goalpoacher Jimmy Greaves played for Barnet at the end of his career in the late 1970s, while fellow internationals Ray Clemence, Alan Mullery and Tony Cottee have all managed the club at some point.

• Barnet's record league goalscorer is Sean Devine with 47 strikes between 1995 and 1999. The club's top appearance maker is defender Paul Wilson, who turned out in 263 games for the Bees between 1991 and 2000.

• In October 1946, the first live televised football match was broadcast by the BBC from Barnet's tiny Underhill Stadium. Around 75

minutes of the Bees' encounter with Wealdstone were screened before it got too dark for the broadcast to continue.

BARNSLEY

Year founded: 1887
Ground: Oakwell (23,009)
Previous name: Barnsley St Peter's
Nickname: The Tykes
Biggest win: 9-0 v Loughborough United (1899)
Heaviest defeat: 0-9 v Notts County (1927)

Founded as the church team Barnsley St Peter's in 1887 by the Rev Tiverton Preedy, the club changed to their present name a year after joining the Football League in 1898.

• The Tykes have spent more seasons (72) in the second tier of English football than any other club and had to wait until 1997 before they had their first taste of life in the top flight.

• The Yorkshiremen's finest hour came in 1912 when they won the FA Cup, beating West Bromwich Albion 1-0 in a replay. The club were nicknamed 'Battling Barnsley' that season as they played a record 12 games during their cup run, including six 0-0 draws, before finally getting their hands on the trophy. Barnsley came close to repeating this feat in 2008, but were beaten in the semi-finals by fellow Championship side Cardiff City after they had sensationally knocked out Liverpool and cup holders Chelsea.

• The youngest player to appear in the Football League is Barnsley striker Reuben Noble-Lazarus, who was 15 years and 45 days old when he faced Ipswich Town in September 2008. Afterwards, Barnsley boss Simon Davey joked Noble-Lazarus would be rewarded with a pizza as he was too young to be paid!

• On 3rd January 2011 Barnsley became the first club to achieve 1,000 wins in the second tier of English football when they beat Coventry City 2-1 at Oakwell.

IS THAT A FACT?
Along with Swindon (1992/93), Burnley (2009/10) and Blackpool (2010/11), Barnsley are one of just four clubs to have spent a single season in the Premier League, the Tykes earning promotion in 1997 only to suffer the agony of relegation a year later.

BAYERN MUNICH

Year founded: 1900
Ground: Allianz Arena (69,901)
Nickname: The Bavarians
League titles: 22
Domestic cups: 15
European cups: 6

The biggest and most successful club in Germany, Bayern Munich were founded in 1900 by members of a Munich gymnastics club. Incredibly, when the Bundesliga was formed in 1963, Bayern's form was so poor they were not invited to become founder members of the league. But, thanks to the emergence in the mid-1960s of legendary players like goalkeeper Sepp Maier, sweeper Franz Beckenbauer and prolific goalscorer Gerd Muller, Bayern rapidly became the dominant force in German football. The club won the Bundesliga for the first time in 1969 and now have a record 22 German championships to their name.

• In 1974 Bayern became the first German club to win the European Cup, defeating Atletico Madrid 4-0 in the only final to go to a replay. Skippered by the imperious Beckenbauer, the club went on to complete a hat-trick of victories in the competition. However, Bayern had to wait another 25 years before winning the trophy again, beating Valencia on penalties in the Champions League final in 2001. More recently, Bayern reached the final again in 2010 and 2012, but lost on both occasions to Inter Milan and Chelsea.

• Bayern are one of just four clubs to have won three different European trophies, having also been triumphant in the Cup Winners' Cup in 1967 and the UEFA Cup in 1996.

• With more than 162,000 registered fans, Bayern have the third-largest membership of any club in the world after Benfica and Barcelona.

• In 2005, following complaints from

their fans that the pitch was too far away from the stands at their old Olympic Stadium ground, Bayern moved to the Allianz Arena in northern Munich. The first player to score at the new venue, in a match against Borussia Monchengladbach, was then Bayern player Owen Hargreaves.

Bayern's players haven't stopped crying since they lost in the 2012 Champions League final

FRANZ BECKENBAUER

Born: Munich, Germany, 11th September 1945
Position: Defender
Club career:
1964-77 Bayern Munich 427 (60)
1977-80 New York Cosmos 105 (19)
1980-82 Hamburg 28 (0)
1983 New York Cosmos 29 (2)
International record:
1965-77 West Germany 103 (14)

Germany's greatest-ever player, Franz Beckenbauer's elegant playing style and outstanding leadership qualities earned him the nickname 'Der Kaiser' ('The Emperor'). Having started out as a midfielder, Beckenbauer created and defined the role of the offensive 'sweeper' in the late 1960s, turning defence into attack with surging runs from the back.

• **Beckenbauer enjoyed huge success at both club and international level. He captained Bayern Munich to three consecutive victories in the European Cup between 1974-76, matching Ajax's treble earlier in the decade. As skipper of West Germany, Beckenbauer led his country to victory in the 1972 European Championships, and two years later he cemented his reputation as a national icon by collecting the World Cup trophy after a 2-1 defeat of Holland in the 1974 final in Munich.**

• His consistent performances won him the European Footballer of the Year award in 1972 and 1976 – the first German player to win the award twice. He was also voted German Footballer of the Year a record four times.

• **More success followed for Beckenbauer in the late 1970s after he accepted a lucrative offer to play in America, his New York Cosmos side winning the NASL Soccer Bowl in 1977, 1978 and 1980.**

• Beckenbauer was appointed manager of West Germany in 1986 and when, four years later, his country triumphed at Italia '90 'Der Kaiser' became the first man to both captain and coach a World Cup-winning team. Later, in 1996, he led Bayern Munich to glory in the UEFA Cup, before becoming the driving force behind Germany's successful bid to host the 2006 World Cup.

DAVID BECKHAM

Born: Leytonstone, 2nd May 1975
Position: Midfielder
Club career:
1993-2003 Manchester United 265 (62)
1995 Preston North End (loan) 5 (2)
2003-07 Real Madrid 116 (13)
2007- LA Galaxy 90 (16)
2009 AC Milan (loan) 18 (2)
2010 AC Milan (loan) 11 (0)
International record:
1996-2009 England 115 (17)

One of the most famous names on the planet, David Beckham's fame extends far beyond the world of football. Yet, for all the interest in his marriage to Spice Girl Victoria Beckham, his fashion sense, his numerous haircuts and tattoos, it shouldn't be forgotten that his celebrity status stems primarily from his remarkable ability on the ball.

• A superb crosser of the ball and free-kick expert, at his peak Beckham was probably the best right-sided midfielder in the world. He twice came close to winning the World Player of the Year award, finishing as runner-up in 1999 and 2001.

• Beckham enjoyed huge success with his first club Manchester United, winning six Premiership titles, two FA Cups and, as the final leg of 'the Treble', the Champions League in 1999. However, his glamorous lifestyle began to irritate United boss Sir Alex Ferguson, and the deteriorating relationship between the pair led to Beckham's departure to Spanish giants Real Madrid in 2003.

• As one of Real's 'galacticos', Beckham was part of a team which was much hyped but frequently failed to deliver. He eventually won the Spanish title with Real in 2007, shortly before making a lucrative move to Major League Soccer in the USA with LA Galaxy. In 2009 he joined AC Milan on loan and performed so well that the Italians were delighted to welcome him back to the San Siro in a similar deal the following year.

• One of just five players to win more than 100 caps for his country and the only England player to have scored at three different World Cups, Beckham captained his country from 2000 to 2006. After being sent off against Argentina at the 1998 World Cup he was made the scapegoat for England's elimination from the competition, but famously bounced

HIGHEST CAPPED ENGLAND PLAYERS

1. Peter Shilton (1970-90) 125 caps
2. David Beckham (1996-2009) 115 caps
3. Bobby Moore (1962-73) 108 caps
4. Bobby Charlton (1958-70) 106 caps
5. Billy Wright (1946-59) 105 caps
6. Ashley Cole (2001-) 98 caps
7. Steven Gerrard (2000-) 96 caps
8. Frank Lampard (1999-) 91 caps
9. Bryan Robson (1980-91) 90 caps
10. Michael Owen (1998-2008) 89 caps

David Beckham in action for the LA Galaxy, showing the dead-ball technique that has brought him dozens of goals

back to score the winning goal from the penalty spot against the same opposition at the 2002 tournament in Japan and South Korea.

• Beckham's England career appeared to be over when he was dropped from the squad by new manager Steve McClaren in 2006. However, he was recalled the following year and was rewarded with his 100th cap by McClaren's successor, his former Real boss Fabio Capello, against France in 2008. The following year he became England's most-capped outfield player, beating the old record set by the great Bobby Moore, when he won his 109th cap against Slovakia. Sadly for Beckham, injury ruled him out of the 2010 World Cup, effectively ending his international career.

BENFICA

Year founded: 1904
Ground: Estadio Da Luz, Lisbon (65,647)
Nickname: The Eagles
League titles: 32
Domestic cups: 27
European cups: 2

Portugal's most successful club, Benfica were founded in 1904 at a meeting of 24 football enthusiasts in south Lisbon. The club were founder members of the Portuguese league in 1933 and have since won the title a record 32 times.

• **With over 215,000 registered members, Benfica is officially the biggest club in the world, ahead of Barcelona.**

• Inspired by legendary striker Eusebio, Benfica enjoyed a golden era in the 1960s when the club won eight domestic championships. In 1961 Benfica became the first team to break Real Madrid's dominance in the European Cup when they beat Barcelona 3-2 in the final in Berne. The following year, the trophy stayed in Lisbon after 'the Eagles' sensationally beat Real 5-3 in the final in Amsterdam.

• **In 1972/73 Benfica went the whole season undefeated – the first Portuguese team to achieve this feat – winning a staggering 28 and drawing just two of their 30 league matches. The great Eusebio struck 40 goals that**

season to top the European scoring charts as Benfica were crowned champions once again.

• Among the big names to have managed Benfica are Sven Göran Eriksson (1989-92), Graeme Souness (1997-99) and Jose Mourinho (a brief spell in 2000). Despite these high profile appointments, the club slipped behind deadly rivals Sporting Lisbon and Porto before landing only their second title in 16 years in 2010.

HONOURS
Portuguese championship 1936, 1937, 1938, 1942, 1943, 1945, 1950, 1955, 1957, 1960, 1961, 1963, 1964, 1965, 1967, 1968, 1969, 1971, 1972, 1973, 1975, 1976, 1977, 1981, 1983, 1984, 1987, 1989, 1991, 1994, 2005, 2010
Portuguese Cup 1930, 1931, 1935, 1940, 1943, 1944, 1949, 1951, 1952, 1953, 1955, 1957, 1959, 1962, 1964, 1969, 1970, 1972, 1980, 1981, 1983, 1985, 1986, 1987, 1993, 1996, 2004
European Cup 1961, 1962

KARIM BENZEMA

Born: Lyon, France, 19th December 1987
Position: Striker
Club career:
2004-09 Lyon 112 (43)
2009- Real Madrid 94 (44)
International record:
2007- France 50 (15)

Real Madrid striker Karim Benzema is the highest-scoring French player ever in Spain's La Liga with 44 goals, passing the legendary Zinedine Zidane's total during the 2011/12 season.

• **Benzema, though, struggled when he first moved to the Spanish capital from French side Lyon in a £30 million deal in 2009. Problems with his fluctuating weight led Real boss Jose Mourinho to describe him as 'listless', but he eventually won over both his manager and the famously**

fickle Bernabeu crowd with some scintillating attacking performances.

• Benzema had previously risen to prominence with his hometown club Lyon, enjoying a superb season in 2007/08 when he was voted Ligue 1 Player of the Year as Lyon stormed to a seventh consecutive title.

• He was aged just 19 when he made his international debut against Austria in 2007, but the following year he was one of a number of younger French players criticised by team-mate William Gallas for being 'insolent'. His struggle for form at Real led to him being left out of the France squad for the 2010 World Cup, but two years later he led his country's attack at Euro 2012.

Karim Benzema of Real Madrid and France

DENNIS BERGKAMP

Born: Amsterdam, Holland,
10th May 1969
Position: Striker
Club career:
1986-93 Ajax 185 (103)
1993-95 Inter Milan 52 (11)
1995-2006 Arsenal 315 (87)
International record:
1990-2000 Holland 79 (37)

One of the most talented overseas players to grace the English game, Dennis Bergkamp spent more than a decade with Arsenal after signing from Inter Milan in 1995. His highly successful striking partnerships with Ian Wright and, later, Thierry Henry helped the Gunners win an armful of honours, including two Doubles in 1998 and 2002.

• **Named after Scottish striker Denis Law by his football-mad parents, Bergkamp began his career with Ajax, with whom he won the European Cup Winners' Cup in 1987, the Dutch league in 1990 and the UEFA Cup in 1992. He was also named Dutch Footballer of the Year on two occasions before moving to Inter in 1993 for £12 million, making him the second most-expensive player in the world at the time. His time in Italy was altogether less successful, although he did win the UEFA Cup again in 1994.**

• After an indifferent start to his Arsenal career, Bergkamp's excellent ball control and visionary passing soon marked him out as one of the Premiership's top performers. Although not a prolific scorer, many of his goals were spectacular, and in September 1997 he became the first player to come first, second and third in *Match of the Day*'s Goal of the Month competition. The following year Bergkamp won the programme's Goal of the Season award, a feat he repeated in 2002 to become only the second player (after Liverpool's John Aldridge) to win the award twice. Bergkamp was voted Footballer of the Year by both his fellow pros and the football writers in 1998, having twice previously finished third in the World Player of the Year poll.

• **Bergkamp's total of 37 international goals made him Holland's all-time leading scorer for a short time, until his tally was beaten by Patrick Kluivert. Dogged by a crippling fear of flying – a phobia which inevitably earned him the nickname 'The non-flying Dutchman' – Bergkamp retired from international football in 2000, as he knew he wouldn't be able to travel to the 2002 World Cup in Japan and Korea.**

• When he eventually retired from club football in 2006 Bergkamp was awarded a testimonial by Arsenal in the first-ever match played at the club's new Emirates Stadium.

GEORGE BEST

Born: Belfast, 22nd May 1946
Died: 25th November 2005
Position: Winger
Club career:
1963-74 Manchester United 361 (138)
1975 Stockport County 3 (2)
1975-76 Cork Celtic 3 (0)
1976-77 Fulham 33 (7)
1977-78 Los Angeles Aztecs 55 (27)
1978-79 Fort Lauderdale 26 (6)
1979-80 Hibernian 22 (3)
1980-81 San Jose Earthquakes 56 (28)
1983 Bournemouth 4 (0)
International record:
1964-78 Northern Ireland 37 (9)

Possibly the greatest natural talent in the history of the British game, George Best was a football genius who thrilled fans everywhere with his dazzling dribbling skills, superb ball control and goalscoring ability.

• **Best left his native Northern Ireland as a youngster to play for Manchester United, making his debut at Old Trafford in 1963 when aged just 17. His most memorable achievements were all packed into the next five years as he helped fire United to two**

TOP 10

GREATEST PAST PLAYERS

1. Pele
2. Diego Maradona
3. Johan Cruyff
4. George Best
5. Zinedine Zidane
6. Ferenc Puskas
7. Michel Platini
8. Bobby Charlton
9. Alfredo di Stefano
10. Franz Beckenbauer

Selected by www.dailymail.co.uk

Opponents were so scared of the brilliant George Best they sometimes didn't bother to turn up...

league titles in 1965 and 1967 and to glory in the European Cup in 1968, Best scoring the vital second goal against Benfica at Wembley. In 1968 he was also named Footballer of the Year and European Footballer of the Year.

• Dubbed 'The Fifth Beatle' for his long hair and good looks, Best was the first footballer to become famous outside the game. He cashed in on his celebrity status by opening a chain of boutiques, appearing in a number of TV ads and dating a seemingly never-ending series of Miss World winners.

• **In 1970 Best scored six goals to set a still-unbeaten United record as the**

BIRMINGHAM CITY

Year founded: 1875
Ground: St Andrew's (30,009)
Previous name: Small Heath Alliance, Small Heath, Birmingham
Nickname: The Blues
Biggest win: 12-0 v Nottingham Forest (1899), Walsall Town Swifts (1892) and Doncaster Rovers (1903)
Heaviest defeat: 1-9 v Blackburn Rovers (1895) and Sheffield Wednesday (1930)

Founded in 1875 as Small Heath Alliance, the club were founder members and the first champions of the Second Division in 1892. Unfortunately, Small Heath were undone at the 'test match' stage (a 19th-century version of the play-offs) and failed to gain promotion to the top flight.

• **The club had to wait until 2011 for the greatest day in their history, when the Blues beat hot-favourites Arsenal 2-1 in the League Cup final at Wembley,** on-loan striker Obafemi Martins grabbing the winner in the final minutes to spark ecstatic celebrations among Birmingham's long-suffering fans. City had previously won the competition back in 1963 after getting the better of arch rivals Aston Villa over a two-legged final, although that achievement was hardly comparable as half the top-flight clubs hadn't even bothered to enter.

• However, on the final day of the 2010 /11 season Birmingham were relegated from the Premier League, to become only the second club (after Norwich City in 1985) to win a major domestic trophy and suffer the drop in the same campaign. It was the 12th time in their history that the Blues had fallen through the top-flight trapdoor, a record of misery unmatched by any other club.

• **In 1956 Birmingham became the first club to reach the FA Cup final without playing a single tie at home, the Midlanders winning at Torquay, Leyton Orient, West Brom and Arsenal before seeing off Sunderland in the semi-final at Hillsbrough. Perhaps, though, their tricky route to Wembley caught up with them, as they lost in the final to Manchester City.**

Red Devils thrashed Northampton 8-2 in an FA Cup fifth-round tie at the Cobblers' old County Ground. "I was so embarrassed that I played the last 20 minutes at left-back," he said years later.

• There appeared to be no limit to what he might achieve, but Best's career nosedived in the 1970s as his hard-drinking, glamorous lifestyle inevitably took its toll. Sacked by Manchester United for repeatedly missing training sessions, Best played for a succession of lesser clubs in Britain and the USA, only occasionally showing flashes of his old brilliance. He eventually ended his playing career in the low-key environment of

Dean Court, making four appearances for Bournemouth in 1983.

• **Easily the finest player ever to represent Northern Ireland, Best never appeared in the final stages of the World Cup or European Championships. Yet he remains idolised in his home country, his standing summed up by the popular Belfast saying: "Maradona good, Pele better, George Best".**

• After a long battle with alcoholism, Best died in November 2005. His passing was marked by a minute's applause at grounds up and down the country – the first British player to receive this continental-style tribute.

• On 15th May 1955 Birmingham became the first English club to compete in Europe when they drew 0-0 away to Inter Milan in the inaugural competition of the Fairs Cup. In 1960 the Blues went all the way to the final of the same tournament to set another first for English clubs in Europe, but lost 4-1 on aggregate to Barcelona. The following year Birmingham were runners-up in the Fairs Cup again, going down 4-2 on aggregate to Roma.

• **The Blues are the only club to have hit double figures in a league fixture on five separate occasions, although they haven't managed the feat since 1915 when they trounced Glossop North End 11-1 in a Second Division fixture.**

• England goalkeeper Gil Merrick played in a record 551 games for Birmingham in all competitions between 1946 and 1959. The club's record goalscorer is inter-war striker Joe Bradford with 249 league goals in the 1920s and 1930s.

• Birmingham's most famous fan is comedian Jasper Carrott, who once summed up the often depressing experience of following the club with the wry remark: "You lose some, you draw some." The Blues' lack of success over the years has been blamed on a 100-year curse put on St Andrew's by discontented gypsies who were evicted from the site when the club moved there in 1906. Various managers attempted to exorcise the curse before it ended in 2006, including '80s boss Ron Saunders who had crucifixes fixed to the stadium's floodlight pylons.

> HONOURS
> **Division 2 champions** *1893, 1921, 1948, 1955*
> **Second Division champions** *1995*
> **League Cup** *1963, 2011*
> **Football League Trophy** *1991, 1995*

IS THAT A FACT?
In the first season in which footballers could be legally paid, 1885/86, Blackburn Rovers spent a total of £615 on players' wages during the whole of the campaign. These days that wouldn't cover a months' wages for the club's tea lady!

BLACKBURN ROVERS

Year founded: 1875
Ground: Ewood Park (31,367)
Nickname: Rovers
Biggest win: 11-0 v Rossendale United (1884)
Heaviest defeat: 0-8 v Arsenal (1933)

Founded in 1875 by a group of wealthy local residents and ex-public school boys, Blackburn Rovers joined the Football League as founder members in 1888. Two years later the club moved to a permanent home at Ewood Park, where they have remained ever since.

• **Blackburn were a force to be reckoned with from the start, winning the FA Cup five times in the 1880s and 1890s. Of all league clubs Rovers were the first to win the trophy, beating Scottish side Queen's Park 2-1 in the final at Kennington Oval in 1884. The Lancashire side went on to win the cup in the two following years as well, setting a record which still stands by remaining undefeated in 24 consecutive games in the competition between 1884-86.**

• Rovers won the cup again in 1890, 1891 and 1928 to make a total of six triumphs in the competition. In the first of these victories they thrashed Sheffield Wednesday 6-1 in the final, with left-winger William Townley scoring three times to become the first player to hit a hat-trick in the final.

• **The club have won the league title three times: in 1912, 1914 and, most memorably, in 1995 when, funded by the millions of local steel magnate Jack Walker and powered by the deadly 'SAS' strikeforce of Alan Shearer and Chris Sutton, Rovers pipped reigning champions Manchester United to the Premiership title. The team soon broke up, though, and Rovers were relegated from the top tier just four years later.**

• Derek Fazackerley made the most appearances for Blackburn, turning out in 596 games between 1970 and 1986. The club's all-time leading scorer is Simon Garner, with 168 league goals between 1978 and 1992, although Alan Shearer's incredible record of 122 goals in just 138 games for the club is

arguably more impressive.

• **In 1891 Blackburn featured in one of the most bizarre matches in the history of the game against bitter local rivals Burnley. After two mass brawls, all the Rovers team except goalkeeper Herby Arthur decided they'd had enough and left the field. Facing the entire Burnley side on his own, Arthur successfully appealed for offside and then refused to take the free kick because he had no one to pass to, forcing the referee to abandon the game.**

• Blackburn won the League Cup for the first and only time to date in 2002, beating Tottenham 2-1 in the final at the Millennium Stadium in Cardiff. A year earlier the club had returned to the Premiership after a two-season absence. However, Rovers slipped back into the Championship in 2012 after a tumultuous season, which saw fans campaigning against the club's Indian owners, Venky's, and unpopular manager Steve Kean.

> HONOURS
> **Division 1 champions** *1912, 1914*
> **Premier League champions** *1995*
> **Division 2 champions** *1975*
> **FA Cup** *1884, 1885, 1886, 1890, 1891, 1928*
> **League Cup** *2002*

BLACKPOOL

Year founded: 1887
Ground: Bloomfield Road (16,220)
Nickname: The Seasiders
Biggest win: 10-0 v Lanerossi Vincenza (1972)
Heaviest defeat: 1-10 v Small Heath (1901)

Founded in 1887 by old boys of St John's School, Blackpool joined the Second Division of the Football League in 1896. The club merged with South Shore in 1899, the same year in which Blackpool lost their league status for a single season.

• **Blackpool's heyday was in the late 1940s and early 1950s when the club reached three FA Cup finals in five years. The Seasiders lost in the finals of 1948 and 1951 but lifted the cup in**

1953 after defeating Lancashire rivals Bolton 4-3 in one of the most exciting Wembley matches ever. Although centre forward Stan Mortensen scored a hat-trick, the match was dubbed the 'Matthews Final' after veteran winger Stanley Matthews, who finally won a winners' medal at the grand old age of 38.

• An apprentice at the time of the Matthews Final, long-serving right-back Jimmy Armfield holds the record for league appearances for Blackpool, with 569 between 1952 and 1971. Now a match summariser for BBC Radio Five Live, Armfield is also Blackpool's most-capped player, having played for England 43 times. In 2011 a nine-foot high statue of the Seasiders legend was unveiled outside Bloomfield Road.

• **The club's record scorer is Jimmy Hampson, who hit 248 league goals between 1927-38, including a season best 45 in the 1929/30 Second Division championship-winning campaign.**

• The club first began wearing their famous tangerine shirts in 1923, following a recommendation by referee Albert Hargreaves, who had officiated at a match between Holland and Belgium and had been impressed by the Dutchmen's bold colours.

• **Blackpool's local derby at home to Bolton on 10th September 1960 was the first league game ever to be televised. The match didn't make great viewing for the Seasiders' fans, however, as their team slumped to a 1-0 defeat.**

• Blackpool are the only club to have gained promotion from three different divisions via the play-offs, most recently rising from the Championship to the Premier League in 2010 after a thrilling 3-2 win over Cardiff City at Wembley. More than 30,000 ecstatic tangerine-clad fans celebrated the club's return to the top flight for the first time since 1971 by bringing the town's famous Golden Mile to a virtual standstill. However, the following year Blackpool dropped back down to the Championship, despite scoring 55 league goals — a record for a relegated Premier League club.

HONOURS
Division 2 champions 1930
FA Cup 1953
Football League Trophy 2002, 2004

SEPP BLATTER

Born: Visp, Switzerland, 10th March 1936

Sepp Blatter tries to hide from his critics

The most powerful man in world football, FIFA President Sepp Blatter was first elected to the post in 1998. Following his most recent re-election in 2011, Blatter is the third-longest serving President of the game's world governing body, after Jules Rimet (1921-54) and Joao Havelange (1974-98).

• **Blatter's tenure has been clouded by allegations of financial mismanagement, notably the claim that bribery played a part in Qatar's successful bid to host the 2022 World Cup. Blatter himself has been criticised for suggesting that female players should wear tighter shorts to make their game more attractive to men, and for arguing that on-field racism should not be investigated by the authorities but resolved by the players involved with 'a handshake'.**

• During his long reign Blatter has introduced a number of significant changes to the game, including the rule that states a player who removes his shirt while celebrating a goal will receive a yellow card. Blatter was also instrumental in a change to the World Cup format in 2002, which meant that the reigning champions no longer qualified automatically for the next tournament.

• **A long-term opponent of goal-line technology, Blatter had a change of heart after the 2010 World Cup following the furore over Frank Lampard's 'goal' against Germany** which was not awarded despite clearly crossing the line. Two years later FIFA sanctioned the use of the 'Hawk Eye' goal-line camera system for the first time in an international when England played Belgium in a pre-Euro 2012 friendly at Wembley, and during the tournament itself Blatter said that the introduction of goal-line technology was "no longer an alternative, but a necessity".

BOLTON WANDERERS

Year founded: 1874
Ground: The Reebok Stadium (28,101)
Previous name: Christ Church
Nickname: The Trotters
Biggest win: 13-0 v Sheffield United (1890)
Heaviest defeat: 1-9 v Preston North End (1887)

The club was founded in 1874 as Christ Church, but three years later broke away from the church after a disagreement with the vicar and adopted their present name (the 'Wanderers' part stemmed from the fact that the club had no permanent home until moving to their former stadium Burnden Park in 1895).

• **Bolton were founder members of the Football League in 1888, finishing fifth at the end of the campaign. The Trotters have since gone on to play more seasons in the top flight without ever winning the title, 73, than any other club.**

• The club, though, have had better luck in the FA Cup. After defeats in the final in 1894 and 1904, Bolton won the cup for the first time in 1923 after beating West Ham 2-0 in the first Wembley final. In the same match Bolton centre forward David Jack enjoyed the distinction of becoming the first player to score a goal at the new stadium. The Trotters went on to win the competition again in 1926 and 1929.

• **In 1953 Bolton became the first, and so far only, team to score three goals in normal time in the FA Cup final yet finish as losers, going down 4-3 to a Stanley Matthews-inspired Blackpool. In 1958 Bolton won the cup for a fourth time, beating Manchester United 2-0 in the final at Wembley. Since then major honours have eluded**

the club, although the Trotters were runners-up in the League Cup in 1995 and 2004.

• The lowest moment in the club's history came at the end of the 1986/87 season when Bolton were relegated to the old Fourth Division for the first time. However, a remarkable recovery saw them reach the Premiership for the first time in 1995. Despite twice being relegated from the top flight in the late 1990s, Bolton bounced back again and under former manager Sam Allardyce established themselves as Premier League regulars. During Allardyce's eight-year reign at the Reebok, Bolton qualified for Europe for the first time after finishing sixth in the Premiership in 2005. However, after an 11-stay in the top flight, the Trotters were relegated back to the Championship on the last day of the 2011/12 season.

• **In 1993, while they were in the third tier, Bolton became the last club from outside the top two flights to knock out the reigning FA Cup holders when they beat Liverpool 2-0 at Anfield in a third-round replay. The following season Wanderers, by then in the second tier, accounted for the holders again, beating Arsenal 3-1 in a fourth round replay at Highbury.**

• Bolton's old Burnden Park stadium was the scene of one of the worst disasters in the history of English football in 1946 when 33 people were killed after two barriers collapsed during a cup tie with Stoke. Amazingly, the match was played to a conclusion on the advice of the police.

• **The club's top scorer is legendary centre forward Nat Lofthouse, who notched 285 goals in all competitions between 1946 and 1960. Lofthouse is also Bolton's most-capped international, making 33 appearances for England. The Trotters' appearance**

record is held by another England international of the same era, goalkeeper Eddie Hopkinson, who turned out 578 times for the club between 1952 and 1970.

• In June 2008 Bolton splashed out a club record £8.2 million to bring Toulouse striker Johan Elmander to the Reebok. The club's record sale was made a few months earlier when Nicolas Anelka joined Chelsea for £15 million.

> **HONOURS**
> **Division 2 champions** 1909, 1978
> **First Division champions** 1997
> **Division 3 champions** 1973
> **FA Cup** 1923, 1926, 1929, 1958, 1999
> **Football League Trophy** 1989

A young Ryan Giggs was very proud of his entry for the 1991 Turner Prize – a sculpture entitled 'Boots'

BOOTS

The first record of a pair of football boots goes back to 1526 when Henry VIII, then aged 35, ordered "45 velvet pairs and one leather pair for football" from the Great Wardrobe. Whether he actually donned the boots for a Royal kick-around in Hampton Court or Windsor Castle is not known.

• **Early leather boots were very different to the synthetic ones worn by modern players, having hard toe-caps and protection around the ankles. Studs were originally prohibited, but were sanctioned after a change in the rules in 1891. Lighter boots without ankle protection were first worn in South America, but did not become the norm in Britain until the 1950s,**

IS THAT A FACT?
In 2011 both Manchester United and Sunderland banned their youth team players from wearing coloured boots, insisting instead that they wore traditional black ones.

following the example of England international Stanley Matthews who had a lightweight pair of boots made for him by a Yorkshire company.

• Herbert Chapman, later Arsenal's manager, is believed to be the first player to wear coloured boots, sporting a yellow pair in the 1900s. White boots first became fashionable in the 1970s when they were worn by the likes of Alan Ball (Everton), Terry Cooper (Leeds) and Alan Hinton (Derby County). In 1996, Liverpool's John Barnes was the first player to wear white boots in an FA Cup final.

• Boots, or rather the lack of them, became a major issue at the 1950 World Cup. After qualifying for the tournament for the first time, India pulled out of the finals after their players were refused permission to play barefoot!

• Today's top players all have individual boot sponsorship deals with the major manufacturers. Stars linked with the various boot companies include Cristiano Ronaldo (Nike), Lionel Messi (Adidas) and Joe Hart (Umbro). In a patriotic gesture at the 2006 World Cup, all the Germany players wore boots made by the nation's leading boots manufacturer, Adidas.

Helped by their secret weapon, a headless giant, Borussia Dortmund were German champions in 2012

BORUSSIA DORTMUND

Year founded: 1909
Ground: Signal Iduna Park (80,720)
Nickname: The Borussians
League titles: 8
Domestic cups: 3
European cups: 2
International cups: 1

German champions Borussia Dortmund were founded by members of a church team in 1909 who decided to form their own club without the involvement of a strict local priest. They chose the name 'Borussia', which means 'Prussia' in Latin, after a nearby brewery.

• In 1966 Dortmund became the first German club to win a European trophy when they beat Liverpool 2-1 in the final of the Cup Winners' Cup at Hampden Park. The greatest day in the club's history, though, came in 1997 when they defeated favourites Juventus 3-1 in the Champions League final. In the same year they lifted the

Intercontinental Cup after beating Brazilian side Cruzeiro.

• The club's Signal Iduna Park stadium (previously known as Westfalenstadion) is the largest in Germany, with a capacity of 80,720. It was the venue for a number of games at the 2006 World Cup, including the semi-final between the hosts and eventual winners Italy.

• In 2012 Dortmund clinched their first ever Double when they smashed Bayern Munich 5-2 in the German Cup final, three weeks after wrapping up the Bundesliga title for a second consecutive year.

> **HONOURS**
> *German League champions 1956, 1957, 1963, 1995, 1996, 2002, 2011, 2012*
> *German Cup 1965, 1989, 2012*
> *Champions League 1997*
> *European Cup Winners' Cup 1966*
> *Intercontinental Cup 1997*

BOURNEMOUTH

Year founded: 1899
Ground: Dean Court (10,700)
Previous name: Boscombe, Bournemouth and Boscombe Athletic
Nickname: The Cherries
Biggest win: 11-0 v Margate (1970)
Heaviest defeat: 0-9 v Lincoln City (1982)

The Cherries were founded as Boscombe FC in 1899, having their origins in the Boscombe St John's club, which was formed in 1890. The club's name changed to Bournemouth and Boscombe FC in 1923 and then to AFC Bournemouth in 1971, when the team's colours were altered to red-and-black stripes in imitation of AC Milan.

BRADFORD CITY

• However, any similarities with the Serie A giants end there, as much of Bournemouth's existence has been spent in the lower divisions struggling with financial difficulties. **The Cherries, though, enjoyed a never-to-be-forgotten day in 1984 when they beat reigning FA Cup holders Manchester United 2-0 in a third round tie at Dean Court.**

• Bournemouth recorded their biggest-ever win in the same competition, smashing fellow seasiders Margate 11-0 at Dean Court in 1970. Cherries striker Ted MacDougall scored nine of the goals, an all-time record for an individual player in the competition.

• **Bournemouth were the first ever winners of the Football League Trophy (then known as the Associate Members' Cup) in 1984, beating Hull City 2-1 in the final at Boothferry Park.**

• The club's record scorer is Ron Eyre (202 goals between 1924 and 1933) while striker Steve Fletcher has pulled on the Cherries' jersey an amazing 617 times since his debut in 1992.

> HONOURS
> *Division 3 champions 1987*
> *Football League Trophy 1984*

BRADFORD CITY

Year founded: 1903
Ground: Valley Parade (25,136)
Nickname: The Bantams
Biggest win: 11-1 v Rotherham United (1928)
Heaviest defeat: 1-9 v Colchester United (1961)

Bradford City were founded in 1903 when a local rugby league side, Manningham FC, decided to switch codes. The club was elected to Division Two in the same year before they had played a single match – a swift ascent into the Football League which is only matched by Chelsea.

• **City's finest hour was in 1911 when they won the FA Cup for the only time in the club's history, beating Newcastle 1-0 in a replayed final at Old Trafford. There were more celebrations in Bradford in 1929 when City won the Third Division (North) scoring 128**

goals in the process – a record for the third tier.

• Sadly, City will forever be associated with the fire that broke out in the club's main stand on 11th May 1985 and killed 56 supporters. The official inquiry into the tragedy found that the inferno had probably been caused by a discarded cigarette butt which set fire to litter under the stand. As a permanent memorial to those who died Bradford added black trimming to their shirt collars and sleeves.

• **West Indian full-back Cec Podd holds Bradford's appearance record, turning out for the club in 502 league games between 1970 and 1984. Northern Ireland international Bobby Campbell is the club's top scorer with 121 league goals in two spells at Valley Parade in the 1980s.**

• Bradford City's coffers have been unexpectedly boosted in recent years by Harry Potter fans who have bought thousands of the club's amber-and-claret scarves as they are identical to Harry's house scarf at Hogwarts School!

> HONOURS
> *Division 2 champions 1908*
> *Division 3 (N) champions 1929*
> *Division 3 champions 1985*
> *FA Cup 1911*

BRAZIL

First international: Argentina 3 Brazil 0, 1914
Most capped player: Cafu, 142 caps (1990-2006)
Leading goalscorer: Pele, 77 goals (1957-71)
First World Cup appearance: Brazil 1 Yugoslavia 2, 1930
Biggest win: Brazil 14 Nicaragua 0, 1975
Heaviest defeat: Uruguay 6 Brazil 0, 1920

The most successful country in the history of international football, Brazil are renowned for an exciting, flamboyant style of play which delights both their legions of drum-beating fans and neutrals alike.

• Brazil is the only country to have won the World Cup five times. The

South Americans first lifted the trophy in 1958 (beating hosts Sweden 5-2 in the final) and retained the prize four years later in Chile. In 1970, a great Brazilian side featuring legends such as Pele, Jairzinho, Gerson and Rivelino thrashed Italy 4-1 to win the Jules Rimet trophy for a third time. Further triumphs followed in 1994 (3-2 on penalties against Italy after a dour 0-0 draw) and in 2002 (after beating Germany 2-0 in the final).

• Brazil is the only country to have appeared at every World Cup (a total of 19) since the tournament began in 1930. The South Americans have also scored the most goals (210) and recorded the most wins (67) at the finals.

• Brazil have worn their famous kit of yellow shirts, blue shorts and white socks since 1954 when a newspaper ran a competition for readers to

Brazil: The most successful country in the history of football

design a new outfit for the national team based around the colours of the Brazilian flag. Originally their shirts were white!

TOP 10

GREATEST BRAZIL PLAYERS

1. Pele (1957-71)
2. Garrincha (1955-66)
3. Zico (1971-89)
4. Zizinho (1942-57)
5. Arthur Friedenreich (1912-35)
   Tostao (1966-72)
7. Didi (1952-62)
8. Leonidas (1932-46)
9. Nilton Santos (1949-62)
   Ronaldo (1994-2011)

Poll by International Federation of Football History & Statistics

• With eight wins to their name, Brazil are the third most successful side in the history of the Copa America (behind Uruguay and Argentina, who have won the trophy 15 and 14 times respectively). Brazil last won the tournament in Venezuela in 2007, beating neighbours Argentina 3-0 in the final.

• In 1970, after Brazil won the World Cup for a third time, they were allowed to keep the Jules Rimet trophy. Unfortunately it was stolen from the Brazilian Football Confederation offices in Rio de Janeiro 13 years later and has never been seen since.

HONOURS

World Cup 1958, 1962, 1970, 1994, 2002

Copa America 1919, 1922, 1949, 1989, 1997, 1999, 2004, 2007

Confederations Cup 1997, 2005, 2009

World Cup record

1930 Round 1
1934 Round 1
1938 Semi-finals
1950 Runners-up
1954 Quarter-finals
1958 Winners
1962 Winners
1966 Round 1
1970 Winners
1974 Fourth place
1978 Third place
1982 Round 2
1986 Quarter-finals
1990 Round 2
1994 Winners
1998 Runners-up
2002 Winners
2006 Quarter-finals
2010 Quarter-finals

BRENTFORD

Year founded: 1889
Ground: Griffin Park (12,763)
Nickname: The Bees
Biggest win: 9-0 v Wrexham (1963)
Heaviest defeat: 0-7 v Swansea Town (1926), v Walsall (1957) and v Peterborough (2007)

Brentford were founded in 1889 by members of a local rowing club. After playing at a number of different venues, the club settled at Griffin Park in 1904.

• **The club enjoyed its heyday in the decade prior to World War II. In 1929/30 Brentford won all 21 of their home games in the Third Division (South) to set a record which remains to this day. Promoted to the First Division in 1935, the Bees finished in the top six in the next three seasons before being relegated in the first post-war campaign.**

• Despite winning the League Two Championship in 2008/09, Brentford have achieved little of note since those glory days. Supporters, though, have ample opportunity to drown their sorrows as the club's ground, Griffin Park, has a pub on all four corners – including one, The Princess Royal, which is owned by the club.

• **The club's most-capped player is John Buttigieg who played 22 times for Malta while at Griffin Park between 1989-91.**

• Singer Rod Stewart had trials at Brentford in 1961 before concentrating on his music career, while TV presenter Bradley Walsh played for the club's reserve team in the late 1970s. Other famous names associated with the club are former BBC director general Greg Dyke, who is Brentford's chairman, and Hollywood actress Cameron Diaz, a keen fan of the Bees.

HONOURS
Division 2 champions 1935
Division 3 (S) champions 1933
Division 4 champions 1963
Third Division champions 1999
League Two champions 2009

IS THAT A FACT?
Brighton are the only non-league club to have won the Charity Shield, beating Aston Villa 1-0 in 1910 in the days when the match was contested between the Football League and Southern League champions.

BRIGHTON AND HOVE ALBION

Year founded: 1900
Ground: AMEX Stadium (22,374)
Previous name: Brighton and Hove Rangers
Nickname: The Seagulls
Biggest win: 10-1 v Wisbech (1965)
Heaviest defeat: 0-9 v Middlesbrough (1958)

Founded originally as Brighton and Hove Rangers in 1900, the club changed to its present name the following year. In 1920 Brighton joined Division Three as founder

After winning promotion to the Championship and moving to a new ground in 2011, the Seagulls of Brighton have been squawking with delight

members but had to wait another 38 years before gaining promotion to a higher level.

• The club reached the final of the FA Cup for the only time in their history in 1983, holding favourites Manchester United to a 2-2 draw at Wembley. The Seagulls were unable to repeat their heroics in the replay, however, and crashed to a 4-0 defeat. In the same year Brighton were relegated from the old First Division, ending a four-season stint in the top flight.

• A decade earlier, The Seagulls were briefly managed by the legendary Brian Clough. His time in charge of the club, though, was not a successful one and included an 8-2 thrashing by Bristol Rovers – the worst home defeat in Brighton's history.

• Brighton's record scorer is 1920s striker Tommy Cook, with 114 league goals. Cult hero Peter Ward, though, enjoyed the most prolific season in front of goal for the club, notching 32 times as the Seagulls gained promotion from the old Third Division in 1976/77. Ernie 'Tug' Wilson made the most appearances for the south coast outfit, with 509 between 1922 and 1936.

• Brighton enjoyed a year to remember in 2011. Not only did they win the League One title under manager Gus Poyet, a former midfield star with Chelsea and Tottenham, but they finally waved goodbye to the ramshackle Withdean Stadium, an athletics venue which had been their 'temporary' home for 12 long years, and moved into their spanking new £93 million ground, the 22,500-capacity AMEX Stadium.

• Famous fans of the club include TV presenters Des Lynam and Jamie Theakston, and DJ Norman Cook.

HONOURS
Division 3 (S) champions 1958
Second Division champions 2002
League One champions 2011
Division 4 champions 1965
Third Division champions 2001

BRISTOL CITY

Year founded: 1894
Ground: Ashton Gate (21,497)
Previous name: Bristol South End
Nickname: The Robins
Biggest win: 11-0 v Chichester City (1960)
Heaviest defeat: 0-9 v Coventry City (1934)

Founded as Bristol South End in 1894, the club took its present name when it turned professional three years later. In 1900 City merged with Bedminster, whose ground at Ashton Gate became the club's permanent home in 1904.

• The Robins enjoyed a golden decade in the 1900s, winning promotion to the top flight for the first time in 1906 after a campaign in which they won a joint record 14 consecutive games. The following season City finished second behind champions Newcastle then, in 1909, they reached the FA Cup final for the first and only time in their history, losing 1-0 to Manchester United at Crystal Palace.

• Since then the followers of Bristol's biggest club have had to endure more downs than ups. The Robins returned to the top flight after a 65-year absence in 1976, but financial difficulties led to three consecutive relegations in the early 1980s (City being the first club ever to suffer this ghastly fate).

• City's strikers were on fire in 1962/63 as the Robins scored 100 goals in Division Three. Sadly for their fans, City could only finish 14th in the league – the lowest place ever by a club hitting three figures.

• With 314 goals in 597 league games for the club between 1951 and 1966, England international striker John Atyeo is both the Robins' top scorer and record appearance maker. Following his death in 1993, a stand at Ashton Gate was named after him.

• Between October 1932 and December 1933 Bristol City conceded at least one goal in 49 consecutive Division Three (South) fixtures – a record for any division.

• Bristol City are the only club to have won both the Welsh Cup (1934) and the Anglo-Scottish Cup (1978).

• Famous fans of the club include comedy genius John Cleese and excitable BBC football commentator Jonathan Pearce.

• To the delight of their fans, the Robins have had the upper hand in their clashes with rivals Bristol Rovers, winning 42 games against Rovers' total of 28.

Bristol City, proud winners of both the Welsh Cup and the Anglo-Scottish Cup!

HONOURS
Division 2 champions 1906
Division 3 (S) champions 1923, 1927, 1955
Football League Trophy 1986
Welsh Cup 1934

BRISTOL ROVERS

Year founded: 1893
Ground: Memorial Stadium (12,011)
Previous name: Black Arabs, Eastville Rovers, Bristol Eastville Rovers
Nickname: The Pirates
Biggest win: 15-1 v Weymouth (1900)
Heaviest defeat: 0-12 v Luton Town (1936)

Bristol Rovers can trace their history back to 1883 when the Black Arabs club was founded at the Eastville Restaurant in Bristol. The club was renamed Eastville Rovers the following year in an attempt to attract more support from the local area, later adding 'Bristol' to their name before finally settling on plain old 'Bristol Rovers' in 1898.

• Rovers have lived up to their name by playing at no fewer than nine different grounds. Having spent much of their history at Eastville Stadium, they are based at the Memorial Stadium, which they share with Bristol Rugby Club.

• The only Rovers player to have appeared for England while with The Pirates, Geoff Bradford is the club's record scorer, netting 242 times in the league between 1949 and 1964. The club's record appearance maker is Stuart Taylor, who turned out in 546 league games between 1966 and 1980.

• Rovers legend Ronnie Dix is the youngest player ever to score in the Football League, getting off the mark in a 3-0 win against Norwich City in 1928 when he was aged just 15 years and 180 days.

• Rovers were the first club from the bottom tier of the Football League to win an FA Cup tie at a Premier League ground, beating Derby County 3-1 at Pride Park in the third round in 2002.

HONOURS
Division 3 (S) champions 1953
Division 3 champions 1990

GIANLUIGI BUFFON

Born: Carrara, Italy, 28th January 1978
Position: Goalkeeper
Club career:
1995-2001 Parma 168
2001- Juventus 325
International record:
1997- Italy 120

Gianluigi Buffon became the world's most expensive goalkeeper when he moved from Parma to Juventus in 2001 for a staggering £32.6 million. He soon proved his worth, though, helping Juve win consecutive titles in his first two seasons with the Turin club, having previously lifted the UEFA Cup with Parma in 1999.

• Since making his international debut against Russia in 1997, Buffon has been a fixture between the posts for Italy. In 2006 he won a World Cup winners' medal with the Azzurri, after Italy beat France in a penalty shoot-out in the final in Berlin. Buffon's outstanding form – he kept five clean sheets in the tournament – earned him the Yashin Award for the best goalkeeper in the competition. At the end of the year he was runner-up to Italian team-mate Fabio Cannavaro in the European Footballer of the Year poll, the first goalkeeper to be ranked so highly since Italian legend Dino Zoff also came second in 1973.

• Buffon would have had two more Serie A titles to his name had Juventus not

Gianluigi Buffon, the world's most expensive goalkeeper

been stripped of their 2005 and 2006 championship victories for their part in a match-fixing scandal. The club was also punished with relegation to Serie B in 2006 but, to the surprise of many, Buffon decided to stay put and help Juve win promotion the following year.

• Serie A Goalkeeper of the Year on a record eight occasions and the third highest capped Italian international ever, Buffon was appointed Italy captain in 2011.

BURNLEY

Year founded: 1882
Ground: Turf Moor (22,546)
Nickname: The Clarets
Biggest win: 9-0 v Darwen (1892), v New Brighton (1957) and v Penrith (1984)
Heaviest defeat: 0-11 v Darwen (1885)

One of England's most famous old clubs, Burnley were founded in 1882 when the Burnley Rovers rugby team decided to switch to the round ball game. The club was a founder member of the Football League in 1888 and has since won all four divisions of the league – a feat matched only by Preston and Wolves.

• Burnley have twice won the league championship, in 1921 and 1960. The first of these triumphs saw the Clarets go on a 30-match unbeaten run, the longest in a single season until Arsenal went through the whole of 2003/04 undefeated. In its own way, Burnley's 1960 title win was just as remarkable, as the Clarets only ever topped the league on the last day of the season after a 2-1 win at Manchester City.

• The club's only FA Cup triumph came in 1914 when they defeated Liverpool 1-0 in the last final at Crystal Palace. After the final whistle Burnley's captain Tommy Boyle became the first man to receive the cup from a reigning monarch, King George V.

• On 16th April 2011 Burnley defender Graham Alexander became only the second outfield player in the history of English football to make 1,000 professional appearances when he came on as a sub in the Clarets' 2-1 win over Swansea City. Alexander is also the most successful penalty taker ever in the domestic game, with 78 goals from the spot in 86 attempts.

• Burnley splashed out a club record £3 million on Hibs striker Steven Fletcher shortly after they gained promotion to the Premier League in 2009. A year later, after they were relegated back to the Championship, Fletcher moved to Wolves for £6 million to become Burnley's most expensive sale.

TOP 10

LONGEST UNBEATEN RUNS IN THE TOP FLIGHT

1.	Arsenal, 2003-04	49 games
2.	Nottingham Forest, 1977-78	42 games
3.	Chelsea, 2004-05	40 games
4.	Leeds United, 1968-69	34 games
5.	Liverpool, 1987-88	31 games
6.	Burnley, 1920/21	30 games
7.	Leeds United, 1973-74	30 games
8.	Arsenal, 2002-03	30 games
9.	Chelsea, 2008-09	29 games
10.	Manchester United, 2010-11	29 games

• Burnley splashed out a club record £3 million on Hibs striker Steven Fletcher shortly after they gained promotion to the Premier League in 2009. Three years later the Clarets sold winger Jay Rodriguez to Southampton for a club record fee of £7 million.

HONOURS
Division 1 champions 1921, 1960
Division 2 champions 1898, 1973
Division 3 champions 1982
Division 4 champions 1992
FA Cup 1914

BURTON ALBION

Year founded: 1950
Ground: Pirelli Stadium (6,912)
Nickname: The Brewers
Biggest win: 12-1 v Coalville Town (1954)
Heaviest defeat: 0-10 v Barnet (1970)

Burton Albion were founded at a public meeting at the Town Hall in 1950. The town had previously supported two Football League clubs, Burton Swifts and Burton Wanderers, who merged to form Burton United in 1901 before folding nine years later.

• The Brewers gained promotion to the Football League for the first time in 2009, going up as Conference

IS THAT A FACT?

At the 2006 World Cup in Germany Gianluigi Buffon conceded just two goals in seven games, a record for a World Cup-winning goalkeeper (which was equalled by Spain's Iker Casillas at the 2010 tournament).

champions. Since then Burton have consolidated their position in the fourth tier, including a spell under the management of Paul Peschisolido, the husband of West Ham director Karren Brady.

• The Brewers' top scorer in league football is Shaun Harrad with 31 goals, including an impressive 21 in 2009/10 – another club record.

• In 2006 Burton achieved the greatest result in their history when they held mighty Manchester United to a 0-0 draw at home in the third round of the FA Cup. A record visiting contingent at Old Trafford of 11,000 Brewers fans attended the replay, but they had little to cheer about as United strolled to an emphatic 5-0 victory. Five years later the Brewers reached the fourth round of the cup for the first time, before their hopes of making further progress were dashed by Burnley.

HONOURS
Conference champions 2009

BURY

Year founded: 1885
Ground: Gigg Lane (11,840)
Nickname: The Shakers
Biggest win: 12-1 v Stockton (1897)
Heaviest defeat: 0-10 v Blackburn Rovers (1887) and West Ham (1982)

The club with the shortest name in the Football League, Bury were founded in 1885 at a meeting at the Old White Horse Hotel in Bury, as successors to two other teams in the town, the Bury Unitarians and the Bury Wesleyans. Bury were founder members of the Lancashire League in 1889, joining the Second Division of the Football League five years later.

• Bury have won the FA Cup on two occasions, in 1900 and 1903. In the second of these triumphs, The Shakers thrashed Derby County 6-0 at Crystal Palace to record the biggest ever victory in an FA Cup final.

• On 27th August 2005 Bury became the first club to score 1,000 goals in all four tiers of the Football League. The landmark was reached when Brian Barry-

Murphy scored the first of the Shakers' goals in their 2-2 home draw with Wrexham in a League Two fixture.

• The following year Bury set a less-happy record, when they became the first club to be thrown out of the FA Cup for fielding an ineligible player – Stephen Turnbull, a loan signing from Hartlepool United.

• In 2011 veteran striker Ryan Lowe scored in a club record nine consecutive league games, a prolific run which helped Bury win promotion to League One at the end of the season.

HONOURS
Division 2 champions 1895
Division 3 champions 1961
Second Division champions 1997
FA Cup 1900, 1903

SIR MATT BUSBY

Born: Orbiston, North Lanarkshire, 26th May 1909
Died: 20th January 1994
Managerial career:
1945-69 Manchester United
1970-71 Manchester United
1958 Scotland (part-time)

The second longest serving post-war manager in English football, Manchester United legend Sir Matt Busby was in charge at Old Trafford for a total of 25 years until he retired in 1971. In that time he won five league championships

(1952, 1956, 1957, 1965 and 1967) and the FA Cup in 1948 and 1963.

• Busby was also the first manager to win the European Cup with an English club, United defeating Benfica 4-1 at Wembley in 1968. Shortly after this triumph, Busby was knighted.

• It had long been Busby's dream to win club football's greatest prize, and it was one he might have fulfilled much earlier but for the Munich air crash of 1958, in which eight members of his brilliant United side (nicknamed the 'Busby Babes' because they were so young) were killed. Busby himself suffered multiple injuries in the crash and spent two months in hospital before returning to Old Trafford to rebuild his shattered team.

• Ironically, Busby's playing career was spent with United's two great rivals, Liverpool and Manchester City (with whom he won the FA Cup in 1934). A defensive midfielder, he won one cap for Scotland against Wales in 1933. Some 25 years later he briefly managed the Scots on a part-time basis, during which time he gave an international debut to future United star Denis Law.

• In 1993, a year before Busby died, the local council honoured the legendary United boss by renaming the main road opposite Old Trafford 'Sir Matt Busby Way'. Three years later a bronze statue of Busby was erected outside the ground as United made their own lasting tribute to the most significant figure in their history.

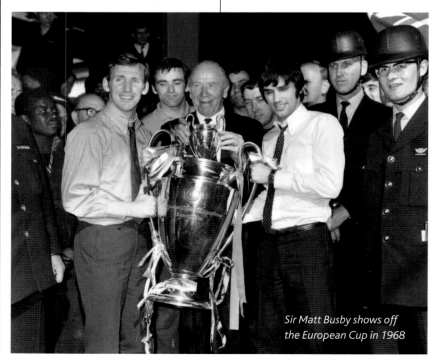

Sir Matt Busby shows off the European Cup in 1968

ERIC CANTONA

Born: Paris, France, 24th May 1966
Position: Striker
Club career:
1983-88 Auxerre 81 (23)
1985-86 Martigues (loan) 15 (4)
1988-91 Marseille 40 (13)
1988-89 Bordeaux (loan) 11 (6)
1989-90 Montpellier (loan) 33 (10)
1991-92 Nimes 17 (2)
1992 Leeds United 28 (9)
1992-97 Manchester United 144 (64)
International record:
1987-95 France 45 (20)

Maverick Frenchman Eric Cantona is one of the most successful foreign players in Premiership history, winning the league championship in five of his six seasons in English football and landing the Double twice.

• **In 1993, Cantona became the first-ever player to win back-to-back league titles with two different clubs when he fired Manchester United to the championship just 12 months after helping Leeds do the same. Amazingly for such an influential figure, Cantona's switch across the Pennines cost the Old Trafford side just £1.2 million in November 1992.**

• The signing of the inspirational Cantona proved to be the catalyst for a decade of dominance by United in the 1990s. In 1994 the former Marseille star was voted PFA Player of the Year as United won the Double for the first time in their history, Cantona coolly slotting home two penalties in his side's 4-0 thrashing of Chelsea in the FA Cup final to become the first Frenchman to win the trophy.

Two years later, United won the Double for a second time and again Cantona was their match-winner in the FA Cup final, scoring the only goal of the game against Liverpool. Another PFA Player of the Year award duly followed.

• **However, the period in between these triumphs saw Cantona serve an eight-month ban after he launched a 'kung fu' kick at an abusive Crystal Palace fan in a match at Selhurst Park in January 1995. The hot-headed Frenchman was also fined £10,000 by the FA and ordered to complete 120 hours of community service after being found guilty of assault.**

• Since his retirement from the game in 1997 when he was aged just 30, Cantona has pursued a successful career as an actor, starring as himself in the 2009 film Looking for Eric.

Manchester United legend, kung fu king, beach footballer, actor... is there no end to Eric Cantona's talents?

CAPS

Legendary goalkeeper Peter Shilton has won more international caps than any other British player. 'Shilts' played for England 125 times between 1970 and 1990 and would have won many more caps if he had not faced stiff competition for the No. 1 shirt from his great rival Ray Clemence, who won 61 caps during the same period. Along with Billy Wright, Sir Bobby Charlton, Bobby Moore and David Beckham, Shilton is one of just five players to have won over 100 caps for England.

• **The first international caps were awarded by England in 1886, following a proposal put forward by the founder of the Corinthians, NL Jackson. To this day players actually receive a handmade 'cap' to mark the achievement of playing for their country. England caps are made by a Bedworth-based company called Toye, Kenning & Spencer, who also provide regalia for the freemasons.**

• The most-capped player in the history of the game is Egypt midfielder Ahmed Hassan, who has played an

C

CAPS

IS THAT A FACT?

England captain Billy Wright became the first player in the world to win 100 caps for his country when he led his team out against Scotland at Wembley in 1959.

CARDIFF CITY

astonishing 184 times for his country since making his debut in 1995. The women's record is held by Kristine Lilly, who made an extraordinary 352 appearances for the USA between 1987 and 2010.

• A handful of players have won caps for more than one country, including the great Real Madrid striker Alfredo di Stefano who represented Spain and Colombia as well as his native Argentina.

CARDIFF CITY

Year founded: 1899
Ground: Cardiff City Stadium (26,828)
Previous name: Riverside
Nickname: The Bluebirds
Biggest win: 8-0 v Enfield (1931)
Heaviest defeat: 2-11 v Sheffield United (1926)

Founded as the football branch of the Riverside Cricket Club, the club changed to its present name in 1908, three years after Cardiff was awarded city status.

• **Cardiff are the only non-English club to have won any of the three main English honours, lifting the FA Cup in 1927 after a 1-0 victory over Arsenal at Wembley. They came close to repeating that feat in 2008, but were beaten 1-0 by Portsmouth in only the second FA Cup final staged at the new Wembley.**

• On 7th April 1947 a crowd of 51,621 squeezed into Cardiff's old Ninian Park stadium for the club's match against Bristol City – an all-time record attendance for the third tier of English football.

• **Cardiff, who missed out on promotion to the Premier League in 2010, 2011 and 2012 in the play-offs, have won the Welsh Cup 22 times, just one short of Wrexham's record. The Bluebirds' domination of the tournament in the 1960s and 1970s earned them regular qualification for the European Cup Winners' Cup and in 1968 they reached the semi-finals of the competition before losing 4-3 on aggregate to Hamburg.**

• Cardiff's record appearance maker is defender Phil Dwyer, who turned out 476 times for the club between 1972-1985.

The Bluebirds' record scorer is Len Davies, who banged in 128 league goals in the 1920s.

> HONOURS
> **Division 3 (S) champions** 1947
> **Third Division champions** 1993
> **FA Cup** 1927
> **Welsh Cup** 1912, 1920, 1922, 1923, 1927, 1928, 1930, 1956, 1959, 1964, 1965, 1967, 1968, 1969, 1970, 1971, 1973, 1974, 1976, 1988, 1992, 1993

CARLISLE UNITED

Year founded: 1903
Ground: Brunton Park (18,202)
Nickname: The Blues
Biggest win: 8-0 v Hartlepool (1928) and v Scunthorpe (1952)
Heaviest defeat: 1-11 v Hull City (1939)

Carlisle United were formed in 1903 following the merger of two local clubs, Shaddongate United and Carlisle Red Rose. The Blues joined the Third Division (North) in 1928 and were long-term residents of the bottom two divisions until 1965, when they won promotion to the second tier for the first time.

• **The club's finest moment came in 1974 when, in their one season in the top flight, they sat on top of the old First Division after three games. Sadly, the Cumbrians were soon knocked off their lofty perch and finished the campaign rock bottom.**

• A long period of decline meant that by 1999 Carlisle were facing relegation from the Football League. However, needing a win against Plymouth on the last day of the season to stay up, United were saved when on-loan goalkeeper Jimmy Glass went up for a corner and scored a dramatic last-gasp winner. They were eventually relegated to the Conference in 2004 but bounced back the following year after a play-off victory over Stevenage Borough.

• **Carlisle have reached the final of the Football League Trophy on a record six occasions, and in 1995 became the first and only team to lose an English trophy on the 'golden goals' rule when they conceded in extra-time in the final against Birmingham City.**

> HONOURS
> **Division 3 (S) champions** 1965
> **Third Division champions** 1995
> **League Two champions** 2006
> **Football League Trophy** 1997, 2011

TOP 10

MOST EXPENSIVE PREMIER LEAGUE PLAYERS

1. Fernando Torres (Liverpool to Chelsea, 2011) £50m
2. Sergio Aguero (Atletico Madrid to Manchester City, 2011) £38m
3. Andy Carroll (Newcastle to Liverpool, 2011) £35m
4. Robinho (Real Madrid to Manchester City, 2008) £32.5m
5. Eden Hazard (Lille to Chelsea, 2012) £32m
6. Andrei Shevchenko (AC Milan to Chelsea, 2006) £30.8m
7. Dimitar Berbatov (Tottenham to Manchester United, 2008) £30.75m
8. Rio Ferdinand (Leeds United to Manchester United, 2002) £29.1m
9. Juan Sebastian Veron (Lazio to Manchester United, 2001) £28.1m
10. Edin Dzeko (Wolsburg to Manchester City, 2011) £27m

ANDY CARROLL

> **Born:** Gateshead, 6th January 1989
> **Position:** Striker
> **Club career:**
> 2006-11 Newcastle United 80 (31)
> 2007-08 Preston North End (loan) 11 (1)
> 2011-12 Liverpool 42 (6)
> 2012- West Ham (loan)
> **International record:**
> 2010- England 7 (2)

The most-expensive British player in Premier League history, Andy Carroll joined Liverpool from Newcastle for an eye-watering £35 million at the end of the January transfer window in 2011. Despite scoring in both the FA Cup semi-final and final the following year, he struggled to hold down a starting place with the Reds and in August 2012 joined West Ham on a season-long loan.

• A powerfully built striker who is especially strong in the air, the pony-tailed Carroll made his Newcastle debut in a UEFA Cup tie against Palermo in November 2006. Aged 17 and 300 days at the time, he set a record as the youngest ever player to appear for the Geordies in Europe. He had to wait a while before establishing himself in the team, but after contributing 17 league goals to Newcastle's Championship title success in 2010 he was hailed as one of the hottest properties in English football.

• Carroll made his England debut against France at Wembley in November 2010,

and the following year scored his first goal for the Three Lions with a fierce drive in a 1-1 friendly draw against Ghana.

• However, before that match then England boss Fabio Capello suggested that Carroll needed to cut back his alcohol intake, saying, "He needs to improve, to drink less." Capello's concerns, though, did not seem to trouble his successor, Roy Hodgson, who picked Carroll as one of his four strikers for the Euro 2012 tournament and the big man justified his selection with a brilliant headed goal in England's 3-2 win against Sweden.

IKER CASILLAS

Born: Madrid, 20th May 1981
Position: Goalkeeper
Club career:
1999- Real Madrid 457
International record:
2000- Spain 138

Spain captain Iker Casillas is the only goalkeeper to have skippered his country to success in both the European Championships and the World Cup. The Real Madrid star pulled off the first leg of this double when Spain beat Germany in the Euro 2008 final in Vienna, before

landing the biggest prize of all two years later after Spain's 1-0 defeat of Holland in the 2010 World Cup final in Johannesburg. He then made it a hat-trick as Spain retained the European championship in 2012.

• **In 2000 Casillas became the youngest goalkeeper to play in the Champions League final, appearing in Real's 3-0 victory over Valencia just four days after his 19th birthday. He won the competition again two years later, after coming on as a sub in Real's 2-1 defeat of Bayer Leverkusen in the final in Glasgow.**

• Casillas is the highest capped international in Spanish football history, passing fellow goalkeeper Andoni Zubizarreta's record of 126 games for Spain in 2011. The following year he set a new record of 73 international clean sheets when Spain beat Serbia 2-0, extending his total to an incredible 79 games by the end of Euro 2012.

• **Thanks in part to Spain's huge success in recent years, Casillas now holds the record for playing in the most international victories. He passed Liliam Thuram's old record of 94 wins when he came on as a sub in Spain's 3-1 friendly defeat of South Korea in May 2012 and became the first player ever to win 100 internationals when Spain thrashed Italy 4-0 in the final of Euro 2012.**

since been beaten by Edwin van der Sar).

• **He had previously set a similar national record in his native Czech Republic, clocking up 855 minutes without conceding in the 2001/02 season while with Sparta Prague.**

• Cech was a member of the Czech Republic side which reached the semi-finals of Euro 2004 before losing to eventual winners Greece. He has since gone on to win 94 caps for his country, making him the second highest appearance maker for the Czech Republic behind Karel Poborsky.

• **In October 2006 Cech suffered a depressed fracture of the skull following a challenge by Reading's Stephen Hunt. He returned to action after three months out of the game wearing a rugby-style headguard for protection, and has gone on to make 369 appearances in all competitions for Chelsea – a club record for an overseas player.**

• In 2012 Cech became the first ever goalkeeper to win the FA Cup four times when he played in Chelsea's 2-1 defeat of Liverpool in the final at Wembley. Two weeks later he starred in the Blues' Champions League final victory over Bayern Munich, blocking a penalty from former team-mate Arjen Robben in extra-time and then saving two more in the shoot-out.

PETR CECH

Born: Plzen, Czech Republic, 20th May 1982
Position: Goalkeeper
Club career:
1999-2001 Chmel Blsany 27
2001-02 Sparta Prague 27
2002-04 Rennes 70
2004- Chelsea 256
International record:
2002- Czech Republic 94

A brilliant shot-stopper who dominates his penalty area with his imposing physique, Cech joined Chelsea from French club Rennes for £10 million in 2004. During the Blues' title-winning season in 2004/05, Cech set two Premiership records by keeping 25 clean sheets and going 1,025 minutes without conceding a goal (the second record has

'If I don't save it with my hands I'll stop it with my nose'

CELTIC

Year founded: 1888
Ground: Celtic Park (60,832)
Nickname: The Bhoys
Biggest win: 11-0 v Dundee (1895)
Heaviest defeat: 0-8 v Motherwell (1937)

The first British team to win the European Cup, Celtic were founded by an Irish priest in 1887 with the aim of raising funds for poor children in Glasgow's East End slums. The club were founder members of the Scottish League in 1890, winning their first title three years later.

• **Celtic have won the Scottish Cup more times than any other club, with 35 victories in the final. The Bhoys first won the cup in 1892, beating Queen's Park 5-1 in a replay.**

• Under legendary manager Jock Stein Celtic won the Scottish league for nine consecutive seasons in the 1960s and 1970s, with a side featuring great names like Billy McNeill, Jimmy Johnstone, Bobby Lennox and Tommy Gemmell. This extraordinary run of success equalled a world record established by MTK Budapest of Hungary in the 1920s but, painfully for Celtic fans, was later matched by bitter rivals Rangers in the 1990s.

• **The greatest-ever Celtic side, managed by Stein and dubbed the 'Lisbon Lions', became the first British club to win the European Cup when they beat Inter Milan 2-1 in the Portuguese capital in 1967. Stein was central to the team's triumph, scoring an early point by sitting in Inter**

Inside the Celtic 'huddle': 'OK, you hide the ball under your jersey, run down the other end, then whack it into the net...'

manager Helenio Herrera's seat and refusing to budge and then urging his players forward after they went a goal down to the defensive-minded Italians. Sticking to their attacking game plan, Celtic fought back with goals by Gemmell and Steve Chalmers to spark jubilant celebrations at the end among the travelling Celtic fans. Remarkably, all the 'Lisbon Lions' were born and bred within a 30-mile radius of Celtic Park.

• That 1966/67 season was the most successful in the club's history as they won every competition they entered: the Scottish League, Scottish Cup and Scottish League Cup, as well as the European Cup. To this day, no other British side has won a similar 'Quadruple'.

• **The skipper of the Lisbon Lions was Billy McNeill, who went on to play in a record 790 games for Celtic in all**

competitions between 1957 and 1975. He later managed the club, leading Celtic to the Double in their centenary season in 1987/88. The club's most-capped player is goalkeeper Pat Bonner, who made 80 appearances for the Republic of Ireland between 1981 and 1996.

• Jimmy McGrory, who played for the club between 1922 and 1938, scored a staggering 397 goals for Celtic – a British record by a player for a single club. His most prolific season for the Bhoys was in 1935/36 when he hit a club record 50 league goals.

• **In 1957 Celtic won the Scottish League Cup for the first time, demolishing Rangers 7-1 in the final at Hampden Park. The victory stands as the biggest by either side in an Old Firm match and is also a record for a major Scottish cup final. Celtic**

IS THAT A FACT?
Petr Cech holds the record for keeping 100 Premier League clean sheets in the fewest appearances, 180, reaching the landmark on 13th April 2010 after Chelsea's 1-0 win over Bolton at Stamford Bridge.

went on to enjoy more success in the League Cup, appearing in a record 14 consecutive finals (winning six) between 1965 and 1978.

• Celtic hold the record for the longest unbeaten run in Scottish football, with 62 matches undefeated (49 wins, 13 draws) from 13th November 1915 until 21st April 1917 when Kilmarnock finally beat the men from Glasgow 2-0. The club also holds the record for the most points in a single league season, racking up 103 when winning the SPL in 2002.

• Two years later, during the 2003/04 season, Celtic won an incredible 25 SPL games on the trot. The run was a Scottish record and has only ever been bettered by three clubs worldwide.

• A vast crowd of 136,505 attended Celtic's European Cup semi-final match against Leeds United at Hampden Park in 1970, the highest ever attendance for a European club competition fixture.

• Celtic's fans are known throughout the world for their passionate and devoted support. In 2003, 80,000 of them pitched up in Seville for the UEFA Cup final defeat by Porto, the largest away following to travel abroad for a match in the history of the game.

HONOURS

Division 1 champions 1893, 1884, 1896, 1898, 1905, 1906, 1907, 1908, 1909, 1910, 1914, 1915, 1916, 1917, 1919, 1922, 1926, 1936, 1938, 1954, 1966, 1967, 1968, 1969, 1970, 1971, 1972, 1973, 1974
Premier Division champions 1977, 1979, 1981, 1982, 1986, 1988, 1998
SPL champions 2001, 2002, 2004, 2006, 2007, 2008, 2012
Scottish Cup 1892, 1899, 1900, 1904, 1907, 1908, 1911, 1912, 1914, 1923, 1925, 1927, 1931, 1933, 1937, 1951, 1954, 1965, 1967, 1969, 1971, 1972, 1974, 1975, 1977, 1980, 1985, 1988, 1989, 1995, 2001, 2004, 2005, 2007, 2011
League Cup 1957, 1958, 1966, 1967, 1968, 1969, 1970, 1975, 1983, 1998, 2000, 2001, 2006
European Cup 1967

CHAMPIONS LEAGUE

The most prestigious competition in club football, the Champions League replaced the old European Cup in 1992. Previously a competition for domestic league champions only, runners-up from

the main European nations were first admitted in 1997 and the tournament has subsequently expanded to include up to four entrants per country.

• Spanish giants Real Madrid won the first European Cup in 1956, defeating French side Reims 4-3 in the final in Paris. Real went on to win the competition in the next four years as well, thanks largely to the brilliance of their star players Alfredo Di Stefano and Ferenc Puskas. With six wins in the European Cup and three in the Champions League, Real have won the competition a record nine times.

• The first British club to win the European Cup were Celtic, who famously beat Inter Milan in the final in Lisbon in 1967. The following year Manchester United became the first English club to triumph, beating Benfica 4-1 at Wembley. The most successful British club in the

tournament, though, are Liverpool, with five wins in 1977, 1978, 1981, 1984 and 2005 followed by Manchester United with three (1968, 1999 and 2008). Three other English clubs, Nottingham Forest (in 1979 and 1980), Aston Villa (in 1982)

IS THAT A FACT?
Sinan Bolat of Standard Liege is the only goalkeeper to score from open play in the Champions League, netting a last-minute headed equaliser in his side's 1-1 draw with AZ Alkmaar in 2009.

and Chelsea (in 2012) have also won the tournament.

• Veteran Spanish striker Raul is the leading scorer in the competition, with an incredible 71 goals for Real Madrid and Schalke. Raul also holds the record for the most appearances, having played in 144 games in the tournament.

• Real Madrid winger Francisco Gento is the most successful player in the history of the competition with six winners' medals (1956-60 and 1966).

• Between March 2005 and May 2006 Arsenal went a record 995 minutes without conceding a goal in the Champions League. The Gunners' defence was eventually breached by Barcelona, who beat the north Londoners in the 2006 final in Paris.

• Manchester United were unbeaten in a record 25 games in the Champions League between 2007-09. This impressive run finally came to an end when they lost 2-0 to Barcelona in the 2009 final in Rome.

• Evergreen United midfielder Ryan Giggs is the oldest player to score in the competition, netting in a 2011 group stage match against Benfica aged 37 and 289 days.

• Feyenoord recorded the biggest win in the competition in 1969 when they thrashed KR Reykjavik 12-2 in the first round. Benfica hold the record for the biggest aggregate victory with an 18-0 first-round humiliation of Luxembourg no-hopers Stade Dudelange in 1965.

CHAMPIONS LEAGUE FINALS

1993 Marseille 1 AC Milan 0
1994 AC Milan 4 Barcelona 0
1995 Ajax 1 AC Milan 0
1996 Juventus 1* Ajax 1
1997 Borussia Dortmund 3 Juventus 1
1998 Real Madrid 1 Juventus 0
1999 Man United 2 Bayern Munich 1
2000 Real Madrid 3 Valencia 0
2001 Bayern Munich 1* Valencia 1
2002 Real Madrid 2 Bayer Leverkusen 1
2003 AC Milan 0* Juventus 0
2004 Porto 3 Monaco 0
2005 Liverpool 3* AC Milan 3
2006 Barcelona 2 Arsenal 1
2007 AC Milan 2 Liverpool 1
2008 Man United 1* Chelsea 1
2009 Barcelona 2 Man United 0
2010 Inter Milan 2 Bayern Munich 0
2011 Barcelona 3 Man United 1
2012 Bayern Munich 1 Chelsea 1*

* Won on penalties

Liverpool fans are the loudest in the Premier League... and that's official!

CHANTS

A survey by www.fanchants.com during the 2010/11 season found that Liverpool fans were the loudest in the Premier League, their chants averaging an impressive 97 decibels. They were followed by fans of Manchester United and Aston Villa, while Fulham supporters were the quietest.

• In 2004, in a competition sponsored by Barclaycard, Birmingham fan Jonny Hurst was chosen as England's first 'Chant Laureate' by a judging panel chaired by then Poet Laureate Andrew Motion. Bizarrely, Hurst's winning entry, set to the tune of the Barry Manilow song Copacabana, was about Colombian striker Juan Pablo Angel – who, at the time, was playing for Brum's arch rivals Aston Villa!

• Possibly the oldest football chant is

TOP 10

FOOTBALL RINGTONES

1. Chelsea, Chelsea
2. We're By Far The Greatest Team (Arsenal version)
3. United Road Take Me Home (Manchester United)
4. We Love You Arsenal
5. Keep The Blue Flag Flying High (Chelsea)
6. Fields Of Anfield Road (Liverpool)
7. Blue Moon (Manchester City)
8. Liverpool, Liverpool, Liverpool!
9. Manchester Is Wonderful (Manchester United)
10. Come On Chelsea!

Source: Ringtone requests on www.fanchants.com

'Who ate all the pies?', which researchers at Oxford University have discovered dates back to 1894 when it was playfully directed by Sheffield United fans at their 22-stone goalkeeper William 'Fatty' Foulke. The chant stemmed from an incident when the tubby custodian got up early at the team hotel, sneaked down into the dining room and munched his way through all the pies that were laid out for the players' breakfast.

HERBERT CHAPMAN

Born: Kiveton Park, Yorkshire, 19th January 1878
Died: 6th January 1934
Managerial career:
1907-12 Northampton Town
1912-19 Leeds City
1921-25 Huddersfield Town
1925-34 Arsenal

Herbert Chapman rivals Arsène Wenger as Arsenal's greatest-ever manager. Previously trophyless, the Gunners won two league titles and the FA Cup during Chapman's nine years at the club and went on to dominate English football in the years after his sudden death from pneumonia in January 1934.

• One of the game's first modernisers, Chapman introduced new tactics and training methods, as well as championing floodlights, shirt numbers and a Europe-wide football competition years before they all became an accepted part of the game. He is also credited with adding white sleeves to Arsenal's previously all-red shirts after admiring the outfit of

a staff member in the Arsenal club offices who came to work sporting a white shirt with a red tank top.

• Before he joined Arsenal in 1925, Chapman managed Northampton, Leeds City and Huddersfield Town. His four-year spell with Huddersfield was easily the most successful in the club's history, the Terriers winning the FA Cup and two league titles under his management, with a third following the season after he left. While he was at Arsenal, Chapman also took charge of two England games in 1933.

• In recognition of his achievements with the Gunners, a bronze bust of Chapman stands inside the Emirates Stadium.

CHARLTON ATHLETIC

Year founded: 1905
Ground: The Valley (27,111)
Nickname: The Addicks
Biggest win: 8-1 v Middlesbrough (1953)
Heaviest defeat: 1-11 v Aston Villa (1959)

Charlton Athletic were founded in 1905 when a number of youth clubs in the south-east London area, including East Street Mission and Blundell Mission, decided to merge. The club, whose nickname 'the Addicks' stemmed from the haddock served by a local chippy, graduated from minor leagues to join the Third Division (South) in 1921.

• **Charlton's heyday was shortly before and just after World War II. After becoming the first club to win successive promotions from the Third to First Division in 1935/36 the Addicks finished runners-up, just three points behind league champions Manchester City, in 1937. After losing in the 1946 FA Cup final to Derby County, Charlton returned to Wembley the following year and this time lifted the cup thanks to a 1-0 victory over Burnley in the final.**

• Charlton's home ground, The Valley, used to be one of the biggest in English football. In 1938 a then record crowd of 75,031 squeezed into the stadium to see the Addicks take on Aston Villa in a fifth round FA Cup tie. In 1985, though,

financial problems forced Charlton to leave the Valley and the Addicks spent seven years as tenants of West Ham and Crystal Palace before making an emotional return to their ancestral home in 1992.

• **When the play-offs were introduced in season 1986/87, Charlton figured among the first finalists, beating Leeds to preserve their First Division status. In 1998, during the long managerial reign of Alan Curbishley, the Addicks triumphed in possibly the most gripping Wembley play-off final, beating Sunderland 7-6 on penalties after a 4-4 draw to earn promotion to the Premiership.**

• Sam Bartram, who was known as 'the finest 'keeper England never had', played a record 623 games for the club between 1934 and 1956. Bearded striker Derek Hales is Charlton's record goalscorer, notching 168 in two spells at the club in the 1970s and 1980s.

• In 2012 Charlton returned to the Championship after winning the League One title with 101 points, matching Fulham's record points tally for the third tier set in 1998/99.

HONOURS
First Division champions 2000
Division 3 (S) champions 1929, 1935
League One champions 2012
FA Cup 1947

SIR BOBBY CHARLTON

Born: Ashington, 11th October 1937
Position: Midfielder
Club career:
1956-73 Manchester United 606 (199)
1973-74 Preston North End 38 (8)
1975 Waterford 31 (18)
International record:
1958-70 England 106 (49)

One of English football's greatest ever players, Sir Bobby Charlton had a magnificent career with Manchester United and England. He remains the highest scorer for both club and country, with 249 goals in all competitions for the Reds and 49 goals in 106 international appearances.

• **Charlton broke into the United first team in 1956, scoring twice on his debut against Charlton Athletic. Two years later he was one of the few**

United players to survive the Munich Air Crash, after being hauled from the burning wreckage by goalkeeper Harry Gregg.

• During the 1960s Charlton won everything the game had to offer, winning the league title twice (1965 and 1967), the FA Cup (1963), the European Cup (scoring twice in the final against Benfica at Wembley in 1968) and the World Cup with England in 1966 (along with his brother, Jack). Probably his best performance for his country came in the semi-final against Portugal at Wembley, when he scored both goals (including a trademark piledriver) in a 2-1 victory.

• **European Footballer of the Year in 1966, Charlton eventually left United in 1973 to become player-manager of Preston. He returned to Old Trafford as a director in 1984 and was knighted a decade later.**

A young Bobby Charlton, years before he became the record goalscorer for both Manchester United and England

CHEATING

The most famous instance of on-pitch cheating occurred at the 1986 World Cup in Mexico when Argentina's Diego Maradona punched the ball into the net to open the scoring in his side's quarter-final victory over England. Maradona was unrepentant afterwards, claiming the goal was scored by "the hand of God, and the head of Diego".

• **In a similar incident in 2009 France captain Thierry Henry clearly handled the ball before crossing for William Gallas to score the decisive goal in a World Cup play-off against Ireland. "I will be honest, it was a handball – but I'm not the ref," a sheepish Henry admitted after the match.**

• In a 1989 World Cup qualifier Brazil were leading Chile 1-0 when a firecracker landed near Chilean goalkeeper Roberto Rojas. He fell to the ground, blood pouring from his head and, when his team-mates insisted it was unsafe to continue playing, the referee abandoned the match. Video evidence, however, revealed that Rojas had cut his own head with a razor blade hidden inside his glove. FIFA awarded Brazil a 2-0 victory which knocked Chile out of the 1990 World Cup and they were also excluded from the 1994 tournament. Rojas, who had hoped his self-inflicted injury would produce a rematch at a neutral venue, was banned from football for life.

• **In September 2009 IFK Gothenburg goalkeeper Kim Christensen was caught by TV cameras using his feet to push the bottom of his posts a few centimetres inwards before a match against Orebro. The referee eventually spotted that the posts had been moved and pushed them back into the correct position. Christensen later admitted that he had moved the goalposts in several earlier matches.**

• In 2009 a number of players in Zimbabwe were revealed to be using the identities of younger relatives in a bid to play longer in junior football, thus increasing their chances of being spotted by a scout from a European club. Age falsification among players has also been an issue in other African countries, notably Nigeria.

CHELSEA

Year founded: 1905
Ground: Stamford Bridge (41,837)
Nickname: The Blues
Biggest win: 13-0 v Jeunesse Hautcharage (1971)
Heaviest defeat: 1-8 v Wolves (1953)

Founded in 1905 by local businessmen Gus and Joseph Mears, Chelsea were elected to the Football League in that very same year. At the time of their election, the club had not played a single match – only Bradford City can claim a similarly swift ascent into league football.

• **Thanks to the staggering wealth of their Russian owner, Roman Abramovich, Chelsea are now one of the richest clubs in the world. Since taking over the Londoners in 2003, Abramovich has pumped hundreds of millions into the club and has been rewarded with back-to-back Premiership titles in 2005 and 2006, the FA Cup in 2007, 2009 and 2012, the Carling Cup in 2005 and 2007 and, under former manager Carlo Ancelotti, the league and cup Double in 2010. After watching his team come agonisingly close on numerous occasions, Abramovich finally saw Chelsea win the Champions League in 2012 when, led by caretaker manager Roberto di Matteo, the Blues beat Bayern Munich on penalties in the final.**

• Chelsea clinched the title in 2010 with an 8-0 thrashing of Wigan, a resounding victory that meant the Blues finished the season with a Premier League record 103 goals and a top-flight best ever goal difference of 71.

• **The Blues' recent success is in marked contrast to their early history. For the first 50 years of their existence Chelsea won precisely**

One for Roman's scrapbook...

nothing, finally breaking their duck by winning the league championship in 1955. After a succession of near misses, the club won the FA Cup for the first time in 1970, beating Leeds 2-1 at Old Trafford in the first post-war final to go to a replay. Flamboyant striker Peter Osgood scored in every round of the cup run and remains the last player to achieve this feat.

• The following year, the Blues won the European Cup Winners' Cup, beating Real Madrid in Athens after another replay. Defending their trophy the next season, Chelsea thrashed Luxembourg minnows Jeunesse Hautcharage 21-0 to set a European record aggregate score. In 1998 club legend Gianfranco Zola scored the only goal of the final against Stuttgart as the Blues became the only British side to lift the Cup Winners' Cup on two occasions.

• The club's fortunes declined sharply in the late 1970s and 1980s, the Blues spending much of the period in the Second Division while saddled with large debts. However, an influx of veteran foreign stars in the mid-1990s, including Zola, Ruud Gullit and Gianluca Vialli, sparked an exciting revival capped when the Blues won the

FA Cup in 1997, their first major trophy for 26 years.

• In the final against Middlesbrough, Italian midfielder Roberto di Matteo scored with a long-range shot after just 43 seconds – at the time the fastest-ever goal in a Wembley final. Further silverware followed in the League Cup in 1998 and the FA Cup in 2000, in the last final played at the old Wembley.

• Chelsea's arrival as one of England's top clubs was finally confirmed when charismatic manager Jose Mourinho led the Blues to the Premiership title in 2005. The club's tally of 95 points set a record for the competition, while goalkeeper Petr Cech went a then record 1,025 minutes during the season without conceding a goal. A second Premiership title followed in 2006, before Mourinho was sensationally sacked a year later. When the club first won the championship way back in 1955, they did so with a record low of just 52 points.

• In 2007 Chelsea won the first-ever FA Cup final at the new Wembley, Ivorian striker Didier Drogba scoring the only goal against Manchester United. In the same year the Blues won the Carling Cup, making them just the third English

team after Arsenal (1993) and Liverpool (2001) to claim a domestic cup double. The Blues also won the FA Cup in 2009 and 2010, making them the first team to retain the trophy at the new Wembley.

• Hardman defender Ron 'Chopper' Harris is Chelsea's record appearance maker, turning out an incredible 795 times for the club in all competitions between 1962 and 1980. Harris' team-mate Bobby Tambling is the Blues' top scorer, with 202 goals between 1958 and 1970. Legendary striker Jimmy Greaves scored the most goals in a single season, with 41 in 1960/61.

• Between 2004 and 2008 the Blues were unbeaten in 86 consecutive home league matches, a record for both the Premiership and the Football League. The impressive run was eventually ended by Liverpool, who won 1-0 at Stamford Bridge on 26th October 2008.

• The club's record signing is Fernando Torres who cost a British record £50 million when he moved to west London from Liverpool in January 2011. In 2007 the Blues sold Dutch winger Arjen Robben to Real Madrid for a club record £24 million.

• Among the many celebrities who support the Blues are England cricketer

Kevin Pietersen, Madness frontman Suggs, broadcaster Johnny Vaughan and veteran film director Richard Attenborough, who is the club's Life Vice-President.

CHELTENHAM TOWN

Year founded: 1892
Ground: Whaddon Road (7,066)
Nickname: The Robins
Biggest win: 12-0 v Chippenham Rovers (1935)
Heaviest defeat: 1-10 v Merthyr Tydfil (1952)

Cheltenham were founded in 1892 but didn't play in the Football League until 1999, the year that the club won the Conference under manager Steve Cotterill. The star of the Robins' promotion-winning side was 41-year-old winger Clive Walker, a former favourite at Chelsea, Sunderland and Fulham.

• The Robins have since twice gained promotion to the third tier via the play-offs, defeating Rushden 3-1 in the final at the Millennium Stadium in 2002 and Grimsby 1-0 four years later at the same venue, but missed out on a hat-trick when they lost 2-0 to Crewe in the 2012 final. The club also won the FA Trophy in 1998, beating Southport 1-0 at Wembley Stadium.

• Cheltenham splashed out a club record £60,000 in 2003 when they signed Jermaine McGlashan from West Ham. The most expensive player to leave Whaddon Road is Steven Gillespie, who signed for Colchester United for a cool £400,000 in June 2008.

• During the 2008/09 season Cheltenham fielded no fewer than

51 different players, many of them loan signings, over the course of a campaign which ended in relegation to League Two.

CHESTERFIELD

Year founded: 1866
Ground: B2net Stadium (10,400)
Previous name: Chesterfield Town
Nickname: The Spireites
Biggest win: 10-0 v Glossop North End (1903)
Heaviest defeat: 0-10 v Gillingham (1987)

The fourth-oldest club in the UK, Chesterfield were founded in 1866. The club was elected to the Second Division in 1899 as Chesterfield Town but lost its league status a decade later, only to return as plain Chesterfield when Division Three (North) was created in 1921.

• Chesterfield fans still complain about a refereeing decision in the 1997 FA Cup semi-final against Middlesbrough which they believe denied their team a place in the final at Wembley. TV replays showed that Jonathan Howard's shot had crossed the Boro line but referee David Elleray thought otherwise. The game went to a replay in which the Spireites were eventually beaten.

• In the 1923/24 campaign Chesterfield goalkeeper Arthur Birch scored five goals, all of them penalties, for the club – a record tally by a keeper in a single season.

• In 2011 Chesterfield became only the second club (after Doncaster) to win the fourth tier title three times when they topped League Two. Sadly for their fans, they were relegated from League One the following season, but they did manage to win the Football League Trophy for the first time, beating Swindon 2-0 in the final.

PAPISS CISSÉ

Born: Dakar, Senegal, 3rd June 1985
Position: Striker
Club career:
2003-04 Douanes Dakar 26 (23)
2005-09 Metz 95 (36)
2005-06 Cherbourg (loan) 28 (11)
2008-09 Chateauroux (loan) 15 (4)
2009-12 Freiburg 65 (37)
2012- Newcastle United 14 (13)
International record:
2009- Senegal 19 (10)

Pap's the way to do it! Cissé celebrates yet another goal

After arriving at St James' Park from German club Freiburg for around £10 million in January 2012, Senegalese striker Papiss Cissé enjoyed a sensational start to his Newcastle career, scoring 10 goals in his first nine games. Only Micky Quinn has reached double figures more quickly in the Premier League era, taking just six games for Coventry City in 1992/93.

• Cissé's goalscoring exploits first attracted attention when he was at French club Metz, but following a £1.5 million move to Freiburg in 2009 he became even more of a hot property. His total of 22 goals in the Bundesliga in 2010/11 was an all-time record for an African player, and made him the league's second-highest scorer behind Bayern Munich's Mario Gomez.

• With fellow Senegalese international Demba Ba providing valuable support, Cissé finished his first half season in the Premier League with an impressive 13 goals in 14 games. His best strike, a swerving shot from outside the area against Chelsea at Stamford Bridge, was chosen as the BBC's 'Goal of the Season'.

• First capped by Senegal in 2009, Cissé averaged a goal every other game in his first 19 appearances to date for his country.

CLEAN SHEETS

Former Manchester United goalkeeper Edwin van der Sar holds the British record for league clean sheets, keeping the ball out of his net for 14 Premiership games and a total of 1,311 consecutive minutes in the 2008/09 season. He was finally beaten on 4th March 2009 by Newcastle's Peter Lovenkrands in United's 2-1 victory at St James' Park.

• The world record for clean sheets is held by Brazilian goalkeeper Mazaropi of Vasco de Gama who went 1,816 minutes without conceding in 1977/78, while the European record belongs to Dany Verlinden of Bruges (1,390 minutes in 1990).

• Italy's long-serving goalkeeper Dino Zoff holds the international record, going 1,142 minutes without having to pick the ball out of his net between September 1972 and June 1974. Another Italian goalkeeper, Walter Zenga, holds the record for clean sheets at the World Cup, with a run of 518 minutes at the 1990 tournament.

• England's overall clean sheet record is held by Peter Shilton who shut out the opposition in 66 of his 125 international appearances between 1970 and 1990. The international record is held by Spain's Iker Casillas with 74 in 131 appearances.

• Chelsea hold the Premier League record for clean sheets in a season, with 24 in 2004/05. Three clubs jointly hold the record for fewest clean sheets, Birmingham (2007/08), Derby (2007/08) and Norwich (2011/12) managing just three each.

BRIAN CLOUGH

Born: Middlesbrough, 21st March 1935
Died: 20th September 2004
Managerial career:
1965-67 Hartlepool United
1967-73 Derby County
1973-74 Brighton
1974 Leeds United
1975-93 Nottingham Forest

The first post-war manager to win the league championship with two different clubs, Brian Clough is a legendary figure at both Derby County and Nottingham Forest. He transformed the fortunes of both clubs, leading Derby from the old Second Division to the title in 1972 before repeating the trick with newly-promoted Forest in 1978.

• The following year Clough guided Forest to success in the European Cup, new £1 million signing Trevor Francis grabbing the winner against Malmo in the final. The Midlanders retained the trophy in 1980 too, beating Hamburg 1-0 in the final in Madrid. During his 18 years with Forest, Clough also won the League Cup four times, but his final season with the club ended in anguish when Forest were relegated from the Premiership in 1993.

• Brash, opinionated and outspoken, Clough was a prolific striker with Middlesbrough and Sunderland before a knee injury forced his retirement from the game aged 29. He also won two caps for England in 1959.

• Since his death from stomach cancer in 2004 the stretch of the A52 linking Nottingham and Derby has been renamed Brian Clough Way and a statue of one of English football's greatest managers and biggest characters has been unveiled in his home town of Middlesbrough.

CLUB WORLD CUP

A competition contested between the champion clubs of all six continental confederations of FIFA, the Club World Cup was first played in Brazil in 2000 but has only been an annual tournament

TOP 10		
PREMIER LEAGUE CLEAN SHEETS 2011/12		
1.	Manchester United	20
2.	Manchester City	17
3.	Newcastle United	15
4.	Swansea City	14
5.	Tottenham	14
6.	Arsenal	13
7.	Everton	12
	Liverpool	12
	Sunderland	12
10.	Fulham	11

'Now, young man, you don't take a picture of Brian Clough without asking his permission first!'

since 2005 when it replaced the old Intercontinental Cup.

• **Manchester United's participation in the first Club World Cup led to the Red Devils pulling out of the FA Cup in 2000, a tournament they had won in the previous season. United's decision attracted a lot of criticism at the time, not least from many of their own fans.**

• Barcelona have the best record in the competition, having won two finals – 2-1 against Estudiantes in 2009 and 4-0 against Santos in 2011 – as well as finishing as runners-up to Brazilian club Internacional in 2006.

• **Manchester United became the first British winners of the tournament when a goal by Wayne Rooney saw off Ecuadorian side Quito in the 2008 final in Yokohama.**

COLCHESTER UNITED

Year founded: 1937
Ground: The Colchester Community Stadium (10,084)
Nickname: The U's
Biggest win: 9-1 v Bradford City (1961) and v Leamington (2005)
Heaviest defeat: 0-8 v Leyton Orient (1989)

Founded as the successors to amateur club Colchester Town in 1937, Colchester United joined the Football League in 1950. The club lost its league status in 1990, but regained it just two years later after topping the Conference.

• **The greatest day in the club's history, though, was in 1971 when the U's sensationally beat Leeds United, then the most powerful side in the country, 3-2 in an epic fifth-round FA Cup tie at their old Layer Road ground. Even a 5-0 defeat at Everton in the next round failed to wipe the smiles off the faces of the Colchester fans.**

• The first brothers to be sent off in the same match while playing for the same team were Colchester's Tom and Tony English against Crewe in 1986.

• **In 1971, the U's became the first English club to win a tournament in a penalty shoot-out after defeating West Brom 4-3 on penalties in the final of the Watney Cup at the Hawthorns.**

• Club legend Martyn King is Colchester's leading scorer with 131 goals between 1959-65.

HONOURS
Conference champions 1992

ASHLEY COLE

Born: Stepney, 20th December 1980
Position: Defender
Club career:
2000-06 Arsenal 156 (8)
2000 Crystal Palace (loan) 14 (1)
2006- Chelsea 181 (6)
International record:
2001- England 98 (0)

Speedy left-back Ashley Cole is the most successful player ever in the history of the FA Cup, having won the competition seven times in total with Arsenal and Chelsea.

• **When Cole helped Chelsea triumph in the FA Cup a week after the Blues' 2009/10 Premier League title success he became the first English player ever to win the Double with two different clubs, having previously achieved the same feat with Arsenal in 2002.**

• England's first-choice left back for a decade, Cole is now the highest-capped full back in his country's history and has played in more games at tournament finals (22) than any other Three Lions player. Somewhat less impressively, he has played more games without scoring than any other outfield England player.

• **Cole was often in the newspapers for his on/off relationship with singer and former X-Factor panellist Cheryl Tweedy. He made the headlines for the wrong reasons again in 2011 when he accidentally shot a young Chelsea staff member with an air rifle he had taken to the club's training ground.**

Ashley Cole, the only player to win the FA Cup seven times

CHRIS COLEMAN

Born: Swansea, 10th June 1970
Managerial career:
2003-07 Fulham
2007-08 Real Sociedad
2008-10 Coventry City
2011-12 Larissa
2012- Wales

Chris Coleman was appointed manager of Wales in January 2012 following the tragic death of his predecessor, Gary Speed. After passing over managerial duties to his assistant for the Gary Speed Memorial Match against Costa Rica, Coleman first took charge of Wales for a 2-0 defeat to Mexico on 27th May 2012.

• **Coleman's first experience of management came at Fulham, where he was the youngest ever Premier League manager when he was put in charge of the Cottagers, aged 32 and 10 months, in April 2003.**

• After parting company with the west Londoners in 2007, Coleman managed Spanish side Real Sociedad and Coventry, where he was sacked after leading the Midlanders to their lowest position – 19th in the Championship – for 45 years in 2010.

• **A tough centre-back in his playing days with Swansea, Crystal Palace, Blackburn and Fulham, Coleman won 32 caps for Wales before his career was ended by a bad car crash in 2002.**

Craig Bellamy sports the new Cardiff kit after the club controversially switched from their traditional blue to red in 2012

COLOURS

In the 19th century, players originally wore different coloured caps, socks and armbands – but not shirts – to distinguish between the two sides. The first standardised kits were introduced in the 1870s, with many clubs opting for the colours of the schools or other sporting organisations from which they had emerged.

• In the period after World War II, clothing restrictions forced many teams in Britain to wear unusual kits. For instance, Oldham Athletic, who traditionally wore blue and white, spent two seasons in red-and-white shirts borrowed from a local rugby league club while Scottish club Clyde turned out in khaki.

• Thanks largely to the longstanding success of Arsenal, Liverpool and Manchester United, teams wearing red have won more trophies in England than those sporting any other colour. Teams wearing stripes have fared less well, their last FA Cup success coming in 1987 (Coventry City) and their last league triumph way back in 1936 (Sunderland).

• In April 1996 Manchester United became the first English team to completely change their kit at half-time during a Premiership match at Southampton. Trailing 3-0 at the break, the United players complained that they found it hard to spot each other in the club's grey away shirts and came out for the second half (which they 'won' 1-0) in blue-and-white stripes. After that the dreaded grey shirts were never seen again.

COMMUNITY SHIELD

The Community Shield was originally known as the Charity Shield and since 1928 has been an annual fixture usually played at the start of the season between the reigning league champions and the FA Cup winners. Founded in 1908 to provide funds for various

IS THAT A FACT?
In 2012 Cardiff's new Malaysian owners decided to change the club's home shirts from blue to red, because the latter colour is believed to be 'luckier' in the Far East.

charities, the Charity Shield was initially played between the league champions and the Southern League champions, developing into a game between select teams of amateurs and professionals in the early 1920s.

• **Manchester United were the first club to win the Charity Shield, defeating QPR 4-0 in a replay at Stamford Bridge. With 15 outright wins and four shared, United are also the most successful side in the history of the competition.**

• United were also involved in the highest-scoring Charity Shield match, beating Swindon Town 8-4 in 1911.

• **In the first Charity Shield played at Wembley in 1974, Liverpool's Kevin Keegan and Leeds's Billy Bremner were sent off for fighting, becoming the first British players to be dismissed at the national stadium. To make matters worse, they tore their shirts off as they left the pitch and both were subsequently banned for five weeks.**

• Manchester United's Ryan Giggs is the most successful player in the history of the Shield, with eight wins in 14 appearances (another record).

CONFERENCE

Formed in 1979 as the Alliance Premier League, the Football Conference is the pinnacle of the non-league National League System which feeds into the Football League. The Conference itself has been divided into three sections – National, North and South – since 2004.

• **Promotion and relegation between the Football League and the Conference became automatic in 1987, when Scarborough United replaced Lincoln City.**

• However, clubs have to satisfy the Football League's minimal ground requirements before their promotion can be confirmed and Kidderminster Harriers, Macclesfield Town and Stevenage Borough all failed on this count in the mid-1990s after topping the Conference table.

• **The Conference is known as the Blue Square Bet Premier after its sponsors. Previously, the league was sponsored by Gola (1984-86), Vauxhall (1986-98) and the Nationwide Building Society (1998-2007).**

• Crawley Town won the Conference with a record total of 105 points in 2011, while the biggest win in the league is 9-0, a record jointly held by Sutton United (1990), Hereford United (2004) and Rushden & Diamonds (2009).

COPA AMERICA

The oldest surviving international football tournament in the world, the Copa America was founded in 1916. The first championships were held in Argentina as part of the country's independence centenary commemorations, with Uruguay emerging as the winners from a four-team field. Originally known as the South American Championship, the tournament was renamed in 1975. Previously, the Copa America was held every two years but in 2007 it was decided to stage future tournaments at four-year intervals.

• **Uruguay have won the tournament a record 15 times and hold the trophy at the time of writing, while Argentina are second in the winners' list, lifting the trophy on 14 occasions.**

• Norberto Mendez of Argentina and Zizinho of Brazil share the tournament record of 17 goals. Three players have scored a record nine goals in a single tournament: Jair Pinto (Brazil, 1949), Humberto Maschio (Argentina, 1957) and Javier Ambrois (Uruguay, 1957).

TOP 10

MOST POINTS IN A CONFERENCE SEASON

1. Crawley Town (2010/11)   105 points
2. Fleetwood Town (2011/12)   103 points
3. Aldershot Town (2007/08)   101 points
4. Stevenage Borough (2009/10)   99 points
5. Dagenham & Redbridge (2006/07)   95 points
6. Yeovil Town (2002/03)   95 points
7. Colchester United (1991/92)   94 points
   Wycombe Wanderers (1991/92)   94 points
9. Runcorn (1981/82)   93 points
10. Chester City (2003/04)   92 points

Uruguay have won the Copa America a record 15 times, most recently in 2011

COPA LIBERTADORES

The Copa Libertadores is the South American equivalent of the Champions League, played annually between top clubs from all the countries in the continent (in recent years, leading clubs from Mexico have also participated). Argentine club Independiente have the best record in the competition, winning the trophy seven times, including four in a row between 1972 and 1975.

• **Ecuadorian striker Albert Spencer is the leading scorer in the history of the competition with 54 goals (48 for Uruguayan club Penarol, helping them to win the first two tournaments in 1960 and 1961, and six for Ecuadorian outfit Barcelona de Guayaquil).**

• In a first round match in 1970, Penarol thrashed Venezuelan club Valencia 11-2 to record the biggest ever win in the competition.

• **Argentinian clubs have won the trophy a record 22 times, six more than those from Brazil. The most successful player in the Copa Libertadores is Argentinian defender Francisco Sa, who won the tournament six times in the 1970s with Independiente and Boca Juniors.**

CORNERS

Corner kicks were first introduced in 1872, but goals direct from a corner were not allowed until 1924. The first player to score from a corner in league football was Billy Smith of Huddersfield in the 1924/25 season. On 2nd October 1924 Argentina's Cesareo Onzari scored direct from a corner against reigning Olympic champions Uruguay in Buenos Aires, the first goal of this sort in an international fixture.

• **The first Football League match to feature no corners was the Division One game between Newcastle and Portsmouth at St James' Park on 5th December 1931. Unsurprisingly, the match finished 0-0.**

• A corner count has been proposed as an alternative to penalty shoot-outs as a way of deciding drawn cup ties. This method was used to determine the result of the 1965 All-African Games football tournament, with Congo beating Mali 7-2 on corners after a 0-0 draw.

• **Former Yugoslav international Dejan Petkovic holds the world record for the most goals scored direct from a corner with eight, his last effort coming for Brazilian side Flamengo in 2009.**

The Copa Libertadores trophy is bigger than some of the players who lift it

COVENTRY CITY

Year founded: 1883
Ground: Ricoh Arena (32,609)
Previous name: Singers FC
Nickname: The Sky Blues
Biggest win: 9-0 v Bristol City (1934)
Heaviest defeat: 2-11 v Berwick Rangers (1901)

Coventry were founded in 1883 by workers from the local Singer's bicycle factory and were named after the company until 1898. The club was elected to the Second Division in 1919, but their league career started unpromisingly with a 5-0 home defeat to Tottenham Hotspur.

• **A club with a history of ups and downs, Coventry were the first team to play in seven different divisions: Premier, Division One, Two, Three, Four, Three (North) and Three (South). The Sky Blues have also played in the Championship and, following their relegation in 2012, started the 2012/13 season in League One.**

• Coventry's greatest moment came in 1987 when the club won the FA Cup for the only time, beating Tottenham 3-2 in an exciting Wembley final. Two years later, though, the Sky Blues were dumped out of the cup by non-league Sutton United in one of the competition's biggest ever upsets.

• **Under innovative manager Jimmy Hill Coventry rose from the Third to the First Division in the mid-1960s and remained there for 34 years until dropping out of the Premiership at the end of the 2000/01 season. After 11 years in the Championship, Coventry slid back into the third tier in 2012.**

• Long-serving goalkeeper Steve Ogrizovic played in a club record 504 league games between 1984 and 2000. The Sky Blues' leading scorer is Clarrie Bourton, who banged in 173 goals between 1931 and 1937.

• **The Ricoh Arena, Coventry's home since they moved from Highfield Road in 2005, was one of six venues to host the 2012 Olympic Games football tournament.**

HONOURS
Division 2 champions 1967
Division 3 champions 1964
Division 3 (S) champions 1936
FA Cup 1987

CRAWLEY TOWN

Year founded: 1896
Ground: Broadfield Stadium (5,996)
Nickname: The Red Devils
Biggest win: 8-0 v Droylsden (2008)
Heaviest defeat: 0-7 v Bath City (2000)

Founded in 1896, Crawley Town started out in the West Sussex League, eventually rising to the Conference in 2004. Dubbed 'the Manchester City of non-league', Crawley splashed out more than £500,000 on new players at the start of the 2010/11 season, an investment which paid off when the club won promotion to the Football League at the end of the campaign.
• Runaway Conference champions, Crawley's haul of 105 points set a new record for the division, while they also equalled the records for fewest defeats (3), most wins (31) and best goal difference (63). The following season Crawley enjoyed a second successive promotion, after finishing third in League Two behind Swindon and Shrewsbury.
• Crawley reached the fifth round of the FA Cup for the first time in their history in 2011 after knocking out Swindon, Derby and Torquay. To their fans' delight they were then paired with Manchester United, and their team did them proud, only losing 1-0 at Old Trafford.
• Five players, including two from Crawley, were sent off following a post-match brawl after the Red Devils won 2-1 at Bradford City on 27th March 2012, equalling the record for the most dismissals in an English league game.

> HONOURS
> *Conference champions 2011*

CREWE ALEXANDRA

Year founded: 1877
Ground: Alexandra Stadium (10,153)
Nickname: The Railwaymen
Biggest win: 8-0 v Rotherham (1932)
Heaviest defeat: 2-13 v Tottenham Hotspur (1960)

Founded by railway workers in 1877, the Crewe Football Club added 'Alexandra' to their name in honour of Princess Alexandra, wife of the future king, Edward VII. The club were founder members of the Second Division in 1892, although they lost their league status four years later before rejoining the newly formed Third Division (North) in 1921.
• Helped by a club-record 19-match unbeaten run Crewe were League Two play-off winners in 2012, but they have never won a major trophy. The Railwaymen did, however, win the Welsh Cup in 1936 and 1937 before being later barred from the competition for not being a Welsh club.
• Alex fans endured a miserable spell in the mid-1950s when their club failed to win away from home for a record 56 consecutive matches. The depressing run finally ended with a 1-0 win at Southport in April 1957.
• Club legend Herbert Swindells scored a record 126 goals for Crewe between 1927 and 1937. Crewe's appearance record is held by Tommy Lowry who turned out in 475 games between 1966 and 1977.
• John Pearson is the only Crewe player to represent England, making one appearance in 1892. He later became a referee, taking charge of the 1911 FA Cup final between Bradford City and Newcastle United.

> HONOURS
> *Welsh Cup 1936, 1937*

Action from the 2012 League Two play-off final when Crewe (in black) beat Cheltenham

The rather inappropriately named Peter Crouch is England's tallest ever player

PETER CROUCH

Born: Macclesfield, 30th January 1981
Position: Striker
Club career:
2000-01 QPR 42 (10)
2001-02 Portsmouth 37 (18)
2002-04 Aston Villa 37 (6)
2003 Norwich City (loan) 15 (4)
2004-05 Southampton 27 (12)
2005-08 Liverpool 85 (22)
2008-09 Portsmouth 35 (11)
2009-11 Tottenham Hotspur 71 (12)
2011- Stoke City 32 (10)
International record:
2005-10 England 42 (22)

At 6ft 7in, Peter Crouch is the tallest player to appear for England. When he first played for Liverpool his extraordinary height prompted Reds fans to chant, "He's big, he's red, his feet stick out the bed!"

• **With his gangly physique and stick-thin legs, Peter Crouch may look more like a basketball player than a footballer, but he has proved himself to be an exceptionally effective striker at both club and international level. Nor is he simply a towering targetman; Crouch has a surprisingly deft touch on the ground.**

• After initially failing to make the grade at Tottenham, Crouch moved to QPR in 2000 and subsequently played for Portsmouth, Aston Villa, Norwich (on loan) and Southampton, before joining Liverpool in 2005. The following year he won the FA Cup with the Merseysiders and in 2007 played as a sub in the Champions League final defeat to AC Milan. However, in the summer of 2008 Crouch returned to Portsmouth in an estimated £11 million deal. A year later he was on the move again, his career coming full circle when he rejoined his first club, Tottenham, for a fee of £10 million. Then on transfer deadline day in August 2011 he moved to Stoke City.

• Crouch made his England debut against Colombia in 2005 and, despite being in and out of the starting XI, enjoyed a prolific scoring record at international level. However, although he enjoyed a good first season at Stoke which saw him named the club's Player of the Year, he wasn't selected for the England squad at Euro 2012.

JOHAN CRUYFF

Born: Amsterdam, Holland, 5th April 1947
Position: Midfielder/Striker
Club career:
1964-73 Ajax 240 (190)
1973-78 Barcelona 142 (48)
1979-80 Los Angeles Aztecs 27 (16)
1980-81 Washington Diplomats 32 (12)
1981 Levante 10 (2)
1981-83 Ajax 36 (14)
1983-84 Feyenoord 33 (11)
International record:
1966-78 Holland 48 (33)

Arguably the greatest European player ever, Johan Cruyff was captain of the brilliant Holland side which reached the final of the 1974 World Cup and of the outstanding Ajax team which won the European Cup three times on the trot in the early 1970s.

• **Unquestionably the best player in the world at the time, Cruyff became the first man to win the European Player of the Year award three times, topping the poll in 1971, 1973 and 1974.**

• Fast, skilful, creative and a prolific scorer, Cruyff was also a superb organiser on the pitch. His talents prompted Barcelona to shell out a world record £922,000 fee to bring him to the Nou Camp in 1973 and the following year Cruyff helped the Catalans win their first title for 14 years.

• **After his retirement, Cruyff coached both Ajax and Barcelona. He led the Spanish giants to four consecutive league titles between 1991-94 and, in 1992, guided them to their first-ever European Cup success, with a 1-0 victory over Sampdoria at Wembley.**

• Cruyff's magnificent contribution to football in Holland was recognised in a 2004 poll when he was voted the sixth greatest Dutch person ever, ahead of two of the world's finest painters, Rembrandt and Vincent Van Gogh.

CRYSTAL PALACE

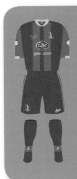

Year founded: 1905
Ground: Selhurst Park (26,309)
Nickname: The Eagles
Biggest win: 9-0 v Barrow (1959)
Heaviest defeat: 0-9 v Burnley (1909) and v Liverpool (1989)

The club was founded in 1905 by workers at the then cup final venue at Crystal Palace, and was an entirely separate entity to the amateur club of the same name which was made up of groundkeepers at the Great Exhibition and reached the first ever semi-finals of the FA Cup in 1871.

• After spending their early years in the Southern League, Palace were founder members of the Third Division (South) in 1920. The club had a great start to their league career, going up to the Second Division as champions in their first season.

• Palace's greatest moment came in 1990 when they reached the FA Cup Final. In the final at Wembley against Manchester United, Ian Wright came off the bench to score twice in a thrilling 3-3 draw before the Eagles went down 1-0 in the replay.

• Pre-war striker Peter Simpson is the club's all-time leading scorer with 153 league goals between 1930 and 1936. Rugged defender Jim Cannon holds the club appearance record, making 660 appearances between 1973 and 1988.

• Palace hold the record for the biggest victory by a non-league side against a Football League club, thrashing Chelsea 7-1 in 1905.

IS THAT A FACT?
Crystal Palace have been relegated a record four times from the Premier League, being particularly unlucky when they first experienced the drop in 1992/93 as they went down with a 49 points – a record points tally for a demoted team.

Crystal Palace have been relegated from the Premier League a record four times

• On 31st March 1961 a crowd of 37,774 turned up for Crystal Palace's derby against Millwall at Selhurst Park – an all-time record for the fourth tier of English football.

HONOURS
Division 2 champions 1979
First Division champions 1994
Division 3 (S) champions 1921

CUP WINNERS' CUP

A competition for the domestic cup winners of all European countries, the European Cup Winners' Cup ran for 39 seasons between 1960/61 until 1998/99. The first winners were Italian club Fiorentina, who beat Rangers 4-1 on aggregate in a two-legged final.

• In 1963 Tottenham Hotspur became the first British club to win the competition and the first to win a major European trophy, when they thrashed Atletico Madrid 5-1 in Rotterdam – a record score for a European final.

• English clubs won the cup eight times – a figure unmatched by any other country. England's successful teams were Tottenham (1963), West Ham (1965), Manchester City (1970), Chelsea (1971 and 1998), Everton (1985), Manchester United (1991) and Arsenal (1994).

• In 1963 Sporting Lisbon tonked APOEL Nicosia 16-1 in a second round, first leg tie to record the biggest ever win in any European fixture.

DAGENHAM & REDBRIDGE

Year founded: 1992
Ground: Victoria Road (6,078)
Previous name: Dagenham
Nickname: The Daggers
Biggest win: 8-1 v Woking (1994)
Heaviest defeat: 0-9 v Hereford United (2004)

The self-styled 'pub team from Essex' were formed in 1992 following the merger of local rivals Dagenham and Redbridge Forest, the latter having previously incorporated the once-famous amateur clubs Ilford, Leytonstone and Walthamstow Avenue.

• In 2007 Dagenham & Redbridge were promoted to the Football League for the first time in their history after winning the Conference. Just three years later the Daggers went up to League One via the play-offs, only to come back down the following season. Nonetheless, the club's 6-0 win over Morecambe in the semi-final set a new record for the biggest ever play-off win.

• Dagenham's record appearance maker, Tony Roberts, is the only goalkeeper to have scored in the FA Cup from open play, netting in a fourth qualifying round tie against Basingstoke in 2001. Less impressively, the Welsh international is the only keeper to have been sent off in the competition while in the opposition penalty area. The bizarre incident happened late on in the Daggers' 5-2 loss to Southend in 2008 when Roberts went up for a corner and was red carded for headbutting a Shrimpers defender.

• The Daggers' coffers received a welcome boost in August 2009 when they sold midfielder Solomon Taiwo to Cardiff City for a club record £200,000.

• The first Dagenham player to win international honours was striker Jon Nurse who played for Barbados against Dominica in 2008.

• Dagenham attracted a record crowd of 5,949 to Victoria Road for a third round FA Cup game vs Ipswich Town, but failed to rise to the occasion, losing 4-1.

HONOURS
Conference champions 2007

KENNY DALGLISH

Born: Glasgow, 4th March 1951
Position: Striker
Club career:
1968-77 Celtic 204 (112)
1977-90 Liverpool 354 (118)
International record:
1971-87 Scotland 102 (30)

Kenny Dalglish was the first man to score 100 league goals in both the Scottish and English leagues. He began his career at Celtic, winning nine major trophies before moving to Liverpool in 1977 for a then British record fee of £440,000. A true Anfield legend, Dalglish won nine championships, two FA Cups and four League Cups with the Reds, plus the European Cup in 1978, 1981 and 1984. He was voted Footballer of the Year in 1979 and 1983.

• A clever striker with a superb first touch, Dalglish won a record 102 caps for Scotland and scored 30 goals – a figure matched only by Denis Law. He represented his country at three World Cups in 1974, 1978 and 1982.

• In 1986 he became the first player-manager to lead a club to the title when he won the championship with Liverpool, and he secured two more titles in 1988 and 1990 before suddenly resigning in 1991.

• Eight months later he took over at Blackburn and in 1995 steered Rovers to the Premiership title, becoming only the third manager to win the title with two different clubs. In 1997 Dalglish became Newcastle manager, but was sacked after a poor start to the 1998/99 season.

• He was briefly manager of Celtic but was out of the game for nine years before going back to Liverpool in 2009, initially as youth academy coach. In January 2011 Dalglish replaced Roy Hodgson as manager but, despite winning the Carling Cup the following year and guiding the Reds to the 2012 FA Cup final, the Kop legend was sacked at the end of the 2011/12 season after a poor league campaign.

DIXIE DEAN

Born: Birkenhead, 22nd January 1907
Died: 1st March 1980
Position: Striker
Club career:
1923-25 Tranmere Rovers 30 (27)
1925-37 Everton 399 (349)
1938-39 Notts County 9 (3)
1939 Sligo Rovers 7 (10)
International record:
1927-32 England 16 (18)

Everton legend Dixie Dean scored an all-time record 60 league goals for the Toffees when they won the championship in 1927/28. His tally included a hat-trick in the final match of the campaign against Arsenal, enabling Dean to pass the then record of 59 goals, established the previous season by Middlesbrough's George Camsell.

• Easily Everton's all-time leading scorer, Dean scored a total of 379

*Liverpool legend
Kenny Dalglish*

league goals with the Toffees, Tranmere and Notts County. In the history of English league football only Arthur Rowley has scored more (434 with West Brom, Fulham, Leicester and Shrewsbury between 1946 and 1965).

• During the 1930/31 season Dean scored in 12 consecutive games for Everton, a record for English football which has only been bettered by the brilliant Pele (14 games) in the world game.

• **Famed for his heading ability, Dean hit an impressive 18 goals in 16 appearances for England, including hat-tricks in consecutive games against Belgium and Luxembourg in 1927.**

• His nickname 'Dixie' was given to him by fans in reference to his dark complexion and curly hair which, they believed, were similar to African Americans in the southern United States. However, Dean disliked the moniker and preferred to be called by his real name, Bill.

• **Dean, who won two league titles and one FA Cup with Everton, died in 1980 after suffering a heart attack while watching a Merseyside derby. In 2001 a sculpture of the club's greatest striker was erected outside Goodison Park carrying the inscription 'Footballer, Gentleman, Evertonian'.**

DEATHS

The first recorded death as a direct result of a football match came in 1889 when William Cropper of Derbyshire side Staveley FC died of a ruptured bowel sustained in a collision with an opponent.

• **In 1931 Celtic's brilliant young international goalkeeper John Thompson died in hospital after fracturing his skull in a collision with Rangers forward Sam English. Some 40,000 fans attended his funeral, many of them walking the 55 miles from Glasgow to Thompson's home village in Fife. In the same decade two other goalkeepers, Jimmy Utterson of Wolves and Sunderland's Jimmy Thorpe, also died from injuries sustained on the pitch. Their deaths led the Football Association to change the rules so that goalkeepers could not be tackled while they had the ball in their hands.**

• Two players were killed by lightning in the 1948 Army Cup final at Aldershot Military Stadium. Six other players, two spectators and the referee were also struck by the bolt but survived after receiving treatment in hospital.

• **In May 2010 Goran Tunjic collapsed**

and died from a heart attack while playing for Croatian county level side Mladost FC. Unfortunately, the referee completely failed to comprehend the unfolding tragedy...and gave Tunjic a yellow card for diving.

• British players to collapse on the pitch and subsequently die in recent years include Robbie James (Llanelli, 2000), Matt Gadsby (Hinckley United, 2006) and Phil O'Donnell (Motherwell, 2007).

DEBUTS

The best debut by an England player was probably that of Blackpool striker Stan Mortensen who scored four times in a 10-0 rout of Portugal in Lisbon in 1947. The 'Blackpool Bombshell' went on to notch an impressive 24 goals for his country in just 25 appearances.

• **Conrad Warner, on the other hand, will have had few fond memories of his England debut against Scotland at Hampden Park in 1878. The Upton Park FC goalkeeper conceded seven goals in a 7-2 thrashing and, unsurprisingly, never played international football again.**

• Freddy Eastwood scored the fastest goal on debut, netting after just seven seconds for Southend against Swansea in 2004. Almost as impressively, goalkeeper Tony Coton was just 83 seconds into his debut with Birmingham City in 1980 when he saved a penalty with his first

touch in top-flight football.

• **The worst debut ever has to be that of hapless Halifax Town goalkeeper Stanley Milton, who let in 13 goals against Stockport in 1934.**

• The only player to score a hat-trick on his Premier League debut is Middlesbrough's Italian striker Fabrizio Ravenelli, who scored all of his team's goals in a 3-3 draw with Liverpool on the opening day of the 1996/97 season.

DERBIES

So called because they matched the popularity of the Epsom Derby horserace, 'derby' matches between local sides provoke intense passions among fans and players alike.

• **Probably the most intense derby match in Britain, and possibly the whole world, is between bitter Glasgow rivals Rangers and Celtic. In the 2010/11 season the two teams met a record seven times, the clashes provoking so many violent incidents in Glasgow that the chairman of the Scottish Police Federation called for future Old Firm matches to be banned.**

• Other famous derbies include Liverpool v Everton, Arsenal v Tottenham, Manchester City v Manchester United, Newcastle v Sunderland and, on mainland Europe, Inter v AC Milan, Betis v Sevilla and Lazio v Roma. Strangely, the match often described as 'the world's greatest derby',

They may not be neighbours, but Barcelona v Real Madrid is 'the world's greatest derby'

the 'El Clasico' clash between Barcelona and Real Madrid, is not a derby in the strict sense.

• Manchester derbies have produced many dramatic moments, notably in 1974 when former United legend Denis Law scored for City with a cheeky backheel in the closing stages at Old Trafford. The goal doomed United to relegation from the First Division and prompted thousands of their fans to invade the pitch in an attempt to get the match abandoned. They succeeded in their aim, but the result (a 1-0 win for City) stood. More recently, City triumphed by the same score in the first ever Wembley meeting between the sides in the 2011 FA Cup semi-final and in a virtual title decider at Eastlands the following year thanks to Vincent Kompany's header.

• Possibly the most important goal in an English derby game, though, came at Tottenham's White Hart Lane in 1971 when Arsenal's Ray Kennedy scored with a last-minute header to win his side the league championship and the first leg of a famous Double.

• In 1986 and 1989 the Merseyside derby came to Wembley as Liverpool and Everton contested the FA Cup final. Liverpool won on both occasions, with Welsh international striker Ian Rush scoring twice in each game. The sides also met in the 1984 League Cup final, the Reds again winning after a replay.

DERBY COUNTY

Year founded: 1884
Ground: Pride Park (33,597)
Nickname: The Rams
Biggest win: 12-0 v Finn Harps (1976)
Heaviest defeat: 2-11 v Everton (1890)

Derby were formed in 1884 as an offshoot of Derbyshire Cricket Club and originally wore an amber, chocolate and blue strip based on the cricket club's colours. Perhaps wisely, they changed to their traditional black and white colours in the 1890s.

• The club were founder members of the Football League in 1888 and seven years later moved from the ground they shared with the cricketers to the Baseball Ground (so named because baseball was regularly played there in the 1890s). Derby had to oust a band of gypsies before they could move in, one of whom is said to have laid a curse on the place as he left. No doubt, then, the club was pleased to leave the Baseball Ground for Pride Park in 1997... although when Derby's first game at the new stadium had to be abandoned due to floodlight failure there were fears that the curse had followed them!

• Runners-up in the FA Cup final in 1898, 1899 and 1903, Derby reached their last final in 1946. Before the match the club's captain, Jack Nicholas, visited a gypsy encampment and paid for the old curse to be lifted. It worked, as Derby beat Charlton 4-1 after extra-time.

• Under charismatic manager Brian Clough, Derby took the top flight by storm after winning promotion to the First Division in 1969. Three years later they won the league in one of the closest title races ever. Having played all their fixtures ahead of their title contenders, Derby's players were actually sitting on a beach in Majorca when they heard news of their victory. The following season Derby reached the semi-finals of the European Cup and, in 1975 under the management of former skipper Dave Mackay, they won the championship again.

• Sadly, the club have failed to live up to those glory days in the decades since. By the early 1980s the Rams had sunk as low as the Third Division and were only saved from extinction when publisher Robert Maxwell bailed them out. The club enjoyed a reasonable spell in the Premiership in the late 1990s, but their most recent season in the top flight in 2007/08 was an utter disaster – the Rams managing just one win in the whole campaign, equalling a Football League record set by Loughborough in 1900.

• Striker Deon Burton is Derby's most-capped international, playing 42 times for Jamaica in a five-year spell at the club between 1997 and 2002.

• Derby's best-ever goalscorer was one of the true greats of the game in the late 19th and early 20th centuries, Steve Bloomer. He netted an incredible 332 goals in two spells at the club between 1892 and 1914. Striker Kevin Hector, a two-time title winner with the club in the 1970s, played in a record 485 league games for the Rams during two spells at the Baseball Ground.

ROBERTO DI MATTEO

Born: Schaffhausen, Switzerland, 29th May 1970
Managerial career:
2008-09 MK Dons
2009-11 West Bromwich Albion
2012- Chelsea

Chelsea boss Roberto di Matteo enjoyed the best ever start to a managerial career at an English club when he won the FA Cup and Champions League in 2012, just two months after taking over the reins at Stamford Bridge on a caretaker basis following the dismissal of Andre Villas-Boas.

• Di Matteo's superb achievements earned him a permanent two-year contract at the Bridge, although he will know that the Chelsea job is one of the most insecure in the Premier League, with owner Roman Abramovich having gone through seven previous managers since he pitched up in west London in 2003.

• A Swiss-born Italian, Di Matteo cut his managerial teeth at MK Dons, who he led to the League One play-off semi-final in 2009. The following year he guided West Brom to automatic promotion to the Premier League, but was dismissed in February 2011 after a poor run of results. Four months later he was appointed assistant manager to Villas-Boas at Chelsea.

• An elegant midfielder in his playing days, Di Matteo first joined Chelsea from Lazio in 1996 for a then club record £4.9 million. The following May he scored the fastest ever goal in the FA Cup final at Wembley, when he struck a brilliant 30-yarder against Middlesbrough after just 42 seconds – a record which stood until 2009. He also scored in the 1998 League Cup final, again against Boro, and hit the winner for the Blues against Aston Villa in the 2000 FA Cup final – the last to be played at the old Wembley. Before a triple leg fracture ended his career in September 2000 he had won 34 caps for Italy.

DISASTERS

The worst disaster at a British football stadium occurred on 15th April 1989 at Hillsborough when 96 Liverpool fans were killed and a further 170 injured during their team's FA Cup semi-final with Nottingham Forest. The tragedy, which occurred when police opened the gates to the stadium as the game kicked off and fans poured into an already overcrowded section of the Leppings Lane end of the ground, led to the introduction of all-seater stadiums and the abolition of perimeter fencing.

• Four years earlier fighting between Liverpool and Juventus fans before the 1985 European Cup final at the Heysel Stadium in Brussels resulted in 39 (mostly Italian) supporters being crushed to death when a wall collapsed in a corner of the ground. Liverpool fans were largely blamed for the disaster, which led to English clubs being banned from European competition for the next five years.

• Rangers' Ibrox Stadium has been the scene of two major disasters, the first in 1902 when 26 people died after a stand collapsed during a Home International between Scotland and England. Then, in 1971, 66 fans were killed in a crush on a steep stairway after an Old Firm fixture.

• In 1982 at least 66 people were killed just before the end of a match between Spartak Moscow and Haarlem at the Lenin Stadium in Moscow. According to some reports, as many as 340 fans died in the tragedy, which was caused when supporters leaving early attempted to get back into the stadium via an icy ramp when Spartak scored a late goal.

• The worst disaster in African football took place at the Accra Sports Stadium in Ghana near the end of a match in 2001 between two top clubs, Hearts of Oak and Asante Kotoko. After seeing their team concede two late goals to go down to a 2-1 defeat, the Asante fans began tearing up their seats and throwing them on the pitch. The police responded by firing tear gas, leading the Asante supporters to rush to the exits. However, these turned out to be locked and 126 people were killed in the ensuing crush.

• On 1st February 2012 at least 79 people were killed at the end of a match between Egyptian sides Al-Masry and Al-Ahly when hundreds of Al-Masry fans attacked their rivals with knives, clubs, stones and fireworks. The remainder of the Egyptian football season was subsequently cancelled after the incident, which many believe was politically motivated.

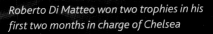

Roberto Di Matteo won two trophies in his first two months in charge of Chelsea

IS THAT A FACT?
In a match in the Democratic Republic of Congo in 1998 11 players were killed by a bolt of lightning. Incredibly, all those who died were members of the visiting team, leading accusations of witchcraft to be levelled at the players from the home side, Busanga.

D

DISCIPLINE

Yellow and red cards were introduced into English league football on 2nd October 1976, and on the same day Blackburn's David Wagstaffe received the first red card during his side's match with Leyton Orient. Five years later cards were withdrawn by the Football Association as referees were getting 'too flashy', but the system was re-introduced in 1987.

• **A stormy last 16 match between Holland and Portugal in 2006 was the most ill-disciplined in the history of the World Cup. Russian referee Valentin Ivanov was the busiest man on the pitch as he pulled out his yellow card 16 times and his red one four times, with the match ending as a nine-a-side affair.**

• David Beckham and Wayne Rooney are the only two England players to have been sent off twice while playing for their country. Beckham was famously red carded against Argentina in the 1998 World Cup and also had first use of the showers against Austria in 2005, while Rooney was dismissed against Portugal in the 2006 World Cup quarter-final and in a Euro 2012 qualifier away to Montenegro in 2011.

• **Roy McDonough, a journeyman striker for Walsall, Colchester, Southend and Exeter in the 1970s and 1980s, was sent off a record 21 times during his career, earning himself the nickname 'Red Card Roy'.**

• Richard Dunne, Duncan Ferguson and Patrick Vieira share the record for receiving the most red cards in Premier League matches, with eight each. Bolton striker Kevin Davies has been shown the yellow card on a record 100 occasions.

• **When a mass brawl erupted in the middle of the pitch during a match between Argentinian sides Victoriano Arenas and Claypole on 26th February 2011 referee Damian Rubino showed red cards to all 22 players and 14 substitutes as well as coaches and technical staff. The total of 36 players sent off set a new world record, smashing the previous 'best' of 20!**

DONCASTER ROVERS

Year founded: 1879
Ground: Keepmoat Stadium (15,231)
Nickname: The Rovers
Biggest win: 10-0 v Darlington (1964)
Heaviest defeat: 0-12 v Small Heath (1903)

Founded in 1879 by Albert Jenkins, a fitter at Doncaster's Great Northern Railway works, Doncaster turned professional in 1885 and joined the Second Division of the Football League in 1901.

• **Remarkably, Doncaster hold the record for the most wins in a league** season (33 in 1946/47) and for the most defeats (34 in 1997/98). At the end of the latter campaign Rovers were relegated to the Football Conference, but they bounced back to reach the heady heights of the Championship by 2008. Sadly for their fans, Rovers' four-year stay in the second tier came to an end in 2012.

• Doncaster were the first club to be champions of the fourth tier of League football on more than two occasions – winning the title three times, in 1966, 1969 and 2004.

• **In 1946 Doncaster were involved in the longest-ever football**

'Sorry Mario, but you've got to admit that haircut deserves a red card!'

TOP 10

FEWEST POINTS IN A SEASON (3 PTS FOR A WIN)

1.	Derby County, 2007/08	11 points
2.	Sunderland, 2005/06	15 points
3.	Stoke City, 1984/85	17 points
4.	Sunderland, 2002/03	19 points
	Portsmouth, 2009/10	19 points*
6.	Doncaster Rovers, 1997/98	20 points
7.	Cambridge United, 1984/85	21 points
8.	Cambridge United, 1983/84	24 points
	West Brom, 1985/86	24 points
	Derby County, 1990/91	24 points
	Watford, 1999/00	24 points

* 9 points deducted

match, a Third Division (North) cup tie against Stockport County at Edgeley Park which the referee ruled could extend beyond extra-time in an attempt to decide a winner. Eventually, the game was abandoned after 203 minutes due to poor light.
• Doncaster were the first club to win a League Cup tie on penalties, defeating Lincoln City 4-2 on spot-kicks following a drawn first round replay at the City Ground, Nottingham in 1976.

> **HONOURS**
> *Division 3 (North) champions 1935, 1947, 1950*
> *Division 4 champions 1966, 1969*
> *Third Division champions 2004*
> *Football League Trophy 2007*

DOUBLES

The first club to win the Double of League Championship and FA Cup were Preston North End, in the very first season of the Football League in 1888/89. The Lancashire side achieved this feat in fine style, remaining undefeated in the league and keeping a clean sheet in all their matches in the FA Cup.
• Arsenal and Manchester United have both won the Double a record three times. The Reds' trio of successes all came within a five-year period in the 1990s (1994, 1996 and 1999), with the last of their Doubles comprising two-thirds of a legendary Treble which also included the Champions League. Arsenal first won the Double in 1971, since when the Gunners have twice repeated the feat under manager Arsene Wenger in 1998 and 2002.
• Perhaps, though, the most famous Double of all was achieved by Tottenham Hotspur in 1961 as it was the first such success in the 20th century. Under legendary manager Bill Nicholson, Spurs clinched the most-prized honour in the domestic game with a 2-0 victory over Leicester City in the FA Cup final. The other English clubs to win the Double are Aston Villa (1897), Liverpool (1986) and Chelsea (2010).
• Northern Ireland side Linfield have won a world record 23 Doubles. Rangers, with 18 Doubles, lie in second place, while Greek outfit Olympiacos (15 Doubles) are in third place.

DRAWS

Everton have drawn more matches in the top flight than any other club, having finished on level terms in 1,057 out of 4,252 matches. Even the Toffees, though, can't match Norwich City's record of 23 draws in a single season, set in the First Division in 1978/79.
• The highest scoring draw in the top division of English football was 6-6, in

The 1961 Tottenham Double team show off their trophies

D

DROGBA

TOP 10

MOST PREMIER LEAGUE DRAWS

1.	Aston Villa	240 draws
2.	Everton	218 draws
3.	Arsenal	204 draws
	Tottenham Hotspur	204 draws
4.	Chelsea	199 draws
5.	Liverpool	194 draws
6.	Newcastle United	186 draws
7.	Blackburn Rovers	184 draws
8.	Manchester United	163 draws
9.	West Ham United	158 draws

a match between Leicester City and Arsenal in 1930. That bizarre scoreline was matched in a Second Division encounter between Charlton and Middlesbrough at The Valley in 1960, with a certain Brian Clough grabbing a hat-trick for the visitors.

• Crystal Palace and Notts County have both twice drawn seven consecutive home league games, while Watford drew an incredible nine away games on the trot in the 1996/97 season.

• The fourth qualifying round of the FA Cup between Alvechurch and Oxford United in 1971 went to five replays before Alvechurch finally won 1-0 in the sixth game between the clubs. The total playing time of 11 hours is a record for an FA Cup tie.

• The last team not to draw a single match in a league season were Darwen, the northerners winning 14 and losing 16 of their 30 Division Two fixtures in 1896/97.

DIDIER DROGBA

Born: Abidjan, Ivory Coast, 11th March 1978
Position: Striker
Club career:
1998-2002 Le Mans 63 (12)
2002-03 En Avant Guingamp 45 (20)
2003-04 Marseille 35 (18)
2004-12 Chelsea 226 (100)
2012- Shanghai Shenhua
International record:
2002- Ivory Coast 87 (55)

Chelsea legend Didier Drogba is the only player to have scored in four FA Cup finals, his goals helping the Blues win the trophy in 2007, 2009, 2010 and 2012.

Didier Drogba in action for Shanghai Shenhua in China

In the last of those years he also played a vital part in the Londoners' first-ever Champions League success, heading the equaliser against Bayern Munich in the final and then calmly scoring in the penalty shoot-out to secure the Blues' historic triumph.

• After rising to prominence with Marseille, Drogba moved to Chelsea for a then club record fee of £24 million in the summer of 2004. In his first season at the Bridge he helped the Londoners win their first-ever Premier League title and also scored in the Blues' Carling Cup final victory over Liverpool.

• The following year Drogba won a second league title, but was widely criticised by opposition fans and the media for falling over too easily around the penalty box. He responded to the critics in fine style, topping the

Premiership scoring charts in 2006/07 and scoring Chelsea's winning goals in both the Carling Cup final victory over Arsenal and the Blues' FA Cup final defeat of Manchester United in the first final played at the new Wembley.

IS THAT A FACT?
Didier Drogba became the first African player ever to score 100 Premier League goals when he netted Chelsea's winner in a 1-0 victory against Stoke City at Stamford Bridge on 10th March 2012.

• Drogba enjoyed his best season with the Blues in 2009/10, scoring the winner in the FA Cup final against Portsmouth. He also fired in a career-best 29 league goals to win the Golden Boot for a second time. However, during the following season he was diagnosed with malaria and understandably failed to show his top form.

• The all-time leading goalscorer for the Ivory Coast by some distance, Drogba was voted African Footballer of the Year in 2006.

DUNDEE

Year founded: 1893
Ground: Dens Park (11,856)
Nickname: The Dee
Biggest win: 10-0 v Alloa (1947), v Dunfermline (1947) and v Queen of the South (1962)
Heaviest defeat: 0-11 v Celtic (1895)

Dundee were founded in 1893 following the merger of two local clubs, Dundee Our Boys and Dundee East End.

• The club's proudest moment came in 1962 when they were crowned Scottish champions under the managership of Bob Shankley, brother of the more famous Bill. The following season Dundee reached the semi-finals of the European Cup, before losing to eventual winners AC Milan.

• Dundee have won the Scottish Cup just once, beating Clyde 2-1 in a second replay in 1910. The club have enjoyed more success in the League Cup, winning the trophy three times including consecutive triumphs in 1952 and 1953 which made Dundee the first team to retain the trophy.

• The club's record scorer is Scottish international Alan Gilzean, who banged in an incredible 113 goals in 134 games before he moved south to join Tottenham in 1964.

• After a seven-year absence, Dundee returned to the SPL in 2012 when, after finishing second in the Scottish First Division at the end of the 2011/12 season, they were voted into the top flight to take the place of Rangers who were demoted for financial irregularities.

HONOURS
Division 1 champions 1962
Division 2 champions 1947
First Division champions 1979, 1992
Scottish Cup 1910
League Cup 1952, 1953, 1974

DUNDEE UNITED

Year founded: 1909
Ground: Tannadice Park (14,209)
Previous name: Dundee Hibernian
Nickname: The Terrors
Biggest win: 14-0 v Nithsdale Wanderers (1931)
Heaviest defeat: 1-12 v Motherwell (1954)

Originally founded as Dundee Hibernian by members of the city's Irish community in 1909, the club changed to its present name in 1923 to attract support from a wider population.

• The club emerged from relative obscurity to become one of the leading clubs in Scotland under long-serving manager Jim McLean in the 1970s and 1980s, winning the Scottish Premier Division in 1983. The club's success, allied to that of Aberdeen, led to talk of a 'New Firm' capable of challenging the 'Old Firm' of Rangers and Celtic for major honours.

• United reached the semi-finals of the European Cup in 1984 and the final of the UEFA Cup in 1987, where they lost to Gothenburg. The club's European exploits also include four victories over Barcelona – a 100 per cent record against the Catalans which no other British team

can match. United have played 104 games in Europe, a figure only surpassed by Celtic, Rangers and Aberdeen among Scottish clubs.

• After being losing finalists on six previous occasions, Dundee United finally won the Scottish Cup in 1994 when they beat Rangers 1-0 in the final. They won the trophy for a second time in 2010, following a comfortable 3-0 win against shock finalists Ross County.

• Dundee United are known as the Terrors because of the lion in the club's badge. Their supporters, though, are called 'The Arabs', the name possibly stemming from a game the club won on a heavily sanded pitch in the early 1960s.

• Defender David Narey made an astonishing 612 league appearances for the club between 1973 and 1994. Full back Maurice Malpas is United's most-capped player, winning 55 caps for Scotland between 1984 and 1992.

• In a BBC poll in 2006 Dundee United fan Zippy from Rainbow was voted Britain's favourite celebrity football fan. The show's presenter, Geoffrey Hayes, a longstanding Terrors' fan, had previously insisted on the puppet's bright orange colour to reflect United's famous tangerine shirts.

• Tannadice Park, Dundee United's home since their foundation, is situated just a few hundred yards from Dundee's Dens Park, making the two clubs the closest neighbours in British football.

HONOURS
Premier League champions 1983
Division 2 champions 1925, 1929
Scottish Cup 1994, 2010
Scottish League Cup 1980, 1981

City pride is at stake in the Dundee derby

Watching England take penalties is never much fun... unless you're Scottish!

ENGLAND

First international:
Scotland 0 England 0,
1872
Most capped player:
Peter Shilton, 125 caps
(1971-90)
Leading goalscorer:
Bobby Charlton, 49
goals (1958-70)
**First World Cup
appearance:** England 2 Chile 0, 1950
Biggest win: England 13 Ireland 0,
1882
Heaviest defeat: Hungary 7
England 1, 1954

England, along with their first opponents Scotland, are the oldest international team in world football. The two countries met in the first official international in Glasgow in 1872, with honours being shared after a 0-0 draw. The following year William Kenyon-Slaney of Wanderers FC scored England's first ever goal in a 4-2 victory over Scotland at the Kennington Oval.

• With a team entirely composed of players from England, Great Britain won the first Olympic Games football tournament in 1908 and repeated the feat in 1912.

• England did not lose a match on home soil against a team from outside the British Isles until 1953 when they were thrashed 6-3 by Hungary at Wembley. The following year England went down to their worst ever defeat to the same opposition, crashing 7-1 in Budapest.

• Although Walter Winterbottom was appointed as England's first full-time manager in 1946, the squad was picked by a committee until Alf Ramsey took over in 1963. Three years later England hosted and won the World Cup – the greatest moment in the country's football history by some considerable margin.

• There were many heroes in that 1966 team, including goalkeeper Gordon Banks, skipper Bobby Moore and striker Geoff Hurst, who scored a hat-trick in the 4-2 victory over West Germany in the final at Wembley. Ramsey, too, was hailed for his part in the success and was knighted soon afterwards.

• Since then, however, England fans have experienced more than their fair share of disappointment. A second appearance in the World Cup final was within the grasp of Bobby Robson's team in 1990 but, agonisingly, they lost on penalties in the semi-final to the eventual winners, Germany.

• In 1996 England hosted the European Championships and were again knocked out on penalties by Germany at the semi-final stage. England have since lost four more times on penalties at major tournaments, most recently going out of Euro 2012 on spot-kicks to Italy, to leave them with the worst shoot-out record (one win in seven) of any country in the world.

• With 49 goals for England, Bobby Charlton is England's leading scorer. His 1960s team-mate Jimmy Greaves scored a record six hat-tricks for the Three Lions.

• The only England player to have appeared in the finals of six major tournaments is Sol Campbell, who played in three European Championships and three World Cups between 1996 and 2006.

• Four players have scored five goals for England in a match, the most recent being Malcolm Macdonald who notched all the Three Lions' goals in a 5-0 thrashing of Cyprus at Wembley in 1975.

TOP 10

ENGLAND GOALSCORERS

1.	Bobby Charlton (1958-70)	49
2.	Gary Lineker (1984-92)	48
3.	Jimmy Greaves (1959-67)	44
4.	Michael Owen (1998-2008)	40
5.	Tom Finney (1946-58)	30
	Nat Lofthouse (1950-58)	30
	Alan Shearer (1992-2000)	30
8.	Vivian Woodward (1903-11)	29
	Wayne Rooney (2003-)	29
10.	Steve Bloomer (1895-1907)	28

• Arsenal winger David Rocastle holds the record for playing the most games for England, 14 between 1988 and 1992, without ever finishing on the losing side.
• **Legendary striker Tommy Lawton scored England's fastest-ever goal, netting after just 17 seconds in a 10-0 rout of Portugal in Lisbon on 25th May 1947.**

HONOURS
World Cup 1966
World Cup record
1930 Did not enter
1934 Did not enter
1938 Did not enter
1950 Round 1
1954 Quarter-finals
1958 Round 1
1962 Quarter-finals
1966 Winners
1970 Quarter-finals
1974 Did not qualify
1978 Did not qualify
1982 Round 1
1986 Quarter-finals
1990 Semi-finals
1994 Did not qualify
1998 Round 2
2002 Quarter-finals
2006 Quarter-finals
2010 Round 2

EUROPA LEAGUE

The inaugural Europa League final was played between Atletico Madrid and Fulham in Hamburg in 2010, the Spanish side winning 2-1 thanks to a late winner by Uruguayan striker Diego Forlan. Two years later Atletico won the competition for a second time after beating Athletic Bilbao 3-0 in the final in Bucharest.
• **In 2011 Porto beat Braga 1-0 in Dublin in the first ever all-Portuguese European final. Porto's match-winner was Colombian striker Radamel Falcao, whose goal in the final was his 17th in the competition that season – a record for the tournament.**
• The competition is now in its third incarnation, having previously been known as the Fairs Cup (1955-71) and the UEFA Cup (1971-2009). The tournament was originally established in 1955 as a competition between cities, rather than clubs. The first winners were Barcelona who beat London 8-2 on aggregate in the final, which bizarrely did not take place until 1958!
• **The first team to win the newly-named UEFA Cup were Tottenham Hotspur in 1972, who beat Wolves 3-2 on aggregate in the only all-English final. In all, English clubs have won the competition 10 times... an impressive record, although Spanish teams lead**
the way with 12 victories.
• Liverpool are the most successful English club in the tournament with three triumphs in 1973, 1976 and 2001. The only other clubs to win the trophy three times are Barcelona, Inter Milan, Juventus and Valencia.
• **The leading goalscorer in the competition is Swedish marksman Henrik Larsson, who notched 40 goals for Feyenoord, Celtic and Helsingborgs.**
• The biggest single win in the competition came in 1984 when Ajax thrashed FA Red Boys Differdange 14-0 at home. Another Dutch side, Feyenoord, hold the record for the biggest aggregate victory, tonking US Rumelange 21-0 in 1972.

IS THAT A FACT?
On their way to winning the Europa League for a second time in 2012, Atletico Madrid won 12 games on the trot in the competition to set a new record for the tournament.

Atletico Madrid won the Europa League for a second time in 2012

European champions in 2008 and 2012, Spain are the first country to retain the trophy

EUROPEAN CHAMPIONSHIPS

Originally called the European Nations Cup, the idea for the European Championships came from Henri Delaunay, the then secretary of the French FA. The first championships in 1960 featured just 17 countries (the four British nations, Italy and West Germany were among those who declined to take part). The first winners of the tournament were the Soviet Union, who beat Yugoslavia 2-1 in the final in Paris.

• Germany have the best record in the tournament, having won the trophy three times (in 1972, 1980 and 1996) and been runners-up on a further three occasions. Spain have also won the championships three times (1964, 2008 and 2012) and are the only country to retain the trophy following a 4-0 demolition of Italy in the final at Euro 2012 – the biggest win in any European Championship or World Cup final.

• The most unlikely winners were Denmark in 1992. The Danes had failed to qualify for the finals in Sweden but were invited to compete at the last minute when Yugoslavia were kicked out for political reasons. To the surprise of just about everyone, Denmark – whose players had to be recalled from their holidays to play – went on to lift the trophy after a 2-0 win over Germany in the final.

• **French legend Michel Platini is the leading scorer in the finals of the European Championships with nine goals. England's Alan Shearer is in second place with a total of seven goals at the 1996 and 2000 tournaments.**

• Platini is also the only player to score two hat-tricks at the finals, notching trebles against both Belgium and Yugoslavia in 1984.

• **In the qualifying tournament for the 2008 finals Germany recorded the biggest-ever win in the history of the competition, thrashing minnows San Marino 13-0 on their home patch.**

• Holland's Edwin van der Sar and France's Lilian Thuram share the appearance record at the finals, having both played in 16 games. The pair are also among the eight players to have played in a record four tournaments, both featuring between 1996 and 2008.

EUROPEAN CHAMPIONSHIP FINALS

1960 USSR 2 Yugoslavia 1 (Paris)
1964 Spain 2 USSR 1 (Madrid)
1968 Italy 2 Yugoslavia 0• (Rome)
1972 West Germany 3 USSR 0 (Brussels)
1976 Czechoslovakia 2* West Germany 2 (Belgrade)
1980 West Germany 2 Belgium 1 (Rome)
1984 France 2 Spain 0 (Paris)
1988 Holland 2 USSR 0 (Munich)
1992 Denmark 2 Germany 0 (Gothenburg)
1996 Germany 2 Czech Republic 1 (London)
2000 France 2 Italy 1 (Rotterdam)
2004 Greece 1 Portugal 0 (Lisbon)
2008 Spain 1 Germany 0 (Vienna)
2012 Spain 4 Italy 0 (Kiev)

• After 1-1 draw   * Won on penalties

Cristiano Ronaldo (in 2008) have won the Golden Shoe after topping both the Premiership and European goalscoring charts. Ronaldo also won the Golden Shoe with Real Madrid in 2011, to become the first player to win the award in two different countries.

• **The most controversial winner of the award was Rumania's Rodion Camataru, who scored 20 of his 44 goals for Dynamo Bucharest in the last six games of the 1986/87 season. Suspicions that some of these matches had not been played in a wholly competitive spirit were confirmed by evidence that emerged in the post-Communist era and in 2007 the runner-up in the 1987 list, Austria Vienna striker Toni Polster, was also granted a Golden Boot.**

• Lionel Messi holds the record for the most goals scored by a Golden Boot winner, with 50 in 2011/12. The Argentinian maestro had previously topped the chart in 2009/10, although that season his goal tally was a more mundane 34.

2011 Golden Boot winner Cristiano Ronaldo smiles, but he'll have to hand over the trophy to arch rival Lionel Messi soon

EUROPEAN GOLDEN BOOT

Now officially known as the European Golden Shoe, the European Golden Boot has been awarded since 1968 to the leading scorer in league matches in the top division of every European league. Since 1997 the award has been based on a points system which gives greater weight to goals scored in the leading European leagues.

• **The first winner of the award was the legendary Portuguese international Eusebio who picked up the trophy after knocking in an incredible 43 goals for Benfica. He topped the poll again in 1973, aged 30, with a total of 40 goals.**

• The first British winner of the award was Liverpool's Ian Rush in 1984, and the most recent was Sunderland's Kevin Phillips in 2000. Since then, Thierry Henry (in 2004 and 2005) and

EVERTON

Year founded: 1878
Ground: Goodison Park (40,157)
Previous name: St Domingo
Nickname: The Toffees
Biggest win: 11-2 v Derby County (1890)
Heaviest defeat: 0-7 v Sunderland (1934), v Wolves (1939) and v Arsenal (2005)

The club was formed as the church team St Domingo in 1878, adopting the name Everton (after the surrounding area) the following year. In 1888 Everton joined the Football League as founder members, winning the first of nine league titles three years later.

• **One of the most famous names in English football, Everton hold the proud record of spending more seasons in the top flight than any other club. Relegated only twice, in 1930 and 1951, they have spent just four seasons in total outside the top tier.**

• The club's unusual nickname, the Toffees, stems from a local business called Ye Ancient Everton Toffee House which was situated near Goodison Park. In the early 1930s Everton's precise style of play earned the club the tag 'The School of Science', a nickname which lingers to this day.

• The club's record goalscorer is the legendary Dixie Dean, who notched an incredible total of 383 goals in all competitions between 1925 and 1937. Dean's best season for the club was in the Toffees' title-winning campaign in 1927/28 when his 60 league goals set a Football League record that is unlikely ever to be beaten.

• Everton's most-capped player is long-serving goalkeeper Neville Southall, who made 93 appearances for Wales in the 1980s and 1990s. He is also the club's record appearance maker, turning out in 578 league games.

• **In 1931 Everton won the Second Division title, scoring 121 goals in the process. The following season the Toffees banged in 116 goals on their way to lifting the First Division title, becoming the first (and so far only) club to find the net 100 times in consecutive seasons.**

• The club's most successful decade, though, was in the 1980s when, under manager Howard Kendall, they won the league championship (1985 and 1987), FA Cup (1984) and the European Cup Winners' Cup (in 1985, following a 3-1 win over Austria Vienna in the final). Since those glory days Everton have had to play second fiddle to city rivals Liverpool, although the Toffees did manage to win the FA Cup for a fifth time in 1995, beating Manchester United in the final thanks to a single goal by striker Paul Rideout.

• **The club's record signing is afro-haired midfielder Morouane Fellaini, who cost £15 million when he signed from Standard Liege in 2008. Local boy Wayne Rooney fetched a record £25.6 million when he left Everton for Manchester United after starring for England at the Euro 2004 championships.**

• In 1893 Everton's Jack Southworth became the first player in Football League history to score six goals in a match when he fired a double hat-trick in a 7-1 victory against West Bromwich Albion.

• **Everton's Louis Saha scored the fastest-ever goal in the FA Cup final, when he netted after just 25 seconds against Chelsea at Wembley in 2009. Sadly for David Moyes' men, the Toffees were unable to hold onto their lead and were eventually beaten 2-1 – one of a record eight times Everton have lost in the final.**

• The oldest ground in the Premiership, Goodison Park is the only stadium in the world to have a church, St Luke the Evangelist, inside its grounds. The stadium was the first in England to feature dug-outs (in the 1930s), undersoil heating (in the 1958/59 season) and a three-tiered stand (in 1971). Goodison Park is also the only ground in the UK to have hosted a World Cup semi-final, staging the West Germany v Russia encounter in 1966.

• **Famous fans of the club include snooker player John Parrott, music legend Sir Paul McCartney and Rocky star Sylvester Stallone.**

Morouane Fellaini is Everton's record buy – his hair alone cost them £5 million!

IS THAT A FACT?
Everton were the first club to win a penalty shoot-out in the European Cup, knocking out German side Borussia Monchengladbach 4-3 on spot-kicks in the second round in 1970.

EXETER CITY

Year founded: 1904
Ground: St James Park (8,541)
Nickname: The Grecians
Biggest win: 14-0 v Weymouth (1908)
Heaviest defeat: 0-9 v Notts County (1948) and v Northampton Town (1958)

Exeter City were founded in 1904 following the amalgamation of two local sides, Exeter United and St Sidwell's United. The club were founder members of the Third Division (South) in 1920 and remained in the two lower divisions until they were relegated to the Conference in 2003. Now owned by the Exeter City Supporters Trust, the club rejoined the Football League in 2008.

• After a poor start to the 1910/11 season Exeter decided to scrap their 'unlucky' green-and-white kit. They changed to red-and-white stripes and their fortunes took an instant turn for the better, the club winning five of their next six games.

• In the 1973/74 season Exeter only played 45 of their 46 league games after failing to turn up for a fixture at Scunthorpe, who were awarded the points.

• Famous fans of the club include Coldplay's Chris Martin, singer Joss Stone and the late Michael Jackson, who was made an honorary director of the club after visiting St James Park with his friend, spoon-bending Exeter supporter Uri Geller.

HONOURS
Division 4 champions 1990

EXTRA TIME

Normally consisting of two halves of 15 minutes each, extra time has been played to produce a winner in knockout tournaments since the earliest days of football, although to begin with the playing of the additional time had to be agreed by the two captains. Extra time was first played in an FA Cup final in 1875, Royal Engineers and the Old Etonians drawing 1-1 (Royal Engineers won the replay 2-0). In all, extra time has been played in 18 finals, the most recent in 2007 when Chelsea eventually

Liverpool celebrate an extra-time goal against Cardiff in the 2012 League Cup final

beat Manchester United 1-0.

• The first World Cup final to go to extra time was in 1934, when hosts Italy and Czechoslovakia were tied 1-1 at the end of 90 minutes. Seven minutes into the additional period, Angelo Schiavio scored the winner for Italy. Since then, five other finals have gone to extra time, most recently in 2010 when Spain's Andres Iniesta scored the winner against Holland with just a few minutes to play.

• In an attempt to encourage attacking football and reduce the number of matches settled by penalty shoot-outs, FIFA ruled in 1993 that the first goal scored in extra time would win the match. The first major tournament to be decided by the so-called 'golden goal' rule was the 1996 European Championships, Germany defeating the Czech Republic in the final thanks to a 94th-minute strike by Oliver Bierhoff. The 2000 final of the same competition was also decided in the same manner, David Trezeguet scoring a dramatic

winner for France against Italy in the 117th minute.

• Concerns that the 'golden goal' put too much pressure on referees led UEFA to replace it with the 'silver goal' in 2002. Under this rule, which was used at Euro 2004 but scrapped afterwards, only the first half of extra time was played if either team led at the interval.

• The first European Cup final to require extra time was between Real Madrid and AC Milan in 1962, Real eventually winning 3-2. In all, 15 finals have gone to extra time, but only four produced a winner inside the additional 30 minutes.

• **The very first final of the League Cup in 1961 went to extra time, Aston Villa eventually beating Rotherham United 3-2 on aggregate after a 3-0 win in the second leg at Villa Park. In total, 17 finals have required the additional half hour, most recently in 2012 when Liverpool beat Cardiff City on penalties after the two teams were tied at 2-2 after 120 minutes.**

FA CUP

The oldest knockout competition in the world, the FA Cup dates back to 1871 when it was established under the control of the Football Association. The first round of the first FA Cup was played on 11th November 1871, Clapham Rovers' Jarvis Kenrick scoring the very first goal in the competition in a 3-0 win over Upton Park.

• **The following year Wanderers beat Royal Engineers at Kennington Oval in the first ever FA Cup final. The only goal of the game was scored by Morton Peto Betts, who played under the pseudonym A.H. Chequer.**

• Unlike the League Cup, the FA Challenge Cup – the competition's full title – has always retained the same name despite being sponsored in recent years by Littlewoods (1994-98), AXA (1998-2002), E.ON (2006-11) and Budweiser (2011-).

• There have, however, been four different trophies. The first trophy – known as the 'little tin idol' – was stolen from a Birmingham shop window in September 1895 where it was on display, having been won by Aston Villa a few months earlier. Sixty years later the thief revealed that the trophy was melted down and turned into counterfeit coins. A second trophy was used until 1910 when it was presented to the FA's long-serving President and former five-time cup winner, Lord Kinnaird. A new, larger trophy was commissioned by the FA from Fattorini and Sons Silversmiths in Bradford – and, by a remarkable coincidence, was won in its first year by Bradford City in 1911. This trophy was used until 1992, when it was replaced with an exact replica.

• The only league team to have won the FA Cup in three consecutive years are

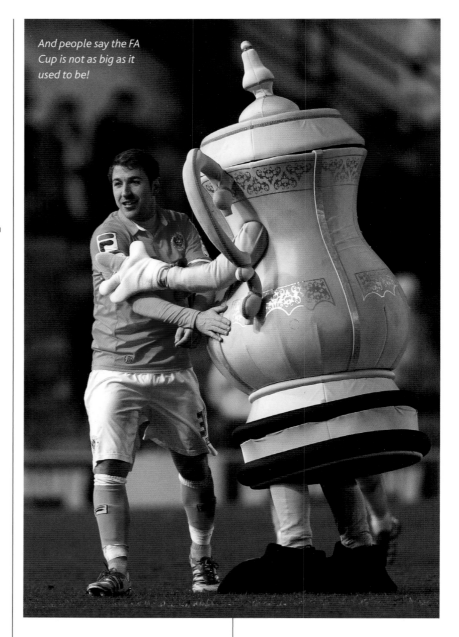

And people say the FA Cup is not as big as it used to be!

Blackburn Rovers, who lifted the trophy in 1884, 1885 and 1886. The most successful club in the competition are Manchester United, who have won the FA Cup a record 11 times.

• **In 2000 Manchester United became the first holders not to defend their title when they failed to enter the FA Cup, opting instead to take part in the inaugural FIFA Club World Championship in Brazil.**

• Five years later United were involved in the first FA Cup final to be decided by penalties, losing 5-4 to Arsenal after a 0-0 draw at the Millennium Stadium, Cardiff. In 2007 the final returned to Wembley, Chelsea becoming the first club to lift the trophy at the new national stadium after a 1-0 victory over Manchester United. The Blues have gone on to dominate the cup in the new Wembley era, winning the trophy in four

of the six seasons since the final returned to London.

• **Tottenham Hotspur are the only non-league side to win the competition, lifting the trophy for the first time in 1901 while members of the Southern League. West Ham were the last team from outside the top flight to win the cup, beating Arsenal 1-0 in the 1980 final.**

• The first player to be sent off in the FA Cup final was Manchester United's Kevin Moran in 1985, who was dismissed for a foul on Everton's Peter Reid. Nonetheless, United went on to win the match 1-0 after extra time.

• **In 1887 Preston North End recorded the biggest win in the history of the competition when they thrashed Hyde 26-0 in a first-round tie.**

• Ashley Cole has won the FA Cup a record seven times. Three of the England

TOP 10

MOST GOALS IN THE FA CUP

1.	Aston Villa	828
2.	Tottenham Hotspur	763
3.	Manchester United	748
4.	Everton	733
5.	Blackburn Rovers	726
6.	Arsenal	707
7.	Sheffield Wednesday	684
8.	Liverpool	673
9.	West Bromwich Albion	671
10.	Chelsea	660

full back's triumphs came with his first club, Arsenal (in 2002, 2003 and 2005), and he has also enjoyed four successes with Chelsea (in 2007, 2009, 2010 and 2012).

• The leading scorer in the FA Cup is Notts County's Henry Cursham, who banged in 49 goals between 1877 and 1888. Liverpool's Ian Rush scored a record five goals in three appearances in the final in 1986, 1989 and 1992, but Chelsea's Didier Drogba is the only player to have scored in four finals (2007, 2009, 2010 and 2012).

CESC FABREGAS

> **Born:** Barcelona, 4th May 1987
> **Position:** Midfielder
> **Club career:**
> 2003-11 Arsenal 212 (35)
> 2011- Barcelona 28 (9)
> **International record:**
> 2006- Spain 69 (10)

One of the most talented midfielders in Europe, Cesc Fabregas is the youngest player ever to appear for Arsenal. He made his debut for the Gunners in a League Cup tie against Rotherham in October 2003, aged just 16 years and 177 days. When he scored against Wolves in a later round of the same competition he also became the club's youngest ever goalscorer.

• Fabregas started out as a trainee with Barcelona before signing for Arsenal in September 2003. A superb passer of the ball who can unpick the tightest of defences, Fabregas was named PFA Young Player of the Year in 2008 and in the same year he was made the Gunners' captain.

• Despite being idolised by Arsenal fans, Fabregas made no secret of his desire to return to Barcelona and in August 2011 his wish was granted when he rejoined the Catalans for an initial £25.4 million, making him the expensive player to leave the Emirates.

• When Fabregas made his debut for Spain in a friendly against Ivory Coast in 2006 he was the youngest player to represent his country for 70 years. Two years later he helped Spain win Euro 2008 in Austria and Switzerland, his country's first trophy for 44 years. Four years later he was a key part of the Spain team that retained the trophy, scoring

the winning penalty in the semi-final shoot-out against Portugal.

• At the 2010 World Cup in South Africa he failed to start a single game, but he came off the bench in the final against Holland to set up the winning goal for team-mate Andres Iniesta with a typically clever pass.

FANS

Manchester United have more fans than any other club in the world. A 2011 survey across 34 different countries by a German sports marketing firm discovered that the Red Devils have around 354 million fans worldwide, equivalent to 5 per cent of the population of the planet. Barcelona (270 million fans) and Real Madrid (174 million fans) were the next most popular clubs.

• A number of fan groups have realised a common supporters' dream by becoming the owners of their clubs. Three Football League clubs (Brentford, Exeter City and AFC Wimbledon) are owned by Supporters' Trusts, while non-league clubs AFC Liverpool and FC United of Manchester were set up by disillusioned supporters of Liverpool

Cesc Fabregas in action for Spain

and Manchester United respectively. Fan-owned clubs, meanwhile, are the norm in Germany, while Spanish titans Athletic Bilbao, Barcelona and Real Madrid are also supporter-owned.

• Formed in 1978, the 92 Club is open to all fans who have attended a competitive first-team fixture at the stadium of every Premiership and Football League club in England and Wales. The club's initial membership of 39 had grown to over 1,000 by the start of the 2012/13 season.

• **With 180,000 members in England and Wales the Football Supporters' Federation is the largest fans' organisation in Britain. The FSF campaigns on a variety of issues affecting fans, including ticket pricing, policing and supporter representation on club boards, as well as organising an annual Fans' Parliament at Wembley stadium. The chairman of the FSF is Malcolm Clarke, a Stoke City fan.**

• Must-have accessories for fans at matches down the decades include the humble football rattle (banned in the 1970s for its potential use by hooligans as a weapon), inflatable bananas (especially popular at Manchester City in the late 1980s), sticks of celery (a Chelsea favourite) and, at the 2010 World Cup in the South Africa, the vuvuzela, a horn-like instrument that emits a loud, distinctive monotone note when blown.

RIO FERDINAND

Born: Peckham, 7th November 1978
Position: Defender
Club career:
1996-2000 West Ham United 127 (2)
1996 Bournemouth (loan) 10 (0)
2000-02 Leeds United 54 (2)
2002- Manchester United 270 (6)
International record:
1997- England 81 (3)

England captain Rio Ferdinand is the world's most expensive defender, having moved from Leeds United to Manchester United for around £30 million in 2002. Nor was that the first time Ferdinand had been transferred for an eye-watering fee. In 2000 he joined Leeds from West Ham, his first club, for £18 million – also a world record at the time for a defender.

• **A composed and commanding centre-** half who likes to bring the ball out from the back to launch attacking moves, Ferdinand won the Premiership title in his first season at Old Trafford. He has since won the title on four further occasions and in 2008 he skippered United when the Reds won the Champions League after beating Premiership rivals Chelsea on penalties in the final in Moscow.

• A mainstay of the England defence for many years, Ferdinand was first capped against Cameroon in 1997, just one week after his 19th birthday. At the time he was the youngest-ever defender to play for England – although this record has since been beaten by Micah Richards. In 2008 Ferdinand captained his country for the first time as then England manager Fabio Capello tried out a number of players in the role before finally handing the armband to the United star's defensive partner, John Terry. When Terry was stripped of the captaincy in 2010 after allegations about his private life, Capello handed Ferdinand the armband on a permanent basis, only for the Chelsea man to regain the captaincy the following year.

Rio Ferdinand wasn't very happy to learn that John Terry had nicked his parking space…

• Ferdinand has played in more games for England, 81, without once appearing at the European championships. He wasn't selected for the 2000 tournament, was banned in 2004 after missing a drugs test and, after England failed to qualify in 2008, he was controversially omitted from Roy Hodgson's squad for Euro 2012.

• Peckham-born Ferdinand hails from a football family. His younger brother Anton plays for QPR while older cousin Les was a prolific striker with QPR, Newcastle, Tottenham and England.

SIR ALEX FERGUSON

Born: Govan, 31st December 1942
Managerial career: 1974 East Stirling
1974-78 St Mirren
1978-86 Aberdeen
1985-86 Scotland (caretaker)
1986- Manchester United

Manchester United boss Sir Alex Ferguson is the most successful British manager in the history of the game.

Over his long career he has won 34 major trophies and is the only manager from these shores to win the Champions League on two occasions.

• Ferguson's reputation was forged at Aberdeen between 1978-86 where he transformed the Dons into Scotland's leading club, breaking the domination of the Glasgow Old Firm in the process. Under Fergie, Aberdeen won three Premier Division titles, four Scottish Cups, one League Cup and the European Cup Winners' Cup in 1983, making him easily the most successful boss in the club's history.

• He moved to Manchester United in 1986 and, after some difficult early years, established the Reds as the dominant force of the 1990s and the new millennium. With United Ferguson has won a record 12 Premiership titles, five FA Cups (another record), three League Cups, the European Cup Winners' Cup and the Champions League in both 1999 and 2008.

• Fergie's 25-year tenure at Old Trafford means he is the longest-serving manager in English football. During the 2011/12 season Ferguson passed Sir Matt Busby's previous record of managing Manchester United for 985 league games, taking his tally to 997 (including 597 victories) by the end of the campaign.

• Ferguson is the only man to guide both Scottish and English clubs to success in all three domestic competitions and in Europe. He is also the only manager to win the English championship in three consecutive seasons with the same club, achieving this feat with United between 1999-2001 and 2007-09. In the first of those years Fergie also won the FA Cup and Champions League to pull off an unprecedented Treble.

• A committed but not especially skilful striker in his playing days in the 1960s and early 1970s, Ferguson scored over 150 goals for a number of Scottish clubs including Dunfermline, Rangers and Falkirk.

• Knighted for services to football in 1999, Ferguson has been named Premier League Manager of the Year on a record ten occasions. Still enthusiastic and motivated after all these years he will, no doubt, be looking to add to his staggering roll of honour in seasons to come.

They love Sir Alex 'Freguson' in Tibet!

Freguson The Tibetian Are Grateful With You!

FIFA

FIFA, the Federation Internationale de Football Association, is the most important administrative body in world football. It is responsible for the organization of major international tournaments, notably the World Cup, and enacts law changes in the game.

• **Founded in Paris in 1904, FIFA is now based in Zurich and has 209 members, 16 more than the United Nations. The President is Sepp Blatter (elected in 1998), while his predecessors include Jules Rimet (1921-54), Sir Stanley Rous (1961-74) and Joao Havelange (1974-98). In 2011 Blatter was re-elected unopposed as President after his rival for the job, Mohammed bin Hammam, withdrew his candidacy following allegations that he offered bribes for votes.**

• Law changes that FIFA have introduced into the World Cup include the use of substitutes (1970), penalty shoot-outs to settle drawn games (1982) and the banning of the professional foul (1990).

• **The British football associations have twice pulled out of FIFA. First, in 1918 when they were opposed to playing matches against Germany after the end of the First World War, and again in 1928 over the issue of payments to amateurs. This second dispute meant that none of the British teams were represented at the first World Cup in 1930.**

• In 1992 FIFA decided to introduce a ranking index for all its member countries. As of August 2012 the three leading nations were Spain (1st), Germany (2nd) and England (3rd). Somewhat surprisingly, Brazil were only ranked 13th behind both Denmark and Greece.

• **Brazil top FIFA's all-time World Cup ranking, with England in 5th place.**

IS THAT A FACT?
To celebrate its 100th anniversary in 2004 FIFA organized a 'Match of the Century' between France and Brazil. The game, at the Stade de France, rather failed to live up to the hype, finishing 0-0.

'The Preston Plumber', Tom Finney in action for England

SIR TOM FINNEY

Born: Preston, 5th April 1922
Position: Winger
Club career:
1946-60 Preston North End 433 (187)
International record:
1947-59 England 76 (30)

One of England's greatest-ever players, flying winger Sir Tom Finney was the first player to be made Footballer of the Year twice. He won the award in 1954, after starring in Preston's run to the FA Cup final, and was honoured for a second time in 1957.

• **Equally adept on either right or left wing, Finney scored a record 187 league goals for Preston but never won a major club trophy. The closest he got was in 1953 when Preston** missed out on the league title on goal average. The following year they lost to West Brom in the FA Cup final, and in 1958 they were again runners-up in the league.

• In his 76 appearances for England, Finney scored an impressive 30 goals – a record at the time shared with Bolton's Nat Lofthouse. Only four players since have scored more goals for England. His Preston team-mate Bill Shankly once said of him: "Tom Finney would have been great in any team, in any match and in any age – even if he had been wearing an overcoat."

• **Before signing as a pro, Finney served his apprenticeship in the family plumbing business – hence his nickname, the 'Preston Plumber'. Unarguably Preston's best-ever player, he was knighted in 1998 and has a stand named after him at the club's Deepdale ground.**

If England could dazzle like these Ukranian floodlights, they would be world-beaters!

FLOODLIGHTS

The first-ever floodlit match was played at Bramall Lane between two representative Sheffield sides on 14th October 1876 in front of a crowd of 10,000 people (around 8,000 of whom used the cover of darkness to get in without paying). The pitch was illuminated by four lamps, powered by dynamos driven by engines located behind the goals.

• For many years the Football Association banned floodlight football, so the first league match played under lights did not take place until 1956, when Newcastle beat Portsmouth 2-0 at Fratton Park. It was hardly the most auspicious of occasions, though, as floodlight failure meant the kick-off was delayed for 30 minutes.

• Arsenal became the first top flight club in England to install floodlights in 1951 – some 20 years after legendary Gunners manager Herbert Chapman had advocated their use. Chesterfield were the last Football League club to install floodlights, finally putting up a set in 1967.

• In the winter of 1997 two Premier League games, at West Ham and Wimbledon, were abandoned because of floodlight failure. What seemed to be an unfortunate coincidence was eventually revealed to be the work of a shadowy Far Eastern betting syndicate, four members of whom were eventually arrested and sentenced to three years each in prison.

• The first match played under the Wembley Stadium floodlights was the Inter-Cities Fairs Cup encounter between London and Frankfurt on 26th October 1955. Among the scorer's for the home team in their 3-2 win was Fulham's Bobby Robson, later the manager of England.

IS THAT A FACT?
England first played under the Wembley floodlights for the final 15 minutes of their friendly against Spain on 30th November 1955. The home side won the match 4-1.

FLEETWOOD TOWN

Year founded: 1997
Ground: Highbury Stadium (5,094)
Previous names: Fleetwood Wanderers, Fleetwood Freeport
Nickname: The Trawlermen
Biggest win: 13-0 v Oldham Town (1998)
Heaviest defeat: 0-7 v Billingham Town (2001)

Established in 1997 as the third incarnation of a club which dates back to 1908, Fleetwood Town have enjoyed a remarkable rise in recent years, culminating in their promotion to the Football League as Conference champions in 2012.

• The Trawlermen's points tally of 103 in 2011/12 was just two short of Crawley Town's Conference record of 105, set in the previous season. Fleetwood's superb campaign also saw them reach the third round of the FA Cup for the first time in their history, their run finally being ended by local rivals Blackpool.

• Fleetwood's climb through the divisions – they were playing in the Conference North as recently as 2010 – has seen their home attendances soar over the past decade. In 2003/04 they were playing in front of an average crowd of just 134, but by 2011/12 that figure had risen to 2,264 – an incredible increase of nearly 11,700 per cent.

HONOURS
Conference champions 2012

The design of the Three Lions badge and the inner workings of Wayne Rooney's mind - just two of the concerns of the Football Association

FOOTBALL ASSOCIATION

Founded in 1863 at a meeting at the Freemasons' Tavern in central London, the Football Association is the oldest football organisation in the world and the only national association with no mention of the country in its name.

• The first secretary of the FA was Ebenezer Cobb Morley of Barnes FC, nicknamed 'The Father of Football', who went on to draft the first set of laws of the game. The most controversial of the 14 laws he suggested outlawed kicking an opponent, known as 'hacking'. The first match to be played under the new laws was between Barnes and Richmond in 1863.

• In 1871 the then secretary of the FA, Charles Alcock, suggested playing a national knock-out tournament similar to the competition he had enjoyed as a schoolboy at Harrow School. The idea was accepted by the FA and the competition, named the FA Challenge Cup, has been running ever since. The FA Cup, as it usually called, has long been the most famous national club competition in world football.

• Since 1992, the FA has run the English game's top division, the Premier League, which was formed when the old First Division broke away from the then four-division Football League.

• The FA is also responsible for the appointment of the management of the England men's and women's football teams. The FA's main asset is the new Wembley Stadium, which it owns via its subsidiary, Wembley National Stadium Limited.

• Among the innovations the FA has fought against before finally accepting are the formation of an international tournament, the use of substitutes and the use of floodlights.

FOOTBALL LEAGUE

The Football League was founded at a meeting at the Royal Hotel, Piccadilly, Manchester in April 1888. The prime mover behind the new body was Aston Villa director William McGregor, who became the league's first President.

• The 12 founder members were Accrington, Aston Villa, Blackburn Rovers, Bolton Wanderers, Burnley, Derby County, Everton, Notts County, Preston North End, Stoke City, West Bromwich Albion and Wolverhampton Wanderers. At the end of the inaugural 1888/89 season, Preston were crowned champions.

• In 1892 a new Second Division, absorbing clubs from the rival Football Alliance, was added to the League and by 1905 the two divisions were made up of a total of 40 clubs. After the First World War, the League was expanded again to include a Third Division (later split between North and South sections).

• A further expansion after 1945 took the number of clubs playing in the league to its long-time total of 92. The formation of the Premier League in 1992 reduced the Football League to three divisions – now known as the Championship, League One and League Two.

• As well as being the governing body for the three divisions, the Football League also organises two knockout competitions: the League Cup (known as the Capital One Cup for sponsorship reasons) and the Football League Trophy (aka the Johnstone's Paint Trophy).

• Liverpool are the most successful club in the history of the Football League, with 18 First Division titles to their name.

FOOTBALLER OF THE YEAR

Confusingly, there are two Footballer of the Year awards in England and Scotland. The Football Writers' award was inaugurated in 1948, and the first winner was England winger Stanley Matthews. In 1974 the PFA (Professional Footballers' Association) set up their own award, Leeds hard man Norman 'Bites Yer Legs' Hunter being the first to be honoured by his peers.

• Liverpool midfielder Terry McDermott was the first player to win both awards in the same season after helping Liverpool retain the title in 1980. A total of 14 different players have won both Footballer of the Year awards in the same season, most recently Arsenal striker Robin van Persie in 2012. Another Arsenal striker, Thierry Henry, has won a record five awards, landing the 'double' in both 2003 and 2004 and also carrying off the Football Writers' award in 2006.

• In 1977 Aston Villa striker Andy Gray became the first player to win both the main PFA award and the Young Player of the Year trophy. Only Cristiano Ronaldo in 2007 has since matched this achievement.

FOOTBALL WRITERS' PLAYER OF THE YEAR (SINCE 1990)
1990 John Barnes (Liverpool)
1991 Gordon Strachan (Leeds United)
1992 Gary Lineker (Tottenham)
1993 Chris Waddle (Sheffield Wednesday)
1994 Alan Shearer (Blackburn Rovers)
1995 Jurgen Klinsmann (Tottenham)
1996 Eric Cantona (Manchester United)
1997 Gianfranco Zola (Chelsea)
1998 Dennis Bergkamp (Arsenal)
1999 David Ginola (Tottenham)
2000 Roy Keane (Manchester United)
2001 Teddy Sheringham (Manchester United)
2002 Robert Pires (Arsenal)
2003 Thierry Henry (Arsenal)
2004 Thierry Henry (Arsenal)
2005 Frank Lampard (Chelsea)
2006 Thierry Henry (Arsenal)
2007 Cristiano Ronaldo (Manchester United)
2008 Cristiano Ronaldo (Manchester United)
2009 Steven Gerrard (Liverpool)
2010 Wayne Rooney (Manchester United)
2011 Scott Parker (West Ham United)
2012 Robin van Persie (Arsenal)

PFA FOOTBALLER OF THE YEAR (SINCE 1990)
1990 David Platt (Aston Villa)
1991 Mark Hughes (Manchester United)
1992 Gary Pallister (Manchester United)
1993 Paul McGrath (Aston Villa)
1994 Eric Cantona (Manchester United)
1995 Alan Shearer (Blackburn Rovers)
1996 Les Ferdinand (Newcastle United)
1997 Alan Shearer (Newcastle United)
1998 Dennis Bergkamp (Arsenal)
1999 David Ginola (Tottenham)
2000 Roy Keane (Manchester United)
2001 Teddy Sheringham (Manchester United)
2002 Ruud van Nistelrooy (Manchester United)
2003 Thierry Henry (Arsenal)
2004 Thierry Henry (Arsenal)

Continued on page 76

2005 John Terry (Chelsea)
2006 Steven Gerrard (Liverpool)
2007 Cristiano Ronaldo
(Manchester United)
2008 Cristiano Ronaldo
(Manchester United)
2009 Ryan Giggs
(Manchester United)
2010 Wayne Rooney (Manchester
United)
2011 Gareth Bale (Tottenham
Hotspur)
2012 Robin van Persie (Arsenal)

FRANCE

First international:
Belgium 3 France 3,
1904
Most capped player:
Lilian Thuram, 142 caps
(1994-2008)
Leading goalscorer:
Thierry Henry, 51 goals
(1997-2010)
**First World Cup
appearance:** France 4 Mexico 1,
1930
Biggest win: France 10 Azerbaijan 0,
1995
Heaviest defeat: France 1
Denmark 17, 1908

One of the most successful football nations of recent years, France won the World Cup for the first and only time on home soil in 1998 with a stunning 3-0 victory over Brazil in the final in Paris. Midfield genius Zinedine Zidane was the star of the show, scoring two of his side's goals.

• Two years later France became the first World Cup holders to go on to win the European Championships when they overcame Italy in the final in Rotterdam. This, though, was a much closer affair with the French requiring a 'golden goal' by striker David Trezeguet in extra time to claim the trophy.

• France had won the European Championships once before, in 1984. Inspired by the legendary Michel Platini, who scored a record nine goals in the tournament, les Bleus beat Spain 2-0 in the final in Paris.

• French striker Just Fontaine scored an all-time record 13 goals at the 1958 World Cup finals in Sweden. His remarkable strike rate helped his country finish third in the tournament.

• When World Cup holders France were beaten 1-0 by Senegal in the 2002 World Cup it was one of the biggest shocks in the history of the tournament. Les Bleus slumped out of the competition in the first round on that occasion, but bounced back to reach the final again in 2006... only to suffer the agony of a penalty shoot-out defeat at the hands of Italy. In 2010, though, the French endured another nightmare campaign, internal disputes between leading players and coach Raymond Domenech contributing to a humiliating first-round exit in South Africa.

• In 1908 France suffered one of the biggest-ever defeats in international football when they were hammered 17-1 by Denmark in the semi-finals of the Olympic Games tournament in London. The French team were so depressed afterwards that they declined to play for the bronze medal against fellow beaten semi-finalists Holland.

• On 13th July 1930 France's Lucien Laurent scored the first-ever goal at the World Cup finals, netting with a 19th-minute volley in his side's 4-1 defeat of Mexico in the Estadio Pocitos in Montevideo, Uruguay.

*The French team
do not always get
along as well as this*

TOP 10

HIGHEST CAPPED FRANCE PLAYERS

1.	Lilian Thuram (1994-2008)	142
2.	Thierry Henry (1997-2010)	123
3.	Marcel Desailly (1993-2004)	116
4.	Zinedine Zidane (1994-2006)	108
5.	Patrick Vieira (1997-2009)	107
6.	Didier Deschamps (1989-2000)	
		103
7.	Laurent Blanc (1989-2000)	97
8.	Bixente Lizarazu (1992-2004)	
		97
9.	Sylvain Wiltord (1999-2006)	92
10.	Fabien Barthez (1994-2006)	87

"Everyone was pleased but we didn't all roll around on the ground," he recalled many years later. "Nobody realised that history was being made."

HONOURS

World Cup 1998
European Championship 1984, 2000
Confederations Cup 2001, 2003

World Cup record
1930 Round 1
1934 Round 1
1938 Round 2
1950 Did not qualify
1954 Round 1
1958 Third place
1962 Did not qualify
1966 Round 1
1970 Did not qualify
1974 Did not qualify
1978 Round 1
1982 Fourth place
1986 Third place
1990 Did not qualify
1994 Did not qualify
1998 Winners
2002 Round 1
2006 Runners-up
2010 Round 1

FREE KICKS

A method for restarting the game after an infringement, free kicks may either be direct (meaning a goal may be scored directly) or indirect (in which case a second player must touch the ball before a goal may be scored).

• In 2000 a new rule was introduced which allowed the referee to punish dissent by moving a free kick ten yards nearer the defenders' goal. The rule change, though, was deemed not to be a success and was unceremoniously scrapped five years later.

• One of the most memorable free kicks ever was taken by England captain David Beckham in a vital World Cup qualifier against Greece at Old Trafford in 2001. With the last kick of the match Beckham curled a superb free kick over the Greek wall and into the corner of the net to earn England a draw which booked the team's passage to the finals of the tournament in Japan and Korea.

• Managers and coaches are forever dreaming up free kick routines which might confuse the opposition and lead to a goal. Serie A side Catania tried a truly bizarre ploy in 2008 when three of their players stood in front of the Torino goalkeeper and dropped their shorts while team-mate Giuseppe Mascara scored with a well-struck free kick.

• On 27th March 2011 Sao Paulo's Rogerio Ceni became the first goalkeeper in the history of football to score 100 career goals when he netted with a free-kick in a 2-1 win against Corinthians. His unlikely century was made up of 56 free-kicks and 44 penalties.

FRIENDLIES

The first official international friendly took place on 30th November 1872 between Scotland and England at the West of Scotland Cricket Ground, Partick, Glasgow. The Scottish side for the match, which ended in a 0-0 draw, was made up entirely of players from the country's leading club, Queen's Park.

• Not all non-competitive matches live up to their 'friendly' billing. The 1934 encounter at Highbury between England and Italy, for instance, was a famously violent affair. Italian captain Luisito Monti suffered a broken toe and his English counterpart Eddie Hapgood a broken nose as the match threatened to disintegrate into a brawl, before some sort of order was eventually restored. England won the match, which became known as 'The Battle of Highbury', 3-2.

• On 6th February 2007 London played host to a record four international friendlies on the same night — and England weren't even one of the eight teams in action! At the Emirates Stadium Portugal beat Brazil 2-0, Ghana thrashed Nigeria 4-1 at Brentford's Griffin Park, South Korea beat European champions Greece 1-0 at Craven Cottage, while at Loftus Road Denmark were 3-1 winners over Australia.

• England's favourite opponents in friendly matches are the USA, the Three Lions winning all seven non-competitive matches against the States. However, it's been a different story in the three competitive encounters between the countries, with the USA winning two and drawing the other.

• Possibly the most bizarre friendly ever took place between Atletic Bilbao and a 200-strong 'team' of local schoolchildren in May 2010. The youngsters' side consisted of 197 outfield players and three goalkeepers, but despite their huge numerical advantage they were defeated 5-3 by their heroes.

FULHAM

Year founded: 1879
Ground: Craven Cottage (25,700)
Previous name: Fulham St. Andrew's
Nickname: The Cottagers
Biggest win: 10-1 v Ipswich Town (1963)
Heaviest defeat: 0-10 v Liverpool (1986)

London's oldest club, Fulham were founded in 1879 by two clergymen. Originally known as Fulham St Andrew's, the club adopted its present name nine years later. After winning the Southern League in two consecutive seasons Fulham were elected to the Football League in 1907.

• Before moving to Craven Cottage in 1896, Fulham had played at no fewer than 11 different grounds. Including a stay at Loftus Road in 2002-04 while the Cottage was being redeveloped, Fulham have played at 13 venues, a total only exceeded by QPR.

• The proudest moment in the club's history came as recently as May 2010 when Fulham met Atletico Madrid in Hamburg in the first Europa League final. Sadly for their fans and their inspirational manager Roy Hodgson, the Cottagers lost 2-1 in extra time despite putting up a spirited fight.

• In 1975 Fulham reached the FA Cup final for the first (and so far only) time,

A sunny Premier League afternoon at the Cottage

losing 2-0 to West Ham. The Cottagers have appeared in the semi-final six times, including a forgettable occasion in 1908 when they were hammered 6-0 by Newcastle, to this day the biggest ever winning margin at that stage of the competition.

• Midfield legend Johnny Haynes holds the club's appearance record, turning out in 594 league games between 1952-70. 'The Maestro', as he was known to Fulham fans, is also the club's most-honoured player at international level, with 56 England caps. Welsh international striker Gordon Davies is Fulham's top scorer with 159 league goals in two spells at the club between 1978 and 1991.

• In 1997 Fulham missed out on the Third Division title on 'goals scored' after finishing level on points with Wigan Athletic, despite having a superior goal difference. Ironically, then Fulham chairman Jimmy Hill had advocated the change to using goals scored, rather than goal difference, to separate teams who were equal on points.

• Bankrolled by multi-millionaire owner Mohamed Al-Fayed, Fulham climbed from the basement division to the Premiership in just four years between 1997-2001 – a year less than the then Harrods boss had predicted. Only Swansea City have made a quicker rise through the divisions, taking just three years between 1978-81.

• **The club have now spent a club record 12 consecutive seasons in the top flight, and have become an established Premier League force thanks to players like Clint Dempsey and Brede Hangeland. During the 2011/12 season Dempsey became the first American to hit 50 Premier League goals while Hangeland was one of only two outfield players to complete all 3,420 minutes of the league campaign.**

• Livewire striker Andrew Johnson is Fulham's record signing, joining the club from Everton for a cool £13 million in 2008. The club's coffers were boosted by a record £12.4 million four years earlier, when Louis Saha left for Manchester United.

• **In 1987 Fulham took part in the longest-ever penalty shoot-out** in British football, losing 11-10 to Aldershot in the Freight Rover Trophy quarter-final after the teams had taken 14 spot-kicks each.

• In April 2011 Mohamed Al-Fayed unveiled a huge statue of pop star Michael Jackson outside Craven Cottage. Many fans were unimpressed by the bizarre new addition, but the Fulham owner was unrepentant, telling them that they could "go to hell" if they didn't like it. Suitably inspired by the statue of the King of Pop, Fulham thrashed Blackpool 3-0 in the match that immediately followed its unveiling.

• **Famous fans of the Cottagers include actor Hugh Grant, singer Lilly Allen and veteran DJ David 'Diddy' Hamilton, who has performed the role of the club's matchday announcer for many years.**

HONOURS

Division 2 champions 1949
First Division champions 2001
Division 3 (S) champions 1932
Second Division champions 1999

PAUL GASCOIGNE

Born: Gateshead, 25th May 1967
Position: Midfielder
Club career:
1985-88 Newcastle United 92 (21)
1988-92 Tottenham Hotspur 92 (19)
1992-95 Lazio 43 (6)
1995-98 Rangers 74 (30)
1998-2000 Middlesbrough 41 (4)
2000-02 Everton 32 (1)
2002 Burnley 6 (0)
2003 Gansu Tianma 4 (2)
2004 Boston United 5 (0)
International record:
1988-98 England 57 (10)

The most talented English midfielder of his generation, Paul Gascoigne could unlock the tightest of defences with a clever pass or a trademark dribble past a couple of opponents. His prodigious skills prompted Tottenham to sign him for £2 million from Newcastle in 1988, making him the most expensive British player at the time.

• Troubled by injuries throughout his career, Gascoigne was at his peak at the 1990 World Cup in Italy when his brilliant performances powered England to the last four. 'Gazzamania' completely swept the country after his tears during the England-Germany semi-final (after he picked up a yellow card which meant he would miss the final) perfectly summed up the mood of disappointment that swept the nation as England went on to lose a penalty shoot-out. A few months later he was voted BBC Sports Personality of the Year – only the second footballer, after Bobby Moore in 1966, to receive the award.

• Gazza also starred at Euro '96, scoring a superb solo goal in the local derby with Scotland at Wembley that many rate as the best England goal ever. However, he was controversially left out of England's 1998 World Cup squad after a series of drunken incidents and never added to his 57 caps.

• At club level, Gascoigne is one of a select band of players to have won both the FA Cup (with Spurs in 1991) and the Scottish Cup (with Rangers in 1996). While at Ibrox he also won two league titles and the League Cup.

• A fun-loving character who was once described as being 'as daft as a brush' by then England manager Bobby Robson, Gazza has sadly struggled with alcohol addiction and mental health problems since quitting the game in 2004.

TOP 10

WORLD'S MOST EXPENSIVE GOALKEEPERS

1. Gianluigi Buffon (Parma to Juventus, 2001) £32.6m
2. David de Gea (Atletico Madrid to Manchester United, 2011) £18m
3. Manuel Neuer (Schalke to Bayern Munich, 2011) £15m
4. Angelo Peruzzi (Inter Milan to Lazio, 2000) £10.5m
5. Fernando Muslera (Lazio to Galatasaray, 2011) £9.93m
6. Craig Gordon (Hearts to Sunderland, 2007) £9m
7. Hugo Lloris (Lyon to Tottenham Hotspur, 2012) £8m
8. Fabien Barthez (Monaco to Manchester United, 2000) £7.8m
   Thibaut Courtois (Racing Genk to Chelsea, 2011) £7.8m
10. Edwin van der Sar (Juventus to Fulham, 2001) £7.1m

DAVID DE GEA

Born: Madrid, 7th November 1990
Position: Goalkeeper
Club career:
2008-09 Atletico Madrid B 35
2009-11 Atletico Madrid 57
2011- Manchester United 29

David De Gea is the most expensive goalkeeper in the history of the British game, costing Manchester United around £18 million when he moved from Atletico Madrid in June 2011.

• After coming through the youth ranks at Atletico, De Gea enjoyed a great first season with the Madrid club helping them win the Europa League following a 2-1 victory against Fulham in the final in Hamburg. At the start of the following campaign he starred in Atletico's UEFA Super Cup victory over Champions League holders Inter Milan, saving a late penalty from Uruguayan striker Diego Milito.

• De Gea confirmed his reputation as one of Europe's most promising young goalkeepers with a string of outstanding performances for the Spain Under-21 side which won the 2011 European Championships in Denmark. Shortly after this triumph De Gea signed for Manchester United, manager Sir Alex Ferguson having targeted the Spaniard for some time as his first-choice replacement for the retired Edwin van der Sar.

• After some unconvincing early performances for United De Gea was dropped by Ferguson, but after winning back his place in the side his form was much improved and he ended the 2011/12 season with the best saves-to-shots ratio, 77.9 per cent, of any Premier League goalkeeper.

David de Gea's impressive quiff is the envy of many

GERMANY

First international: Switzerland 5 Germany 3, 1908
Most capped player: Lothar Matthaus, 150 caps (1980-2000)
Leading goalscorer: Gerd Muller, 68 goals (1966-74)
First World Cup appearance: Germany 5 Belgium 2, 1934
Biggest win: Germany 16 Russia 0, 1912
Heaviest defeat: Austria 6 Germany 0, 1931

Germany (formerly West Germany) have the third-best record in the World Cup behind Brazil and Italy, having won the tournament three times and reached the final on seven occasions (a record shared with Brazil). They have also won the European Championships a record three times and been losing finalists on another three occasions.

• **Germany are the only country to have won the World Cup after falling two goals behind in the final, fighting back to beat Hungary 3-2 in Bern in 1954 – a match which became known in Germany as 'The Miracle of Bern'. Their other triumphs in the competition came on home soil against Holland in 1974 and at Italia 90 against Argentina.**

• Lothar Matthaus, a powerhouse in the German midfield for two decades, played in a record 25 matches at the World Cup in five tournaments between 1982-98. His total of 150 caps for Germany is also a national record.

• **With a total of 14 goals at the 1970 and 1974 World Cups German striker**

Gerd 'der Bomber' Muller set a record for the tournament which stood for 32 years until it was topped by Brazil's Ronaldo in 2006.

• Germany's Oliver Kahn is the only goalkeeper to win the Player of the Tournament award at a World Cup, topping the poll for his performances in 2002 in Japan and Korea.

• **Germany have played a record 99 games at the World Cup finals. Along with Brazil, Germany are the only country to have appeared in three consecutive World Cup finals (1982, 1986 and 1990).**

HONOURS

World Cup 1954, 1974, 1990
European Championship 1972, 1980, 1996

World Cup record
1930 Did not enter
1934 Third place
1938 Round 1
1950 Did not enter
1954 Winners
1958 Fourth place
1962 Quarter-finals
1966 Runners-up
1970 Third place
1974 Winners
1978 Round 1
1982 Runners-up
1986 Runners-up
1990 Winners
1994 Quarter-finals
1998 Quarter-finals
2002 Runners-up
2006 Third place
2010 Third place

STEVEN GERRARD

Born: Whiston, 30th May 1980
Position: Midfielder
Club career:
1998- Liverpool 405 (89)
International record:
2000- England 96 (19)

Liverpool captain Steven Gerrard is the only player to have scored in the FA Cup final, the League Cup final, the UEFA Cup final and the Champions League final. He achieved this feat between 2001-06 while winning all four competitions with the Reds (and, indeed, earning winners' medals in the FA Cup and League Cup on two occasions).

• A dynamic midfielder who is famed for his surging runs and thunderous shooting, Gerrard made his Liverpool debut in 1998. Five years later, then Anfield boss Gerard Houllier made the Kop idol his skipper and he has retained the armband ever since. A Red to his very core, Gerrard has twice turned down lucrative moves to Chelsea.

• In the 2006 FA Cup final Gerrard scored two stunning goals against West Ham, including a last-minute equaliser which many rate as the best ever goal in the final. Liverpool went on to win the match on penalties and Gerrard's heroics were rewarded with the 2006 PFA Player of the Year award – the first Liverpool player to top the poll since John Barnes in 1988.

• **Gerrard made his international debut for England against Ukraine in 2000 and scored his first goal for his country**

Liverpool captain Steven Gerrard in typical pose

IS THAT A FACT?
In their successful 1954 World Cup campaign West Germany scored 25 goals, a record for the champions, but also conceded 14 goals – again, a record for the tournament winners.

At the 1950 World Cup in Brazil, for instance, England sensationally lost 1-0 to an unheralded United States team. The result was so unexpected that many people assumed it was a misprint when they saw it in the newspapers. Other major World Cup shocks include North Korea's 1-0 victory over Italy in 1966, Cameroon's 1-0 defeat of holders Argentina in 1990 and Senegal's 1-0 win over holders France in 2002.

RYAN GIGGS

Born: Cardiff, 29th November 1973
Position: Winger/midfielder
Club career:
1991- Manchester United 638 (112)
International record:
1991-2007 Wales 64 (12)

In a glorious career with Manchester United, Ryan Giggs has become the most-decorated player in English football history. At the last count he had won 21 major honours: 12 Premier League titles, four FA Cups, three League Cups and two Champions League trophies. In 2009 he was voted PFA Player of the Year by his fellow professionals.

• Formerly a flying winger but now more likely to be seen in a deep-lying midfield role, Giggs is the only player to have played and scored in every season since the Premier League was formed in 1992, having made his debut for United the previous year against Everton. He holds the Premier League appearance record, 598 games, moving ahead of the previous record holder, David James, at the start of the 2011/12 season.

• When Giggs played for United in their 2008 Champions League final victory over Chelsea in Moscow it was his 759th appearance for the Reds in all competitions, one more than the club record previously set by Bobby Charlton.

• Giggs enjoyed his best-ever year in 1999 when he won the Premiership, FA Cup and Champions League with United. His goal against Arsenal in that season's FA Cup semi-final, when he dribbled past four defenders before smashing the ball into the roof of the net from a tight angle, is often recalled as one of the greatest ever.

• The oldest goalscorer ever in the Champions League, Giggs has also played more games in the competition (139)

Ryan Giggs is the most decorated player in English football

with a superb 20-yarder in the famous 5-1 thrashing of Germany in Berlin in 2001. In the absence of regular skipper Rio Ferdinand, he captained England at the 2010 World Cup and, after being appointed the permanent captain by new boss Roy Hodgson, he led his country at the 2012 European championships.

• Gerrard just missed out on leading Liverpool to the Premier League title in 2009, but was rewarded with the Footballer of the Year award at the season's end.

GIANT-KILLING

Many of the most remarkable instances of giant-killing have occurred in the FA Cup, with a number of non-league clubs claiming the scalps of top-flight opposition. One of the biggest such shocks came in 1989 when Coventry

City, who had won the FA Cup just two years earlier, were knocked out of the competition by non-league Sutton United in the third round.

• Hereford United's 2-1 defeat of Newcastle in the third round in 1972 is often remembered as one of the biggest giant-killing acts ever, being particularly memorable for Ronnie Radford's long-range equaliser which preceded Ricky George's winner. "The action is constantly replayed on the TV every year, and that shows what a big shock it was," said George recently.

• In their non-league days Yeovil Town beat a record 20 league teams in the FA Cup. The Glovers' most famous win came in the fourth round in 1949 against First Division Sunderland, who they defeated 2-1 on their notorious sloping pitch at Huish Park.

• Giant-killings also happen occasionally at international level.

and scored more goals (29) than any other British player.

• Once Wales's youngest-ever player, Giggs previously played for England Schoolboys under the name Ryan Wilson (the surname being that of his father, a former Welsh rugby league player). However, having no English grandparents, Giggs was ineligible to play for the England national team and was proud to represent Wales on 64 occasions before retiring from international football in 2007.

GILLINGHAM

Year founded: 1893
Ground: Priestfield Stadium (11,582)
Previous name: New Brompton
Nickname: The Gills
Biggest win: 12-1 v Gloucester City (1946)
Heaviest defeat: 2-9 v Nottingham Forest (1950)

Founded by a group of local businessmen as New Brompton in 1893, the club changed to its present name in 1913. Seven years later Gillingham joined the new Third Division but in 1938 were voted out of the league in favour of Ipswich Town. They eventually returned in 1950.

• **The only Kent-based team in the Football League, Gillingham recovered** from a financial crisis in the mid-'90s to enjoy a first spell in the second tier between 2000-05 although they have since plummeted back to the basement division.

• In 1952 the Gills' Jimmy Scarth notched three goals in just two minutes and 30 seconds against Leyton Orient to set a record for the fastest Football League hat-trick which stood until 2004.

• In their 1995/96 promotion campaign Gillingham only conceded 20 goals – a record for a 46-game season in the Football League.

> **HONOURS**
> *Division 4 champions 1964*

SHAY GIVEN

> **Born:** Lifford, Republic of Ireland, 20th April 1976
> **Position:** Goalkeeper
> **Club career:**
> 1994-97 Blackburn Rovers 2
> 1995 Swindon Town (loan) 5
> 1996 Sunderland (loan) 17
> 1997-2009 Newcastle United 354
> 2009-11 Manchester City 50
> 2011- Aston Villa 32
> **International record:**
> 1996-2012 Republic of Ireland 125

The highest-capped Republic of Ireland player ever, Shay Given was a fixture between the posts for his country for well over a decade, before retiring from international football in 2012.

• Given started out with Celtic but failed to make a first-team appearance before moving to Blackburn. Again, he failed to establish himself at Ewood Park, and his career only really got going after he joined Newcastle for £1.5 million in 1997. During a 12-year stay at St James's Park Given was twice voted into the PFA Team of the Season and played in a near record total of 462 games for the Magpies.

• Frustrated by Newcastle's failure to win major honours, Given put in a transfer request in January 2009 and the following month joined Manchester City for around £6 million. Despite playing well for his new club, he eventually lost his place to England goalkeeper Joe Hart and had to be content with a place on the bench throughout the 2010/11 season. In July 2011 he joined Aston Villa for around £3.5 million.

• An excellent shot-stopper, Given made his international debut for the Republic of Ireland against Russia in 1996 and represented his country with distinction at the 2002 World Cup. In 2009 he became only the second player to make 100 appearances for the Republic in a World Cup qualifier against Montenegro.

GOAL CELEBRATIONS

The days when players celebrated a goal by exchanging a simple handshake among team-mates before jogging back to the halfway line are long gone. In today's game the celebrations can be even more spectacular than the goals themselves – think, for instance, of the impressive gymnastic routines performed by Manchester United's Nani.

• In the 1990s Middlesbrough striker Fabrizio Ravanelli would regularly celebrate by pulling his shirt over his head after scoring. Soon players were removing their shirts altogether, sometimes to reveal personal, political or religious messages written on a T-shirt. In 2003 FIFA decided that the craze had got out of hand and ruled that any player removing his shirt would be booked. The first player to be sent off after falling foul of this new law was Everton's Tim Cahill, who was shown a second yellow against Manchester City in 2004.

• Denmark striker Nicklas Bendtner was fined a record £80,000 by UEFA after celebrating a goal against Portugal at Euro 2012 by revealing a betting company

Fortunately this 'shorts on head' goal celebration by Montenegro striker Marko Vucinic hasn't really caught on…

logo on his underwear. Fortunately for Bendtner, the company paid the fine for him.

• In one of the most bizarre goal celebrations ever Manchester United star Carlos Tevez produced a baby's dummy from his shorts and sucked on it after scoring against Birmingham at Old Trafford in 2008. He later explained that the routine was a tribute to his young daughter, Florencia. Earlier in his career, Tevez was sent off while playing for Boca Juniors against arch rivals River Plate when he celebrated a goal in front of the opposition fans by imitating a chicken.

• In 2004 Servette midfielder Paulo Diogo celebrated a goal he had created against FC Schaffhausen by jumping on a metal perimeter fence. Unfortunately, his wedding ring caught in the fence and when he jumped down he left much of his finger behind. To add insult to injury, Diogo was then shown a yellow card by the referee for leaving the pitch without permission.

• In a Euro 2012 qualifier in England's group, Montenegro striker Marko Vucinic celebrated his winning goal against Switzerland by whipping off his shorts and putting them on his head. The referee failed to see the funny side and showed Vucinic a yellow card.

GOAL OF THE SEASON

The Goal of the Season award has been awarded by BBC TV's flagship football programme *Match of the Day* since 1971 (apart from the years 2001-04 when, for broadcasting rights reasons, the award was given by ITV). The first winner was Coventry City's Ernie Hunt, whose spectacular volley against Everton at Highfield Road topped the poll.

• Liverpool's John Aldridge is the only player to win Goal of the Season in

Goals – like this one by England's Joleon Lescott against France at Europe 2012 – are the essence of football

consecutive seasons, taking the award in 1988 and 1989 for his FA Cup strikes against Nottingham Forest and Everton respectively, the second of these goals coming in the final itself. Manchester United striker Wayne Rooney is the only player to win the award three times, most recently in 2011 for a spectacular overhead kick against local rivals Manchester City.

• Only two players have won the award for goals scored for their countries rather than their clubs: Scotland's Kenny Dalglish in 1983 and England's Bryan Robson in 1986.

• Liverpool players have won the Goal of the Season award a record six times, most recently in 2006 when Steven Gerrard's 30-yarder in the FA Cup final against West Ham topped the list. Arsenal have conceded the Goal of the Season a record five times, most recently in 1999 when Ryan Giggs dribbled through the Gunners' defence to score the winner in the FA Cup semi-final for Manchester United.

GOALS

Manchester United have scored more league goals than any other English club. Up to the start of the 2012/13 season, the Red Devils had managed 7,497 goals, 166 more than second-placed Wolves. Liverpool, though, have scored most goals at home, with 4,510.

• Peterborough United hold the record for the most league goals in a season, banging in 134 in 1960/61 on their way to claiming the Fourth Division title. Less impressively, Darwen conceded a record 141 goals in the Second Division in 1898/99.

• Aston Villa hold the top flight record,

with 128 goals in 1930/31. Despite their prolific attack, the Villans were pipped to the First Division title by Arsenal (amazingly, the Gunners managed 127 goals themselves). Title-winners Chelsea became the first team to score a century of goals in the Premier League era in 2009/10, the Blues taking their tally to 103 with an 8-0 thrashing of Wigan on the final day of the season.

• Arthur Rowley scored a record 434 Football League goals between 1946 and 1965, notching four for West Brom, 27 for Fulham, 251 for Leicester City and 152 for Shrewsbury. Former Republic of Ireland international John Aldridge is the overall leading scorer in post-war English football, with an incredible total of 476 goals in all competitions for Newport County, Oxford United, Liverpool and Tranmere between 1979 and 1998.

• Joe Payne set an English Football League record for goals in a game by scoring ten times for Luton against Bristol Rovers on 13th April 1936.

• A record 209 league goals were scored in the Football League on 1st February 1936, while the most prolific day in top-flight history was on Boxing Day 1963 when 66 goals hit the back of the net in just 10 games – the highest score was at Craven Cottage where Fulham stuffed Ipswich 10-1.

• A Premier League record average of 2.81 goals per game were scored in the 2011/12 season – the highest in the top flight since 1967/68, when the average was 3.03.

• Iranian striker Ali Daei is the leading scorer in international football with an incredible 109 goals, including a record 35 in World Cup qualifiers, between 1993 and 2006.

IS THAT A FACT?

In an internet poll in 2012 Eric Cantona's pirouette and haughty pose after he scored with a delicate chip against Sunderland in 1996 was voted the best Premier League goal celebration ever.

Jimmy Greaves wasn't called a 'goal hanger' for nothing…

JIMMY GREAVES

Born: East Ham, 20th February 1940
Position: Striker
Club career:
1957-61 Chelsea 157 (124)
1961-62 AC Milan 14 (9)
1962-70 Tottenham 321 (220)
1970-71 West Ham United 38 (13)
International record:
1959-67 England 57 (44)

With 44 goals for England, Jimmy Greaves is his country's third highest-ever goalscorer behind Bobby Charlton and Gary Lineker. He scored on his international debut in 1959 in a 4-1 defeat by Peru, and went on to bag a record six hat-tricks for his country. Famously, Greaves also scored on his debut for all the clubs he played for.

• A quicksilver striker who always carefully picked his spot when shooting, Greaves began his career at Chelsea. In the 1960/61 season he hit an incredible 41 league goals for the Blues – a post-war record for the top flight – and also scored a record 13 goals for England.

• After a brief spell with AC Milan, Greaves moved to Tottenham where he helped the club claim two major trophies, the European Cup Winners' Cup in 1963 and the FA Cup in 1967. His haul of 220 league goals for Spurs remains a club record.

• At 21, Greaves was the youngest player to score 100 league goals. He netted his 200th aged 23 years and 290 days, coincidentally exactly the same age at which Dixie Dean reached the same landmark with Everton.

• Arguably English football's most consistent-ever striker, Greaves was top scorer in the First Division six times and notched a total of 357 league goals – both top flight records that are unlikely to be broken.

• He experienced the lowest point of his career in 1966 when, after starting in England's opening matches at the World Cup, he was left out of the team for the triumphant final against West Germany. Bitterly disappointed, he was the only member of the squad not to attend the victory bash in a London hotel.

• After hanging up his boots Greaves overcame alcoholism to launch a new career as a TV personality, his double act with former Liverpool star Ian St John being especially popular with viewers.

RUUD GULLIT

Born: Amsterdam, 1st September 1962
Position: Sweeper/midfielder/striker
Club career:
1979-82 Haarlem 91 (32)
1982-85 Feyenoord 85 (31)
1985-87 PSV Eindhoven 68 (46)
1987-93 AC Milan 117 (35)
1993-94 Sampdoria 31 (16)
1994 AC Milan 8 (3)
1994-95 Sampdoria 22 (9)
1995-98 Chelsea 32 (4)
International record:
1981-94 Holland 66 (17)

Once described as 'the Dutch Duncan Edwards', Ruud Gullit was a brilliant performer in a variety of positions, including sweeper, attacking midfielder and striker. In 1987 he became the world's most-expensive player when he moved from PSV to AC Milan for a cool £6.5 million.

• In the same year Gullit became only the third player – after Paolo Rossi and Michel Platini – to be voted both World and European Footballer of the Year in the same season. He dedicated his awards to Nelson Mandela, then still in prison in South Africa.

• After helping Milan win the Serie A title in 1988 Gullit played a huge part in the club's European Cup success the following year, scoring twice in the Italian club's 4-0 demolition of Steaua Bucharest in the final. In all he won three league titles and two European Cups with Milan.

• In 1988 he became the first Dutch captain to lift major international silverware when his side beat the Soviet Union 2-0 in the final of the European Championships, Gullit netting the first goal with a trademark power header.

• In 1997, as player-manager of Chelsea, Gullit became the first foreign boss to win a major domestic competition when the Blues beat Middlesbrough in the FA Cup final at Wembley. The following year, though, he was sacked and replaced by Gianluca Vialli, one of a number of big-name players he had brought to Stamford Bridge. Gullit later managed Newcastle, Feyenoord and LA Galaxy and, most recently, was the boss of Russian side Terek Grozny before being sacked by the club's President who accused him of spending too much time in the local bars and nightclubs.

If anyone can stop a shot that seems destined for the net it's England's Joe Hart!

JOE HART

Born: Shrewsbury, 19th April 1987
Position: Goalkeeper
Club career:
2003-06 Shrewsbury Town 54
2006- Manchester City 126
2007 Tranmere Rovers (loan) 6
2007 Blackpool (loan) 5
2009-10 Birmingham City (loan) 36
International record:
2008- England 22

Now firmly established as England's No. 1, Joe Hart is only the second goalkeeper (after Liverpool's Pepe Reina) to retain the Premier League Golden Gloves award for keeping the most clean sheets in the division, claiming the honour in both 2011 and 2012. In the second of those years Hart was a pivotal figure for his club, Manchester City, as they won their first-ever Premier League title.

• **Hart began his career with his hometown club, Shrewsbury Town. His assured performances with the Shrews soon attracted the attention of bigger clubs and in 2006 he moved to City for an initial £600,000 fee. After loan spells at Tranmere, Blackpool and Birmingham, where his superb displays earned him a place in the 2010 PFA Team of the Year, he returned to Eastlands to claim the keeper's jersey ahead of Shay Given.**

• While a regular between the sticks for the England Under-21 side, Hart moved up to the senior squad and in June 2008 made his full debut as a sub in a 3-0 win over Trinidad and Tobago.

• **Hart was one of three goalkeepers selected by England coach Fabio Capello for the World Cup in South Africa, but he failed to get off the bench. However, the Italian installed him as a regular for the Euro 2012 qualifiers and he retained his place at the tournament proper under new boss Roy Hodgson.**

HARTLEPOOL UNITED

Year founded: 1908
Ground: Victoria Ground (7,856)
Previous name: Hartlepools United, Hartlepool
Nickname: The Pool
Biggest win: 10-1 v Barrow (1959)
Heaviest defeat: 1-10 v Wrexham (1962)

The club were founded as Hartlepools United in 1908 as a professional team to emulate the success of West Hartlepools, winners of the FA Amateur Cup three years earlier. In 1968 they became 'Hartlepool', adding the word 'United' in 1977.

• **The Pool, as they are nicknamed, had to apply for re-election to the Football League a record 11 times, including five times between 1960 and 1964 when they finished bottom or second bottom of the old Fourth Division in** five consecutive seasons. On each occasion, though, they earned a reprieve and in recent years they have twice climbed out of the bottom tier into League One.

• Hartlepool's Victoria Ground was the first ever football stadium to be bombed, its wooden stand being destroyed by a bomb dropped from a German Zeppelin airship in 1917, during the First World War. The ground is also notable for being one of just two (along with Old Trafford) which has staged two football league matches on the same day, hosting both Hartlepool v Cardiff and Middlesbrough v Port Vale on 23rd August 1983 (Boro's Ayresome Park ground having been shut after the club went into liquidation).

• **The only player to be capped at international level while with Hartlepool is midfielder Ambrose Fogarty, who played for the Republic of Ireland in a 5-1 defeat to Spain in Seville in 1964.**

• Hartlepool's most famous fan is Jeff Stelling, presenter of Sky Sports' *Soccer Saturday*.

IS THAT A FACT?
The legendary Brian Clough started his managerial career at Hartlepool in 1965 – aged just 30 he was the youngest manager in the Football League at the time.

HAT-TRICKS

Geoff Hurst is the only player to have scored a hat-trick in a World Cup final, hitting three goals in England's 4-2 defeat of West Germany at Wembley in 1966.

• **Eighteen-year-old Tony Ross scored the fastest hat-trick in football history in 1964, taking just 90 seconds to complete a treble for Ross County in a Highland League match against Nairn County.**

• In 2004 Bournemouth's James Hayter struck the fastest hat-trick in English football league history, finding the net three times in just two minutes and 20 seconds against Wrexham. Incredibly, he was only on the pitch for six minutes after coming on as a late substitute! Ten years earlier, Liverpool's Robbie Fowler hit the fastest hat-trick in Premier League history, grabbing three goals in under five minutes against Arsenal at Anfield.

• **The legendary Dixie Dean scored a record 37 hat-tricks during his career, while his contemporary George Camsell scored a record nine hat-tricks for Middlesbrough in the 1925/26 season.**

• Paraguayan international Jose Luis Chilavert is the only goalkeeper to have notched a hat-trick, scoring three penalties for Argentinean side Velez Sarsfield in their 6-1 win over Ferro Carril Oeste in 1999.

• **The last player to score a hat-trick in an FA Cup final was Blackpool's Stan Mortensen in his side's 4-3 victory over Bolton in 1953. Despite Mortensen's feat, the match is remembered as 'the Matthews final', after a brilliant display by his veteran team-mate Stanley Matthews.**

• Alan Shearer holds the record for the most Premier League hat-tricks, hitting 11 in total for Blackburn Rovers and Newcastle United.

EDEN HAZARD

Born: Louviere, Belgian, 7th January 1991
Position: Midfielder
Club career:
2007-12 Lille 147 (36)
2012- Chelsea
International record:
2008- Belgium 29 (2)

Chelsea playmaker Eden Hazard

A creative midfielder whose dribbling skills have earned comparisons with both Lionel Messi and Cristiano Ronaldo, Belgian international Eden Hazard became the fifth most expensive Premier League player ever when he moved from Lille to Chelsea for an eye-watering £32 million in May 2012.

• **The son of footballers – his father played in the Belgian second tier, while his mother was a striker in the women's league – Hazard joined Lille when he was 14, making his debut for the first team just two years later. In his first full season, 2008/09, he became the first non-French player to win the Young Player of the Year award. He scooped the award again the following season to become the first player to win it twice.**

• In 2011, after completing a league and cup double with Lille, Hazard was voted Player of the Year – aged 20, he was the youngest player to win the award. He topped the poll again the following year to become only the second player to retain the trophy.

• **Hazard was first capped by Belgium, aged 17, against Luxembourg in 2008. He hasn't always been able to transfer his scintillating club form to the international stage, however, and in 2011 he was criticised for leaving the stadium after being substituted against Turkey, choosing to eat a burger with his family rather than watch the rest of the match.**

HEADERS

In 2011 Ryujiro Ueda, a defender with Fagiano Okayama, scored with a header from 58.6 metres in a J-League match against Yokohama to set a record for the longest distance headed goal. He was helped, though, by some dodgy goalkeeping, the Yokohama keeper allowing the ball to bounce over his head and dribble into the net.

• **Huddersfield striker Jordan Rhodes scored the fastest headed hat-trick in Football League history in 2009, nodding in three goals against Exeter City in eight minutes and 23 seconds to smash a record previously held by Everton legend Dixie Dean.**

• Alan Shearer holds the Premier League record for headed goals with 46 for Blackburn Rovers and Newcastle. At the opposite end of the scale, Damien Duff has scored the most Premier League goals,

David Healy, Northern Ireland's record goalscorer

goals for his country include 13 in the qualifiers for Euro 2008, a record for the European championships.

• Those 13 goals included hat-tricks against Spain, in an historic 3-2 defeat of the soon-to-be European and world champions, and Liechtenstein, making Healy the only Northern Ireland player ever to hit two hat-tricks for his country. Perhaps, though, Healy's most famous international goal came in a 1-0 win over England at Windsor Park during the 2006 World Cup qualifying campaign to give Northern Ireland their first victory over the Three Lions since 1972.

• In an itinerant club career, Healy has failed to hit the same heights. He started out at Manchester United, but only made one league appearance before moving on to Preston for £1.5 million in December 2000. He later played for Leeds, Fulham and Sunderland, as well as having loan spells at four other clubs.

• In January 2011 Healy joined Rangers, initially on a six-month loan, and marked his debut for the Scottish giants with a goal in a 6-0 hammering of Motherwell.

HEART OF MIDLOTHIAN

Year founded: 1874
Ground: Tynecastle (17,420)
Nickname: Hearts
Biggest win: 21-0 v Anchor (1880)
Heaviest defeat: 1-8 v Vale of Leven (1883)

Hearts were founded in 1874, taking their unusual and romantic-sounding name from a popular local dance hall which, in turn, was named after the famous novel The Heart of the Midlothian by Sir Walter Scott. The club were founder members of the Scottish league in 1890, winning their first title just five years later.

• The club enjoyed a golden era in the late 1950s and early 1960s, when they won two league championships and five cups. In the first of those title triumphs in 1958 Hearts scored 132 goals, many of them coming from the so-called 'Terrible Trio' of Alfie Conn, Willie Bauld and Jimmy Wardhaugh.

TOP 10

MOST HEADED PREMIER LEAGUE GOALS

1. Alan Shearer		46
2. Dion Dublin		45
3. Les Ferdinand		43
4. Dwight Yorke		38
5. Duncan Ferguson		35
6. Peter Crouch		33
7. Tim Cahill		31
8. Andy Cole		29
9. Robbie Fowler		28
9. Emile Heskey		28

50, without once netting with his head.

• The world record for non-stop heading of the ball is held by Tomas Lundman from Sweden, who kept it bouncing off his bonce for eight hours, 32 minutes and three seconds on 27th February 2004.

DAVID HEALY

Born: Killyleagh, 5th August 1979
Position: Striker
Club career:
1999-2001 Manchester United 1 (0)
2000 Port Vale (loan) 16 (3)
2000-01 Preston North End (loan) 2 (1)
2001-04 Preston North End 137 (44)
2003 Norwich City (loan) 13 (2)
2004-07 Leeds United 111 (29)
2007-08 Fulham 30 (4)
2008-11 Sunderland 13 (1)
2010 Ipswich Town (loan) 12 (1)
2010-11 Doncaster Rovers (loan) 8 (2)
2011-12 Rangers 19 (4)
International record:
2000- Northern Ireland 93 (35)

Veteran striker David Healy is, by some considerable distance, Northern Ireland's all-time leading goalscorer. His 35

The total is still a record for the top flight in Scotland. In the same year Hearts conceded just 29 goals, giving them the best-ever goal difference in British football, an incredible 103.

• In 1965 Hearts came agonisingly close to winning the championship again when they were pipped by Kilmarnock on goal average after losing 2-0 at home to their title rivals on the last day of the season. Twenty-one years later they suffered a similar fate, losing the title on goal difference to Celtic after a surprise last-day defeat against Dundee. Annoyingly for their fans, on both occasions Hearts would have won the title if the alternative method for separating teams level on points had been in use.

• In 1990 Hearts chairman Wallace Mercer proposed that Hearts should merge with their Edinburgh rivals Hibs to form a single club with better prospects of successfully competing with Celtic and Rangers. Understandably, fans of both Hearts and Hibs were appalled at the idea and their noisy protests helped ensure that the scheme was thwarted.

• Hearts won the Scottish Cup in 2012, thrashing local rivals Hibs 5-1 in the final at Hampden Park – the biggest victory in the final since Hearts themselves were tonked by the same score by Rangers in 1996. It was the eighth time that Hearts had won the Scottish Cup, making them the fourth most successful club in the competition after Celtic, Rangers and Queen's Park.

• When Craig Gordon joined Sunderland from Hearts in 2007 for £9 million he became the most expensive goalkeeper in British football history and the most expensive Scottish player ever.

• The club's record goalscorer is John Robertson with 214 goals between 1983 and 1998, and the record appearance holder is Gary Mackay, who played in 640 games between 1980-97. Hearts' highest-capped international is Steven Pressley, who won 32 caps for Scotland between 2000-06.

• Famous fans of Hearts include pint-sized comedian Ronnie Corbett, snooker star Steven Hendry and Alex Salmond, Scotland's First Minister.

HONOURS
Division 1 champions *1895, 1897, 1958, 1960*
First Division champions *1980*
Scottish Cup *1891, 1896, 1901, 1906, 1956, 1998, 2006, 2012*
League Cup *1955, 1959, 1960, 1963*

THIERRY HENRY

Born: Paris, 17th August 1977
Position: Striker
Club career:
1994-98 Monaco 105 (20)
1999 Juventus 16 (3)
1999-2007 Arsenal 254 (174)
2007-10 Barcelona 80 (35)
2010- New York Red Bulls 54 (27)
2012 Arsenal (loan) 4 (1)
International record:
1997-2010 France 123 (51)

Arguably Arsenal's greatest-ever player, Thierry Henry is the Gunners' all-time top goalscorer. During an eight-year stay in North London after signing from Juventus for a bargain £10.5 million in 1999 he scored 224 goals, many of them memorable ones. He briefly returned to Arsenal on loan from New York Red Bulls in 2012, adding two more goals to his Gunners' account.

• Frighteningly quick and a reliably clinical finisher, Henry started out with Monaco who he helped win the French title in 1997. He was even more successful at Arsenal, winning two league titles and three FA Cups, and in 2006 become the first-ever player to win the Footballer of the Year award three times. The following year he joined Barcelona, with whom he won the Spanish league title and the Champions League in 2009.

• Henry's total of 175 league goals for Arsenal puts him third in the list of all-time Premiership scorers behind Alan Shearer and Andy Cole. In both 2004 and 2005 he won the European Golden Boot, sharing the award with Villarreal's Diego Forlan in 2005.

Arsenal's record goalscorer Thierry Henry

• A member of the French squad that won the World Cup in 1998, Henry collected a European Championship winners' medal two years later. In 2006 he had to settle for a runners-up medal in the World Cup final.

• In October 2007 Henry scored twice against Lithuania to become France's all-time leading goalscorer, passing Michel Platini's previous record of 41 goals. Capped 123 times, he stands second behind Lilian Thuram in France's all-time top appearance makers.

HIBERNIAN

Year founded: 1875
Ground: Easter Road (20,421)
Previous name: Hibernians
Nickname: Hibs
Biggest win: 22-1 v 42nd Highlanders (1881)
Heaviest defeat: 0-10 v Rangers (1898)

Founded in 1875 by Irish immigrants, the club took its name from the Roman word for Ireland, Hibernia. After losing many players to Celtic the club disbanded in 1891, but reformed and joined the Scottish League two years later.

• Hibs won the Scottish Cup for the first time in 1887 and lifted the same trophy again in 1902. Since then, however, the club have reached the final on a further nine occasions, most recently in 2012 when they lost to local rivals Hearts, but failed to win once.

• The club enjoyed a golden era after the Second World War, winning the league championship in three out of five seasons between 1948-52 with a side managed by Hugh Shaw that included the 'Famous Five' forward line of Bobby Johnstone, Willie Ormond, Lawrie Reilly, Gordon Smith and Willie Turnbull. All of the Famous Five went on to score 100 league goals for Hibs, a feat only achieved for the club since by Joe Baker.

• When Baker made his international debut against Northern Ireland in 1959 he became the first man to represent England while playing for a Scottish club. In the same season Baker scored an incredible 42 goals in just 33 league games to set a club record.

• Hibs originally wore green-and-white-hooped shirts but switched to their famous green shirts with white sleeves in 1938, imitating the kit style of the great Arsenal side of that era.

• In 1955 Hibs became the first British side to enter the European Cup, having been invited to participate in the new competition partly because their Easter Road ground had floodlights. They did Scotland proud, reaching the semi-finals of the competition before falling 3-0 on aggregate to French side Rheims.

• Hibs hold the British record for the biggest away win, thrashing Airdrie 11-1 on their own patch on 24th October 1959. As if to prove that astonishing result was no fluke, they also hit double figures at Partick later that season, winning 10-2.

• No player has turned out more often for Hibs than popular left-winger Arthur Duncan, who made 446 league appearances between 1969 and 1984. Lawrie Reilly is the club's record scorer, notching 234 league goals in the 1940s and 1950s, and is also Hibs' highest-capped player, having played 38 times for Scotland.

• Famous fans of Hibs include Trainspotting author Irvine Welsh and tennis superstar Andy Murray.

HONOURS
Division 1 champions 1903, 1948, 1951, 1952
Division 2 champions 1894, 1895, 1933
First Division champions 1981, 1999
Scottish Cup 1887, 1902
League Cup 1972, 1991, 2007

GLENN HODDLE

Born: Hayes, 27th October 1957
Position: Midfielder
Club career:
1975-87 Tottenham Hotspur 377 (88)
1987-90 Monaco 69 (27)
1991-93 Swindon Town 64 (1)
1993-95 Chelsea 31 (1)
International record:
1979-88 England 53 (8)

An extravagantly gifted midfielder, Glenn Hoddle gained 53 caps for England and might have won many more but for doubts about his work-rate and tackling ability.

• During a 12-year playing career with Tottenham Hotspur, Hoddle won the FA Cup twice (in 1981 and 1982) and the UEFA Cup (in 1984). He joined Monaco in 1987, where he played under Arsène Wenger, and the following year became the first Englishman to be part of a championship-winning side in France. "I couldn't understand why he hadn't been appreciated in England," Wenger said of him. "Perhaps he was a star in the wrong period, years ahead of his time."

• As player-manager of Swindon, Hoddle led the Wiltshire club into the top flight for the first time in their history in 1993. In the same role at Chelsea the following year he guided the Blues to their first FA Cup final for nearly a quarter of a century.

• In May 1996 Hoddle was appointed England manager, succeeding Terry Venables after Euro '96. Aged 38, he was the youngest man to fill the position since Walter Winterbottom.

• Hoddle led England to the 1998 World Cup in France, where they were unlucky

IS THAT A FACT?
Glenn Hoddle (Chelsea, 1994) is one of just three player-managers to have appeared in the FA Cup final, along with Kenny Dalglish (Liverpool, 1986) and Dennis Wise (Millwall, 2004). Of this trio, only Dalglish finished on the winning side.

to lose to Argentina in a penalty shoot-out. The following year, though, he was dismissed from the job after suggesting in a newspaper interview that disabled people were somehow paying for sins committed in a previous life. He has subsequently managed Southampton, Tottenham and Wolves and now runs a football academy in southern Spain.

ROY HODGSON

Born: Croydon, 9th August 1947
Managerial career:
1976-80 Halmstads
1982 Bristol City
1983-85 Orebro
1985-90 Malmo
1990-92 Neuchatel Xamax
1992-95 Switzerland
1995-97 Inter Milan
1997-98 Blackburn Rovers
1999 Inter Milan
1999-2000 Grasshoppers
2000-01 Copenhagen
2001 Udinese
2002-04 United Arab Emirates
2004-05 Viking
2006-07 Finland
2007-2010 Fulham
2010-11 Liverpool
2011-12 West Bromwich Albion
2012- England

England boss Roy Hodgson is one of the most experienced managers in the game, having managed four Premier League clubs, four different national teams and club sides in five continental countries.
• **Hodgson is the oldest man to be appointed England manager, taking charge of the Three Lions in May 2012 at the age of 64 and then leading them to the quarter-finals of the European championships. He is also the first England boss to have international experience, having previously managed Switzerland, United Arab Emirates and Finland.**
• After failing to make the grade

as a player at Crystal Palace, Hodgson spent much of his early managerial career in Sweden. He won the title with Halmstads in 1979 before leading Malmo to a Swedish record five consecutive championships between 1985 and 1989.
• **Hodgson has enjoyed mixed fortunes with Premier League clubs, being sacked by both Blackburn and Liverpool after brief spells at the helm of those clubs, but doing much better with Fulham and West Brom. His time at Liverpool in the 2010/11 season was particularly forgettable, as he led the Reds to their worst start in 82 years and was eventually shown the door after just 31 games in charge, making his the shortest managerial reign in the history of the Anfield club.**

'The object I'm holding up is the ball.' England boss Roy Hodgson gets back to basics.

• His three-year stint at his previous club, Fulham, on the other hand, was much happier. In his first season at Craven Cottage Hodgson guided his team to an unlikely escape from relegation after the west Londoners won their final three Premier League fixtures. Two years later, in 2010, he easily topped that achievement, by taking Fulham to the Europa League final. Although the Cottagers lost out to Atletico Madrid, Hodgson picked up the League Managers' Association Manager of the Year award for his efforts.
• **His other great success came**

with Switzerland, who he took to the last 16 of the World Cup in 1994 – the country's best performance for 40 years. Hodgson also earned plaudits during two spells with Inter Milan, taking the Italian giants to the UEFA Cup final in 1997, where they were beaten on penalties by Schalke.

HOLLAND

First international: Belgium 1 Holland 4, 1905
Most capped player: Edwin van der Sar, 130 caps (1995-2008)
Leading goalscorer: Patrick Kluivert, 40 goals (1994-2004)
First World Cup appearance: Holland 2 Switzerland 1, 1934
Biggest win: Holland 11 San Marino 0, 2011
Heaviest defeat: England amateurs 9 Holland 1, 1909

Long associated with an entertaining style of attacking football, Holland have only won one major tournament, the European Championship in 1988. In the final that year the Dutch beat Russia with goals from their two biggest stars of the time, Ruud Gullit and Marco van Basten.
• Holland have never won the World Cup, although they have been runners-up three times. On the first two occasions they had the misfortune to meet the hosts in the final, losing to West Germany in 1974 and Argentina in 1978. Then, in the 2010 final, they went down 1-0 in extra-time to Spain in Johannesburg following a negative, at times brutal, Dutch performance which was totally at odds with the country's best footballing traditions.
• A professional league wasn't formed in Holland until 1956, and it took some years after that before the country was taken seriously as a football power. Their lowest ebb was reached in 1963 when they were humiliatingly eliminated from the European Championships by minnows Luxembourg.
• The following decade, though, saw a renaissance in Dutch football. With exciting players like Johan Cruyff, Johan Neeskens and Ruud Krol in their side, the Dutch were considered the best team in Europe. Pivotal to their success was the revolutionary 'Total Football' system devised by manager Rinus Michels which allowed the outfield players to constantly switch positions during the game.
• Holland have lost four of the five penalty shoot-outs they have been involved in at major tournaments. Only England have a worse record from the spot, with just one win in seven shoot-outs.

HONOURS
European Championship 1988

World Cup record
1930 *Did not enter*
1934 *Round 1*
1938 *Round 1*
1950 *Did not enter*
1954 *Did not enter*
1958 *Did not qualify*
1962 *Did not qualify*
1966 *Did not qualify*
1970 *Did not qualify*
1974 *Runners-up*
1978 *Runners-up*
1982 *Did not qualify*
1986 *Did not qualify*
1990 *Round 2*
1994 *Quarter-finals*
1998 *Fourth place*
2002 *Did not qualify*
2006 *Round 2*
2010 *Runners-up*

HOME AND AWAY

Brentford hold the all-time record for home wins in a season. In 1929/30 the Bees won all 21 of their home games at Griffin Park in Division Three (South). However, their away form was so poor they missed out on promotion to champions Plymouth.
• Chelsea hold the record for the longest unbeaten home run in the league, remaining undefeated at Stamford Bridge between February 2004 and October 2008. Ironically, the Blues' 86-game run was eventually broken by Liverpool, the previous holders of the same record.
• The Blues also hold the record for the most consecutive away wins, with 11 in the Premier League in 2008. The highest number of straight home wins is 25, a record set by Bradford Park Avenue in the Third Division (North) in 1926/27.
• Doncaster Rovers won a record 18 out of 21 away games while topping the Third Division (North) table in 1946/47.

• Millwall scored a record 87 goals at home in 1927/28, a total which helped the London club top the Third Division (South) table that season. The away record is held by Arsenal, who scored 60 goals on their travels in their 1930/31 championship-winning campaign.
• Sunderland are the only club to have won all their home games in a top-flight season, picking up maximum points in all 13 matches they played at their old Blue House Field ground on their way to claiming the title in 1891/92. In the Premier League era Chelsea (2005/06), Manchester United (2010/11) and Manchester City (2011/12) have come close to matching Sunderland's feat, winning all but one of their 19 home games.

HUDDERSFIELD TOWN

Year founded: 1908
Ground: Galpharm Stadium (24,500)
Nickname: The Terriers
Biggest win: 11-0 v Heckmondwike (1909)
Heaviest defeat: 1-10 v Manchester City (1987)

Huddersfield Town were founded in 1908 following a meeting held at the local Imperial Hotel some two years earlier – it took the club that long to find a ground to play at! The club were elected to the Second Division of the Football League two years later.
• The Terriers enjoyed a golden era in the 1920s when, under the shrewd management of the legendary Herbert Chapman, they won three consecutive league titles between 1924-26 – no other club had matched this feat at the time and only three have done so since. The Terriers also won the FA Cup in 1922.
• Huddersfield won the first of their league titles in 1924 by pipping Cardiff City on goal average, the first time the champions had been decided by this method.
• The early 1970s were a desperate time for Huddersfield, who slumped from the First to the Fourth Division in just four seasons, becoming the first league champions to be relegated to the bottom tier.

• However, recent seasons have been happier for the Terriers, who made it back into the Championship in 2012 after a dramatic penalty shoot-out play-off victory over Yorkshire rivals Sheffield United at Wembley. With both sides taking 11 spot-kicks it was the longest shoot-out in play-off history. Huddersfield's promotion push was helped by a Football League record unbeaten run of 43 games during most of 2011.

• Outside left Billy Smith made a record 521 appearances, scoring 114 goals, for Huddersfield between 1913-34. Smith and his son Conway, who started out with the Terriers before playing for QPR and Halifax, were the first father and son to both hit a century of goals in league football.

• In 1957 Huddersfield were beaten 7-6 at Charlton, the only time in Football League history that a team has scored six goals and still lost the match.

HONOURS
Division 1 champions 1924, 1925, 1926
Division 2 champions 1970
Division 4 champions 1980
FA Cup 1922

MARK HUGHES

Born: Wrexham, 1st November 1963
Managerial career:
1999-04 Wales
2004-08 Blackburn Rovers
2008-09 Manchester City
2010-11 Fulham
2012- QPR

Appointed QPR boss in January 2012, following the departure from Loftus Road of Neil Warnock, Mark Hughes fulfilled his brief by keeping Rangers in the Premier League. It was, though, an agonisingly close thing as Rangers only survived by a single point on a dramatic last day of the season.

• Known throughout the football world as 'Sparky', Hughes began his managerial career on a part-time basis with Wales in 1999 while he was still playing in the Premier League with Southampton. He almost led his country to the finals of Euro 2004 but they were pipped in a play-off by Russia.

• In 2004 Hughes was appointed

'Anyone want to buy this shirt?' asks Mark Hughes. 'C'mon, I'll do you a good deal!'

manager of Blackburn Rovers. He stay at Ewood Park for four years before succeeding Sven Goran Eriksson as boss of Manchester City in the summer of 2008. However, after a season and a half at the Etihad he was replaced by Roberto Mancini, with whom he has since had an extremely frosty relationship. His next job was at Fulham, but he only stayed one season before deciding to quit.

• In a glittering playing career, Hughes won the FA Cup four times with Manchester United and Chelsea – a record for the 20th century. He also won two league titles with United and the European Cup Winners' Cup in 1991, when his two goals for the Red Devils secured victory in the final against his former club Barcelona in Rotterdam.

HULL CITY

Year founded: 1904
Ground: KC Stadium (25,586)
Nickname: The Tigers
Biggest win: 11-1 v Carlisle United (1939)
Heaviest defeat: 0-8 v Wolves (1911)

Hull City were formed in 1904, originally sharing a ground with the local rugby league club. The club joined the Football League in 1905 but failed to achieve promotion to the top flight until 2008.

England's Geoff Hurst (left) claims that his shot crossed the line in the 1966 World Cup final against West Germany. Now, it's all down to the Russian linesman…

• Burdened by financial problems, Hull only narrowly avoided relegation to the Conference in 1998 and 1999, finishing a worst-ever third bottom in the lowest tier in the first of these years.

• **However, their fortunes turned around and in 2008 Hull made it into the Premier League thanks to a play-off final victory over Bristol City, local boy Dean Windass scoring the vital goal. That triumph meant that Hull had climbed from the bottom tier to the top in just five seasons – a meteoric rise only bettered in the past by Swansea City and Wimbledon – but their stay at the top only lasted two years**

• The club's record goalscorer is Chris Chilton, who banged in 193 league goals in the 1960s and 1970s. His sometime team-mate Andy Davidson has pulled on a Hull shirt more than any other player, making 520 league appearances between 1952 and 1968.

• **In his first spell at Hull between 1991 and 1996, goalkeeper Alan Fettis played a number of games as a striker during an injury crisis. He did pretty well too, scoring two goals!**

• In 2009 Hull splashed out a club record £5 million to bring midfielder Jimmy Bullard to Humberside from Fulham. In the same year the Tigers received a record £4 million when they sold defender Michael Turner to Sunderland.

SIR GEOFF HURST

Geoff Hurst is the only player to have scored a hat-trick in the World Cup final. His famous treble against West Germany at Wembley helped England to a legendary 4-2 triumph in 1966.

• **Along with Ian Rush, Hurst is the leading scorer in the history of the League Cup with an impressive total of 49 goals. He is also the last player to hit six goals in a top-flight league match, netting a double hat-trick in West Ham's 8-0 thrashing of Sunderland at Upton Park in 1968.**

• A well-built centre forward who was strong in the air and possessed a powerful shot, Hurst won an FA Cup winners' medal with West Ham in 1964 and, the following year, helped the Hammers win the European Cup Winners' Cup.

• **In 1979 he was appointed manager of Second Division side Chelsea but was sacked two years later after a dismal run of results. However, Hurst's great achievements on the pitch remain part of English folklore and earned him a knighthood in 1998.**

ZLATAN IBRAHIMOVIC

Born: Malmo, Sweden, 3rd October 1981
Position: Striker
Club career:
1999-2001 Malmo 40 (16)
2001-04 Ajax 74 (35)
2004-06 Juventus 70 (23)
2006-09 Inter Milan 88 (57)
2009-11 Barcelona 29 (16)
2010-11 AC Milan (loan) 29 (14)
2011-12 AC Milan 32 (28)
2012- Paris St Germain
International record:
2001- Sweden 80 (33)

An exceptionally gifted striker with an individualistic style of play, Sweden captain Zlatan Ibrahimovic is something of a lucky talisman, having won eight consecutive league titles with five different clubs between 2004 and 2011.
• His incredible run began with Ajax, who he had joined from his first club Malmo in 2001, when the Amsterdam giants won the Dutch league in 2004. Ibrahomivic's golden touch continued with his next club, Juventus, where he won back-to-back Serie A titles,

Andres 'The Brain' Iniesta computes his next move...

although these were later scrubbed from the record books following Juve's involvement in a match-fixing scandal.
• At his next club, Inter Milan, Ibrahimovic fared even better, helping the Nerazzurri win a hat-trick of titles in 2007, 2008 and 2009. He then moved to Barcelona, with Samuel Eto'o joining Inter as part of the deal, and despite failing to see eye-to-eye with Barca boss Pep Guardiola won a La Liga title medal in 2010. Returning to Italy, his astonishing run of success continued with AC Milan, who were crowned Serie A champions in 2011.
• In the summer of 2012 Ibrahimovic was transferred to newly-moneyed Paris

St Germain for £31 million, taking his combined transfer fee up to a world record £150 million, the highest for any player ever.
• Inevitably, perhaps, Ibrahimovic has been less fortunate at international level, but his impressive strike rate of 33 goals in 80 games for Sweden has made him a firm favourite with his country's fans.

ANDRES INIESTA

Born: Albacete, Spain, 11th May 1984
Position: Midfielder
Club career:
2001-03 Barcelona B 54 (5)
2002- Barcelona 271 (27)
International record:
2006- Spain 72 (10)

Attacking midfielder Andres Iniesta became an iconic figure for the whole Spanish nation when he scored the winning goal in the 2010 World Cup final against Holland at the Soccer City stadium in Johannesburg. To cap a great

£150 million man Zlatan Ibrahimovic

day for the Barcelona star he also picked up the Man of the Match award and was shortlisted for the Golden Ball.

• Nicknamed 'El Cerebro' ('The Brain') for his brilliant reading of the game, Iniesta made his debut for Spain in 2006 and scored his first goal for his country the following year in a 1-0 friendly win against England at Old Trafford. In 2008 he helped Spain win their first major honour for 44 years, the European Championships in Austria and Switzerland, and four years later he picked up the Player of the Tournament award as Spain retained the trophy in Poland and the Ukraine.

• A product of the Barcelona youth system, La Masia, he is now revered as one of the great Spanish players of his generation. Even before his World Cup heroics, a study by a social media marketing company revealed that he was the most popular Spanish sportsman on the internet, ahead of the likes of Real Madrid goalkeeper Iker Casillas, tennis star Rafael Nadal and racing driver Fernando Alonso.

• As well as his international honours, Iniesta has won five league titles with Barcelona plus a hat-trick of Champions League titles in 2006, 2009 and 2011.

INTER MILAN

Year founded: 1908
Ground: San Siro (80,018)
Nickname: Nerazzurri (The black and blues)
League titles: 18
Domestic cups: 7
European cups: 6
International cups: 3

Founded in 1908 as a breakaway club from AC Milan, Internazionale (as they are known locally) are the only Italian team never to have been relegated from Serie A. The dominant force in Italian football in the last decade, Inter have 18 title wins to their name – a total only bettered by Juventus.

• Inter were the first Italian club to win the European Cup twice, beating the mighty Real Madrid 3-1 in the 1964 final before recording a 1-0 defeat of Benfica the following year.

They had to wait 45 years, though, before making it a hat-trick with a 2-0 defeat of Bayern Munich in Madrid in 2010 – a victory that, with the domestic league and cup already in the bag, secured Inter their first ever treble.

• Under legendary manager Helenio Herrera, Inter introduced the 'catenaccio' defensive system to world football in the 1960s. Playing with a sweeper behind two man-markers, Inter conceded very few goals as they powered to three league titles between 1963 and 1966.

• The club endured a barren period domestically until they were awarded their first Serie A title for 17 years in 2006 after Juventus and AC Milan, who had both finished above them in the league table, had points deducted for their roles in a match-fixing scandal. Inter went on to win the championship in more conventional style in the following four years, the last two of these triumphs coming under former Chelsea boss Jose Mourinho.

• England boss Roy Hodgson was twice manager of Inter in the 1990s. Only two English players, meanwhile, have played for the club: striker Gerry Hitchens, who joined from Aston Villa in 1961, and Paul Ince, who made a £7 million move from Manchester United in 1995.

HONOURS
Italian champions 1910, 1920, 1930, 1938, 1940, 1953, 1954, 1963, 1965, 1966, 1971, 1980, 1989, 2006, 2007, 2008, 2009, 2010
Italian Cup 1939, 1978, 1982, 2005, 2006, 2010, 2011
European Cup/Champions League 1964, 1965, 2010
UEFA Cup 1991, 1994, 1998
Intercontinental Cup/Club World Cup 1964, 1965, 2010

IS THAT A FACT?
When Inter Milan won their fifth consecutive Serie A title in 2010 they equalled a record originally set by Juventus in the 1930s and matched by Torino a decade later.

INVERNESS CALEDONIAN THISTLE

Year founded: 1994
Ground: Caledonian Stadium (8,000)
Previous name: Caledonian Thistle
Nickname: Caley Thistle
Biggest win: 8-1 v Annan Athletic (1998))
Heaviest defeat: 0-6 v Airdrie (2001)

Founded as Caledonian Thistle in 1994 following the amalgamation of Highland league sides Caledonian and Inverness Thistle, the club was elected to the Scottish Third Division in the same year. In 1996, at the request of Inverness District Council, the club added 'Inverness' to its name.

• The club has steadily climbed up the league ladder in the years since, eventually gaining promotion to the SPL in 2004 after winning the First Division title. The club was relegated from the SPL in 2009 but bounced back the following season under manager Terry Butcher, a former England international defender.

• In February 2000 Thistle pulled off one of the biggest-ever shocks in the Scottish Cup when they beat Celtic 3-1 in the third round at Parkhead. The Sun newspaper famously reported this famous giant-killing under the witty headline "Super Caley go ballistic, Celtic are atrocious".

• Incredibly, Caley went 'ballistic' again in 2003 when they knocked Celtic out of the cup for a second time, winning 1-0 at their tiny Caledonian Stadium. The club went on to reach the semi-final of the Scottish Cup for the first time in their history, before losing to Dundee. The following season they got to the semi-finals again, only to be beaten by Dunfermline in a replay.

• Amazingly, Inverness were unbeaten away from home in the league throughout the whole of 2010 – a run of 19 matches in the Scottish First Division and SPL which a stunned Butcher described as 'a fairy tale'.

HONOURS
First Division champions 2004, 2010
Third Division champions 1997

IPSWICH TOWN

Year founded: 1878
Ground: Portman Road (30, 311)
Nickname: The Blues
Biggest win: 10-0 v Floriana (1962)
Heaviest defeat: 1-10 v Fulham (1963)

The club was founded at a meeting at the town hall in 1878 but did not join the Football League until 1938, two years after turning professional.

• Ipswich were the last of just four clubs to win the old Second and First Division titles in consecutive seasons, pulling off this remarkable feat in 1962 under future England manager Alf Ramsey. The team's success owed much to the strike partnership of Ray Crawford and Ted Phillips, who together scored 61 of the club's 93 goals during the title-winning campaign.

• Two years after that title win, though, Ipswich were relegated after conceding 121 goals. Only Blackpool in 1930/31 (125 goals against) have had a worse defensive record in the top flight.

• However, the club enjoyed more success under Bobby Robson, another man who went on to manage England, in the following two decades. In 1978 Ipswich won the FA Cup, beating favourites Arsenal 1-0 in the final at

'Well played, Italy, you were unlucky... to come up against a team as brilliant as us!'

Wembley, and three years later they won the UEFA Cup with attacking midfielder John Wark contributing a record 14 goals during the club's continental campaign.

• Ipswich were founder members of the Premier League in 1992 but were relegated in 1995 after a dismal season which included a 9-0 thrashing against Manchester United at Old Trafford – the biggest defeat in Premiership history.

• With 203 goals for the Tractor Boys between 1958 and 1969, Ray Crawford is the club's record goalscorer. Mick Mills is the club's record appearance maker, turning out 591 times between 1966 and 1982. Another defender from that era, Allan Hunter, is Ipswich's most-capped international, winning 47 of his 53 caps for Northern Ireland while at Portman Road.

• Ipswich made their record signing back in 2001 when they bought goalkeeper Matteo Sereni from Italian side Sampdoria for £4.75 million. More recently, the club received a record cheque for £12 million when they sold highly-rated teenage striker Conor Wickham to Sunderland in June 2011.

TOP 10

MOST AWAY GOALS CONCEDED IN A PREMIER LEAGUE SEASON

1.	Ipswich Town, 1994/95	59
2.	Swindon Town, 1993/94	55
3.	Wigan Athletic, 2009/10	55
4.	Burnley, 2009/10	52
5.	Middlesbrough, 1992/93	48
	Leeds United, 2003/04	48
7.	Barnsley, 1997/98	47
	Sheffield Wednesday, 1999/2000	47
9.	Norwich City, 1992/93	46
	Watford, 1999/2000	46
	Wimbledon, 1999/2000	46
	Derby County, 2007/08	46
	Hull City, 2009/10	46

HONOURS

Division 1 champions 1962
Division 2 champions 1961
Division 3 (S) champions 1954, 1957
FA Cup 1978
UEFA Cup 1981

ITALY

First international: Italy 6 France 2, 1910
Most capped player: Fabio Cannavaro, 136 caps (1997-2010)
Leading goalscorer: Luigi Riva, 35 goals (1965-74)
First World Cup appearance: Italy 7 USA 1, 1934
Biggest win: Italy 11 Egypt 3, 1928
Heaviest defeat: Hungary 7 Italy 1, 1924

Italy have the best record of any European nation at the World Cup, having won the tournament four times (in 1934, 1938, 1982 and 2006). Only Brazil, with five wins, have done better in the competition.

• The Azzurri, as they are known to their passionate fans, are the only country to have been involved in two World Cup final penalty shoot-outs. In 1994 they lost out to Brazil, but in 2006 they beat France on penalties after a 1-1 draw in the final in Berlin.

• When Italy won 1-0 at Wembley in 1997 in a World Cup qualifier they became the first country to beat England on home soil in a World Cup match.

• The most humiliating moment in Italy's sporting history came in 1966 when they lost 1-0 to minnows

North Korea at the World Cup in England. The Italians had a remarkably similar embarrassment at the 2002 tournament when they were knocked out by hosts South Korea after a 2-1 defeat. Fortunately for the Azzurri, neither 'East Korea' or 'West Korea' exist as independent countries!

• To the dismay of their fans, Italy had another World Cup to forget in 2010 when they defended their trophy in lamentable style, finishing bottom of their group behind Paraguay, Slovakia and, most embarrassingly, New Zealand.

• Italy have won the European Championship just once, beating Yugoslavia 2-0 in the final in Rome in 1968. They reached the final again in 2000 but lost to France, and endured more disappointment in 2012 when they were hammered 4-0 by Spain in the final in Kiev.

HONOURS

World Cup 1934, 1938, 1982, 2006
European Championship 1968
World Cup record
1930 Did not enter
1934 Winners
1938 Winners
1950 Round 1
1954 Round 1
1958 Did not qualify
1962 Round 1
1966 Round 1
1970 Runners-up
1974 Round 1
1978 Fourth place
1982 Winners
1986 Round 2
1990 Third place
1994 Runners-up
1998 Quarter-finals
2002 Round 2
2006 Winners
2010 Round 1

IS THAT A FACT?
Italy are the only World Cup hosts who have been required to go through a qualifying stage, the Azzurri comfortably beating Greece 4-0 in 1934 to book their place at the tournament proper.

NIKICA JELAVIC

Born: Capljina, Bosnia & Herzegovina, 27th August 1985
Position: Striker
Club career:
2002-07 Hadjuk Split 35 (8)
2007-08 Zulte Waregem 23 (3)
2008-10 Rapid Vienna 71 (27)
2010-12 Rangers 45 (30)
2012- Everton 13 (9)
International record:
2009- Croatia 22 (3)

Signed for a bargain £5 million from Rangers in January 2012, Nikica Jelavic enjoyed a glorious start to his Everton career, becoming the quickest player to hit double figures for the club for a century.

• When Jelavic scored twice in a thrilling 4-4 draw at Manchester United in April 2012 he became the first Everton player since Duncan McKenzie in the 1977/78 season to hit the target in five successive away games. His brace helped him win the Premier League Player of the Month award, the first Croatian player to be so honoured.

• After spells in Croatia, Belgium and Austria, Jelavic joined Rangers for £4 million in August 2010 from Rapid Vienna. In his one full season at Ibrox he helped the Glasgow giants win the league and League Cup, and he also claimed the SFA Goal of the Season award for a spectacular strike against Aberdeen.

• An instinctive finisher in the penalty box who also works hard for his team, Jelavic won his first cap for Croatia in a friendly against Qatar in 2009. He scored his first competitive goal for his country at the 2012 Euros in a 3-1 victory over the Republic of Ireland.

Nikica Jelavic of Everton and Croatia

J

JENNINGS

TOP 10

HIGHEST CAPPED NORTHERN IRELAND PLAYERS

1. Pat Jennings (1964-86) 119 caps
2. David Healey (2000-) 92 caps
3. Mal Donnaghy (1980-94) 91 caps
4. Sammy McIlroy (1972-87) 88 caps
   Maik Taylor (1999-2011) 88 caps
6. Keith Gillespie (1995-2008) 86 caps
7. Aaron Hughes (1998-) 80 caps
8. Jimmy Nicholl (1976-86) 73 caps
9. Michael Hughes (1992-2004) 71 caps
10. David McCreery (1976-90) 67 caps

PAT JENNINGS

Born: Newry, 12th June 1945
Position: Goalkeeper
Club career:
1961-63 Newry
1963-64 Watford 48
1964-77 Tottenham Hotspur 472
1977-85 Arsenal 237
International record:
1964-86 Northern Ireland 119

In an international career spanning 22 years, Pat Jennings made a record 119 appearances for Northern Ireland. He won his first cap in 1964 against Wales and his last against Brazil, on his 41st birthday, during the 1986 World Cup. At the time he was the oldest-ever player to appear in the finals.

• For four years Jennings held the world record for the most international caps, until his total was surpassed by England keeper Peter Shilton at the 1990 World Cup finals.

• Jennings is the only goalkeeper in the modern era to have played for both Arsenal and Tottenham. He won the FA Cup with Spurs in 1967, before repeating the feat with the Gunners 12 years later.

• Voted Footballer of the Year in 1973, Jennings is one of a handful of goalkeepers to have scored with a kick from his hands, his huge punt downfield bouncing over Manchester United 'keeper Alex Stepney and into the net during the 1967 Charity Shield.

MARTIN JOL

Born: The Hague, Holland, 16th January 1956
Managerial career:
1996-98 Roda JC
1998-2004 RKC Waalwijk
2004-07 Tottenham Hotspur
2008-09 Hamburg
2009-10 Ajax
2011- Fulham

Appointed as Fulham manager in June 2011, Martin Jol enjoyed a decent first season with the Cottagers, guiding them to ninth place in the Premier League, just two places below their best-ever top flight finish.

• Jol began his managerial career with Den Haag, with whom he won the Dutch Cup in 1997. The following year he moved on to RKC Waalwijk, where he was named the Dutch Football Writers' Coach of the Year in 2001. He joined Tottenham as assistant manager in 2004, stepping up to replace Jacques Santini as number one that autumn. In his time with the club he guided Spurs to two fifth-place finishes, but his failure to bring Champions League football to White Hart Lane saw him brutally sacked during a UEFA Cup tie in 2007.

• After a season with Hamburg, Jol returned to his native Holland to take over the reins at Ajax in 2009. The following year he led the Amsterdam giants to success in the Dutch Cup before quitting the club a few months later in December 2010.

• A tough-tackling midfielder in his playing days, Jol won the Dutch Cup with Den Haag in 1975 and later played for Bayern Munich, FC Twente, West Brom and Coventry. In 1980 he won three caps for Holland in a friendly tournament in Uruguay.

JUVENTUS

Year founded: 1897
Ground: Juventus Stadium (41,000)
Nickname: The Zebras
League titles: 28
Domestic cups: 9
European cups: 8
International cups: 2

Juventus have won the Italian league trophy – held aloft here by skipper Alessandro Del Piero in 2012 – a record 28 times

The most famous and the most successful club in Italy, Juventus were founded in 1897 by pupils at a school in Turin – hence the team's name, which means 'youth' in Latin. Six years later the club binned their original pink shirts and adopted their distinctive black-and-white-striped kit after an English member of the team had a set of Notts County shirts shipped out to Italy.

• Juventus emerged as the dominant force in Italian football in the 1930s when they won five titles in a row. They have a record 28 titles to their name and are the only team in Italy allowed to wear two gold stars on their shirts, signifying 20 Serie A victories. Juve's most recent triumph in 2012 saw them go through the whole league season undefeated, only the third time this impressive feat has been achieved.

• When, thanks to a single goal by their star player Michel Platini, Juventus beat Liverpool in the European Cup final in 1985 they became the first-ever club to win all three European trophies. However, their triumph at the Heysel Stadium in Brussels was overshadowed by the death of 39 of their fans, who were crushed to death as they tried to flee from crowd trouble before the kick-off.

• Juventus have won the Italian Cup nine times, a record matched only by Roma, although they haven't raised the trophy since 1995.

HONOURS
Italian champions *1905, 1926, 1931, 1932, 1933, 1934, 1935, 1950, 1952, 1958, 1960, 1961, 1967, 1972, 1973, 1975, 1977, 1978, 1981, 1982, 1984, 1986, 1995, 1997, 1998, 2002, 2003, 2012*
Italian Cup *1938, 1942, 1959, 1960, 1965, 1979, 1983, 1990, 1995*
European Cup/Champions League *1985, 1996*
European Cup Winners' Cup *1984*
UEFA Cup *1977, 1990, 1993*
European Super Cup *1984, 1996*
Club World Cup *1985, 1996*

SHINJI KAGAWA

Born: Kobe, Japan, 17th March 1989
Position: Winger
Club career:
2006-10 Cerezo Osaka 125 (55)
2010-12 Borussia Dortmund 49 (21)
2012- Manchester United
International record:
2008- Japan 33 (11)

Japanese international Shinji Kagawa became the most expensive Asian player in the history of the Premier League when he joined Manchester United from Borussia Dortmund for around £17 million in the summer of 2012.

• A winger who can also operate in midfield, Kagawa was the first player in Japan to sign a professional contract while still at school when, aged 17, he joined Cerezo Osaka. After scoring an impressive 55 goals in 125 appearances for Osaka he moved to Borussia Dortmund in 2010.

• In his first season with the German club, Kagawa helped Dortmund win the league although he missed the second half of the campaign through injury. He returned for the start of the 2011/12 and starred as Dortmund won the league and cup Double for the first time in their history.

• Kagawa made his debut for Japan in a 1-0 friendly win over Ivory Coast in 2008, but was a surprise omission from his country's squad for the World Cup in South Africa two years later. Since then, however, he has established himself as one of the key players in the Japanese team.

Manchester United's Shinji Kagawa is the most expensive Asian footballer ever

KAKA

Born: Brasilia, Brazil, 22nd April 1982
Position: Midfielder
Club career:
2001-03 Sao Paulo 59 (23)
2003-09 AC Milan 193 (70)
2009- Real Madrid 65 (20)
International record:
2002- Brazil 82 (27)

Ricardo Izecson dos Santos Leite, better known as 'Kaka', is one of the most famous names in modern football. In 2009 he joined Real Madrid from AC Milan for a then world record fee of £56 million but, following a couple of injury-hit seasons at the Bernabeu, only really started to pay back that investment in the 2011/12 season when he helped the Spanish giants win La Liga.

• After impressing with Brazilian club Sao Paulo, Kaka moved to Italy in 2003 for £5 million – a fee later described by Milan owner Silvio Berlusconi as "peanuts". It certainly appeared so as Kaka played a central role in Milan's Serie A title success in 2004, and then starred in their Champions League triumph in 2007, when he scored 10 goals en route to the final against Liverpool in Athens. In the same year he was named FIFA World Footballer of the Year.

• Kaka first played for Brazil in 2002 and was a member of his country's squad which won the World Cup in the same year – although he actually only appeared on the pitch for 25 minutes of the tournament. Since then he has gone on to win over 80 caps for the South Americans.

• When he was 18 Kaka suffered a spinal fracture in a swimming pool accident that could easily have left him in a wheelchair for the rest of his life. A committed Christian who wears a T-shirt bearing the legend 'I belong to Jesus' under his football jersey, he attributed his remarkable recovery to the power of God.

ROBBIE KEANE

Born: Dublin, 8th July 1980
Position: Striker
Club career:
1997-99 Wolves 74 (24)
1999-2000 Coventry City 31 (12)
2000-01 Inter Milan 6 (0)
2001 Leeds United (loan) 18 (9)
2001-02 Leeds United 28 (4)
2002-08 Tottenham Hotspur 197 (80)
2008-09 Liverpool 19 (5)
2009-11 Tottenham Hotspur 41 (11)
2010 Celtic (loan) 16 (12)
2011 West Ham United (loan) 9 (2)
2011- LA Galaxy 20 (8)
2012 Aston Villa (loan) 6 (3)
International record:
1998- Republic of Ireland 120 (53)

Livewire striker Robbie Keane is the Republic of Ireland's all-time top scorer, with an impressive haul of 53 goals in 120 appearances. He has also captained his country a record 55 times since taking over the armband in 2006.

• Keane began his club career with Wolves, for whom he scored twice on his debut against Norwich in 1997. Two years later, aged 19, he joined Coventry City for £6 million – then a record fee for a teenager.

Robbie Keane, the Republic of Ireland's record goalscorer

• After brief spells with Inter Milan and Leeds, Keane moved to Tottenham in 2002. While at White Hart Lane he finally won the first trophy of his career, the Carling Cup in 2007/08 – a season in which he hit a personal best ever 23 goals in all competitions.

• His goals record prompted Liverpool to pay £20 million for him in the summer of 2008. It was a dream move for Keane, a childhood fan of the Reds, but he was used irregularly by then Liverpool boss Rafa Benitez and, in the January 2009 transfer window, he returned to Tottenham for £15 million. However, he soon found himself surplus to requirements at White Hart Lane and, after loan spells at Celtic and West Ham, Keane signed for LA Galaxy in a £3.5 million deal in the summer of 2011. He briefly returned from America to play on loan at Aston Villa during the second half of the 2011/12 season.

ROY KEANE

Born: Cork, 10th August 1971
Position: Midfielder
Club career:
1989/90 Cobh Ramblers 12 (1)
1990-93 Nottingham Forest 114 (22)
1993-2005 Manchester United 323 (33)
2005-06 Celtic 10 (1)
International record:
1991-2005 Republic of Ireland 66 (9)

Manchester United legend Roy Keane is the club's most successful captain ever, leading the Reds to nine major trophies while wearing the armband between 1997 and 2005.

• The driving force in United's midfield for over a decade after arriving from Nottingham Forest for a then British record fee of £3.75 million in 1993, Keane won seven league titles and four FA Cups while at Old Trafford but he missed out on the Reds' 1999 Champions League triumph through suspension.

• A fiery, volatile character, Keane was sent off 13 times during his career – a record for the top flight. He set another unwanted record in 2002 when he was fined £150,000 by the FA for bringing the game into disrepute when he admitted in his autobiography that he had intended to hurt an opponent, Manchester City's Alf-Inge Haaland.

• Keane starred for the Republic of Ireland at the 1994 World Cup, being named his country's best player. However, before the 2002 tournament in Japan and Korea he stormed out of Ireland's training camp on the Pacific island of Saipan after a furious row with manager Mick McCarthy. Despite the intervention of Irish Prime Minister Bertie Ahern, Keane refused to return, although he later played for his country again under new boss Brian Kerr.

• Once tipped by Sir Alex Ferguson to succeed him at Old Trafford, Keane became manager of Sunderland in 2006 but walked out in November 2008. Five months later he was unveiled as the new manager of Ipswich Town, but after a poor run of results he was sacked in January 2011.

KEVIN KEEGAN

Born: Doncaster, 14th February 1951
Position: Striker
Club career:
1968-71 Scunthorpe United 124 (18)
1971-77 Liverpool 230 (68)
1977-80 Hamburg 90 (32)
1980-82 Southampton 68 (37)
1982-84 Newcastle United 78 (48)
International record:
1972-82 England 63 (21)

A busy, all-action striker with a sharp eye for goal, Kevin Keegan is the only British player to have twice been voted European Footballer of the Year and he was only the second player – after the great Johan Cruyff – to win the award in consecutive seasons (1978 and 1979).

• Keegan was also the first English player to appear in the European Cup final with two different clubs. In 1977 he was a winner with Liverpool against Borussia Monchengladbach, but three years later he had to settle for a runners-up medal after Hamburg were beaten by Nottingham Forest.

• Uniquely, Keegan's first three England appearances were all against the same opposition, Wales. He went on to win 63 caps, 31 of them as captain.

• Nicknamed 'Mighty Mouse' during his spell with Hamburg, Keegan had a top 10 hit in Germany with Head Over Heels in 1979. The single fared less well in the UK, stalling at number 31.

• Keegan finished his playing days at

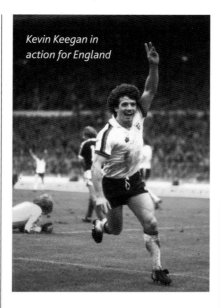
Kevin Keegan in action for England

Newcastle in the early 1980s, returning to St James' Park a decade later as manager. But, after five years in charge, he dramatically quit the club a few months after his entertaining Toon team had narrowly missed out on the Premiership title. A brief second spell in charge of the Geordies ended in similar fashion in 2008 following a long-running disagreement with owner Mike Ashley about the club's management structure.

• Keegan also walked out on the England job in October 2000 just a few minutes after his team had lost a vital World Cup qualifier to Germany in the last ever match played at the old Wembley. He had only been in charge for 18 months, but had increasingly come under fire after a poor England showing at Euro 2000.

KICK-OFF

Scottish club Queen's Park claim to have been the first to adopt the traditional kick-off time of 3pm on a Saturday, which allowed those people who worked in the morning time to get to the match.

• The fastest-ever goal from a kick-off was scored in just two seconds by Nawaf Al Abed, a 21-year-old striker for Saudi Arabian side Al Hilal in a cup match against Al Shoalah in 2009. After a team-mate tapped the ball to him, Al Abed struck a fierce left-foot shot from the halfway line which sailed over the opposition 'keeper and into the net.

• Until the start of the 20th century teams used to change ends before kicking off after every goal.

• The start of the 1974 World Cup final between hosts West Germany and Holland was delayed when English

referee Jack Taylor spotted that there were no corner flags – so much for German efficiency!

• Singer Diana Ross was supposed to kick off the 1994 World Cup in the USA by kicking a ball into an enormous inflatable goal, but she missed!

KILMARNOCK

Year founded: 1869
Ground: Rugby Park (18,128)
Nickname: Killie
Biggest win: 13-2 v Saltcoats Victoria (1896)
Heaviest defeat: 1-9 v Celtic (1938)

The oldest professional club in Scotland, Kilmarnock were founded in 1869 by a group of local cricketers who were keen to play another sport during the winter months. Originally, the club played rugby (hence the name of Kilmarnock's stadium, Rugby Park) before switching to football in 1873.

• That same year Kilmarnock entered the inaugural Scottish Cup and on 18th October 1873 the club took part in the first-ever match in the competition, losing 2-0 in the first round to Renton.

• Kilmarnock's greatest moment was back in 1965 when they travelled to championship rivals Hearts on the last day of the season requiring a two-goal win to pip the Edinburgh side to the title on goal average. To the joy of their travelling fans, Killie won 2-0 to claim the title by 0.04 of a goal.

• Kilmarnock have won the Scottish Cup three times, and claimed their first ever League Cup in the 2012 when they beat Celtic 1-0 in the final at Hampden Park, Belgian striker Dieter van Tornhout scoring the winning goal six minutes from time.

• During the 2010/11 campaign Kilmarnock scored in 23 consecutive SPL matches, their best ever such run in a single season.

HONOURS
Division 1 champions 1965
Division 2 champions 1898, 1899
Scottish Cup 1920, 1929, 1997
Scottish League Cup 2012

FRANK LAMPARD

Born: Romford, 20th June 1978
Position: Midfielder
Club career:
1995-2001 West Ham United 148 (24)
1995-96 Swansea City (loan) 9 (1)
2001- Chelsea 376 (126)
International record:
1999- England 91 (23)

With 150 goals to his name, Frank Lampard is the highest-scoring midfielder in Premier League history and the only player to hit double figures in the league in nine consecutive seasons (2004-12). The vast majority of those strikes have come for Chelsea, who Lampard joined from West Ham in an £11 million deal back in 2001.

• A key figure in Chelsea's success in recent years, Lampard has won the league three times and the FA Cup four times during his nine years with the Blues, including the Double in 2010. After numerous near misses, he finally won the Champions League with Chelsea in 2012, scoring one of his team's penalties in the shoot-out victory over Bayern Munich in the final.

• A model of consistency, Lampard played in a then record 164 consecutive Premier League games until illness forced him out of Chelsea's visit to Manchester City in December 2005. Goalkeepers David James and Brad Friedel have since passed his total, but Lampard still holds the Premier League record for an outfield player.

• Now on 186 goals for Chelsea in all competitions, Lampard is the third-highest goalscorer in the Blues' history behind 1960s striker Bobby Tambling (202) and 1980s club legend Kerry Dixon (193).

• The son of former England and West Ham defender Frank senior, Lampard made his international debut in 1999 against Belgium, but took a while to establish himself in the England team. He starred at the European Championships in 2004, scoring in three of his country's four games, but fared less well at the 2006 World Cup where he was one of three England players to miss a penalty in the quarter-final shoot-out defeat at the hands of Portugal. His luck was also out at the 2010 tournament in South Africa, when the officials failed to spot that his shot in England's second-round defeat by Germany had clearly crossed the line after bouncing down off the crossbar.

Frank Lampard holds aloft the Champions League trophy, aka 'the cup with big ears'

DENIS LAW

Born: Aberdeen, 24th February 1940
Position: Striker
Club career:
1956-60 Huddersfield Town 81 (16)
1960-61 Manchester City 44 (21)
1961-62 Torino 27 (10)
1962-73 Manchester United 309 (171)
1973-74 Manchester City 24 (9)
International record:
1958-74 Scotland 55 (30)

Along with Kenny Dalglish, Denis Law is Scotland's leading scorer with 30 international goals. Law, though, scored his goals in roughly half the number of games as 'King Kenny'.

• Law made his international debut in 1958, scoring in a 3-0 win against Wales. Aged 18, he was the youngest player to appear for Scotland since before the war. He went on to represent Scotland for 16 years, taking his bow at the 1974 World Cup in Germany.

• On two occasions Law was sold for fees that broke the existing British transfer record. In 1960 he moved from Huddersfield to Manchester City for a record £55,000, and two years later his £115,000 transfer from Torino to Manchester United set a new benchmark figure.

• With United, Law won two league titles and the FA Cup in 1963, but he missed out on the club's European Cup triumph in 1968 through a knee injury. He remains the only Scottish player to have been voted European Footballer of the Year, an award he won in 1964.

• The last goal Law scored, a clever backheel for Manchester City against United at Old Trafford in 1974, gave him no pleasure at all as it condemned his old club to relegation to the Second Division. "I have seldom felt so depressed as I did that weekend," he remarked later.

• In 2002 a statue of Law was unveiled at Old Trafford, scene of many of his greatest triumphs. The following year the Scottish Football Association marked UEFA's Jubilee by naming him as Scotland's 'Golden Player' of the previous 50 years.

LAWS

Thirteen original laws of association football were adopted at a meeting

of the Football Association in 1863, although these had their roots in the 'Cambridge Rules' established at Cambridge University as far back as 1848.

• No copy of those 1848 rules now exists, but they are thought to have included laws relating to throw-ins, goal-kicks, fouls and offside. They even allowed for a length of string to be used as a cross bar.

• Perhaps the most significant rule change occurred in 1925 when the offside law was altered so that an attacking player receiving the ball would need to be behind two opponents, rather than three. The effect of this rule change was dramatic, with the average number of goals per game in the Football League rising from 2.55 in 1924/25 to 3.44 in 1925/26.

• The laws of the game are governed by the International Football Association Board, which was founded in 1886 by the four football associations of the United Kingdom. Each of these associations still has one vote on the IFAB, with FIFA having four votes. Any changes to the laws of the game require a minimum of six votes.

• In recent years the most important change to the laws of the game was the introduction of the 'back pass' rule in 1992, which prevented goalkeepers from handling passes from their own

team-mates. The rule was introduced to discourage time-wasting and overly defensive play, following criticisms of widespread negative tactics at the 1990 World Cup.

LEAGUE CUP

With eight wins to their name, most recently in the 2012 final against Cardiff, Liverpool have won the League Cup more often than any other club. The Reds have also appeared in the most finals, 11.

• The competition has been known by more names than any other in British football. Originally called the Football League Cup (1960-81), it has subsequently been rebranded through sponsorship deals as the Milk Cup (1981-86), Littlewoods Cup (1986-90), Rumbelows Cup (1990-92), Coca-Cola Cup (1992-98), Worthington Cup (1998-2003), Carling Cup (2003-12) and, since 2012, the Capital One Cup.

• Ian Rush won a record five winners' medals in the competition with Liverpool (1981-84 and 1995) and, along with Geoff Hurst, is also the leading scorer in the history of the League Cup with 49 goals. In the 1986/87 season Tottenham's Clive Allen scored a record 12 goals in the competition.

• Oldham's Frankie Bunn scored a record six goals in a League Cup match when Oldham thrashed Scarborough 7-0 on 25th October 1989.

• Liverpool won the competition a record four times in a row between 1981-84, going undefeated for an unprecedented 25 League Cup matches.

Liverpool have won the League Cup a record eight times

• Liverpool were also the first club to win the trophy on penalties, beating Birmingham City 5-4 in the shoot-out in 2001 in the first final to be played at the Millennium Stadium, Cardiff.

• Norman Whiteside, the youngest player ever to score in an FA Cup final (for Manchester United v Brighton in 1983), is also the youngest man ever to score in the League

Cup final (for Manchester United v Liverpool, also in 1983), aged 17 years and 324 days.

• The youngest player ever to feature in a League Cup match is Leicester City's Ashley Chambers, who was aged 15 years and 203 days when he came on as a sub against Blackpool in 2005.

• The first League Cup final to be played at Wembley was between West Brom and QPR in 1967. QPR were then a Third Division side and pulled off a major shock by winning 3-2. Prior to 1967, the final was played on a home and away basis over two legs. The first club to win the League Cup at the new Wembley were Tottenham, who beat London rivals Chelsea 2-1 after extra-time in 2008.

• The first player to score in every round of the League Cup was West Brom's Tony Brown in the 1965/66 season.

• Chelsea striker Didier Drogba scored a record four goals in League Cup finals, finding the target against Liverpool in 2005, Arsenal in 2007 (two goals) and Tottenham in 2008.

• In 1983 West Ham walloped Bury 10-0 to record the biggest-ever victory in the history of the League Cup. Three years later Liverpool equalled the Hammers' tally with an identical thrashing of Fulham.

TOP 10

LEAGUE CUP FINAL APPEARANCES

1.	Liverpool	11 (8 won, 3 lost)
2.	Aston Villa	8 (5 won, 3 lost)
3.	Manchester United	8 (4 won, 4 lost)
4.	Tottenham Hotspur	7 (4 won, 3 lost)
5.	Arsenal	7 (2 won, 5 lost)
6.	Chelsea	6 (4 won, 2 lost)
7.	Nottingham Forest	6 (4 won, 2 lost)
8.	Leicester City	5 (3 won, 2 lost)
9.	Norwich City	4 (2 won, 2 lost)
10.	Birmingham City	3 (2 won, one lost)
	Manchester City	3 (2 won, one lost)

LEEDS UNITED

Year founded: 1919
Ground: Elland Road (39,460)
Nickname: United
Biggest win: 10-0 v Lyn Oslo (1969)
Heaviest defeat: 1-8 v Stoke City (1934)

Leeds United were formed in 1919 as successors to Leeds City, who had been expelled from the Football League after making illegal payments to their players. United initially joined the Midland League before being elected to the Second Division in 1920.

• Leeds' greatest years were in the 1960s and early 1970s under legendary manager Don Revie. The club were struggling in the Second Division when he arrived at Elland Road in 1961 but, building his side around the likes of Jack Charlton, Billy Bremner and Johnny Giles, Revie soon turned Leeds into a formidable force.

• During the Revie years Leeds won two league titles in 1969 and 1974, the FA Cup in 1972, the League Cup in 1968, and two Fairs Cup in 1968 and 1971. There were any number of near misses, too, as the Yorkshiremen's unique blend of skill and steel saw them challenge for just about every trophy going.

• Leeds also reached the final of the European Cup in 1975, losing 2-0 to Bayern Munich. Sadly, rioting by the club's fans resulted in Leeds becoming the first English club to be suspended from European competition. The ban lasted three years.

• Peter Lorimer, another Revie-era stalwart, is the club's leading scorer, hitting 168 league goals in two spells at Elland Road: 1962-79 and 1983-86. Jack Charlton holds the club appearance record, turning out in 773 games in total between 1952 and 1973.

• On 15th April 1970 Leeds appeared in front of the biggest crowd ever to watch a European Cup tie when 135,826 fans crammed into Hampden Park in Glasgow to see Celtic beat them 2-1 in the semi-final second leg.

• In 1992 Leeds pipped Manchester United to the title to become the last club to win the old First Division before it became the Premiership.

Ironically, Leeds' star player at the time, Eric Cantona, joined the Red Devils the following season. The club remained a force over the next decade, even reaching the Champions League semi-final in 2001, but financial mismanagement saw them plummet to League One in 2007 before they climbed back into the Championship three years later.

• Incredibly, Leeds failed to win a single FA Cup tie between 1952 and 1963 – the worst-ever run by a league club in the post-war era.

• Rio Ferdinand is both Leeds' record buy and record sale, joining the club from West Ham for £18 million in 2000 before leaving for Manchester United for a then British record £29.1 million two years later.

> **HONOURS**
> *Division 1 champions* 1969, 1974, 1992
> *Division 2 champions* 1924, 1964, 1990
> *FA Cup* 1972
> *League Cup* 1968
> *Fairs Cup* 1968, 1971

LEICESTER CITY

Year founded: 1884
Ground: King Power Stadium (32,262)
Pevious name: Leicester Fosse
Nickname: The Foxes
Biggest win: 13-0 v Notts Olympic (1894)
Heaviest defeat: 0-12 v Nottingham Forest (1909)

Founded in 1884 as Leicester Fosse by old boys from Wyggeston School, the club were elected to the Second Division a decade later. In 1919 they changed their name to Leicester City, shortly after Leicester was given city status.

• The Foxes have enjoyed great success in the League Cup, winning the trophy three times. Their first victory came against Stoke in 1964 and more recently they won the trophy twice under then manager Martin O'Neill, against Middlesbrough in 1997 and Tranmere Rovers in 2000.

• Only Crystal Palace can match Leicester's record of playing in four Championship play-off finals since the system was introduced in 1987. The club's record in these games is mixed with two wins and two defeats.

• In 1909, while still known as Leicester Fosse, the club suffered their worst-ever defeat, losing 12-0 to East Midland neighbours Nottingham Forest. The score is still a record for a top-flight match.

• Leicester City are the only club to have played in four FA Cup finals and lost them all. Beaten in 1949, 1961 and 1963, they were defeated again by Manchester City in 1969 – the same season that they were relegated from the First Division. Only four other teams, most recently Portsmouth in 2010, have suffered a similar double blow.

• Leicester made their record sale in 2000, when England striker Emile Heskey moved to Liverpool for £11 million. In the same year the Foxes forked out £5 million on Wolves' Ade Akinbiyi, their record purchase.

• Arthur Chandler holds the club goalscoring record, netting 259 times between 1923 and 1935. Remarkably, he scored in a record 16 consecutive matches during the 1924/25 season. The club's appearance record is held by defender and ex-Leicestershire county cricketer Graham Cross, who turned out 599 times in all competitions for the Foxes between 1960 and 1976.

• Dr Who actor, Matt Smith, played for Leicester at Under-16 level before a back injury forced him to give up his football dreams and concentrate on acting instead.

> **HONOURS**
> *Division 2 champions* 1925, 1937, 1954, 1957, 1971, 1980
> *League One champions* 2009
> *League Cup* 1964, 1997, 2000

IS THAT A FACT?
In 1954 in a match at Chelsea, Leicester City conceded a unique 'shared own goal', defenders Stan Milburn and Jack Froggart attempting to clear the ball at the same time but only managing to send it flying into their own net. Doh!

Neil Lennon has developed terrible dandruff since taking over at Celtic

NEIL LENNON

Born: Lurgan, 25th June 1971
Managerial career:
2010- Celtic

Celtic manager since 2010, when he stepped up from his position as first team coach to replace Tony Mowbray, Neil Lennon enjoyed his biggest success to date when he brought the SPL title to Celtic Park in 2012. The previous year he had guided his team to the Scottish Cup after a 3-0 defeat of Motherwell in the final.

• Lennon's two years in charge of the Glasgow giants have been littered with controversy. A fiery character, Lennon was twice banned from the touchline during the 2010/11 season, the second time after a post-match confrontation with then Rangers assistant manager Ally McCoist.

• Shortly after that incident, Lennon was attacked by a crazed Hearts fan while he stood in the technical area at Tynecastle during Celtic's 3-0 win. Even worse, a parcel bomb was sent to Lennon in April 2011 but, fortunately, the package was intercepted by the Royal Mail before it was delivered to his house. Nine years earlier, in 2002, Lennon, a Catholic from Northern Ireland, received death threats from Protestant extremists after suggesting that he would like to play for a United Ireland team. The threats prompted his retirement from international football.

• A hard-working midfielder, Lennon twice won the League Cup with Leicester before leaving in 2000 for Celtic, where he won the SPL five times and the Scottish Cup three times.

CRAIG LEVEIN

Born: Dunfermline, 22nd October 1964
Managerial career:
1997-2000 Cowdenbeath
2000-04 Hearts
2004-06 Leicester City
2006 Raith Rovers
2006-09 Dundee United
2009- Scotland

Appointed as Scotland manager in December 2009 as the successor to George Burley, Craig Levein got off to a great start when his team beat the Czech Republic 1-0 at Hampden Park in his first match in charge of the national team. Incredibly, the victory was Scotland's first in a home friendly for 14 years.

• The following year, however, Levein was roundly criticised by fans and media when he fielded an ultra-defensive 4-6-0 formation against the Czechs in a Euro 2012 qualifier in Prague – the first time in Scotland's history that the national team had taken to the field without a recognised striker. Unfortunately for Levein, his negative tactics flopped as Scotland went down to a 1-0 defeat, a result which contributed to their failure to qualify for Euro 2012.

• Levein began his managerial career at Cowdenbeath, before moving to Hearts in 2000. In four years with the Edinburgh club he guided them to consecutive third-place finishes in the SPL, but was unable to break the Old Firm's monopoly of the top two positions.

• After spells at Leicester and Raith, he became boss of Dundee United in 2006. He spent three years at Tannadice before taking the Scotland job, the highlight coming in 2008 when he led the Terrors to the League Cup final, which United eventually lost to Rangers on penalties.

• A tough-tackling defender in his playing days, Levein started out at Cowdenbeath before spending many years at Hearts. He also won 16 caps for Scotland, representing his country at the 1990 World Cup in Italy.

LEYTON ORIENT

Year founded: 1881
Ground: Brisbane Road (9,271)
Pevious name: Eagle FC, Clapton Road, Orient
Nickname: The O's
Biggest win: 9-2 v Aldershot (1934) and v Chester (1962)
Heaviest defeat: 0-8 v Aston Villa (1929)

Originally founded by members of a local cricket team, the club chose the name 'Orient' in 1888 following a suggestion by one of the players who worked for the Orient Shipping Company.

• **Over 40 Orient players and staff fought in the First World War, three of them dying in the conflict. In recognition of this sacrifice, The Prince of Wales (later King Edward VIII) watched an Orient match in 1921 – the first time a member of the Royal Family had attended a Football League fixture.**

• Orient are the only club to have played league matches at the old Wembley stadium. During the 1931/32 season, while still named Clapton Orient, the club played matches against Brentford and Southend at 'the home of football' after their own Lea Bridge ground was temporarily closed for failing to meet official standards.

• **Success has generally proved elusive for the eastenders, but the club did enjoy a single season in the top flight in 1962/63 and in 1978 the O's reached the semi-finals of the FA Cup before losing 3-0 to Arsenal.**

• Orient's record scorer is Tommy Johnston, who banged in 121 goals in two spells at the club between 1956-61. In 2009 the South Stand at Brisbane Road was named after the prolific striker.

• In the Third Division play-off final in 2001, Orient's Chris Tate scored against Blackpool after just 27 seconds – the fastest-ever goal at the Millennium Stadium. Sadly for the O's, they lost the game 4-2.

HONOURS
Division 3 (S) champions 1956
Division 3 champions 1970

GARY LINEKER

Born: Leicester, 30th November 1960
Position: Striker
Club career:
1978-85 Leicester City 194 (95)
1985-86 Everton 41 (30)
1986-89 Barcelona 103 (43)
1989-92 Tottenham Hotspur 105 (67)
1992-94 Nagoya Grampus 8 23 (9)
International record:
1984-92 England 80 (48)

Now a popular BBC sports presenter known for his excruciating puns, Gary Lineker is England's second-highest scorer, with 48 goals, just one behind the legendary Bobby Charlton. He had a great chance to beat the record, but failed to score in any of his final six matches and even missed a penalty to equal Charlton's tally against Brazil.

• **He is, though, England's leading scorer at the finals of the World Cup with ten goals. At the 1986 tournament in Mexico Lineker scored six goals to win the Golden Boot, and he added another four at Italia '90.**

• Lineker is the only player to have twice scored all four England goals in a match, grabbing all his side's goals in 4-2 away wins over Spain in 1987 and Malaysia in 1991. In all, he hit five hat-tricks in his 80 international appearances.

• **At club level Lineker won the European Cup Winners' Cup with Barcelona in 1989 and the FA Cup with Spurs two years later. He was also voted PFA Player of the Year in 1986 after a single goal-filled season with Everton.**

• In his last international, against Sweden at the 1992 European championships, Lineker was controversially substituted by England boss Graham Taylor. The move backfired as England lost the match and were eliminated.

IS THAT A FACT?
Anfield was the first ground to be visited by the Match of the Day cameras when the programme started on 22nd August 1964, Liverpool's Roger Hunt grabbing the first goal for the reigning champions in a 3-2 win over Arsenal.

• A revered figure in his hometown, Lineker has a stand named after him at Leicester's King Power Stadium.

LIVERPOOL

Year founded: 1892
Ground: Anfield (45,522)
Nickname: The Reds
Biggest win: 11-0 v Stromsgodset (1974)
Heaviest defeat: 1-9 v Birmingham City (1954)

Liverpool were founded as a splinter club from local rivals Everton following a dispute between the Toffees and the landlord of their original ground at Anfield, John Houlding. When the majority of Evertonians decided to decamp to Goodison Park in 1892, Houlding set up Liverpool FC after his attempts to retain the name 'Everton' had failed.

• **With 18 league titles to their name, Liverpool are the second most successful club in the history of English football behind deadly rivals Manchester United. However, the Reds have failed to lift the championship trophy for over two decades, their last title coming way back in 1990.**

• Liverpool dominated English football in the 1970s and 1980s after the foundations of the club's success were laid by legendary manager Bill Shankly in the previous decade. Under Shankly's successor, Bob Paisley, the Reds won 13 major trophies – a haul only surpassed by Sir Alex Ferguson.

• **Liverpool are the most successful English side in Europe, having won the European Cup/Champions League on five occasions. The Reds first won the trophy in 1977, beating Borussia Monchengladbach 3-1 in Rome, and the following year became the first British team to retain the cup (after a 1-0 win in the final against Bruges at Wembley, club legend Kenny Dalglish grabbing the all-important goal).**

• In 1984 Liverpool became the first club

to win the European Cup on penalties when they beat Roma by this method after a 1-1 draw. In 2005 the Reds won the trophy on spot-kicks again, this time against AC Milan, and remain the only club to have twice triumphed in the competition after a penalty shoot-out.

• Liverpool have won the League Cup a record eight times, including four times in a row between 1981-84, and are the only club to win the trophy twice on penalties (in 2001 and 2012). Reds striker Ian Rush is the joint leading scorer in the history of the competition with 49 goals, hitting all but one of these for Liverpool in two spells at the club in the 1980s and 1990s.

• Rush also scored a record five goals in three FA Cup finals for Liverpool in 1986, 1989 and 1992 – all of which were won by the Reds. In all, the Merseysiders have won the trophy seven times, most recently in 2006 when they became only the second team (after Arsenal the previous year) to claim the cup on penalties.

• When the Reds' recorded their biggest ever victory, 11-0 against Norwegian no-hopers Stromsgodset in the Cup Winners Cup in 1974, no fewer than nine different Liverpool players got on

the scoresheet to set a British record for the most scoring players in a competitive match.

• In 1986 Liverpool became only the third English side in the 20th century to win the Double, pipping rivals Everton to the league title and then beating the Toffees 3-1 in the FA Cup final at Wembley with a line-up that featured not a single English player – a first for the final.

• England international striker Roger Hunt is the club's leading scorer in league games, with 245 goals between 1958 and 1969. His team-mate Ian Callaghan holds the Liverpool appearance record, turning out in 640 league games between 1960 and 1978.

• Pony-tailed striker Andy Carroll is the club's record signing, joining the Reds from Newcastle for £35 million in January 2011. In the same month Spanish hitman Fernando Torres left Anfield for Chelsea, the Reds picking up a British record fee of £50 million from the Londoners.

Dirk Kuyt celebrates scoring during Liverpool's 2012 League Cup win

• In 2001 Liverpool became only the second English club to win the League Cup and FA Cup in the same season. For good measure, the Reds made it a 'Treble' by lifting the UEFA Cup as well after a thrilling 5-4 victory over Spanish club Alaves in the final.

• Kop hero Steven Gerrard is the club's most-capped international, having played 96 games for England since making his debut in 2000.

• Famous Liverpool fans include former Conservative Party leader Michael Howard, veteran comedian Jimmy Tarbuck and singer Elvis Costello.

HONOURS

Division 1 champions *1901, 1906, 1922, 1923, 1947, 1964, 1966, 1973, 1976, 1977, 1979, 1980, 1982, 1983, 1984, 1986, 1988, 1990*
Division 2 champions *1894, 1896, 1905, 1962*
FA Cup *1965, 1974, 1986, 1989, 1992, 2001, 2006*
League Cup *1981, 1982, 1983, 1984, 1995, 2001, 2003, 2012*
Double *1986*
European Cup/Champions League *1977, 1978, 1981, 1984, 2005*
UEFA Cup *1973, 1976, 2001*
European Super Cup *1977, 2001, 2005*

DAVID LUIZ

Born: Diadema, Brazil, 22nd
April 1987
Position: Defender
Club career:
2006-07 Vitoria 26 (1)
2007 Benfica (loan) 10 (0)
2007-11 Benfica 72 (4)
2011- Chelsea 32 (4)
International record:
2010- Brazil 11 (0)

Flamboyant centre-back David Luiz joined Chelsea from Benfica in January 2011 for £21.3 million, making him the Blues' most expensive ever defensive purchase.

• The frizzy-haired Brazilian's skills on the ball soon made him a cult figure at Stamford Bridge, with stallholders outside the stadium doing a roaring trade in 'David Luiz wigs'. However, his occasionally erratic approach to the basics of defending led to some criticism, notably from Sky Sports pundit Gary Neville who, after one haphazard display by Luiz, said that he played as though 'controlled by a ten-year-old on a PlayStation.'

• Luiz answered his critics in the best possible manner by playing a starring role in Chelsea's run to the 2012 Champions League final and then bravely stepping up to score one of his team's penalties in the shoot-out victory over Bayern Munich which brought the trophy to London for the first time.

• In 2010 Luiz made his debut for Brazil in a 2-0 friendly win over the USA.

People are starting to take David Luiz seriously now... well, er, sometimes!

ALLY McCOIST

Born: Bellshill, 24th September 1962
Position: Striker
Club career:
1979-81 St Johnstone 57 (22)
1981-83 Sunderland 56 (8)
1983-98 Rangers 418 (251)
1998-2001 Kilmarnock 59 (12)
International record:
1986-98 Scotland 61 (19)

Rangers legend Ally McCoist is the highest scorer in the Gers' history with an incredible 355 goals for the Ibrox outfit in all competitions. His tally of 251 league goals is also a club record.

• **During a 15-year career with Rangers, McCoist won no fewer than 10 league titles (including nine in a row between 1989 and 1997), nine Scottish League Cups and one Scottish Cup. His haul of medals is unmatched by any other Scottish player in the last quarter of a century.**

• In 1992 McCoist hit a personal best 34 goals and won the European Golden Boot. In the same year he was voted Scottish Player of the Year. A Scotland international for over a decade, his total of 19 goals for his country is only bettered by four players.

• **In 2007 McCoist became assistant manager of Rangers and was promoted to the top job in 2011 following Walter Smith's retirement. His first season in charge of the Glasgow giants was an extremely difficult one as Rangers were plunged into an ever-deepening financial catastrophe, a crisis which eventually resulted in the club's liquidation and demotion from the SPL.**

MANAGER OF THE YEAR

Manchester United boss Sir Alex Ferguson has won the FA Premier League Manager of the Year award a record 10 times, once more than all the other winning managers put together. He also won the old Manager of the Year award in 1993, giving him a total of 11 triumphs.

• Arsène Wenger (in 1998, 2002 and 2004) and Jose Mourinho (2005 and 2006) are the only other managers to win the award more than once since it was introduced in the 1993/94 season.

• Only three managers have won the award while in charge of a club which did not win the title that season: George Burley, who was honoured in 2001 after leading Ipswich to fifth place in the Premiership a year after winning promotion; Harry Redknapp, who claimed top spot in 2010 after guiding Tottenham to fourth place and a Champions League place; and Newcastle boss Alan Pardew, who collected the award after the Magpies finished fifth in 2012.

• **The most successful manager in the pre-Premiership era was Liverpool's Bob Paisley, who won six Manager of the Year awards between 1976 and 1983.**

MANCHESTER CITY

Year founded: 1887
Ground: Etihad Stadium (47,726)
Previous name: Ardwick
Nickname: The Citizens
Biggest win: 12-0 v Liverpool Stanley (1890)
Heaviest defeat: 1-9 v Everton (1906)

City have their roots in a church team which was renamed Ardwick in 1887 and became founder members of the Second Division five years later. In 1894, after suffering financial difficulties, the club was reformed under its present name.

• **Now owned by Sheikh Mansour of the Abu Dhabi Royal Family, City are the richest club in the world. Following a massive spending spree on the likes of Mario Balotelli, David Silva and Yaya Toure, the Sheikh received the first return on his huge investment in 2011 when City won the FA Cup, their first trophy for 35 years, after beating Stoke City 1-0 in the final at Wembley. More silverware followed the next season as City won the Premier League, their first league title since 1968. It was a close run thing, though, as the Citizens only pipped their arch rivals Manchester United on goal difference thanks to Sergio Aguero's last-minute winner against QPR in the final match of the season, making the 2011/12 title race the closest in Premier League history.**

• Prior to the modern era, the late 1960s were the most successful period in City's history, a side featuring the likes of Colin Bell, Francis Lee and Mike Summerbee winning the league title (1968), the FA Cup (1969), the League Cup (1970) and the European Cup Winners' Cup (also in 1970) and for a short time usurping Manchester United as the city's premier club.

• **City also won the league title in 1937. Incredibly, the following season they were relegated to the Second Division despite scoring more goals than any other side in the division. To this day they remain the only league champions to suffer the drop in the following campaign.**

• Eric Brook, an ever-present in that initial title-winning season, is City's joint leading scorer (along with 1920s marksman Tommy Johnson) with 158 league goals between 1928 and 1940. The club's record appearance maker is Alan Oakes, who turned out 564 times in the sky blue shirt between 1958 and 1976.

Manchester City lift their first league trophy since 1968

• Apart from their most recent triumph City have won the FA Cup four other times and, in 1926, were the first club to reach the final and be relegated in the same season. A 1-0 defeat by Bolton at Wembley ensured a grim season ended on a depressing note.

• The 1957/58 season was more enjoyable, especially for fans who like goals, as City scored 104 times while conceding 100 – the first and only time this 'double century' has been achieved. At the other end of the scale, City managed to score just ten goals at home in the 2006/07 season, the lowest-ever total by an English club.

• City have won the title for the second tier of English football a record seven times, most recently in 2002 when they returned to the Premiership under then manager Kevin Keegan. Four years earlier the club experienced their lowest-ever moment when they dropped into the third tier for the first and only time in their history – the first European trophy winners to sink this low.

• The highest attendance ever at an English club ground, 84,569, saw City beat Stoke 1-0 at their old Maine Road stadium in the sixth round of the FA Cup in 1934.

• The club's most expensive purchase is Argentinian wonderkid Sergio Aguero, who signed from Atletico Madrid for around £38 million in July 2011. Shaun Wright-Phillips, now with QPR, boosted the club's coffers by a record £21 million when he joined Chelsea in 2005.

TOP 10

MOST PREMIER LEAGUE POINTS IN A SEASON

1.	Chelsea (2004/05)	95 points
2.	Manchester United (1993/94)	92 points
3.	Manchester United (1999/2000)	91 points
4.	Chelsea (2005/06)	91 points
5.	Arsenal (2003/04)	90 points
	Manchester United (2008/09)	90 points
7.	Blackburn Rovers (1994/95)	89 points
	Manchester United (2006/07)	89 points
	Manchester City (2011/12)	89 points
	Manchester United (2011/12)	89 points

• City's most famous supporters are the Gallagher brothers, Liam and Noel, formerly of rock band Oasis, while boxer Ricky Hatton is also a devoted fan of the club.

MANCHESTER UNITED

Year founded: 1878
Ground: Old Trafford (75,811)
Previous name: Newton Heath
Nickname: Red Devils
Biggest win: 10-0 v Anderlecht (1956)
Heaviest defeat: 0-7 v Blackburn (1926), v Aston Villa (1930) and v Wolverhampton Wanderers (1931)

The club was founded in 1878 as Newton Heath, a works team for employees of the Lancashire and Yorkshire Railway. In 1892 Newton Heath (who played in yellow-and-green-halved shirts) were elected to the Football League but a decade later went bankrupt, only to be immediately reformed as Manchester United with the help of a local brewer, John Davies.

• United are the most successful club in the history of English football, having won the league title a record 19 times and the FA Cup a record 11 times. The Red Devils have been the dominant force of the Premiership era, winning the title a record 12 times under long-serving manager Sir Alex Ferguson and never finishing outside the top three since the league

Usain Bolt: The world's fastest Man Utd fan!

was formed in 1992.

• United were the first English club to win the Double on three separate occasions, in 1994, 1996 and 1999. The last of these triumphs was particularly memorable as the club also went on to win the Champions League, beating Bayern Munich 2-1 in the final in Barcelona thanks to two late goals by Teddy Sheringham and Ole Gunner Solskjaer, to record English football's first ever Treble.

• Under legendary manager Sir Matt Busby United became the first ever English club to win the European Cup in 1968, when they beat Benfica 4-1 in the final at Wembley. Victory was especially sweet for Sir Matt who, a decade earlier, had narrowly survived the Munich air crash which claimed the lives of eight of his players as the team returned from a European Cup fixture in Belgrade. United also won European football's top club prize in 2008, beating Chelsea in the Champions League final on penalties in Moscow.

• United won the FA Cup for the first time in 1909, beating Bristol City 1-0 in the final. The club's total of 18 appearances in the final (11 wins, seven defeats) is a record for the competition.

• The club's history, though, has not always been glorious. The 1930s were a particularly

IS THAT A FACT?
Somewhat confusingly for their fans at the time, Manchester United signed three unrelated players with the surname Robertson (Alex, Tom and another Alex) in the space of just five days in May 1903.

grim decade for United, who were threatened with relegation to the old Third Division on the final day of the 1933/34 season. In a bid to change their luck, United swapped their red shirts for cherry and white hoops for the first and only time, and beat Millwall 2-0 away to stay in the Second Division.

• Old Trafford has the highest capacity of any club ground in Britain but, strangely, when United set an all-time Football League attendance record of 83,260 for their home game against Arsenal on 17th January 1948 they were playing at Maine Road, home of local rivals Manchester City. This was because Old Trafford was badly damaged by German bombs during the Second World War, forcing United to use their neighbours' ground in the immediate post-war period.

• **United's leading appearance maker is 37-year-old veteran Ryan Giggs, who has played in an incredible 909 games in all competitions for the club since making his debut in 1991. He is also the only player to have scored at least one goal in every Premier League season.**

• The club's highest goalscorer is Sir Bobby Charlton, who banged in 199 league goals for the club between 1956 and 1973. Charlton is also United's most capped international, playing 106 times for England in an illustrious career. Denis Law, another 1960s United legend, scored a record 18 hat-tricks for the club.

• **United recorded the biggest-ever victory in Premier League history on 4th March 1995 when they thrashed Ipswich 9-0 at Old Trafford, with striker Andy Cole scoring five of the goals to set another Premiership record.**

• In the last of a record-equalling three consecutive title-winning campaigns, in 2008/09, United went a record 14 league games (a total of 1,334 minutes) without conceding a single goal.

• **Known for many years as a big-spending club, United's record signing is Bulgarian international striker Dimitar Berbatov, who cost £30.75 million when he moved from Tottenham in 2008. The club's most expensive sale is former Old Trafford hero Cristiano Ronaldo, who joined Real Madrid for a world record £80 million in 2009.**

• One of the most widely supported clubs around the world, United are

followed by a host of celebrity fans including actor Steve Coogan (aka Alan Partridge), golfer Rory McIlroy and Stone Roses singer Ian Brown.

HONOURS

Division 1 champions 1908, 1911, 1952, 1956, 1957, 1965, 1967
Premier League champions 1993, 1994, 1996, 1997, 1999, 2000, 2001, 2003, 2007, 2008, 2009, 2011
Division 2 champions 1936, 1975
FA Cup 1909, 1948, 1963, 1977, 1983, 1985, 1990, 1994, 1996, 1999, 2004
League Cup 1992, 2006, 2009, 2010
Double 1994, 1996, 1999
European Cup/Champions League *1968, 1999, 2008*
European Cup Winners' Cup 1991
European Super Cup 1991
Intercontinental Cup/Club World Cup 1999, 2008

Born: Jesi, Italy, 27th November 1964
Managerial career:
2001-02 Fiorentina
2002-04 Lazio
2004-08 Inter Milan
2009- Manchester City

Roberto Mancini became the first Manchester City manager since Tony Book in 1976 to lead his club to a major trophy when his side beat Stoke 1-0 in the 2011 FA Cup final at Wembley. The following year Mancini was faced with the biggest test of his managerial career when Argentinian striker Carlos Tevez refused to play for the club, but he rose to the challenge brilliantly, rallied his players behind him and guided City to their first top-flight title since 1968.

• **Mancini began his managerial career at cash-strapped Fiorentina, who he led to the Coppa Italia before moving to Lazio in 2002. He won another Coppa Italia with the Rome club, but after two years moved on to Inter Milan.**

'Hey Fergie, look what I've got!'

• During a four-year stint at the San Siro, Mancini turned Inter into the dominant force in Italian football. His team were awarded the 2006 Serie A title after Juventus were stripped of the honour, but the following season Inter won the championship in some style, winning an Italian record 17 consecutive league games at one stage and ending the campaign with a record 97 points – an amazing 22 points ahead of runners-up Roma. A third title followed in 2008, but Mancini's incredible domestic success was counterbalanced by repeated failures in the Champions League and he was sacked at the end of the season.

• **An intelligent striker in his playing days, Mancini won the Scudetto and the Cup Winners' Cup with both Sampdoria and Lazio and played 36 times for Italy. He also enjoyed a brief spell in the Premier League with Leicester City in 2001 before moving into management.**

DIEGO MARADONA

Born: Buenos Aires, 30th October 1960
Position: Striker/midfielder
Club career:
1976-80 Argentinos Juniors 167 (115)
1980-82 Boca Juniors 40 (28)
1982-84 Barcelona 36 (22)
1984-91 Napoli 186 (83)
1992-93 Sevilla 25 (4)
1995-97 Boca Juniors 29 (7)
International record:
1977-94 Argentina 91 (34)

Diego Maradona: Arguably the greatest player of all time

The best player in the world in the 1980s, Diego Maradona is considered by many to be the greatest footballer ever.

• During his career in his native Argentina, then in Spain and Italy, he smashed three transfer records. First, his £1 million move from Argentinos Juniors to Boca Juniors in 1980 was a world record for a teenager. Then he broke the world transfer record when he joined Barcelona from Boca for £4.2 million in 1982, and again when he signed for Napoli for £6.9 million in 1984.

• A superb dribbler who used his low centre of gravity to great effect, Maradona was almost impossible to mark. He was idolised at Napoli, who he led to a first-ever Italian title in 1987 and a first European trophy two years later, when they won the UEFA Cup.

• He made his international debut aged 16 in 1977 and went on to play at four World Cups, captaining his country in a record 16 games at the finals. His greatest triumph came in 1986 when, after scoring the goals that beat England (including the infamous 'Hand of God' goal which he punched into the net) and Belgium in the quarter and semi-finals, he skippered Argentina to victory in the final against West Germany. He also led his side to the 1990 final against the same opponents.

• However, Maradona's international career ended in disgrace when he was thrown out of the 1994 World Cup in the USA after failing a drugs test. He had previously been hit with a worldwide 15-month ban from football in 1991 after testing positive for cocaine.

• **Despite these blots on his reputation, Maradona was voted 'The Player of the Century' by more than half of those who took part in a worldwide FIFA internet poll in 2000. In 2008 he became head coach of Argentina, but resigned two years later after his side were thrashed 4-0 by Germany in the World Cup quarter-finals.**

MASCOTS

In one of the most bizarre football sights ever, Wolves mascot Wolfie traded punches with his Bristol City counterpart City Cat during a half-time penalty shoot-out competition at Ashton Gate in 2002. City Cat, who was backed up by three little piggies representing a local company, got the better of the fracas which had to be broken up by stewards.

• **Bury mascot Robbie the Bobby – who, ironically, has the appearance of a policeman – was sent off from the touchline three times in as many months in 2001. Two of his dismissals were for over-exuberant goal celebrations, while the third was**

IS THAT A FACT?
Oldham mascot Chaddy the Owl ruptured ankle ligaments and had to be rushed to hospital after falling off a BMX bike before the Latics' match away to Carlisle in 2009.

for fighting with Cardiff City mascot, Barclay the Bluebird.

• In April 2012 Borussia Dortmund manager Jurgen Klopp had to apologise after the club mascot, a bumblebee called Emma, was caught on camera pretending to urinate on the Bayern Munich team bus after Dortmund had beaten Bayern at home in the Bundesliga.

• The Mascot Grand National, an annual race over hurdles between football and other sporting mascots, has been held at Huntingdon Racecourse since 1999. The first winner was Birmingham's Beau Brummie Bulldog, while Oldham's Chaddy the Owl was the first mascot to retain the title.

• Luis Moreno of Deportivo Pereira became the most hated man in Colombia in 2011 when he cruelly booted the owl mascot of opposing club Atletico Junior de Barranquilla off the pitch after it was stunned by the ball. The owl later died, while Moreno was fined and suspended for two games.

• The first World Cup mascot, a Union Jack-draped lion called World Cup Willie, was designed for the 1966 tournament in England. The most recent mascot, for the 2010 tournament in South Africa, was Zakumi, a green-haired lion.

MATCH-FIXING

The first recorded incidence of match-fixing occurred in 1900 when Jack Hillman, goalkeeper with relegation-threatened Burnley, was alleged to have offered a bribe to the Nottingham Forest captain. Hillman was found guilty of the charges by a joint Football Association and Football League commission and banned for one year.

• Nine players received bans after Manchester United beat Liverpool at Old Trafford in April 1915. A Liverpool player later admitted the result had been fixed in a Manchester pub before the match. For his part in the scandal, United's Enoch West was banned for life – although the punishment was later waived... when West was 62!

• In the mid-1960s English football was rocked by a match-fixing scandal when former Everton player Jimmy Gauld revealed in a newspaper interview that a number of games had been rigged as part of a betting coup. Gauld implicated three Sheffield Wednesday players in the scam, including England internationals Tony Kay and Peter Swan. The trio were later sentenced to four months in prison and banned for life from football. Ringleader Gauld fared even worse, receiving a four-year prison term.

• In 1978 World Cup hosts Argentina needed to beat Peru by four clear goals to reach the final of the competition.

It has been alleged (though never proved) that the Argentinian military junta offered the Peruvian government 35,000 tonnes of free grain and the unfreezing of $50 million in credits for their team to play below par. Argentina cruised to a 6-0 victory and went on to win the tournament.

• Following a match-fixing scandal in South Korea in 2011 ten players were given life bans from the game, while all other players suspected of cheating in the future were warned that they would have to take a lie detector test to prove their innocence.

• In 2005 German referee Robert Hoyzer was jailed for more than two years after admitting fixing, or trying to fix, nine matches for a Croatian organised crime syndicate who rewarded him with £46,000 in cash and a flat-screen TV.

• In 2011 former Italy international Giuseppe Signori was among dozens of people arrested by police as part of an investigation into a match-fixing ring. Suspicion focused on a number of Serie B and Serie A fixture, with the most serious allegation being that players had their drinks spiked with drugs by team-mates in an attempt to hamper their performance.

Sir Alex Ferguson always consults Fred the Red on tactics

SIR STANLEY MATTHEWS

Born: Stoke, 1st February 1915
Died: 23rd February 2000
Position: Winger
Club career:
1932-47 Stoke City 259 (51)
1947-61 Blackpool 379 (17)
1961-65 Stoke City 59 (3)
International record:
1934-57 England
54 (11)

Nicknamed 'the Wizard of the Dribble' for his magnificent skills on the ball, Stanley Matthews was one of the greatest footballers of all time. His club career spanned a record 33 years and, incredibly, he played his last game in the First Division for Stoke City five days after his 50th birthday. He remains the oldest player to appear in the top flight.

• **Matthews' England career was almost as lengthy, his 54 appearances for his country spanning 23 years between 1934 and 1957. He made his last appearance for the Three Lions at the age of 42, setting another record.**

• A brilliant winger who possessed superb close control, Matthews inspired Blackpool to victory in the 1953 FA Cup final after the Seasiders came back from 3-1 down to beat Bolton 4-3. Despite a hat-trick by his team-mate Stan Mortensen, the match is remembered as 'the Matthews final'. He had never won an FA Cup winners' medal before and the whole country (outside of Bolton) was willing Matthews to succeed.

• **The first player to be voted Footballer of the Year (in 1948) and European Footballer of the Year (another first in 1956), Matthews was knighted in 1965 – the only footballer to be so honoured while still playing. When he died in 2000 more than 100,000 people lined the streets of Stoke to pay tribute to one of the true legends of world football.**

LIONEL MESSI

Born: Rosario, Argentina, 24th June 1987
Position: Winger
Club career:
2004- Barcelona 214 (169)
International record:
2005- Argentina 71 (27)

Rated by many as the best player in the world, Lionel Messi is Barcelona's all-time leading scorer with 253 goals in all competitions. No fewer than 70 of those came in the 2011/12 season and with the little Argentinian also hitting the target twice for his country, his total of 72 goals set a new world record for a player in a single campaign.

Spanish defenders saw this famous goal celebration 70 times in 2011/12!

• Life, though, could have been very different for Messi, who suffered from a growth hormone deficiency as a child in Argentina. However, his outrageous talent was such that Barcelona were prepared to move him and his family to Europe when he was aged just 13 and pay for his medical treatment.

• Putting these problems behind him, he has flourished to the extent that in 2009 he was named both World Player of the Year and European Player of the Year, a year after being runner-up in both polls, and in 2010 he was the inaugural winner of the FIFA Ballon d'Or – an award he retained the following year. A brilliant dribbler who can bamboozle the most experienced of defenders with his mesmeric ball skills, Messi helped Barcelona win La Liga and the Champions League in both 2009 and 2011. The next year he became the first player to be top scorer

in four consecutive Champions League campaigns (2009-12) and he also set another record for the competition when he hit five goals in a single game against Bayer Leverkusen.

• Messi made his international debut in 2005 but it was a forgettable occasion – he was sent off after just 40 seconds for elbowing a Hungarian defender who was pulling his shirt.

Happier times followed in 2007 when he was voted Player of the Tournament at the Copa America and in 2008 when he won a gold medal with the Argentine football team at the Beijing Olympics. At the 2010 World Cup in South Africa Messi produced some thrilling displays, but he failed to score a single goal and was left in tears after Argentina's 4-0 thrashing by Germany at the quarter-final stage.

• The legendary Diego Maradona has hailed Messi as his true successor, saying, "He has something different to any other player in the world."

IS THAT A FACT?
Along with Mario Gomez, Filippo Inzaghi and Michael Owen, the brilliant Lionel Messi is one of just four players to have scored three hat-tricks in the Champions League.

TOP 10

TOP SCORERS IN LA LIGA 2011/12

1. Lionel Messi (Barcelona) 50 goals
2. Cristiano Ronaldo (Real Madrid) 46 goals
3. Falcao (Atletico Madrid) 24 goals
4. Higuain (Real Madrid) 22 goals
5. Karim Benzema (Real Madrid) 21 goals
6. Roberto Soldado (Valencia) 17 goals
7. Fernando Llorente (Athletic Bilbao) 17 goals
8. Ruben Castro (Real Betis) 16 goals
9. Arouna Kone (Levante) 15 goals
   Miguel Perez Cuesta (Rayo Vallecano) 15 goals

MIDDLESBROUGH

Year founded: 1876
Ground: Riverside Stadium (34,988)
Nickname: Boro
Biggest win: 11-0 v Scarborough (1890)
Heaviest defeat: 0-9 v Blackburn Rovers (1954)

Founded by members of the Middlesbrough Cricket Club at the Albert Park Hotel in 1876, the club turned professional in 1889 before reverting to amateur status three years later. Winners of the FA Amateur Cup in both 1895 and 1898, the club turned pro for a second time in 1899 and was elected to the Football League in the same year.

• In 1905 Middlesbrough became the first club to sign a player for a four-figure transfer fee when they forked out £1,000 for Sunderland and England striker Alf Common. On his Boro debut Common paid back some of the fee by scoring the winner at Sheffield United... the Teesiders' first away win for two years!

• The club had to wait over a century before winning a major trophy but finally broke their duck in 2004 with a 2-1 victory over Bolton in the League Cup final at the Millennium Stadium, Cardiff.

MILLWALL

• Two years later Middlesbrough reached the UEFA Cup final, after twice overturning three-goal deficits earlier in the competition. There was no happy ending, though, as Boro were thrashed 4-0 by Sevilla in the final in Eindhoven.

• In 1997 the club were deducted three points by the FA for calling off a Premier League fixture at Blackburn at short notice after illness and injury ravaged their squad. The penalty resulted in Boro being relegated from the Premier League at the end of the season. To add to their supporters' disappointment the club was also beaten in the finals of the League Cup and FA Cup in the same campaign.

• The lowest moment in Middlesbrough's history, though, came in the summer of 1986 when a financial crisis led to the club almost being wound up. At the last minute a consortium led by chairman Steve Gibson stepped in to save the club from bankruptcy.

• In 1926/27 striker George Camsell hit an astonishing 59 league goals, including a record nine hat-tricks, for Boro as the club won the Second Division championship. His tally set a new Football League record and, although it was beaten by Everton's Dixie Dean the following season, Camsell still holds the divisional record. An ex-miner, Camsell went on to score a club record 325 league goals for Boro and also notched an impressive 18 goals in just nine appearances for England.

• Middlesbrough's record signing is Brazilian striker Afonso Alves, who moved to Teeside from Dutch club Heerenveen in 2008 for £12.8 million but, disappointingly for Boro' fans, failed to live up to his hefty transfer fee.

HONOURS
Division 2 champions 1927, 1929, 1974
First Division champions 1995
League Cup 2006
FA Amateur Cup 1895, 1898

MILLWALL

Year founded: 1885
Ground: The New Den (20,146)
Previous name: Millwall Rovers
Nickname: The Lions
Biggest win: 9-1 v Torquay (1927) and v Coventry (1927)
Heaviest defeat: 1-9 v Aston Villa (1946)

The club was founded as Millwall Rovers in 1885 by workers at local jam and marmalade factory, Morton and Co. In 1920 they joined the Third Division, gaining a reputation as a club with some of the most fiercely partisan fans in the country.

• In 1988 Millwall won the Second Division title to gain promotion to the top flight for the first time in their history. The Lions enjoyed a few brief weeks at the top of the league pyramid in the autumn of 1988 but were brought back to earth with a bump when they were relegated two years later.

• The club's greatest moment, though, came in 2004 when they reached their first FA Cup final. Despite losing 3-0 to Manchester United, the Lions made history by becoming the first club from outside the top flight to contest the final in the Premier League era, while substitute Curtis Weston set a new record for the youngest player to appear in the final (17 years and 119 days).

• Neil Harris is the club's all-time leading scorer with 125 goals in two spells at the Den between 1998 and 2011. Hardman defender Barry Kitchener has made more appearances for Millwall than any other player, turning out in 602 games in all competitions between 1967 and 1982.

• On their way to winning the Division Three (South) championship in 1928 Millwall scored 87 goals at home, an all-time Football League record.

• In 1974 Millwall hosted the first league match to be played on a Sunday. To get around the law at the time, admission for the Lions' game with Fulham was by 'programme only' – the cost of the programme being the same as a match ticket.

• In 1999 Millwall took 47,000 fans to Wembley for the final of the Football League Trophy – the most ever by a club in a final at the national stadium. Despite only bringing around 8,000 fans down to London, their opponents Wigan still won the game 1-0.

HONOURS
Division 2 champions 1988
Division 3 (S) champions 1928, 1938
Second Division champions 2001
Division 4 champions 1962

MILTON KEYNES DONS

Year founded: 2004
Ground: stadium:mk (22,000)
Nickname: The Dons
Biggest win: 6-0 v Nantwich Town (2011)
Heaviest defeat: 0-5 v Hartlepool (2005), v Huddersfield (2006), v Tottenham (2006) and v Rochdale (2007)

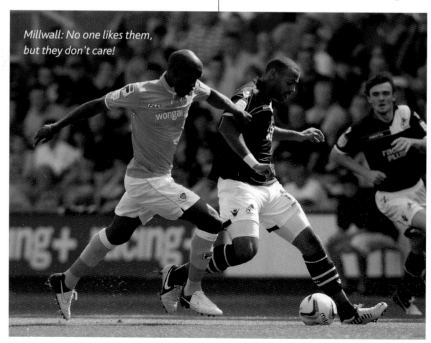

Millwall: No one likes them, but they don't care!

The club was effectively formed in 2004 when Wimbledon FC were controversially allowed to re-locate to Milton Keynes on the ruling of a three-man FA commission despite the opposition of the club's supporters, the Football League and the FA.

• **Despite pledging to Wimbledon fans that they would not change their name, badge or colours, within a few seasons all three of these things had happened, reinforcing the impression amongst many in the game that the MK Dons are English football's first 'franchise'.**

• The MK Dons have since handed back to Merton Council all the honours and trophies won by Wimbledon FC and claimed by AFC Wimbledon, the club started up by angry Wimbledon supporters which was promoted to the Football League in 2011 despite the claim by the FA Commission that the creation of such a team would "not be in the wider interests of football".

• **The MK Dons won their first trophy in 2008 when, under then manager Paul Ince, they beat Grimsby Town 2-0 in the Football League Trophy final at Wembley. Later that season they lifted the League Two title.**

• Appointed MK Dons boss in 2010 when he was just 29, Karl Robinson is the youngest manager in the Football League.

> HONOURS
> *League Two champions 2008*
> *Football League Trophy 2008*

MLS

Founded in 1993 as part of the United States' bid to hold the following year's World Cup, Major League Soccer (MLS) is made up of 16 American and three Canadian clubs, all of whom are owned by the league. Owing to the huge distances teams have to travel, the MLS is split into Eastern and Western sections with the club gaining the most points at the end of the season claiming the Supporters' Shield.

• **Along with LA Galaxy, D.C. United have won a record four Supporters' Shields since the league began in 1996. The Washington DC-based outfit have also won a record four MLS Cup championship finals, a play-off competition for the top 10 clubs at the end of the regular season.**

• Among the former Premier League stars to have played in the MLS towards the end of their careers are David Beckham (LA Galaxy), Thierry Henry (New York Red Bulls) and Freddie Ljungberg (Seattle Sounders).

LUKA MODRIC

> **Born:** Zagreb, 9th September 1985
> **Position:** Midfielder
> **Club career:**
> 2003-08 Dinamo Zagreb 112 (31)
> 2003 Zrinjski Mostar (loan) 22 (8)
> 2004 Inter Zapresic (loan) 18 (4)
> 2008-12 Tottenham Hotspur 127 (13)
> 2012- Real Madrid
> **International record:**
> 2006- Croatia 57 (8)

A highly creative midfielder who can pass, dribble and shoot with both feet, Luka Modric signed for Real Madrid from Tottenham in August 2012 for around £30 million.

• **Before joining Spurs in 2008, Modric had helped Dinamo Zagreb win the Croatian league three times on the trot, and in 2007 his superb displays earned him the Croatian Player of the Year award.**

• The slightly-built playmaker recovered from a broken leg in 2009 to help Spurs qualify for the Champions League for the first time the next year. In the summer of 2011, though, he agitated for a move to Chelsea, but was forced to honour his contract by Spurs chairman Daniel Levy. The following season Modric was one of Spurs' best players as the north Londoners just missed out on Champions League qualification despite finishing fourth in the Premier League.

• **Modric won his first cap for Croatia in a 3-2 friendly win over Argentina in 2006. He was an influential figure for the Croats as they twice beat England in the qualifiers for Euro 2008 and at the finals he became only the second ever Croatian player to be voted into the UEFA Team of the Tournament.**

IS THAT A FACT?
During the 2011/12 season, Tottenham midfielder Luka Modric made more passes (1,440) in the opposition half than any other Premier League player.

A picture England fans will never tire of looking at: Bobby Moore holds aloft the World Cup trophy in 1966

BOBBY MOORE

Born: Barking, 12th April 1941
Died: 24th February 1993
Position: Defender
Club career:
1958-74 West Ham United 544 (22)
1974-77 Fulham 124 (1)
1976 San Antonio Thunder 24 (1)
1978 Seattle Sounders 7 (0)
International record:
1962-73 England 108 (2)

The first and only Englishman to lift the World Cup, Bobby Moore captained England on 90 occasions – a record shared with Billy Wright.

• **Moore's total of 108 caps was a record until it was surpassed by Peter Shilton in 1989, but he was England's most-capped outfield player until David Beckham passed him in 2009.**

• At club level, Moore won the FA Cup with West Ham in 1964 and the European Cup Winners' Cup the following year. Then, in 1966, he made it a Wembley treble when England beat West Germany in the World Cup final. England boss Sir Alf Ramsey later paid tribute to his skipper and most reliable defender, saying, "He was the supreme professional. Without him England would never have won the World Cup."

• **In the same year Moore was voted the BBC Sports Personality of the Year – the first footballer to win the honour.**

• The world of football mourned Moore's death when he died of cancer in 1993, but he has not been forgotten. A decade later he was selected by the FA as England's 'Golden Player' of the previous 50 years

and, in 2007, a huge bronze statue of England's greatest captain was unveiled outside the new Wembley.

MORECAMBE

Year founded: 1920
Ground: Globe Arena (6,476)
Nickname: The Shrimps
Biggest win: 8-0 v Fleetwood Town (1993)
Heaviest defeat: 0-7 v Leek Town (1998)

Founded in 1920 after a meeting at the local West View Hotel, Morecambe joined the Lancashire Combination League that same year and subsequently spent the next 87 years in non-league football.

• **The greatest moment in the club's history came in 2007 when The Shrimps beat Exeter 2-1 in the Conference play-off final at Wembley to win promotion to the Football League.**

• Morecambe's first outing in the League Cup in 2007 saw them pull off a major shock when they beat Championship outfit Preston 2-1 at Deepdale. The Shrimps then knocked out Wolves before crashing out to Sheffield United, who beat them 5-0 in the third round.

• **In 2010 Morecambe reached the League Two play-offs, but a 6-0 hammering by Dagenham and Redbridge – the biggest-ever play-off defeat – in the first leg of the semi-final ended their promotion hopes.**

Morecambe (in red) take on Everton in a pre-season friendly in July 2012

MOTHERWELL

Year founded: 1886
Ground: Fir Park (13,742)
Nickname: The Well
Biggest win: 12-1 v Dundee United (1954))
Heaviest defeat: 0-8 v Aberdeen (1979)

Motherwell were founded in 1886 following the merger of two local factory-based sides, Alpha and Glencairn. The club turned pro in 1893 and, in the same year, joined the newly formed Scottish Second Division.

• **The club enjoyed its heyday in the 1930s, winning the league title for the first and only time in 1932 and finishing as runners-up in the Scottish Cup three times in the same decade.**

• Striker Willie McFadyen scored a remarkable 52 league goals for The Well when they won the title in 1931/32, a Scottish top flight record that still stands today. The club's all-time leading scorer, though, is Hugh Ferguson, who notched 284 goals between 1916 and 1925.

• **Motherwell had to wait until 1952 before they won the Scottish Cup for the first time, and they did it in some style thrashing Dundee 4-0 in the final. Another success followed in 1991, The Well beating Dundee United 4-3 in an exciting final.**

• Scottish international striker John Spencer is the most expensive player to arrive at Fir Park, costing £500,000 when he joined the club from Everton in 1999. Five years earlier Motherwell received a club record £1.75 million when they sold Phil O'Donnell to Celtic. O'Donnell returned to Fir Park later but, tragically, died after collapsing on the pitch during a match against Dundee United in 2007.

• **In May 2010 Motherwell were involved in the highest-scoring game ever in the SPL, coming from 6-2 down to draw 6-6 with Hibs.**

HONOURS
Division 1 champions 1932
First Division champions 1982, 1985
Division 2 champions 1954, 1969
Scottish Cup 1952, 1991
League Cup 1951

JOSE MOURINHO

Born: Setubal, Portugal, 26th January 1963
Managerial career:
2000 Benfica
2001-02 Uniao Leiria
2002-04 Porto
2004-07 Chelsea
2008-10 Inter Milan
2010- Real Madrid

Outspoken Real Madrid manager Jose Mourinho is one of just four coaches to have won the domestic title in four different countries and the only one to have claimed the championship in England, Italy and Spain.

• **Mourinho started out as Bobby Robson's assistant at Sporting Lisbon, Porto and Barcelona before briefly managing Benfica in 2000. Two years later he returned to Porto, where he won two Portuguese league titles and the UEFA Cup before becoming Europe's most sought-after young manager when his well-drilled side claimed the Champions League trophy in 2004.**

• Shortly after this triumph, Mourinho replaced Claudio Ranieri as Chelsea manager, styling himself as a "Special One" in his first press conference. He certainly lived up to his billing, as his expensively-assembled Blues team won back-to-back Premier League titles in 2005 and 2006, the FA Cup in 2007 and the League Cup in both 2005 and 2007.

• **Often embroiled in controversy, Mourinho was fined a record £200,000 (later reduced to £75,000 on appeal) in 2005 for breaking Premier League rules by secretly meeting Arsenal defender Ashley Cole to talk about a possible move to Chelsea. Two years later he sensationally left the club after falling out with Blues owner Roman Abramovich.**

• A year after quitting Chelsea, Mourinho took charge of Italian giants Inter Milan and led them to the Serie A title in 2009. The following year he did even better, guiding Inter to a treble which included the Champions League, before leaving the San Siro to take over the reins at Real Madrid. He had to be satisfied with the Spanish Cup in his first season at the Bernabeu, but in 2012 his Real team raced to the title in some style, racking up a record 100 points tally while also scoring a record number of goals, 121.

Jose Mourinho's introduction of 'the Haka' caused a stir when he arrived at Real Madrid

DAVID MOYES

Born: Glasgow, 25th April 1963
Managerial career:
1998-2002 Preston North End
2002- Everton

Having joined Everton in 2002 as successor to fellow Scot Walter Smith, David Moyes is now the third longest-serving Premier League manager behind Arsène Wenger and Sir Alex Ferguson.

• **Moyes' first managerial job was at Preston who he led to the Division Two (now League One) title in 2000. The following year North End almost made it into the Premiership, but lost out to Bolton in the play-off final.**

• In his first season in charge at Goodison Park in 2002/03, Moyes was voted the League Managers' Association Manager of the Year after guiding the Toffees to a creditable seventh place in the Premier League. Two years later he won the award again after Everton finished fourth, one place ahead of deadly rivals Liverpool, and qualified for the preliminary stage of the Champions League.

• **A journeyman centre half in his playing days, Moyes won a championship medal with Celtic in 1982 and later played for a number of clubs, including Bristol City, Dunfermline and Preston.**

NANI

Born: Cape Verde, 17th November 1986
Position: Winger
Club career:
2005-07 Sporting Lisbon 58 (9)
2007- Manchester United 124 (25)
International record:
2006- Portugal 59 (13)

GARY NEVILLE

Born: Bury, 18th February 1975
Position: Defender
Club career:
1992-2011 Manchester United 400 (5)
International record:
1995-2007 England 85 (0)

Luis Carlos Almeida da Cunha, or Nani as he is better known, was one of just four Premier League players short-listed for the prestigious FIFA Ballon d'Or in 2011 after enjoying his best season to date with Manchester United in 2010/11, his exciting wing play helping the Red Devils top the Premier League table and earning himself a place in the PFA Premier League Team of the Year.

• Abandoned by his parents and brought up by an aunt in Portugal, Nani had a difficult childhood, but his talent with a ball at his feet was always evident and he graduated from a small local team to sign for Lisbon giants Sporting. In his last season at the club in 2007 he won the Portuguese Cup before moving to Manchester United in a £14 million deal.

• Nani was a bit-part player in his early years at Old Trafford and rather in the shadow of fellow Portuguese winger Cristiano Ronaldo, but he still made a valuable contribution to United's Premier League and Champions League double success in 2008, coming off the bench to score one of the penalties in the shoot-out against Chelsea in Moscow.

• Famed for his back-flip goal celebration as well as his trickery on the flanks, Nani scored on his debut for Portugal in a friendly against Denmark in 2006 and now has 59 international caps.

England's highest-capped right-back, Gary Neville is one of the most decorated players in the modern game, winning eight Premier League titles, three FA Cups, two League Cups and the Champions League in an illustrious career with his one and only club, Manchester United.

• A fixture in his country's defence for over a decade, Neville played in more games in the finals of the European Championships, 11, than any other England player. Along with his younger brother Phil, Neville also holds the record for the most England games played by a pair of brothers, 144 – three more than the Charltons of 1966 World Cup fame managed in total. In addition, the Nevilles played in 31 England games together, to set another record.

• After retiring from the game during the 2010/11 season, Neville became a pundit for Sky Sports, earning rave reviews for his thought-provoking insights into the game and surprising those who feared he would be biased towards Manchester United with his impartial viewpoint in his new role.

• In 2012 Neville joined Roy Hodgson's backroom staff on a four-year contract, and was part of the coaching team that assisted the new Three Lions boss at the European championships in Poland and the Ukraine.

'Just call me Nani, it'll be a lot quicker!', says Luis Carlos Almeida da Cunha

NEYMAR

Born: Mogi das Cruzes, Brazil, 5th
February 1992
Position: Striker
Club career:
2009- Santos 88 (42)
International record:
2010- Brazil 18 (9)

Voted South American Footballer of the
Year in 2011 by a record margin, 20-year-
old Neymar has become a transfer target
for every big European club, with the
likes of Real Madrid, Chelsea, Manchester
City and Inter Milan all keen to buy the
brilliant Santos youngster.
• **A superbly talented player who
is stronger than his slight frame
suggests, Neymar grabbed the
attention of Brazilian football fans
soon after making his Santos debut**
in 2009 when he scored five goals
in a cup match against Guarani. A
campaign urging then Brazil boss
Dunga to take the teenager to the
2010 World Cup was quickly launched,
with 14,000 people signing a petition,
but in the event Neymar was not
selected for the squad. He eventually
won his first cap just after the
tournament, scoring with a header in a
2-0 friendly win over the USA.
• In April 2011 Neymar was sent off
in bizarre circumstances in a Copa
Libertadores match against Chilean side
Colo Colo. After scoring a magnificent
individual goal he celebrated by donning
a mask of himself thrown onto the pitch
by a Santos supporter. Unfortunately for
Neymar, the referee was unimpressed
by his antics and showed him a second
yellow card.
• **Later that year he helped Santos win
the Copa Libertadores for the first**
time since 1963, earning the Man of
the Match award for his performance
against Penarol in the final. He also
won the much-coveted FIFA Puskas
Award for the best goal scored in
world football in 2011, collecting the
honour for a stunning individual effort
against Flamengo.

NEWCASTLE UNITED

Year founded: 1892
Ground: Sports Direct
Arena (52,381)
Nickname: The Magpies
Biggest win: 13-0 v
Newport County (1946)
Heaviest defeat: 0-9 v
Burton Wanderers (1895)

The club was founded in 1892 following
the merger of local sides Newcastle East
End and Newcastle West End, gaining
election to the Football League just a
year later.
• **In 1895 Newcastle suffered their
worst-ever defeat, going down 9-0
to Burton Wanderers in a Second
Division match. The Magpies recorded
their best ever win in 1946, thrashing
Newport County 13-0 to equal
Stockport County's record for the
biggest ever victory in a Football
League match. Star of the show at
St James' Park was Len Shackleton,
who scored six of the goals on his
Newcastle debut to set a club record.**
• Newcastle have a proud tradition in
the FA Cup, having won the competition
on six occasions. In 1908 the Magpies
reached the final after smashing Fulham
6-0, the biggest-ever win in the semi-
final. Then, in 1924, 41-year-old defender
Billy Hampson became the oldest player
ever to appear in the cup final, when
he turned out for the Toon in their 2-0
defeat of Aston Villa at Wembley.
• **The club's best cup era was in the
1950s when they won the trophy
three times, boss Stan Seymour
becoming the first man to lift the cup
as a player and a manager. Legendary
centre forward Jackie Milburn was
instrumental to Newcastle's success,
scoring in every round in 1951 and
then notching after just 45 seconds
in the 1955 final against Manchester
City... the fastest Wembley cup final**

*Neymar, possibly
praying for a big-money
move to Europe...*

Is Hatem Ben Arfa pointing the way to a trophy for Newcastle? It's sure been a while...

HONOURS
Division 1 champions 1905, 1907, 1909, 1927
Division 2 champions 1965
First Division champions 1993
Championship champions 2010
FA Cup 1910, 1924, 1932, 1951, 1952, 1955
Fairs Cup 1969

NORTHAMPTON TOWN

Year founded: 1897
Ground: Sixfields Stadium (7,653)
Nickname: The Cobblers
Biggest win: 11-1 v Southend United (1909)
Heaviest defeat: 0-11 v Southampton (1901)

goal ever until Roberto di Matteo scored for Chelsea after 43 seconds in 1997.

• Milburn is the club's leading goalscorer in league matches with 178 strikes between 1946 and 1957. However, Alan Shearer holds the overall club goalscoring record, finding the net 206 times in all competitions after his then world record £15 million move from Blackburn Rovers in 1996. Another famous Newcastle centre forward, Hughie Gallacher, scored a record 36 goals in the 1926/27 season to help the Magpies win the last of their four league titles.

• **The club's leading appearance maker is goalkeeper Jimmy Lawrence, who featured in 432 league games between 1904 and 1921. Another goalkeeper, Shay Given, is easily Newcastle's most honoured international with 83 caps for the Republic of Ireland between 1997 and 2009.**

• Newcastle supporters have not had much to cheer about in recent years, their team having failed to win a major trophy since 1969. That was the Fairs Cup, the Magpies beating Hungarian side Ujpest Dozsa 6-2 on aggregate in a two-legged final.

• The mid-1990s, though, promised much. A swashbuckling side managed by Toon legend Kevin Keegan swept to the new First Division title in 1993 before emerging as Premiership title contenders in the 1995/96 season. At one stage during that campaign Newcastle held a 12-point lead over eventual winners Manchester United, but they were unable to hold their advantage and ultimately finished in second place.

• In January 2011 Newcastle sold striker Andy Carroll to Liverpool for a staggering £35 million, the highest fee ever for a British player. Michael Owen is Newcastle's most expensive player, joining the club from Real Madrid for £16 million in 2005.

• **Relegated from the Premier League in 2009, Newcastle bounced back the following season under then manager Chris Hughton with a mammoth total of 102 points – only four short of the all-time Football League record set by Reading in 2005/06.**

• Newcastle are followed by an army of devoted fans who include TV presenters Ant and Dec, former Prime Minister Tony Blair and eccentric racing pundit John McCririck.

IS THAT A FACT?
During the 2011/12 season, Newcastle defender Jonas Gutierrez was fouled more often (86 times) than any other Premier League player.

The club was founded at a meeting of local schoolteachers at the Princess Royal Inn in Northampton in 1897. After turning professional in 1901 Northampton were founder members of the Third Division in 1920.

• **The club's first full-time manager was Herbert Chapman (1907-12), who later became the first manager to win the league title with two different clubs, Huddersfield and Arsenal.**

• No other club can match the extraordinary decade Northampton experienced in the 1960s. After starting the era in the Fourth Division, the Cobblers rose to the First Division in 1965 – in the process becoming the first club to reach the top flight via all three lower divisions – before swiftly plummeting back to the basement by 1969.

• **Northampton's best run in the FA Cup came in 1970 when they reached the fifth round before going down 8-2 at home to Manchester United, with a certain George Best scoring six of the visitors' goals.**

• The Cobblers were managed between 1985 and 1990 by Graham Carr, a former Northampton player from the club's 1960s heyday and father of buck-toothed comedian Alan Carr.

HONOURS
Division 3 champions 1963
Division 4 champions 1987

TOP 10

TOP TEN BIGGEST HOME INTERNATIONAL WINS

1. England 13 Ireland 2, 1899
2. Wales 11 Ireland 0, 1888
3. Scotland 11 Ireland 0, 1901
4. Ireland 2 Scotland 10, 1888
5. England 9 Ireland 0, 1895
6. Ireland 1 England 9, 1890
   Wales 1 England 9, 1896
   Scotland 9 Ireland 1, 1899
9. England 9 Northern Ireland 2, 1949
10. England 9 Scotland 3, 1961

NORTHERN IRELAND

First international:
Northern Ireland 2
England 1, 1923
Most capped player:
Pat Jennings, 119 caps
(1964-86)
Leading goalscorer:
David Healy, 35 goals
(2000-)
First WorldCup appearance: Northern Ireland 1
Czechoslovakia 0 (1958)
Biggest win: 7-0 v Wales, 1930
Heaviest defeat: 2-9 v England, 1949

Until Trinidad and Tobago appeared at the 2006 tournament, Northern Ireland were the smallest country to qualify for a World Cup finals tournament. They have made it on three occasions, reaching the quarter-finals in 1958 and beating the hosts Spain in 1982 on their way to the second round.

• Northern Ireland's Norman Whiteside is the youngest player ever to appear at the World Cup. He was aged just 17 years and 42 days when he played at the 1982 tournament in Spain, beating the previous record set by Pele in 1958.

• When Northern Ireland thrashed Wales 7-0 on 1st February 1930 to record their biggest-ever win striker Joe Bambrick scored six of the goals – a record for a Home International match.

• After going a record ten matches without a goal Northern Ireland's fortunes picked up when Lawrie Sanchez became manager in 2003. Their revival included a famous 1-0 win over England in the 2006 World Cup qualifying campaign and a 3-2

victory over champions-to-be Spain in the Euro 2008 qualifiers.

• During that Euro 2008 campaign Northern Ireland's highest ever scorer David Healy scored 13 goals to set a new record for the competition.

WORLD CUP RECORD	
1930	Did not enter
1934	Did not enter
1938	Did not enter
1950	Did not qualify
1954	Did not qualify
1958	Quarter-finalists
1962	Did not qualify
1966	Did not qualify
1970	Did not qualify
1974	Did not qualify
1978	Did not qualify
1982	Round 2
1986	Round 1
1990	Did not qualify
1994	Did not qualify
1998	Did not qualify
2002	Did not qualify
2006	Did not qualify
2010	Did not qualify

NORWICH CITY

Year founded: 1902
Ground: Carrow Road
(27,033)
Nickname: The Canaries
Biggest win: 10-2 v
Coventry City (1930)
Heaviest defeat: 2-10 v
Swindon Town (1908)

Founded in 1902 by two schoolteachers, Norwich City soon found themselves in hot water with the FA and were expelled from the FA Amateur Cup in 1904 for being 'professional'. The club joined the Football League as founder members of the Third Division in 1920.

• Norwich were originally known as the Citizens, but adopted the nickname Canaries in 1907 as a nod to the longstanding popularity of canary-keeping in the city – a result of 15th-century trade links with Flemish weavers who had brought the birds over to Europe from Dutch colonies in the Caribbean. Soon afterwards, the club changed their colours from blue and white to yellow and green.

• City fans enjoyed the greatest day in their history when Norwich beat Sunderland 1-0 at Wembley in 1985 to win the League Cup. However, joy soon turned to despair when the Canaries were relegated from the top flight at the end of the season, the first club to experience this particular mix of sweet and sour.

• Ron Ashman is the club's leading appearance maker, turning out in 592 league matches between 1947 and 1964. The Canaries' leading scorer is Ashman's team-mate John Gavin, who notched 122 league goals between 1948 and 1958.

• Norwich's most-capped player is Mark Bowen, who played 35 times for Wales during his Carrow Road career.

• In 2006 the Canaries splashed out a club record £3.5 million to bring striker Robert Earnshaw to Carrow Road from West Brom. In the same year Norwich received a club record £7.25 million when they sold striker Dean Ashton to West Ham United.

• Now under the ownership of cook and recipe book author Delia Smith, Norwich came a best ever third in the inaugural Premiership season in 1992/93 – albeit with a goal difference of -4, the worst ever by a team finishing in the top three in the top flight. The club enjoyed a spirited run in the UEFA Cup in the following campaign, defeating Vitesse Arnhem and German giants Bayern Munich before going out to Inter Milan.

• In 2010 lifelong Canaries fan Stephen Fry was appointed to the Board of Directors at Norwich, leading the TV presenter and actor to announce that "I am as proud and pleased as I could be." His first season as a director was one to remember as City went up from the Championship, in the process becoming the first club to win consecutive promotions from the third tier to the top flight since Manchester City in 2000.

• Norwich City's anthem, On the Ball City, is a music hall song that has been associated with the club throughout their history and is believed to be the oldest fans' song anywhere in the world that is still regularly heard at matches.

HONOURS

Division 2 champions 1972, 1986
First Division champions 2004
Division 3 (S) champions 1934
League One champions 2010
League Cup 1985

NOTTINGHAM FOREST

Year founded: 1865
Ground: The City Ground (30,576)
Nickname: The Reds
Biggest win: 14-0 v Clapton (1891)
Heaviest defeat: 1-9 v Blackburn Rovers (1937)

One of the oldest clubs in the world, Nottingham Forest were founded in 1865 at a meeting at the Clinton Arms in Nottingham by a group of former players of 'shinty' (a form of hockey), who decided to switch sports to football.

• Over the following years the club was at the forefront of important innovations in the game. For instance, shinguards were invented by Forest player Sam Widdowson in 1874, while four years later a referee's whistle was first used in a match between Forest and Sheffield Norfolk. In 1890, a match between Forest and Bolton Wanderers was the first to feature goal nets.

• Forest adopted their famous red tops in tribute to the Italian patriot Giuseppe Garibaldi, whose followers were known as the 'redshirts'. In 1886 the club donated a spare kit to newly formed Arsenal and the Londoners have worn red ever since.

• **Forest enjoyed a golden era under charismatic manager Brian Clough, who sat in the City Ground hotseat from 1975 until his retirement in 1993. After winning promotion to the top flight in 1977, the club won the league championship the following season – a feat that no promoted team has achieved since. Even more incredibly, the Reds went on to win the European Cup in 1979 with a 1-0 victory over Malmo in the final. The next year Forest retained the trophy, beating Hamburg 1-0 in the final in Madrid, to become the first and only team to win the European Cup more times than their domestic league.**

• Forest also won the League Cup in 1978, and the following year became the first club to retain the trophy. The Reds' record of four wins in the competition is only bettered by Liverpool and Aston Villa.

• **In 1959, in the days before subs, Forest won the FA Cup despite being reduced to ten men when Roy Dwight, a cousin of pop star Elton John, was carried off with a broken leg after 33 minutes of the final against Luton Town. It was the first time that a club had won the cup with fewer than 11 players.**

• Defender Bobby McKinlay, a member of that 1959 team, is Forest's longest-serving player, turning out in 614 league games in 19 seasons at the club. The Reds' record scorer is Grenville Morris, who fell just one short of a double century of league goals for the club in the years before the First World War.

• **Nottingham Forest's City Ground is just 330 yards from Notts County's Meadow Lane, making the two clubs the nearest neighbours in the Football League.**

• In 2007 Forest's Paul Smith scored the fastest-ever goal by a goalkeeper when he netted after just 23 seconds in the Carling Cup. However, he was helped considerably by opponents Leicester who allowed him to walk through their defence to make the score 1-0 to Forest, as it had been when the original tie between the clubs was abandoned.

HONOURS
Division 1 champions 1978
Division 2 champions 1907, 1922
First Division champions 1998
Division 3 (S) champions 1951
FA Cup 1898, 1959
League Cup 1978, 1979, 1989, 1990
European Cup 1979, 1980
European Super Cup 1979

Nottingham Forest are aiming for a return to the big time

NOTTS COUNTY

Year founded: 1862
Ground: Meadow Lane (20,229)
Nickname: The Magpies
Biggest win: 15-0 v Rotherham (1885)
Heaviest defeat: 1-9 v Aston Villa (1888), v Blackburn (1889) and v Portsmouth (1927)

Notts County are the oldest professional football club in the world. Founded in 1862, the club were founder members of the Football League in 1888.

• In their long history County have swapped divisions more often than any other league club, winning 13 promotions and suffering the agony of relegation 15 times.

• The club's greatest-ever day was way back in 1894 when, as a Second Division outfit, they won the FA Cup – the first time a team from outside the top flight had won the trophy. In the final at Goodison Park County beat Bolton 4-1, with Jimmy Logan scoring the first ever hat-trick in the FA Cup final.

• Striker Henry Cursham scored a record 48 goals for Notts County in the FA Cup between 1880 and 1887, playing alongside his two brothers in the same County team.

• Giant goalkeeper Albert Iremonger played in a club record 564 games for County between 1905-26, the last occasion when he was 42, making him the club's oldest-ever player. A temperamental character, Iremonger was known for running out of his goal to argue with the ref.

• Along with Brentford, Notts County are one of just two clubs to have won the fourth tier of English football under its three historical names: Division 4 in 1971, the Third Division in 1998 (by a record margin of 17 points), and League Two in 2010.

HONOURS
Division 2 champions 1897, 1914, 1923
Division 3 (S) champions 1931, 1950
Division 4 champions 1971
Third Division champions 1998
League Two champions 2010
FA Cup 1894
Anglo-Italian Cup 1995

NUMBERS

Shirt numbers were first used in a First Division match by Arsenal against Sheffield Wednesday at Hillsborough on 25th August 1928. On the same day Chelsea also wore numbers for their Second Division fixture against Swansea at Stamford Bridge.

• In 1933 teams wore numbers in the FA Cup final for the first time. Everton's players were numbered 1-11 while Manchester City's wore 12-22. Six years later, in 1939, the Football League made the use of shirt numbers obligatory for all teams.

• England and Scotland first wore numbered shirts on 17th April 1937 for the countries' Home International fixture at Hampden Park. Scotland won 3-1. The following year numbers were introduced for the World Cup tournament in France.

• Celtic were the last club in Scotland to wear numbers, only sporting them for the first time in 1960.

• Squad numbers were adopted by Premier League clubs at the start of the 1993/94 season. The highest number worn to date by a Premier League player is 62 by Manchester City's Abdul Razak when he came on as a sub against West Brom in 2011.

• In 2000 Aberdeen's Moroccan striker Hicham Zerouaki was allowed to wear the number 0 on his back after being nicknamed 'Zero' by Dons fans. The following season, however, the SPL outlawed the number.

• In 2005 Sao Paulo goalkeeper Rogerio Ceni wore the highest-ever shirt number in football history, 618, to commemorate his record-breaking 618th appearance for the Brazilian club.

• In 2010 Australia's Thomas Oar set a world record for a high shirt number in an international match when he sported '121' on his back for an Asian Cup qualifier against Indonesia.

IS THAT A FACT?
In the 2006 Merseyside derby both Liverpool's Steven Gerrard and Everton's James Beattie wore the number '08', rather than their usual '8', to advertise Liverpool's status as the European City of Culture for 2008.

OLDHAM ATHLETIC

Year founded: 1895
Ground: Boundary Park (10,638)
Previous name: Pine Villa
Nickname: The Latics
Biggest win: 11-0 v Southport (1962)
Heaviest defeat: 4-13 v Tranmere Rovers (1935)

Originally known as Pine Villa, the club was founded by the landlord of the Featherstone and Junction Hotel in 1895. Four years later the club changed to its present name and in 1907 Oldham joined the Second Division, winning promotion to the top flight after three seasons.

• The Latics enjoyed a golden era in the early 1990s under manager Joe Royle, reaching the League Cup final (in 1990), two FA Cup semi-finals (1990 and 1994) and earning promotion to the top flight (1991). The club were founder members of the Premier League in 1992 but were relegated two years later. In 1997 Oldham dropped into the third tier, and they are now the longest-serving members of League One.

• In 1915 Oldham looked almost certain to win the First Division championship, but they blew the opportunity by losing their last two games, at home to Burnley and Liverpool. Everton took full advantage of the Oldham's loss of nerve, by claiming the title by a single point.

• In 1989 Oldham striker Frankie Bunn scored six of his side's goals in a 7-0 hammering of Scarborough in the third round of the League Cup. He remains the only player to have notched a double hat-trick in the competition.

• In February 1992 Oldham received a club record £1.7 million when they sold defender Earl Barrett to Aston Villa. Four months later the Latics returned £750,000 of this cash to Villa when they bought striker Ian Olney, still their most expensive signing.

HONOURS
Division 2 champions 1991
Division 3 (N) champions 1953
Division 3 champions 1974

OLYMPIC GAMES

The first official Olympic Games football tournament was played in London in 1908, Great Britain beating Denmark 2-0 in the final at White City. With the exception of the 1932 games in Los Angeles, football has been played at every Olympiad since, with a women's tournament being added in 1996.

• **The most successful team in Olympic history are Hungary, who have won three gold medals, one silver and one bronze. Hungary striker Ferenc Bene scored a record 12 goals at the 1964 tournament in Tokyo, including one in his side's 2-1 defeat of Czechoslovakia in the final.**

• The USA have dominated the women's football tournament, winning four golds (including one at London 2012) and finishing runners up to the only other winners, Norway, in 2000.

• **With the rise of the World Cup, the football tournament at the Olympics declined in significance but was given a boost in 1984 when the International Olympic Committee decided to admit professional players. Since 1992 all but three players in competing countries' squads must be aged under 23.**

• Mexico won the men's football tournament at the 2012 Olympics, beating Brazil 2-1 in the final at Wembley. Great Britain, managed by Stuart Pearce, reached the quarter-finals before bowing out to bronze medallists South Korea in a penalty shoot-out.

MARTIN O'NEILL

Born: Kilrea, 1st March 1962
Managerial career:
1990-95 Wycombe Wanderers
1995 Norwich City
1995-2000 Leicester City
2000-05 Celtic
2006-10 Aston Villa
2011- Sunderland

Appointed Sunderland manager in December 2011 following the departure of Steve Bruce, Martin O'Neill enjoyed the best start ever by a Black Cats' boss in the Premier League, winning four of the first six games for which he was in charge.

• **One of the brightest, most articulate managers in the game, O'Neill started out at Wycombe Wanderers in 1990, leading the Chairboys out of the Conference and into the third tier before spending a brief spell at Norwich. From Carrow Road he went to Leicester, who he guided into the Premier League via the play-offs in** 1996. The following year he led the Foxes to triumph in the League Cup, a competition the club won again in 2000.

• Later that year O'Neill joined Celtic, where he won the treble in his first season. Dubbed 'Martin the Magnificent' by the fans, O'Neill led the Glasgow titans to two more league titles, four more cups and the final of the UEFA Cup in 2003 before quitting the club in 2005 to care for his sick wife. He returned to management the following year with Aston Villa but, despite taking the club to the League Cup final in 2010, was unable to deposit any silverware in the Villa Park trophy cabinet during his four-year tenure.

• **Formerly a law student at Queen's University in Belfast, O'Neill's playing career was mostly spent at Nottingham Forest under legendary manager Brian Clough. A hard-working midfielder with no little skill, O'Neill won the league championship and two European Cups with Forest, before later playing for Norwich, Manchester City and Notts County. He also won 64 caps for Northern Ireland, captaining his country at the 1982 World Cup in Spain.**

MICHAEL O'NEILL

Born: Portadown, 5th July 1969
Managerial career:
2006-08 Brechin City
2009-11 Shamrock Rovers
2012- Northern Ireland

A surprise choice as Northern Ireland manager in December 2011, Michael O'Neill quickly discovered that international football can be cruel and unforgiving as his team were thrashed 3-0 by Norway and 6-0 by Holland in his first two matches in charge.

• **After a spell in charge of Brechin City, O'Neill rose to prominence as manager of Shamrock Rovers who he led to the League of Ireland title in 2010 and the Setanta Sports Cup the**

Craig Bellamy playing for Team GB at London 2012

following year. In 2011 he became the first manager to lead a League of Ireland side into the group stage of a European competition when Rovers beat Partizan Belgrade in the final qualifying round of the Europa League.

• In his playing days O'Neill turned out for a number of clubs including Dundee United, Hibs and Newcastle, for whom he was the club's leading scorer in the old First Division in 1987/88.

MICHAEL OWEN

Born: Chester, 14th December 1979
Position: Striker
Club career:
1997-2004 Liverpool 216 (118)
2004-05 Real Madrid 35 (13)
2005-09 Newcastle United 71 (26)
2009-12 Manchester United 31 (5)
International record:
1998-2008 England 89 (40)

Former Liverpool, Newcastle and Manchester United striker Michael Owen is England's fourth-highest scorer of all time. He once seemed certain to become his country's record scorer but his international career came to a juddering halt when he was 28.

• Frighteningly quick in his heyday with Liverpool, Owen enjoyed a golden year in 2001 when he won the FA Cup, League Cup and UEFA Cup in the same season with the Merseysiders, scoring both the Reds' goals in their 2-1 FA Cup final defeat of Arsenal at the Millennium Stadium. In the same year he was voted European Footballer of the Year, the last English player to achieve that distinction.

• Owen joined Real Madrid for £8 million in 2004, but the following year moved back to England when he signed for Newcastle for £16 million. His unveiling at St James' Park was attended by 20,000 excited Toon fans, but after failing to set Tyneside alight he made a surprise move to Manchester United in 2009. In his first season at Old Trafford he helped United win the Carling Cup, scoring in the final against Aston Villa before limping off injured, and in 2011 he picked up his first Premier League winners' medal with the Red Devils.

• Owen is the only England player to have scored at four international tournaments, notching at two World Cups and two European

Championships. His strike against Argentina at the 1998 World Cup, when he sped past two defenders before slamming the ball high into the net, is one of the most famous England goals of all time. In the same year he was voted BBC Sports Personality of the Year, becoming only the third footballer to win the award.

• Of Owen's 40 international goals, 26 of them have come in competitive matches – a figure unmatched by any other England player. He is also the only England player to have scored for his country at both the old and new Wembleys.

OWN GOALS

The first-ever own goal in the Football League was scored on the opening day of the inaugural 1888/89 season, the unfortunate George Cox of Aston Villa putting through his own net in his team's 1-1 draw with Wolves.

• The record number of own goals in a single match is, incredibly, 149. In 2002 Madagascan team Stade Olympique l'Emyrne staged a predetermined protest against alleged refereeing bias by constantly whacking the ball into their own net, their match against AS Adema finishing in a 149-0 win for their opponents. The Madagascan FA took a dim view of the incident and promptly handed out long suspensions to four SOE players.

• Three players have scored at both ends in the same FA Cup final: Charlton's Bert Turner in his side's 4-1 defeat to Derby in 1949, Manchester City's Tommy Hutchison in a 1-1 draw with Tottenham in 1981, and Spurs' Gary Mabbutt in a surprise 3-2 defeat to Coventry City in 1987.

IS THAT A FACT?
Two Premier League clubs have conceded a record three own goals in a single match: Sunderland in a 3-1 home defeat to Charlton in 2003, and Portsmouth in a 5-0 thrashing at Manchester United in 2010.

• During the 1934/35 season Middlesbrough's Bobby Stuart scored five own goals – a record for a single campaign.

• A record 43 own goals were scored in the 2009/10 Premier League season, with Manchester United being gifted an incredible 12 of them (another record). The unfortunate Richard Dunne of Aston Villa holds the Premier League own goal record, with an amazing nine strikes at the wrong end.

• **The most notorious own goal ever was scored by Colombia's Andreas Escobar in his country's 2-1 defeat by hosts USA at the 1994 World Cup. Ten days later Escobar was shot dead in his home town, Medellin, reportedly as a punishment for the gambling losses the city's drug lords had suffered as a result of his error.**

• Indonesia defender Mursyid Effendi was banned from international football for life after scoring an intentional own goal in the last minute of a Tiger Cup group match against Thailand in 1998, an encounter neither side wanted to win as defeat would have paired them in the semi-finals with underdogs Singapore rather than hosts and hot favourites Vietnam.

OXFORD UNITED

Year founded: 1893
Ground: Kassam Stadium (12,500)
Previous name: Headington, Headington United
Nickname: The U's
Biggest win: 9-1 v Dorchester Town, 1995
Heaviest defeat: 0-7 v Sunderland, 1998

The club was founded by a local vicar and doctor in 1893 as Headington, primarily as a way of allowing the cricketers of Headington CC to keep fit during the winter months. The name Oxford United was adopted in 1960, six years before Oxford were elected to the Football League.

• In 1964 Oxford became the first Fourth Division side to reach the quarter-finals of the FA Cup. However, despite being backed by a record crowd of 22,750 at their old Manor Ground, the U's went down 2-1 to eventual finalists Preston.

• The club enjoyed a golden era under controversial owner Robert Maxwell in the 1980s, although the decade began badly when the newspaper proprietor proposed that Oxford and Reading should merge as the 'Thames Valley Royals'. The fans' well-organised campaign against the idea was successful, and their loyalty was rewarded when Oxford gained consecutive promotions to reach the top flight in 1985.

• **The greatest day in the club's history, though, came in 1986 when Oxford defeated QPR 3-0 at Wembley to win the League Cup. The following two decades saw a period of decline, however, and by 2006 Oxford had become the first major trophy winners to sink down into the Conference.**

• Winger John Shuker played in a record 478 league games for Oxford between 1962 and 1977.

> HONOURS
> *Division 2 champions 1985*
> *Division 3 champions 1968, 1984*
> *League Cup 1986*

ALEX OXLADE-CHAMBERLAIN

> **Born:** Portsmouth, 15th August 1993
> **Position:** Winger
> **Club career:**
> 20010-11 Southampton 36 (9)
> 2011- Arsenal 16 (2)
> **International record:**
> 2012- England 5 (0)

One of the most exciting attacking talents to emerge in the Premier League for many years, Alex Oxlade-Chamberlain became the youngest English scorer in the Champions League when he netted for Arsenal against Olympiacos at the start of the 2011/12 campaign.

• **'The Ox', as he has been dubbed by fans for his powerful, direct style of play, began his career at Southampton where he became the club's second youngest player (behind Theo Walcott) when he made his debut as a substitute against Huddersfield on 2nd March 2010, aged 16.**

• The following season he helped the Saints gain promotion to the Championship, his thrilling displays earning him a place in the League One Team of the Year. A transfer target for numerous Premier League clubs, he moved to Arsenal for an initial fee of £12 million in August 2011.

• **After a number of outstanding performances for the Under-21s, Oxlade-Chamberlain made his first appearance for the full England side as a sub against Norway in May 2012. New England boss Roy Hodgson clearly liked what he saw, taking the youngster to the Euros and giving him a first competitive start in the 0-0 draw with France, where he became his country's second-youngest player (behind Wayne Rooney in 2004) at the tournament.**

• Oxlade-Chamberlain is one of just four England players to have a father who also represented the Three Lions, his dad Mark earning eight caps on the wing during the early 1980s.

BOB PAISLEY

> **Born:** Sunderland, 23rd January 1919
> **Died:** 14th February 1996
> **Managerial career:**
> 1974-83 Liverpool

The most successful manager in Liverpool's history, Bob Paisley won no fewer than 13 major trophies in his nine years in charge of the club between 1974 and 1983: six league titles, three European Cups, three League Cups and one UEFA Cup.

• **Paisley was the first manager to win the European Cup with the Merseysiders, leading his team to a 3-1 victory over Borussia Monchengladbach in Rome in 1977. On arriving in the Italian capital, referring to his wartime**

Watch out! 'The Ox' is on the charge!

exploits, Paisley had quipped: "The last time I was here I was in a tank!" Two more triumphs in the competition followed in 1978 and 1981 to make Paisley the first manager to win the European Cup three times with the same club.

• After taking over from the equally legendary Bill Shankly in 1974, Paisley won at least one trophy every season apart from his first in the Anfield hot seat. His success was rewarded with six Manager of the Year awards – a total only surpassed by Sir Alex Ferguson, with 11.

• **As a player Paisley won the league title with Liverpool in 1947 and later captained the club. He joined the back-room staff as a physiotherapist after retiring in 1954, serving the club in a variety of roles before becoming manager.**

• Paisley died in 1996, aged 77, after a long illness. His memory was subsequently honoured by the club with the opening of the Paisley Gates at one of the entrances to Anfield.

ALAN PARDEW

Born: Wimbledon,
18th July 1961
Managerial career:
1999-2003 Reading
2003-06 West Ham United
2006-08 Charlton Athletic
2009-10 Southampton
2010- Newcastle United

In his first full season at Newcastle, 2011/12, Alan Pardew became only the second Englishman (after Harry Redknapp in 2010) to win the Premier League Manager of the Year award. The honour reflected Pardew's feat in guiding the Toon into the Europa League just two years after they had won promotion from the Championship.

• **Pardew began his managerial career at Reading, who he led to promotion from the third tier in 2002. He enjoyed more success in his next job, taking West Ham to their first FA Cup final for 26 years in 2006 – however, the Hammers lost to Liverpool on penalties and Pardew was sacked just six months later.**

• He soon returned to management with Charlton, but could not prevent the Addicks from sliding out of the Premier League in 2007. The following year he left The Valley by mutual consent, and then spent 18 months at Southampton before he moved to Newcastle in December 2010.

• **An industrious midfielder in his playing career, Pardew enjoyed his best days with Crystal Palace, helping the Eagles gain promotion to the top flight in 1989 and scoring the winner against Liverpool in the 1990 FA Cup semi-final.**

Alan Pardew was voted League Manager of the Year 2011/12

PARIS ST GERMAIN

Year founded: 1970
Ground: Parc des Princes (48,712)
Nickname: PSG
League titles: 2
Domestic cups: 8
European cups: 1

Founded as recently as 1970 following a merger between Paris FC and Stade Saint-Germain, Paris St Germain are now one of the richest clubs in the world after being bought by the Qatar Investment Authority in 2011.

• In the same year PSG splashed around £35 million of their new-found wealth on Palermo's Argentinian midfielder Javier Pastore, the most expensive purchase in French football history.

• In 1996 PSG became only the second French club to win a European trophy when they beat Rapid Vienna 1-0 in the final of the Cup Winners' Cup. The Paris outfit had a good chance to become the only club to retain the trophy the following year, but lost in the final to Barcelona.

• Now managed by former Chelsea boss Carlo Ancelotti, a host of famous names have played for PSG in the past, including ex-Spurs winger David Ginola, former World Player of the Year George Weah and Brazilian superstar Ronaldinho.

HONOURS
French league champions 1986, 1994
French Cup 1982, 1983, 1993, 1995, 1998, 2004, 2006, 2010
European Cup Winners' Cup 1996

SCOTT PARKER

Born: Lambeth, 13th October 1980
Position: Midfielder
Club career:
1997-2004 Charlton Athletic 128 (9)
2000 Norwich City (loan) 6 (1)
2004-05 Chelsea 15 (1)
2005-07 Newcastle United 55 (4)
2007-11 West Ham United 107 (9)
2012- Tottenham Hotspur 29 (0)
International record:
2003- England 17 (0)

England's Scott Parker was once most famous for being in a McDonalds ad

Scott Parker is the only England player to have won his first four caps while at four different clubs. He finally broke that trend in the spring of 2011 by sufficiently impressing then England boss Fabio Capello to play in consecutive internationals. The following year he captained his country for the first time in a 3-2 home defeat by Holland.

• A tenacious and tireless midfielder, Parker started out with Charlton, making his first appearance for the Addicks in 1997 when he was still 16. After seven years at the Valley he joined Chelsea for £10 million in 2004 but, after making only a limited impression at Stamford Bridge, soon moved on to Newcastle.

• In 2007 he returned to the capital with West Ham, but his four-year stint at Upton Park ended in heartbreak as the Hammers were relegated to the Championship in 2011. Nonetheless, Parker's gritty displays earned him the Football Writers' Player of the Year award – the first time that this honour has gone to a player with a demoted club. In August 2011 he joined his fourth London club, Tottenham paying £5.5 million for his services.

• Parker first came to public prominence in 1994 when, aged just 13, his keepy-uppy skills were showcased in a McDonald's TV advert to tie in with that year's World Cup in the USA.

PELE

Born: Tres Coracoes, Brazil, 23rd October 1940
Position: Striker
Club career:
1956-74 Santos 412 (470)
1975-77 New York Cosmos 56 (31)
International record:
1957-71 Brazil 92 (77)

Born Edson Arantes do Nascimento, but known throughout the world by his nickname, Pele is generally recognised as the greatest footballer ever to play the game.

• In 1957, aged just 16 years and nine months, he scored on his debut for Brazil against Argentina to become the youngest international goalscorer ever. The following year he made headlines around the globe when he scored twice in Brazil's 5-2 World Cup final defeat of hosts Sweden, in the process making history as the youngest ever World Cup winner.

• Four years later he missed most of Brazil's successful defence of their trophy through injury but was later awarded a winners' medal by FIFA. After being kicked out of the 1966 World Cup, he was back to his best at the 1970 tournament in Mexico, opening the scoring in the final against Italy and inspiring a magnificent Brazilian side to a comprehensive 4-1 victory. He remains the only player in the world with three World Cup winners' medals.

• **Fast, strong, tremendously skilful and powerful in the air, Pele was the complete footballer. He was also a phenomenal goalscorer who remains Brazil's top scorer of all time with an incredible 77 goals (in just 92 games), a record only surpassed in international football by two players. Twelve of those goals came at the World Cup, making him the fifth highest scorer in the history of the tournament.**

• Pele's career total of 1,281 goals in 1,365 top-class matches is officially recognised by FIFA as a world record, although many of his goals came in friendlies for his club Santos. The Brazilian ace's most prolific patch saw him score in 14 consecutive games, to set another world record.

PENALTIES

Penalty kicks were first proposed by goalkeeper William McCrum of the Irish FA in 1890 and adopted the following year. Wolves's John Heath was the first player to take and score a penalty in a Football League match, against Accrington at Molineux on 14th September 1891.

• **Francis Lee holds the British record for the most penalties in a league season, scoring 15 for Manchester City in Division One in 1971/72. He earned many of the penalties himself, leading fans to dub him 'Lee Won Pen'.**

• The first penalty awarded in a World Cup final was scored by Holland's Johan Neeskens after just one minute of the 1974 final against West Germany. Only one player has missed a spot-kick in a World Cup final in normal play, Italy's Antonio Cabrini in 1982.

• **Alan Shearer is the most prolific penalty-taker in the Premier League era, scoring 58 times from the spot.**

• The most penalties ever awarded in a British match is five in the game between Crystal Palace and Brighton at Selhurst Park in 1989. Palace were awarded four penalties (one scored, three missed) while Brighton's consolation goal in a 2-1 defeat also came from the spot.

• **Argentina's Martin Palermo missed a record three penalties in a Copa America match against Colombia in 1999. His first effort struck the crossbar, his second penalty sailed over, but remarkably Palermo still insisted on taking his side's third**

The legendary Pele in his New York Cosmos days

TOP 10

MOST PREMIER LEAGUE PENALTIES CONVERTED

1.	Alan Shearer	58
2.	Frank Lampard	36
3.	Matthew Le Tissier	24
4.	Thierry Henry	23
5.	Teddy Sheringham	21
6.	Ruud van Nistelrooy	19
7.	Danny Murphy	19
8.	Peter Beardsley	18
	Gareth Barry	18
10.	Gary McAllister	17

spot-kick of the match. Perhaps he shouldn't have bothered, as his shot was palmed away by the goalkeeper.

• Ipswich goalkeeper Paul Cooper saved a record eight out of the ten penalties he faced during the 1979/80 season. His technique was to leave a slightly bigger gap on one side of the goal, tempting the penalty taker to shoot there.

• **The first goalkeeper to save a penalty in the FA Cup final at Wembley was Wimbledon's Dave Beasant, who beat away John Aldridge's spot-kick in 1988 to help the Dons record a shock 1-0 win over hot favourites Liverpool.**

PENALTY SHOOT-OUTS

Penalty shoot-outs were first used in England as a way to settle drawn matches in the Watney Cup in 1970. In the first-ever shoot-out Manchester United beat Hull City in the semi-final of the competition, United legend George Best being the first player to take a penalty while his team-mate Denis Law was the first to miss.

• **The third/fourth place play-off between Birmingham and Stoke at St Andrew's was the first FA Cup match to be decided by penalties, Birmingham winning 4-3 after a 0-0 draw.** However, spot-kicks weren't used to settle normal FA Cup ties until the 1991/92 season, Rotherham United becoming the first team to progress by this method when they beat Scunthorpe United 7-6 in the shoot-out after their first-round replay finished 3-3. In 2005 Arsenal became the first team to win the final on penalties, defeating Manchester United 5-4 after a 0-0 draw.

• The first World Cup match to be settled by penalties was the 1982 semi-final between France and West Germany. The Germans won 5-4 in the shoot-out after an exciting 3-3 draw. In 1994 the final was decided by penalties for the first time, Brazil defeating Italy 3-2 on spot-kicks after a dull 0-0 draw. The 2006 final also went to penalties, Italy beating France 5-3. In all, 22 World Cup matches have been settled by penalties.

• **The first country to win a major international tournament on penalties, though, was Czechoslovakia, who beat West Germany 5-3 in the shoot-out of the 1976 European Championship final. The winning penalty was scored by Antonin Panenka with a delicate chip into the middle of the net.**

• Among major nations who have taken part in more than two shoot-outs, Germany have the best record with five wins out of six. England, on the other hand, have the poorest record, with just one win in seven attempts.

• **The longest-ever penalty shoot-out was between KK Palace and Civics in the first round of the 2005 Namibian Cup. After an incredible total of 48 kicks, KK Palace emerged victorious 17-16. At junior level, Under-10 sides Mickleover Lightning Blue Sox and Chellaston required an extraordinary 66 penalties to settle their Derby County Cup match in 1998, before Blue Sox narrowly won 2-1.**

• Brazilian club Palmeiras were the first club to win a penalty shoot-out with an outfield player in goal, defeating Flamengo in 1988 thanks to the heroics of centre-forward Gaucho who saved two spot-kicks.

Will England ever win another penalty shoot-out?

PETERBOROUGH UNITED

Year founded: 1934
Ground: London Road (15,314)
Nickname: The Posh
Biggest win: 9-1 v Barnet (1998)
Heaviest defeat: 1-8 v Northampton Town (1946)

Peterborough were founded in 1934 at a meeting at the Angel Hotel to fill the void left by the collapse of local club Peterborough and Fletton United two years earlier.

• **The club's unusual nickname, The Posh, stemmed from Peterborough and Fletton manager Pat Tirrel's remark in 1921 that the club wanted "Posh players for a Posh team". When the new club played its first game against Gainsborough Trinity in 1934 there were shouts of "Up the Posh!" and the nickname stuck.**

• Peterborough were finally elected to the Football League in 1960... at the 21st attempt. The fans' long wait was rewarded when Peterborough stormed to the Fourth Division title in their first season, scoring a league record 134 goals. Striker Terry Bly notched an amazing 52 of the goals to set a hard-to-beat club record.

• **In 1968 the club became the first since the Second World War to be relegated for non-football reasons, dropping from the Third to the Fourth Division after making illegal payments to players and collecting a 19-point deduction as a punishment.**

• Peterborough broke two club transfer records in the January 2012 transfer window, buying striker Tyrone Barnett from Crawley Town for £1.1 million and selling defender Ryan Bennett to Norwich City for £3.5 million.

HONOURS
Division 4 champions 1961, 1974

PITCHES

According to FIFA rules, a football pitch must measure between 100 and 130 yards in length and 50 and 100 yards in breadth. It's no surprise, then, that different pitches vary hugely in size.

• Of Premier League clubs, Manchester City have the largest pitch, their surface at the Etihad Stadium measuring 116 yards by 77 yards to give a total playing area of 8,932 square yards.

• At the opposite end of the scale, Stoke City have the smallest pitch in the top flight. The playing surface at the Britannia Stadium is just 7,700 square yards (105 x 70yds).

• The first portable natural grass pitch was used for the 1993 America Cup clash between America and England at the Detroit Silverdome. The grass was grown in hexagonal segments in the stadium car park and then reassembled in the covered stadium.

• At the start of the 1981/82 season QPR became the first English club to install an artificial pitch, with Oldham, Luton Town and Preston soon following suit. By 1994, however, Preston were the last club still playing on 'plastic' and at the start of the 1994/95 season the Football League banned all artificial surfaces on the grounds that they gave home clubs an unfair advantage.

• The world's highest pitch was marked out on the summit of Mount Sajama in Bolivia in 2001. Carrying two goalposts and four orange balls, the players climbed 6,542 metres before playing a ten-a-side game (two players having dropped out with altitude sickness) on the snow-capped peak. To prevent other players succumbing to altitude sickness the match lasted just 20 minutes.

MICHEL PLATINI

Born: Joeuf, France, 21st June 1955
Position: Midfielder
Club career:
1972-79 Nancy 181 (98)
1979-82 St Etienne 104 (58)
1982-87 Juventus 147 (68)
International record:
1976-87 France 72 (41)

The only man to be voted European Footballer of the Year in three consecutive years (1983, 1984 and 1985), Platini is a legendary figure in world football.

• An elegant attacking midfielder with a striker's scoring instinct, Platini starred in the French team that reached the World Cup semi-final in 1982 and 1986, only to lose on both occasions to West Germany.

• In between those disappointments, however, Platini captained France to their first ever trophy when, as the host nation, they won the 1984 European Championships. Again, Platini was the main inspiration, scoring a record nine goals in the tournament, including one from a free kick in his side's 2-0 defeat of Spain in the final.

• After playing for Nancy and St Etienne, Platini joined Juventus for £1.2 million in 1982. Three-times top scorer in Serie A, he scored the winning goal for the Italian giants in the 1985 European Cup final against Liverpool, although Juventus' victory was completely overshadowed by the deaths of 39 fans in the Heysel tragedy.

• After managing France for four years between 1988-1992, Platini was elected President of UEFA in 2007. In this role he has opposed the use of goal-line technology but been a firm advocate of 'Financial Fair Play', which would prevent clubs with mega-rich owners from spending more than they earn.

PLAY-OFFS

The play-off system was introduced by the Football League in the 1986/87 season. Initially, one club from the higher division competed with three from the lower division at the semi-final stage but this was changed to four teams from the same division in the 1988/89 season. The following season a one-off final at Wembley replaced the original two-legged final.

• Ipswich Town have featured in the Championship play-offs a record seven times but have only reached the final once, defeating Barnsley 4-2 in 2000.

• The highest-scoring play-off final was a thrilling 4-4 draw between Charlton Athletic and Sunderland in 1998. The Londoners won the subsequent penalty shoot-out 7-6 to gain promotion to the Premier League. Dagenham & Redbridge

IS THAT A FACT? Crystal Palace are the only club to have been promoted to the top flight via the play-offs on three occasions, in 1989, 1997 and 2004.

recorded the biggest-ever play-off victory when they smashed Morecambe 6-0 in the League Two semi-final first leg in 2010.

• The Championship play-off final is the most financially rewarding sporting event in the world, its worth to the winners in prize money, TV and advertising revenue and increased gate receipts being estimated at around £90 million.

• Between 2003 and 2007 Lincoln City reached the League Two play-offs a record five times on the trot, but failed to gain promotion every time.

PLYMOUTH ARGYLE

Year founded: 1886
Ground: Home Park (16,388)
Previous name: Argyle FC
Nickname: The Pilgrims
Biggest win: 8-1 v Millwall (1932) and v Hartlepool (1994)
Heaviest defeat: 0-9 v Stoke City (1960)

The club was founded as Argyle FC in 1886 in a Plymouth coffee house, the name deriving from the Argyll and Sutherland Highlanders who were stationed in the city at the time. The current name was adopted in 1903, when the club became fully professional and entered the Southern League.

• After joining the Football League in 1920, Plymouth just missed out on promotion from the Third Division (South) between 1922 and 1927, finishing in second place in six consecutive seasons... a record of misfortune no other club can match.

• Sammy Black, a prolific marksman during the 1920s and 1930s, is the club's leading goalscorer with 185 league goals. The Pilgrims' longest-serving player is Kevin Hodges, with 530 appearances between 1978 and 1992.

• In 2004 Plymouth beat Chesterfield 7-0 and, amazingly, were 5-0 up after just 17 minutes – the best ever start to a match by an English professional club.

• In one of the most bizarre incidents ever in the history of football, Plymouth conceded a goal scored by the referee in a Division Three fixture against Barrow in 1968. A shot from a Barrow player was heading wide until it deflected off the boot of referee Ivan Robinson and into the Pilgrims' net for the only goal of the match.

• The largest city in England never to have hosted top flight football, Plymouth have won the third tier of English football a record four times, most recently topping the Second Division in 2004.

LUKAS PODOLSKI

Born: Gliwice, Poland, 4th June 1985
Position: Striker
Club career:
2002-04 Cologne II 2 (0)
2003-06 Cologne 81 (46)
2006-09 Bayern Munich 71 (15)
2007-08 Bayern Munich II 2 (0)
2009-12 Cologne 88 (33)
2012- Arsenal
International record:
2004- Germany 101 (44)

Arsenal striker Lukas Podolski is one of just four German players to have scored four goals in a match for his country, filling his boots in a 13-0 demolition of San Marino in 2006.

• When the Polish-born Podolski made his debut for Germany, as a sub against Hungary in 2004, he was the first Second Division player since 1975 to represent his country. He has gone on to win over 100 caps for Germany, his powerful and direct performances winning him the Young Player of the Tournament award at the 2006 World Cup and a place in the UEFA Team of the Tournament at Euro 2008.

• Podolski rose to fame with yo-yo club Cologne, heading the second tier goalscoring charts with 24 goals in 2004/05 to help his team bounce back to the Bundesliga. He moved on to Bayern Munich in 2006 but struggled to establish himself and returned to Cologne three years later.

• Podolski was top scorer for his club in 2011/12 with an impressive haul of 18 goals in 29 games, but couldn't prevent Cologne being relegated from the Bundesliga. In the summer of 2012 he joined Arsenal for an undisclosed fee believed to be around £12 million.

PORT VALE

Year founded: 1876
Ground: Vale Park (19,052)
Previous name: Burslem Port Vale
Nickname: The Valiants
Biggest win: 9-1 v Chesterfield (1932)
Heaviest defeat: 0-10 v Sheffield United (1892) and v Notts County (1895)

Port Vale's name derives from the house where the club was founded in 1876. Initially, the club was known as Burslem Port Vale – Burslem being the Stoke-on-Trent town where the Valiants are based – but the prefix was dropped in 1911.

• **After a 12-year gap Port Vale returned to the Football League in October 1919, replacing the disbanded Leeds City. Bizarrely, the Valiants**

Lukas Podolski applauds Arsenal's kit designers!

inherited the Yorkshiremen's playing record (won four, lost two, drawn two) and went on to finish in a respectable 13th position.

• In their first season as a league club, in 1892/93, Port Vale suffered the worst ever home defeat in Football League history when Sheffield United hammered them 10-0. However, Vale's defence was in much better nick in 1953/54 when they kept a league record 30 clean sheets on their way to the Third Division (North) championship.

• **Loyal defender Roy Sproson is Port Vale's longest-serving player, appearing in a phenomenal 761 league games between 1950 and 1972. Only two other players in the history of league football have made more appearances for the same club. With 154 league goals in two spells at the club between 1923 and 1933 Wilf Kirkham is the Valiants' record goalscorer.**

• Port Vale's most famous fan is singer Robbie Williams, who in 2006 became the club's majority shareholder. Darts legend Phil 'The Power' Taylor is also a keen supporter of the Valiants.

FC PORTO

Year founded: 1893
Ground: Estadio do Dragao (52,000)
Nickname: The Dragons
League titles: 26
Domestic cups: 19
European cups: 5
International cups: 2

Easily the most successful Portuguese side of recent years, Porto were founded in 1893 by a local wine salesman who had been introduced to football on his regular business trips to England.

• **Six league title wins in the last seven seasons have taken Porto's total of domestic championships to 26, five behind arch rivals Benfica. The club was also the dominant force of the 1990s, winning eight titles, including a record five on the trot between 1995 and 1999.**

- Porto have the best record in Europe of any Portuguese side, with two victories in the European Cup/Champions League (in 1987 and 2004) and two in the UEFA Cup (in 2003, 2011), the latter of these triumphs coming under current Tottenham manager Andre Villas-Boas – at 33, the youngest coach ever to win a European competition.
- Porto are the only Portuguese club to have been crowned world champions, claiming the Intercontinental Cup in both 1987 and 2004.

HONOURS
Portuguese League champions 1935, 1939, 1940, 1956, 1959, 1978, 1979, 1985, 1986, 1988, 1990, 1992, 1993, 1995, 1996, 1997, 1998, 1999, 2003, 2004, 2006, 2007, 2008, 2009, 2011, 2012
Portuguese Cup 1922, 1925, 1932, 1937, 1956, 1958, 1968, 1977, 1984, 1988, 1991, 1994, 1998, 2000, 2001, 2003, 2006, 2009, 2011
European Cup/Champions League 1987, 2004
UEFA Cup/Europa League 2003, 2011
European Super Cup 1987
Intercontinental Cup 1987, 2004

PORTSMOUTH

Year founded: 1898
Ground: Fratton Park (20,224)
Nickname: Pompey
Biggest win: 9-1 v Notts County (1927)
Heaviest defeat: 0-10 v Leicester City (1928)

Portsmouth were founded in 1898 by a group of sportsmen and businessmen at a meeting in the city's High Street. After starting out in the Southern League the club joined the Third Division in 1920.
- **In 1949 the club became the first team to rise from the third tier to claim the league championship, and the following year became the first of just five clubs to retain the title since the end of the Second World War.**
- The most influential player in that team was half-back Jimmy Dickinson, who went on to play a record 764 times for Pompey, the second-highest number of Football League appearances with any single club. Dickinson is also Portsmouth's most-decorated international, winning 48 caps for England.
- **Another legendary figure from that period, right-winger Peter Harris is the club's leading marksman, with 193 goals between 1946 and 1960.**
- The club won the FA Cup for the first time in 1939, when Pompey thrashed favourites Wolves 4-1 in the final at Wembley. The club's success was attributed to the 'lucky' white spats worn by manager Jack Tinn throughout the cup run.
- **In 2008 the famous Pompey Chimes ("Play up Pompey, Pompey play up!") were heard at Wembley again as Portsmouth took on Cardiff in only the second FA Cup final to be played at the new national stadium. A single goal by Portsmouth's Nigerian striker Kanu was enough to see off the Welshmen, sparking ecstatic celebrations across the city.**
- Already relegated from the Premier League and suffering grave financial difficulties, Pompey made it to the FA Cup final again in 2010 but their miserable season ended on a low note when they lost 1-0 to champions Chelsea – although it might have been a different story if Kevin Prince-Boateng hadn't missed a penalty at 0-0. To add to their woes, Portsmouth dropped down to League One in 2012, the first time for nearly 30 years they had been in the third tier.

HONOURS
Division 1 champions 1949, 1950
First Division champions 2003
Division 3 (South) champions 1924
Division 3 champions 1962, 1983
FA Cup 1939, 2008

PORTUGAL

First international: Spain 3 Portugal 1, 1921
Most capped player: Luis Figo, 127 caps (1991-2006)
Leading goalscorer: Pauleta, 47 goals (1997-2006)
First World Cup appearance: Portugal 3 Hungary 1, 1966
Biggest win: Portugal 8 Liechtenstein 0, 1994 and 1999
Heaviest defeat: Portugal 0 England 10, 1947

It's been a rollercoaster ride at Pompey over the last few years

Portugal have never won a major trophy, although led by then manager Luiz Felipe Scolari they did reach the final of the European Championships in 2004. Playing on home soil they were hot favourites to beat Greece, but went down to a surprise 1-0 defeat. Eight years later they missed out on a chance to appear in another final when they lost a Euro 2012 semi-final shoot-out to Spain.

• Portugal's best showing at the World Cup was in 1966 when they finished third after going out to hosts England in the semi-finals. Much of their success was down to legendary striker Eusebio, who topped the goalscoring charts at the tournament with nine goals.

• The southern Europeans also reached the semi-finals of the World Cup in 2006, after beating Holland in 'The Battle of Nuremburg' in the last 16 and England on penalties in the quarter-finals. A 1-0 defeat to France, though, ended their hopes of appearing in the final.

• Portugal were the first country to beat West Germany at home in a competitive match, winning 1-0 in Stuttgart in a World Cup qualifier in 1985. That victory booked Portugal's passage to the 1986 World Cup in Mexico where they went out in the first round despite recording a shock 1-0 victory over England in their first match.

WORLD CUP RECORD
1930-38 Did not enter
1950-62 Did not qualify
1966 Third place
1970-82 Did not qualify
1986 Round 1
1990-98 Did not qualify
2002 Round 1
2006 Fourth place
2010 Round 2

PREMIER LEAGUE

The Premier League was founded in 1992 and is now the most watched and most lucrative sporting league in the world, with revenues of over £2 billion in the 2010/11 season.

• Initially composed of 22 clubs, the Premier League was reduced to 20 teams in 1995. A total of 45 clubs have played in the league but just five – Manchester United, Blackburn Rovers, Arsenal, Chelsea

TOP 10

MOST PREMIER LEAGUE APPEARANCES

1.	Ryan Giggs (1992-)	598
2.	David James (1992-2010)	573
3.	Gary Speed (1992-2007)	535
4.	Frank Lampard (1995-)	520
5.	Emile Heskey (1995-)	510
6.	Sol Campbell (1992-2011)	503
7.	Phil Neville (1995-)	484
8.	Jamie Carragher (1996-)	481
9.	Paul Scholes (1994-)	478
10.	Mark Schwarzer (1997-)	468

and Manchester City – have won the title. Of this group, United are easily the most successful, having won the league 12 times.

• The first-ever Premier League goal was scored by Sheffield United striker Brian Deane on 15th August 1992 five minutes into the Blades' 2-1 victory against Manchester United at Bramall Lane.

• Only seven clubs have appeared in the league in every season since its inception: Arsenal, Aston Villa, Chelsea, Everton, Liverpool, Manchester United and Tottenham Hotspur. United lead the all-time table with 1,663 points (including a record 500 wins in 772 games), followed by Arsenal (1,449 points) and Chelsea (1,402 points), and the Red Devils have also scored a record number of goals, 1,541.

• Alan Shearer is the leading scorer in the history of the Premier League with a total of 260 goals for Blackburn Rovers and Newcastle between 1992 and 2006.

• Ryan Giggs holds the Premier League appearance record, turning out in 598 games for Manchester United since the league started in 1992.

PRESTON NORTH END

Year founded: 1879
Ground: Deepdale (23,404)
Nickname: The Lilywhites
Biggest win: 26-0 v Hyde (1887)
Heaviest defeat: 0-7 v Blackpool (1948)

Preston were founded in 1879 as a branch of the North End Cricket and Rugby Club, playing football exclusively from 1881.

• Founder members of the Football League in 1888, Preston won the inaugural league title the following year, going through the entire 22-game season undefeated and conceding just 15 goals (a league record). For good measure the club also won the FA Cup, beating Wolves 3-0 in the final, to become the first club to win the Double. During their cup run, Preston demolished Hyde 26-0 to record the biggest ever win in any English competition, striker Jimmy Ross scoring seven of the goals to set a club record that has never been matched. Ross went on to score 20 goals in the cup that season, a record for the competition.

• Of the 12 founder members of the league, Preston are the only club still playing at the same ground, making Deepdale the oldest league football stadium anywhere in the world.

• The legendary Tom Finney is Preston's most-capped international, turning out for England in 76 games. The flying winger is also the club's highest scorer, with 187 strikes between 1946 and 1960. North End's leading appearance maker is Alan Kelly, who played in goal for the club in 447 league games between 1958 and 1973.

• Along with Wolves and Burnley, Preston are one of just three clubs to have won all four divisions of English football, achieving this feat in 1996 when they topped the Third Division (now League Two).

• Preston have appeared in the play-offs on a record eight occasions but, strangely, have yet to be promoted via this route.

• Famous fans of Preston include former England cricket captain Andrew Flintoff and BBC football pundit Mark Lawrenson, who began his playing career at Deepdale in the mid-1970s.

HONOURS
Division 1 champions 1889, 1890
Division 2 champions 1904, 1913, 1951
Division 3 champions 1971
Second Division champions 2000
Third Division champions 1996
FA Cup 1889, 1938
Double 1889

PROGRAMMES

Football programmes started out in the 1870s as simple teamsheets and have since evolved to become full-colour magazines of 50 or more pages. The programme for the 2007 FA Cup final between Chelsea and Manchester United provided the event's biggest-ever read, running to 146 pages.

• **On 25th December 1948 Chelsea became the first club to issue a 16-page magazine-style programme for their home match against Portsmouth.**

• Between 1904 and 1935 Everton and Liverpool issued a shared programme, which covered both the first-team game of whichever club happened to be at home that week and the reserve-team home game of the other club.

• **Crystal Palace were the first winners of the Football League's 'Best Matchday Programme' award in 2006. Since then, five different clubs have topped the poll, most recently Burnley in 2012, in the process becoming the first club to win the award twice.**

• In 2012 a programme from the 1909 FA Cup final between Bristol City and Manchester United fetched £23,500 at auction, a world record price for a football programme.

PROMOTION

Automatic promotion from the Second to First Division was introduced in the 1898/99 season, replacing the previous 'test match' play-off-style system. The first two clubs to go up automatically were Glossop North End and Manchester City.

• **Birmingham City and Notts County have gained a record 13 promotions, while the Brummies and Leicester have both gone up to the top flight on a record 11 occasions.**

• Not all clubs who have been promoted have done so through playing merit. The most notorious case involved Arsenal in 1919 who were elected to the First Division at the expense of local rivals Tottenham, allegedly thanks to the underhand tactics employed by the Gunners' then chairman, Sir Henry Norris.

• **In the Premier League era promoted clubs have often struggled against relegation the following season. The worst season for the new boys was in 1997/98 when all three promoted clubs – Barnsley, Bolton and Crystal Palace – were relegated at the end of the campaign.**

FERENC PUSKAS

> **Born:** Budapest, 2nd April 1927
> **Died:** 17th November 2006
> **Position:** Striker
> **Club career:**
> 1943-49 Kispest 177 (187)
> 1949-56 Honved 164 (165)
> 1958-66 Real Madrid 182 (157)
> **International record:**
> 1945-56 Hungary 85 (84)
> 1962 Spain 4 (0)

The greatest Hungarian player ever and the all-time top scorer for his country with an incredible 84 goals, Ferenc Puskas is one of the legendary names of world football.

• **Nicknamed 'the Galloping Major' during his time with the Hungarian army team Honved, the left-footed Puskas captained his country to Olympic victory in 1952 and, two years later, to the World Cup final. Although not fully fit, he got on the scoresheet in the biggest match of his career, but finished on the losing side as West Germany recovered from 2-0 down to win 3-2.**

• Puskas skippered Hungary to their most famous victory in 1953, scoring twice as the central Europeans became the first country from outside the British Isles to beat England on home soil. The 6-3 score that day was remarkable, but the next year England went down to their biggest-ever thrashing, losing 7-1 in Budapest with Puskas grabbing another brace.

• **After the Hungarian revolution in 1956, Puskas fled his homeland and was banned from playing by UEFA for two years. He took centre stage again with Real Madrid, starring alongside the brilliant Alfredo di Stefano, where he won five league titles and was top scorer in La Liga on four occasions.**

• In 1960 Puskas won the European Cup with Real, notching four goals in the final as the Spanish giants overwhelmed Eintracht Frankfurt 7-3 at Hampden Park in a game considered by many to be the greatest ever played. Two years later he hit another hat-trick in the final, although Real went down 5-3 to Benfica.

• Puskas later managed Greek side Panathinaikos, who he led to the European Cup final in 1971. A revered figure in Hungary, the national stadium in Budapest was renamed in his honour in 2002 and, following

his death in 2006, he was given a full state funeral.

CARLES PUYOL

> **Born:** Lleida, 13th April 1978
> **Position:** Defender
> **Club career:**
> 1997-2000 Barcelona B 89 (6)
> 1999- Barcelona 374 (10)
> **International record:**
> 2000- Spain 99 (3)

Barcelona centre-back Carles Puyol is the second-highest appearance maker in the Catalans' history, turning out in 559 games in all competitions since graduating from the club's B side in 1999.

• **In his time at the Nou Camp the shaggy-haired defender has enjoyed enormous success, winning five La Liga titles and the Champions League on three occasions, although injury restricted him to a two-minute cameo role in the latest of these triumphs against Manchester United at Wembley in 2011.**

• Few would bet against him adding to those honours, as Puyol's commitment to the cause is second to none. "If he sees you relax at all, he's suddenly at your side demanding more," said his team-mate Xavi on one occasion, summing up Puyol's superb leadership qualities.

• **Puyol made his international debut for Spain against Holland in 2000 and is now closing in on a century of caps. He was a member of the Spain side that won both Euro 2008 and the 2010 World Cup, memorably scoring the winning goal in the semi-final of the latter tournament with a powerful header against Germany.**

QUEEN'S PARK

Year founded: 1867
Ground: Hampden Park (52,500)
Nickname: The Spiders
Biggest win: 16-0 v St Peters (1885)
Heaviest defeat: 0-9 v Motherwell (1930)

Founded in 1867 at a meeting at a house in south Glasgow, Queen's Park are Scotland's oldest club.

• The dominant force in the game north of the border in the 19th century, Queen's Park won the first-ever Scottish Cup in 1874 and held the trophy for the next two years as well. In all, they have won the competition ten times... a cup record only bettered by Old Firm giants Celtic and Rangers.

• Queen's Park's star player of the Victorian era was Charles Campbell, who won a record eight Scottish Cup-winners' medals.

• Queen's Park are the only Scottish side to have played in the final of the FA Cup, losing to Blackburn Rovers in both 1884 and 1885 before the Scottish FA banned its clubs from entering the competition two years later.

• Despite being the only amateur club in senior football anywhere in Britain, Queen's Park play their games at the home of Scottish football, Hampden Park, but rarely attract more than a few hundred spectators to the 52,000-capacity stadium.

HONOURS
Division 2 champions 1923, 1956
Second Division champions 1981
Third Division champions 2000
Scottish Cup 1874, 1875, 1876, 1880, 1881, 1882, 1884, 1886, 1890, 1893

QUEENS PARK RANGERS

Year founded: 1882
Ground: Loftus Road (18,360)
Nickname: The R's
Biggest win: 9-2 v Tranmere Rovers (1960)
Heaviest defeat: 1-8 v Mansfield Town (1965) and v Manchester United (1969)

Founded in 1882 following the merger of St Jude's and Christchurch Rangers, the club was called Queens Park Rangers because most of the players came from the Queens Park area of north London.

• A nomadic outfit in their early days, QPR have staged home matches at no fewer than 19 different venues, a record for a Football League club.

• The club enjoyed its finest moment in 1967 when Rangers came from two goals down to defeat West Bromwich Albion 3-2 in the first-ever League Cup final to be played at Wembley. In the same season the R's won the Third Division title to pull off a unique double.

• Loftus Road favourite Rodney Marsh hit a club record 44 goals that season, 11 of them coming in the League Cup. George Goddard, though, holds the club record for league goals with 37 in 1929/30. Goddard is also the club's leading scorer, notching 174 league goals between 1926 and 1934.

• In 1976 QPR finished second in the old First Division, being pipped to the league championship by Liverpool. Six years later Rangers reached the FA Cup final for the only time in their history but went down 1-0 to Tottenham in a replay.

• No other player has pulled on Rangers' famous hoops more often than Tony Ingham, who made 519 league appearances over 13 years after signing from Leeds in 1950.

• In January 2012 QPR splashed out a club record £6 million when they signed striker Bobby Zamora from Fulham. The west Londoners received a record £6 million when they sold Les Ferdinand to Newcastle in 1995.

• In 1981 QPR became the first club in England to install a plastic pitch. Three years later the R's qualified for the UEFA Cup but were banned from playing home games in the competition on an artificial pitch. In the second round Rangers thrashed Partizan Belgrade 6-2 at Highbury, but lost the return 4-0 in Yugoslavia to go out on the away goals rule – the first time an English club had failed to progress in Europe after taking a four-goal lead in the first leg.

• In 2012 QPR striker Bobby Zamora became only the second Premier League player – after Newcastle's Obafemi Martins – to score from the penalty spot with both his right and left foot.

HONOURS
Division 2 champions 1983
Championship champions 2011
Division 3 (S) champions 1948
Division Three champions 1967
League Cup 1967

QPR's Adel Taarabt

AARON RAMSEY

Born: Caerphilly, 26th December 1990
Position: Midfielder
Club career:
2007-08 Cardiff City 16 (1)
2008- Arsenal 68 (6)
2010-11 Nottingham Forest (loan) 5 (0)
2011 Cardiff City (loan) 6 (1)
International record:
2008- Wales 22 (5)

Rangers will have to play at a lot more tiny grounds like this before they make it back to the SPL...

The youngest player ever to have captained Wales, Aaron Ramsey was aged just 20 and 90 days when he led his country for the first time against England in a Euro 2012 qualifier on 26th March 2011.

• A product of the Cardiff City youth system, Ramsey became the club's youngest ever player when he made his debut as a sub against Hull City on the last day of the 2006/07 season aged 16 and 124 days. He cemented his place in the City team the following season and played in the 2008 FA Cup final against Portsmouth – aged 17, he was the second youngest player ever to appear in the final behind Millwall's Curtis Weston.

• In June 2008 Ramsey signed for Arsenal in a £4.8 million deal, choosing the Gunners ahead of Manchester United and Everton. When he netted his first goal for the north Londoners against Fenerbahce in October 2008 he became only the second player born in the 1990s to score in a Champions League match.

• Twice Welsh Young Player of the Year, Ramsey suffered a double fracture of his right leg playing against Stoke in February 2010 and spent much of the 2010/11 season on loan at Nottingham Forest and Cardiff in a bid to regain match fitness. He returned to the Emirates towards the end of the campaign, and the following season was a fixture in the Arsenal side which finished third in the Premier League.

SIR ALF RAMSEY

Born: Dagenham, 21st January 1920
Died: 28th April 1999
Managerial career:
1955-63 Ipswich Town
1963-74 England
1977-78 Birmingham City

England manager between 1963 and 1974, Alf Ramsey is the only man to have guided the Three Lions to victory in a World Cup final.

• At the 1966 tournament England were one of the favourites, primarily because they had the advantage of being hosts and playing all their matches at Wembley. Ramsey still had to get the team to perform, though, and he did so brilliantly, devising a 4-4-2 formation without wide men which earned England the nickname of 'the Wingless Wonders'.

• His most important single contribution came just after West Germany scored a last-minute equaliser to take the final into extra-time. "You've beaten them once," he told his disappointed players, "now go out there and bloody beat them again." England did precisely that, scoring two more goals to win 4-2.

• Ramsey was sacked from the England job after failing to lead the team to the 1974 World Cup in West Germany. Under his management, England won 69 of 113 matches and only lost 17.

• As a club manager, Ramsey took over Third Division Ipswich Town in 1955, taking them into the second tier in 1957. In 1961 they won the Second Division title and the following season Ipswich were crowned league champions for the first and only time in their history. In recognition of these remarkable achievements a statue of Ramsey was erected outside Portman Road a year after his death in 1999.

• A solid right-back for Southampton and Spurs in his playing days, Ramsey won 32 caps for England and scored three goals, including one from the penalty spot in the infamous 6-3 thrashing by Hungary at Wembley in 1953.

RANGERS

Year founded: 1873
Ground: Ibrox Stadium (51,082)
Nickname: The Gers
Biggest win: 14-2 v Blairgowrie (1934)
Heaviest defeat: 2-10 v Airdrieonians (1886))

The most decorated club in the history of world football, Rangers were founded by a group of rowing enthusiasts in 1873. The club were founder members of the Scottish League in 1890, sharing the

inaugural title with Dumbarton.

• Rangers have won the league title 54 times, a record of domestic success which is unmatched by any club on the planet. Between 1989-97 the Gers topped the league in nine consecutive seasons, initially under Graeme Souness then under Walter Smith, to equal a record previously set by arch rivals Celtic.

• In 2000 Rangers became the first club in the world to win 100 major trophies. The Glasgow giants have since extended their tally to 115, most recently adding the League Cup and SPL title in 2011. The club's tally of seven domestic trebles is also unequalled anywhere in the world.

• Way back in 1898/99 Rangers enjoyed their best-ever league season, winning all 18 of their matches to establish yet another world record.

• The club's record goalscorer is Rangers manager Ally McCoist. In a 15-year Ibrox career between 1983 and 1998 McCoist banged in an incredible 251 goals (355 in all competitions),

including a record 28 hat-tricks. McCoist is also the club's most-capped international, winning 59 of his 61 Scotland caps while with the Gers.

• Rangers also hold two important records in the Scottish League Cup, with more wins (27) and more appearances in the final (33) than any other club. The Gers' first win in the competition came in its inaugural year when they thrashed Aberdeen 4-0 in the final in 1947.

• The club's record in the Scottish Cup is not quite as impressive, the Gers' 33 triumphs in the competition being bettered by Celtic's 35. However, it was in the Scottish Cup that Rangers recorded their biggest ever victory, thrashing Blairgowrie 14-2 in 1934. Striker Jimmy Fleming scored nine of the goals on the day to set a club record.

• Despite all their domestic success, Rangers have only won a single European trophy. That was the Cup Winners' Cup, which they claimed in 1972 after beating Dynamo Moscow 3-2 in the final in Barcelona. The club, though, did reach the final of the same competition in both 1961 and 1967 and were also runners-up in the UEFA Cup in 2008, when an estimated 150,000 (mostly ticketless) Rangers fans followed their team to the final in Manchester.

• No player has turned out in the royal blue shirt of Rangers more often than former captain John Greig, who made 755 appearances in all competitions between 1961 and 1978. The league record, though, is held by Sandy Archibald (513 games between 1917 and 1934).

• In two spells with Rangers between 1994 and 2009 midfielder Barry Ferguson made 82 European appearances, a record for a Scottish player.

• In 2000 Rangers splashed out a club record £12 million when they signed lanky Norwegian striker Tore Andre Flo from Chelsea. Eight years later, in 2008, the Ibrox coffers were boosted by a record £9 million when full back Alan Hutton moved south of the border to join Spurs.

• In 2012 Rangers' massive debts, estimated

IS THAT A FACT?
The Old Firm clash between Rangers and Celtic is the most-played fixture in British football, the two teams having played each other a staggering 399 times since they first met in 1888. Rangers lead the way with 159 victories to Celtic's 144, and there have been 96 draws.

to be over £130 million, forced the club into administration and then liquidation, prompting the other SPL clubs to vote them out of the league – with the result that, for the first time in their history, Rangers will start the 2012/13 season outside the elite tier of Scottish football in the Scottish Third Division.

HONOURS

Division 1 champions 1891 (shared), 1899, 1900, 1901, 1902, 1911, 1912, 1913, 1918, 1920, 1921, 1923, 1924, 1925, 1927, 1928, 1929, 1930, 1931, 1933, 1934, 1935, 1937, 1939, 1947, 1949, 1950, 1953, 1956, 1957, 1959, 1961, 1963, 1964, 1975
Premier League champions 1976, 1978, 1987, 1989, 1990, 1991, 1992, 1993, 1994, 1995, 1996, 1997
SPL champions 1999, 2000, 2003, 2005, 2009, 2010, 2011
Scottish Cup 1894, 1897, 1898, 1903, 1928, 1930, 1932, 1934, 1935, 1936, 1948, 1949, 1950, 1953, 1960, 1962, 1963, 1964, 1966, 1973, 1976, 1978, 1979, 1981, 1992, 1993, 1996, 1999, 2000, 2002, 2003, 2008, 2009
Scottish League Cup 1947, 1949, 1961, 1962, 1964, 1965, 1971, 1976, 1978, 1979, 1982, 1984, 1985, 1987, 1988, 1989, 1991, 1993, 1994, 1997, 1999, 2002, 2003, 2005, 2008, 2010, 2011
European Cup Winners' Cup 1972

RAUL

Born: Madrid, 27th June 1977
Position: Striker
Club career:
1994-2010 Real Madrid 550 (228)
2010- Schalke 66 (28)
International record:
1996-2006 Spain 102 (44)

Raul Gonzalez Blanco, usually known simply as Raul, is the all-time leading scorer in the Champions League, having scored an incredible 71 goals for Real Madrid and Schalke in 144 games (another record for the competition).

• A three-time winner of the Champions League with Real, Raul was the first player to score in two finals of the competition, netting in his side's victories against Valencia in 2000 and Bayer Leverkusen two years later.

• Raul was the club's youngest ever player when he made his debut in 1994 aged 17 and four months. He went on to win six La Liga titles with the Spanish giants and in 2009 became Real's all-time leading scorer when he passed Alfredo di Stefano's longstanding club record of 216 goals. By the time he left for German club Schalke in 2010 he was third on the list of all-time scorers in Spain with 228 goals in La Liga, while his total of 550 La Liga appearances is only exceeded by former Barcelona goalkeeper Andoni Zubizarreta.

• **One of just five players to win over 100 caps for Spain, Raul's total of 44 goals for his country has only been bettered by David Villa's 51. Despite his prolific scoring record, Raul missed out on international honours, failing to be selected for the Spain squad that won Euro 2008 and the 2010 World Cup.**

READING

Year founded: 1871
Ground: Madjeski Stadium (24,161)
Nickname: The Royals
Biggest win: 10-2 v Crystal Palace (1946)
Heaviest defeat: 0-18 v Preston (1894))

Reading were founded in 1871, making them the oldest Football League club south of Nottingham. After amalgamating with local clubs Reading Hornets (in 1877) and Earley FC (in 1889), the club was eventually elected to the new Third Division in 1920.

• **The oldest club still competing in the FA Cup never to have won the trophy, Reading experienced their worst-ever defeat in the competition when they were hammered 18-0 by Preston in 1894.**

• Happier days followed, though, when Reading toured Italy in 1913. After beating AC Milan 5-0 and the Italian national team 2-0, the club were hailed as "the finest foreign team seen in Italy" by the Corriere della Sera newspaper.

• **In the 1985/86 season Reading set a Football League record by winning their opening 13 matches, an outstanding start which provided the launch pad for The Royals to go on to top the old Third**

Division at the end of the campaign.

• Reading's greatest moment, though, came in 2006 when, under manager Steve Coppell, they won promotion to the top flight for the first time in their history. They went up in fine style, too, claiming the Championship title with a Football League record 106 points and going 33 matches unbeaten (a record for the second tier) between 9th August 2005 and 17th February 2006.

• **Prolific marksman Ronnie Blackman holds two scoring records for the club, with a total of 158 goals between 1947 and 1954 and a seasonal best of 39 goals in the 1951/52 campaign.**

• Stalwart defender Martin Hicks is Reading's longest-serving player, making precisely 500 league appearances for the club between 1978 and 1991.

• **In 2001 Reading became the first English club to register their supporters as an official member of the squad when their fans were allotted the vacant number 13 shirt.**

• In 2007 Reading were involved in the Premier League's highest-scoring match, losing 7-4 to Portsmouth in 2007. At the end of the season they were relegated but, after losing in the Championship play-off final to Swansea in 2011, they returned to the top flight in 2012 after winning the second tier title.

HONOURS
Championship champions *2006, 2012*
Division 3 (S) champions *1926*
Division 3 champions *1986*
Second Division champions *1994*
Division 4 champions *1979*

REAL MADRID

Year founded: 1902
Ground: Estadio Bernabeu (85,454)
Previous name: Madrid
Nickname: Los Meringues
League titles: 32
Domestic cups: 18
European cups: 12
International cups: 3

Founded by students as Madrid FC in 1902, the title 'Real' (meaning 'Royal') was bestowed on the club by King Alfonso XIII in 1920.

• **One of the most famous names in world football, Real Madrid won**

the first ever European Cup in 1956 and went on to a claim a record five consecutive victories in the competition with a side featuring greats such as Alfredo di Stefano, Ferenc Puskas and Francisco Gento. Real's total of nine victories in the European Cup/Champions League is also a record.

• The club have dominated Spanish football over the years, winning a record 32 league titles (11 more than nearest rivals Barcelona) including a record five on the trot on two occasions (1961-65 and 1986-90).

• **As Madrid FC, the club won silverware for the first time, the Spanish Cup, in 1905. They went on to win the trophy four times in succession, a record later equalled by their opponents in the final, Athletic Bilbao.**

• Between 17th February 1957 and 7th March 1965 Real Madrid were undefeated at home in the league for an incredible 121 consecutive matches, a sequence unmatched by any European team.

HONOURS
Spanish League *1932, 1933, 1954, 1955, 1957, 1958, 1961, 1962, 1963, 1964, 1965, 1967, 1968, 1969, 1972, 1975, 1976, 1978, 1979, 1980, 1986, 1987, 1988, 1989, 1990, 1995, 1997, 2001, 2003, 2007, 2008, 2012*
Spanish Cup *1905, 1906, 1907, 1908, 1917, 1934, 1936, 1946, 1947, 1962, 1970, 1974, 1975, 1980, 1982, 1989, 1993, 2011*
European Cup/Champions League *1956, 1957, 1958, 1959, 1960, 1966, 1998, 2000, 2002*
UEFA Cup *1985, 1986*
European Super Cup *2002*
Intercontinental Cup *1960, 1998, 2002*

REFEREES

In the 19th century Colonel Francis Marinden was the referee at a record nine FA Cup finals, including eight on the trot between 1883 and 1990. His record will never be beaten as the FA now appoints a different referee for the FA Cup final every year.

• **The first referee to send off a player in the FA Cup final was Peter Willis, who dismissed Manchester United defender Kevin Moran in the 1985 final for a foul on Everton's Peter Reid. Video replays showed that it was a harsh decision.**

Luckily for Real Madrid, the giant water bomb sent by Barcelona failed to explode on their championship celebration party!

PEPE REINA

Born: Madrid, 31st August 1982
Position: Goalkeeper
Club career:
1999-2000 Barcelona B 41
2000-02 Barcelona 30
2002-05 Villarreal 109
2005- Liverpool 254
International record:
2005- Spain 24

A model of consistency since he arrived from Villarreal in 2005, Liverpool goalkeeper Pepe Reina has won the Barclays Golden Glove (awarded to the 'keeper with the most clean sheets in the Premier League) a record three times, collecting the award in three consecutive seasons between 2006 and 2008. In December 2010 he kept his 100th clean sheet in the league for the Reds in his 198th game, making him the fastest Liverpool goalkeeper to reach this landmark.

• **In his seven years on Merseyside, Reina has won just two major honours with the Reds, the FA Cup in 2006 and the Carling Cup in 2012. Both games were settled by penalty shoot-outs with the Madrid-born goalkeeper sensationally saving three of West Ham's penalties in the FA Cup final at the Millennium stadium.**

• In 2007 Reina became only the third player to follow his father by featuring in a European Cup final when he lined up against AC Milan in Athens. Unfortunately, Reina finished on the losing side, just as his father, Miguel, had done in 1974 with Atletico Madrid.

• **Reina made his international debut for Spain in 2005 but has had to be content with being his country's number two behind Real Madrid's Iker Casillas.**

RELEGATION

Birmingham City boast the unwanted record of having been relegated from the top flight more often than any other club, having taken the drop 12 times — most recently in 2010/11. However, the Blues have not experienced that sinking feeling as often as Notts County, who have suffered 15 relegations.

• **In the Premier League era Crystal Palace have been the most unfortunate club, dropping out of the top flight on no fewer than four occasions.**

• Modern-day referees have to put up with plenty of abuse but at least none of them have suffered the unfortunate fate of William Ernest Williams, who was attacked and killed in his dressing room in 1912 after a match between Wattstown and Aberaman Athletic in south Wales. His attacker was later jailed for manslaughter.

• **On 21st August 2010 Michael Oliver became the youngest referee to officiate at a Premier League match when he took charge of Birmingham's home game with Blackburn, aged 25 and 182 days.**

• English referees have taken charge of the World Cup final on a record four occasions: in 1950 (George Reader), 1954 (William Ling), 1974 (Jack Taylor) and 2010 (Howard Webb).

• **The first woman to officiate at a major cup final was Wendy Toms, who** ran the line at the League Cup final between Leicester and Tranmere in 2000.

TOP 10

MOST YELLOW CARDS AWARDED BY PREMIER LEAGUE REFEREES IN 2011/12

1.	Phil Dowd	3.79 per match
2.	Kevin Friend	3.7 per match
3.	Mike Dean	3.6 per match
4.	Andre Marriner	3.45 per match
5.	Mike Jones	3.44 per match
6.	Stuart Attwell	3.3 per match
7.	Martin Atkinson	3.3 per match
8.	Anthony Taylor	3.22 per match
9.	Howard Webb	3.1 per match
10.	Jon Moss	3.09 per match

• Of longstanding members of the Football League or Premier League, Arsenal have the best relegation record, having only once been demoted (in 1913) in a proud 123-year history.

• **When Derby County went down from the Premier League in 2008 they did so with the lowest points total of any club in the history of the English league football. The Rams accumulated only 11 points in a miserable campaign, during which they managed to win just one match out of 38.**

• Chelsea are the only club to have been relegated from the top flight via the play-offs, taking the drop in 1988 after losing in the final to Second Division Middlesbrough. Following crowd violence at the match, the Football League changed the play-off format so that all four competing clubs were from the same division.

REPLAYS

In the days before penalty shoot-outs, the FA Cup fourth qualifying round tie between Alvechurch and Oxford City went to a record five replays before Alvechurch reached the first round proper with a 1-0 win in the sixth match between the two clubs.

• **The first FA Cup final to go to a replay was the 1875 match between Royal Engineers and Old Etonians, Engineers winning 2-0 in the second match. The last FA Cup final to require a replay was the 1993 match between Arsenal and Sheffield Wednesday, the Gunners eventually triumphing 2-1 in the second game. In 1999 the FA scrapped final replays, ruling that any drawn match would be settled on the day by penalties.**

• Five League Cup finals have gone to replays, the first in 1977 between Aston Villa and Everton requiring a third match before Villa eventually won 3-2 at Old Trafford. The 1997 final between Leicester and Middlesbrough was the last major domestic final to be replayed, Leicester winning 1-0 in the second match at Hillsborough.

• **Only one European Cup final went to a**

'Keep looking! I really need to find that contact lens...'

replay, Bayern Munich defeating Atletico Madrid 4-0 in 1974 after the original final ended in a 0-0 draw.

REPUBLIC OF IRELAND

First international: Republic of Ireland 1 Bulgaria 0, 1924
Most capped player: Shay Given 125 caps (1996-)
Leading goalscorer: Robbie Keane, 53 goals (1998-)
First World Cup appearance: Republic of Ireland 1 England 1, 1990
Biggest win: 8-0 v Malta (1983)
Heaviest defeat: 0-7 v Brazil (1982)

The Republic of Ireland enjoyed their most successful period under English manager Jack Charlton in the late 1980s and early 1990s. 'Big Jack' became a legend on the Emerald Isle after guiding the Republic to their first-ever World Cup in 1990, taking the team to the quarter-finals of the tournament before they were eliminated by hosts Italy.

• Under Charlton, Ireland were undefeated in four matches against arch-rivals England, pulling off a famous 1-0 win in the 1988 European Championships and drawing three other competitive matches 1-1. This record prompted the gleeful chant whenever the teams met of, "You'll never beat the Irish!".

• The Republic were the first country from outside the United Kingdom to beat England on home soil, winning 2-0 at Goodison Park in 1949.

• **In 2009, in a World Cup play-off against France, the Republic were on the wrong end of one of the worst refereeing decisions of all time when Thierry Henry's blatant handball went unpunished before he crossed for William Gallas to score the goal that ended Ireland's hopes of reaching the 2010 finals in South Africa.**

• The Republic qualified for their first major tournament since the 2002 World Cup when they beat Estonia in a play-off to reach Euro 2012. However, at the finals the Irish performed poorly, losing all three of their games and conceding nine goals – their worst ever showing in either the World Cup or the European championships.

IS THAT A FACT?
The Republic of Ireland's first ever manager, Mick Meagan, is also his country's least successful boss, his team failing to win a single one of the 12 games for which he was in charge between 1969 and 1971.

WORLD CUP RECORD	
1930 Did not enter	
1934 Did not qualify	
1938 Did not qualify	
1950 Did not enter	
1954-86 Did not qualify	
1990 Quarter-finals	
1994 Round 2	
1998 Did not qualify	
2002 Round 2	
2006 Did not qualify	
2010 Did not qualify	

'Wake up Arjen, the match is about to start!'

SIR BOBBY ROBSON

Born: Sacriston, County Durham, 18th February 1933
Died: 31st July 2009
Managerial career:
1968 Fulham
1969-82 Ipswich Town
1982-90 England
1990-92 PSV Eindhoven
1992-94 Sporting Lisbon
1994-96 Porto
1996-97 Barcelona
1998-99 PSV Eindhoven
1999-2004 Newcastle United

Apart from the legendary Sir Alf Ramsey, who won the trophy in 1966, no other England manager has come closer than Bobby Robson to claiming football's greatest prize. At the 1990 World Cup in Italy Robson's England reached the semi-finals, where they were desperately unlucky to be knocked out by Germany in a nail-biting penalty shoot-out.

• **Robson also guided England to the quarter-finals of the 1986 tournament in Mexico during an eight-year reign as his country's boss. Overall, his record was pretty good, but a failure to qualify for the 1984 European championships and a poor showing at the 1988 finals made him a target for the tabloid press.**

• He made his managerial reputation with Ipswich, who he led to triumphs in the FA Cup (in 1978) and the UEFA Cup (in 1981). His achievements with the unfashionable East Anglian outfit prompted the club to erect a statue of Robson outside Portman Road in 2002. In the same year he received a knighthood for services to football.

• **After resigning as England manager, Robson worked on the continent for a number of famous clubs. He won two league titles with PSV Eindhoven, another brace with Porto and, in 1997, the European Cup Winners' Cup with Barcelona. His ended his managerial career with Newcastle, the club he had supported as a boy, twice leading the Geordies to Champions League qualification.**

• Robson's playing career was spent with Fulham and West Bromwich Albion. He played 20 times for England, scoring twice on his debut in a 4-0 Wembley win over France in 1957. The following year he played in the World Cup in Sweden.

ARJEN ROBBEN

Born: Bedum, Holland, 23rd June 1984
Position: Winger
Club career:
2000-02 Groningen 50 (8)
2002-04- PSV 56 (17)
2004-07 Chelsea 67 (15)
2007-09 Real Madrid 50 (11)
2009- Bayern Munich 62 (40)
International record:
2003- Holland 60 (17)

Flying winger Arjen Robben is one of a handful of players to have won the domestic league title with four clubs in four different countries, having finished top of the pile with PSV (2003), Chelsea (2005 and 2006), Real Madrid (2008) and Bayern Munich (2010).

• **After starting out with Groningen, Robben made his name with PSV, with whom he was named Dutch Young Player of the Year in 2003. The following year he joined Chelsea where, despite suffering a number of injuries and a testicular cancer scare during his three years in London, he enjoyed huge** success, collecting five winners' medals before departing for Real Madrid in 2007 for £24 million – making him the Blues' most expensive sale.

• After two years he was on the move again, to Bayern Munich, where he won the domestic double in his first season and was also voted Player of the Year in Germany – the first Dutchman to receive the honour. Robben, though, was denied a treble when Bayern were beaten in the final of the Champions League by Inter Milan. Two years later, in 2012, he suffered more heartbreak in the same tournament when Bayern were beaten by Chelsea in the final in Munich, although the result could have been very different if Robben had not seen his penalty in extra-time saved by his former team-mate Petr Cech.

• **The pacy wideman has also experienced much disappointment at international level, being part of the Holland team that lost in the 2010 World Cup final to Spain. Two years later he failed to live up to his stellar reputation at Euro 2012, looking a pale shadow of his normal self as the much-fancied Dutch crashed out at the group stage after losing all three of their games.**

BRYAN ROBSON

Born: Chester-le-Street, 11th January 1957
Position: Midfielder
Club career:
1974-81 West Bromwich Albion 198 (40)
1981-94 Manchester United 345 (74)
1994-96 Middlesbrough 25 (1)
International record:
1980-91 England 90 (26)

Dubbed 'Captain Marvel' for his inspirational midfield performances for Manchester United and England, Bryan Robson captained his country on 65 occasions – a figure only surpassed by Billy Wright and Bobby Moore.

• Robson's £1.5 million move from West Bromwich Albion to Manchester United in 1981 broke the British transfer record and he remained the UK's most-expensive player for the next six years. However, it proved money well spent as 'Robbo' went on to lead United to three FA Cups and the European Cup Winners' Cup, as well as winning two Premier League titles later in his career.

• Robson won 90 caps for England, and would have gained many more but for a string of serious injuries. He scored 26 goals for his country, including one after just 27 seconds against France in 1982 which at the time was the fastest goal ever scored at the World Cup.

• In 1994 Robson became player-manager of Middlesbrough. In seven years in charge at the Riverside he led the Teesiders to three Wembley finals, all of which they lost. He has since managed West Brom, Bradford City, Sheffield United and Thailand.

ROCHDALE

Year founded: 1907
Ground: Spotland stadium (10,249)
Nickname: The Dale
Biggest win: 8-1 v Chesterfield (1926)
Heaviest defeat: 1-9 v Tranmere Rovers (1931)

Founded at a meeting at the town's Central Council Office in 1907, Rochdale were elected to the Third Division (North) as founder members in 1921.

• In their long history, Rochdale have gained promotion just twice, climbing into the third tier for the first time in 1969. They stayed there until a disastrous season in 1973/74 when they finished bottom of the pile after winning just two matches... a Third Division record.

• The proudest day in the club's history came in 1962 when they reached the League Cup final. Rochdale lost 4-0 on aggregate to Norwich City, then in the Second Division, but it remains the only time a club from the bottom division has reached a major cup final.

• Rochdale failed to win a single game in the FA Cup for 18 years from 1927 – the longest period of time any club has gone without victory in the competition. The appalling run finally came to an end in 1945 when The Dale beat Stockport 2-1 in a first-round replay.

• Along with Hartlepool, Rochdale have spent more seasons than any other club in the bottom two divisions of English football (84), without ever reaching the top two tiers.

BRENDAN RODGERS

Born: Carnlough, 26th January 1973
Managerial career:
2008-09 Watford
2009 Reading
2010-12 Swansea City
2012- Liverpool

Brendan Rodgers was appointed manager of Liverpool in June 2012 after just one season in the Premier League with Swansea City. Aged 39, he was the third youngest Premier League boss in situ at the start of the 2012/13 season after Tottenham's Andre Villas-Boas and Wigan's Roberto Martinez.

• After injury forced him to retire aged just 20, Rodgers began his coaching career at Reading, where he was youth team manager. He moved to Chelsea to take a similar role at Stamford Bridge in 2006, where he worked under Jose Mourinho.

• He became Watford manager in 2008 but left after a season to return to Reading. However, after a disappointing run of results he was sacked by chairman John Madjeski in December 2009.

• Rodgers' fortunes turned around at Swansea, who he joined in 2010 and led into the Premier League the following year after a play-off final victory against Reading. He

Liverpool boss Brendan Rodgers

then guided Swansea, the first Welsh club to reach the Premier League, to a respectable mid-table finish and earned many plaudits for the Swans' free-flowing passing style.

CRISTIANO RONALDO

Born: Madeira, Portugal, 5th February 1985
Position: Winger/Striker
Club career:
2001-03 Sporting Lisbon 25 (3)
2003-09 Manchester United 196 (84)
2009- Real Madrid 101 (112)
International record:
2003- Portugal 96 (36)

In July 2009 Cristiano Ronaldo became the most expensive footballer ever when he joined Real Madrid from Manchester United for £80 million on a six-year contract worth a reported £10 million a year. He has since provided Real with a superb return on their investment, becoming the second-fastest player in history to reach 100 La Liga goals in 2012. He enjoyed his best season in 2011/12 scoring a club record 60 goals in all competitions and helping Real win the league title.

TOP 10

WORLD'S MOST EXPENSIVE PLAYERS

1. Cristiano Ronaldo (Manchester United to Real Madrid, 2009) £80m
2. Zlatan Ibrahimovic (Inter Milan to Barcelona, 2009) £59m
3. Kaka (AC Milan to Real Madrid, 2009) £56m
4. Zinedine Zidane (Juventus to Real Madrid, 2001) £53m
5. Fernando Torres (Liverpool to Chelsea, 2011) £50m
6. Luis Figo (Barcelona to Real Madrid, 2000) £44m
7. Radamel Falcao (Porto to Atletico Madrid, 2011) £40.7m
8. Hernan Crespo (Parma to Lazio, 2000) £38m
9. Sergio Aguero (Atletico Madrid to Manchester City, 2011) £38m
10. Ronaldo (Inter Milan to Real Madrid, 2002) £37.4m

• Born on the Portuguese island of Madeira, Ronaldo began his career with Sporting Lisbon before joining Manchester United in a £12.25 million deal in 2003. The following year he won his first trophy with the Red Devils, opening the scoring as United beat Millwall 3-0 in the FA Cup final. He later helped United win a host of major honours, including three Premiership titles and the Champions League in 2008.

• In 2007 Ronaldo was voted PFA Player of the Year and Young Player of the Year, the first man to achieve this double since Andy Gray in 1977. The following season he scored a remarkable 42 goals for United in all competitions, and won the European Golden Boot. Three years later, in his second season with Real, he became the first player ever to win the Boot in two different countries.

• Ronaldo made his international debut for Portugal against Kazakhstan in 2003 and the following year played for his country in their surprise Euro 2004 final defeat by Greece. He first captained Portugal in 2007 and now wears the armband on a regular basis.

• Arguably the most exciting talent in world football today, Cristiano Ronaldo is the only player from the Premier League to have been voted World Footballer of the Year, having collected this most prestigious of awards in 2008. In the same year he was also voted European Footballer of the Year.

WAYNE ROONEY

Born: Liverpool, 24th October 1985
Position: Striker
Club career:
2002-04 Everton 67 (15)
2004- Manchester United 251 (129)
International record:
2003- England 76 (29)

When Wayne Rooney scored his first goal for England, against Macedonia in a Euro 2004 qualifier on 6th September 2003, he was aged just 17 years and 317 days... the youngest player ever to find the net for the Three Lions.

• Rooney burst onto the scene with Everton in 2002, scoring his first league goal for the Toffees with a magnificent 20-yarder against reigning champions Arsenal at Goodison Park just five days before his 17th birthday. At the time he was the youngest-ever Premiership scorer, but his record has since been surpassed by both James Milner and James Vaughan.

• After starring for England at Euro 2004 Rooney signed for Manchester United later that summer for £25.6 million, to become the world's most expensive teenage footballer. He started his Old Trafford career in sensational style with a hat-trick against Fenerbahce and has since played a pivotal part in the Red Devils' recent success, winning four Premier League titles, two League Cups and the

Wayne Rooney, England's youngest ever goalscorer

Champions League. He enjoyed his most prolific season in 2011/12, hitting 27 Premier League goals and taking his overall tally in the Champions League to 27 – a record for a British player. It was a return to form for Rooney who, during the previous season, had looked below par after publicly expressing a wish to leave Old Trafford, before eventually signing a new improved contract with the club.

• When Rooney made his England debut against Australia on 12th February 2003 he was his country's youngest-ever player, but he has since lost this particular record to Arsenal's Theo Walcott.

• Famously hot-tempered, Rooney endured his worst moment in an England shirt at the 2006 World Cup when he was sent off in the quarter-final against Portugal after clashing with Ricardo Carvalho. He fared little better at the 2010 finals in South Africa or at Euro 2012, completely failing at both tournaments to live up to his billing as one of the best players in the world.

ROSS COUNTY

Year founded: 1929
Ground: Victoria Park (6,310)
Nickname: The Staggies
Biggest win: 11-0 v St Cuthbert Wanderers (1993)
Heaviest defeat: 1-6 v Alloa (1968) and v Meadowbank (1991)

Founded in 1929, Ross County played in the Highland League until 1994 when they were elected to the Scottish Third Division along with Inverness Caledonian Thistle.

• Ross County enjoyed the greatest day in their history in 2010 when they sensationally beat Celtic in the Scottish Cup semi-final. However, there was to be no fairytale ending for The Staggies as they went down 3-0 to Dundee United in the final at Hampden Park.

• Two years later the club won promotion to the SPL for the first time in their history after a glorious campaign which ended with them a record 24 points clear at the top of the Scottish First Division. The Staggies also put together an incredible 34-match unbeaten run,

matching a record for the Scottish second tier set by Aidrieonians way back in 1955.

• With a capacity of just 6,310, Ross County's tiny Victoria Park is the smallest in the SPL.

HONOURS
First Division champions 2012
Second Division champions 2008
Third Division champions 1999

ROTHERHAM UNITED

Year founded: 1925
Ground: New York Stadium (12,021)
Nickname: The Millers
Biggest win: 8-0 v Oldham Athletic (1947)
Heaviest defeat: 1-11 v Bradford City (1928)

The club had its origins in Thornhill FC (founded in 1878, later becoming Rotherham County) and Rotherham Town, who merged with County to form Rotherham United in 1925.

• The club's greatest moment came in 1961 when they reached the first ever League Cup final, losing 3-2 on aggregate to Aston Villa. Six years earlier Rotherham had missed out on goal average on promotion to the First Division for the first time in the club's history... the closest they've ever been to playing top-flight football.

• In 1991 Rotherham made history by becoming the first side to win a penalty shoot-out in the FA Cup, defeating Scunthorpe United 7-6 on spot-kicks after a first-round replay.

• Less happily, in 1925 Rotherham failed to keep a clean sheet in 45 consecutive league matches. The run was a record at the time, but Bristol City extended it to 49 games seven years later.

• At the start of the 2012/13 season the club moved from the Don Valley stadium in Sheffield to a brand-new ground in Rotherham, the 12,000-capacity New York Stadium.

HONOURS
Division 3 (N) champions 1951
Division 3 champions 1981
Division 4 champions 1989
Football League Trophy 1996

IAN RUSH

Born: St Asaph, 20th October 1961
Position: Striker
Club career:
1979-80 Chester City 34 (18)
1980-87 Liverpool 224 (139)
1987-88 Juventus 29 (8)
1988-96 Liverpool 245 (90)
1996-97 Leeds United 36 (3)
1997-98 Newcastle United 10 (2)
1998 Sheffield United (loan) 4 (0)
1998-99 Wrexham 18 (0)
1999 Sydney Olympic 2 (0)
International record:
1980-96 Wales 73 (28)

One of the most prolific strikers ever, Ian Rush is Liverpool's leading scorer of all time with a total of 346 goals for the club in two spells at Anfield in the 1980s and 1990s.

• Rush has scored more goals in the FA Cup final than any other player, with a total of five for Liverpool in the 1986, 1989 and 1992 finals. His strikes helped the Reds win all three games, two of them against local rivals Everton. With 44 goals in the competition as a whole, Rush is the second-highest scorer in the history of the tournament and the leading FA Cup marksman of the 20th century.

• 'Rushie', as he was known to Liverpool fans, is also the joint leading scorer in the League Cup with Geoff Hurst, the pair both ending their careers on 49 goals. He enjoyed huge success in the tournament, winning the trophy in 1981, 1982, 1983, 1984 and 1995 to become the first player to collect five League Cup winners' medals.

• Rush tops the scoring charts for his native Wales, with 28 goals in 73 appearances. However, he never played in the finals of either the World Cup or the European Championships.

• Rush is the all-time leading scorer in the Merseyside derby with 25 goals against Everton, including a post-war record four goals in a 5-0 thrashing of the Toffees at Goodison Park on 6th November 1982.

• In 1988 Rush returned to Liverpool from Juventus for a then British record £2.7 million. He had only spent a year on the continent and seemed pleased to be back, famously complaining that life in Italy "was like being in a foreign country."

SACKINGS

In May 2007 Leroy Rosenoir was sacked as manager of Conference side Torquay United after just 10 minutes in charge! No sooner had the former West Ham and QPR striker been unveiled as the Gulls' new boss when he was told that the club had been bought by a business consortium and his services were no longer required.

IS THAT A FACT?
Ian Porterfield became the first Premier League manager to be sacked when he was given the boot by Chelsea in February 1993.

• In 1959 Bill Lambton got the boot from Scunthorpe United after just three days in the managerial hot seat, an English league record. His reign at the Old Showground took in just one match – a 3-0 defeat at Liverpool in a Second Division fixture. The shortest Premier League reign, meanwhile, was Les Reed's seven-game stint at Charlton in 2006.

• Crystal Palace have sacked more managers since the Second World War than any other league club. The Eagles have made 43 different managerial appointments since 1945, although Steve Coppell and Steve Kember have filled the role on four occasions each.

• **The safest job in football, on the other hand, is manager of Manchester United. Since the war the Reds have only made eight managerial appointments, helped by the lengthy tenures of Sir Matt Busby (1945-69) and Sir Alex Ferguson, who arrived at Old Trafford way back in 1986.**

• A record 10 Premier League managers were replaced during the 1994/95 season, while just one got the chop in 1992/93.

ST JOHNSTONE

Year founded: 1884
Ground: McDiarmid Park (10,456)
Nickname: The Saints
Biggest win: 13-0 v Tulloch (1887)
Heaviest defeat: 0-12 v Cowdenbeath (1928)

St Johnstone were founded in 1884 by a group of local cricketers in Perth who wanted to keep fit in winter.

• **The club have experienced little in the way of success over the years, but they did reach the League Cup final in 1969 (losing 1-0 to Celtic) and again in 1998 (losing 2-1 to Rangers).**

• The Saints' record scorer is John Brogan, who hit 114 league goals for the club between 1976 and 1984. Stalwart goalkeeper Alan Main played in a record 361 games for St Johnstone in two spells at McDiarmid Park between 1995 and 2010.

• Defensive midfielder Nick Dasovic won a club record 26 international caps for Canada while at St Johnstone between 1996 and 2002.

HONOURS
Division 2 champions 1924, 1960, 1963
First Division champions 1983, 1990, 1997, 2009

ST MIRREN

Year founded: 1877
Ground: St Mirren Park (8,023)
Nickname: The Buddies
Biggest win: 15-0 v Glasgow University (1960)
Heaviest defeat: 0-9 v Rangers (1897)

Named after the patron saint of Paisley, St Mirren were founded in 1877 by a group of local cricketers and rugby players. The club were founder members of the Scottish League in 1890, but have never finished higher than third in the top flight.

• **The Buddies, though, have won the Scottish Cup on three occasions, most recently in 1987 when they beat Dundee United 1-0 in the final after extra time – the last time that the winners have fielded an all-Scottish line-up.**

• St Mirren were the only Scottish club to win the Anglo-Scottish Cup in the six years of its existence, thrashing Bristol City 5-1 on aggregate in 1980. Seven years later they were involved in a short-lived attempt to revive the tournament, but after their match with Coventry City attracted a poor attendance the competition was unceremoniously scrapped.

• **Defender Andy Millen is the oldest player to appear in the SPL, turning out for St Mirren against Hearts for the final time on 15th March 2008 when he was aged 42 and 279 days.**

• In 1986 St Mirren's Alex Miller became the first player to receive three red cards in the same match when he was sent off for fighting a Motherwell opponent, and was then shown a further two red cards for dissent.

HONOURS
Division 2 champions 1968
First Division champions 1977, 2000, 2006
Scottish Cup 1926, 1959, 1987

PETER SCHMEICHEL

Born: Gladsaxe, Denmark, 18th November 1963
Position: Goalkeeper
Club career:
1981-84 Gladsaxe-Hero 46 (0)
1984-87 Hvidovre 78 (6)
1987-91 Brondby 119 (2)
1991-99 Manchester United 292 (0)
1999-2001 Sporting Lisbon 50 (0)
2001-02 Aston Villa 29 (1)
2002-03 Manchester City 29 (0)
International record:
1987-2001 Denmark 129 (1)

One of the greatest goalkeepers ever, Peter Schmeichel played a record 129 times for Denmark. The highlight of his international career came in 1992 when the Danes won the European championship, beating hot favourites Germany 2-0 in the final. Incredibly, Denmark had already been eliminated in the qualifying round, but sneaked into the finals through the back door after the withdrawal of war-torn Yugoslavia.

• **At club level, Schmeichel enjoyed huge success with Manchester United whom he joined from Brondby for £530,000 in 1991 – a deal later described by Sir Alex Ferguson as "the bargain of the century". The Great**

Dane went on to win five Premiership titles and three FA Cups with the Reds, before skippering his side to victory in the 1999 Champions League final against Bayern Munich.

• After winning the Portuguese title with Sporting Lisbon, Schmeichel returned to England with Aston Villa in 2001. In the same year he became the first goalkeeper to score in the Premier League, shooting home from a corner in a 3-2 defeat at Everton.

PAUL SCHOLES

Born: Salford, 16th November 1974
Position: Midfielder
Club career:
1994-2011 Manchester United 466 (102)
2012- Manchester United 16 (4)
International record:
1997-2004 England 66 (14)

Described by Zinedine Zidane as "the greatest midfielder of his generation", Paul Scholes is one of just five players to have made more than 600 competitive appearances for Manchester United.

• A product of United's youth system, Scholes scored twice against Port Vale on his first-team debut in September 1994 before going on to enjoy a glittering career with the club. Among the many honours he won at Old Trafford before announcing his retirement in 2011 were eight Premier League titles, three FA Cups and two Champions League titles. In January 2012 he made a sensational return to the United team, earning rave reviews for some inspired displays as the Red Devils just missed out on the league title.

• Scholes made his England debut against South Africa in 1997 and the following year he played for his country at France '98, scoring in the group stage against Tunisia. In 1999 he hit a hat-trick at Wembley in a European championship qualifier against Poland and, later that year, secured England's place at Euro 2000 with two goals against Scotland in a play-off decider.

• Less happily, Scholes was the first and last England player to be sent off at the old Wembley, receiving his marching orders for a rash tackle in a friendly against Sweden in 2000. He has also crossed referees in the Champions League on a regular basis, collecting a competition record 32 yellow cards.

SCOTLAND

First international: Scotland 0 England 0, 1872
Most capped player: Kenny Dalglish, 102 caps (1971-86)
Leading goalscorer: Denis Law (1958-74) and Kenny Dalglish (1971-86), 30 goals
First World Cup appearance: Scotland 0 Austria 1, 1954
Biggest win: Scotland 11 Ireland 0, 1901
Heaviest defeat: Scotland 0 Uruguay 7, 1954

Along with England, Scotland are the oldest international team in the world. The two countries played the first official international way back in 1872, the match at Hamilton Crescent, Partick, finishing 0-0. Since then, honours have been more or less even between the 'Auld Enemies', with England winning 45 matches, Scotland winning 41 and 20 ending in a draw.

• It took the Scots a while to make an impression on the world scene. After withdrawing from the 1950 World Cup, Scotland competed in the finals for the first time in 1954 but were eliminated in the first round after suffering their worst-ever defeat, 7-0 to reigning champions Uruguay.

• Scotland have taken part in the World Cup finals on eight occasions but have never got beyond the group stage. They have been unlucky, though, going out of the 1974, 1978 and 1982 tournaments only on goal difference.

• Scotland have a pretty poor record in the European Championships, only qualifying for the finals on two occasions, in 1992 and 1996. Again, they failed to reach the knockout stage both times, although they were unfortunate to lose out on the 'goals scored' rule to Holland at Euro '96. More recently, the Scots made a brave

Along with arch rivals England, Scotland are the oldest international football team on the planet

attempt to qualify for Euro 2008 but were narrowly pipped by Italy and France despite beating the French home and away.

• Scotland had a good record in the Home Championships until the tournament was scrapped in 1984, winning the competition 24 times and sharing the title another 17 times. Only England (34 outright wins and 20 shared) have a better overall record.

• Two of Scotland's most famous wins, both against England, came in the Home Championships. In 1928 a Scottish team later dubbed 'the Wembley Wizards' won 5-1 at the Twin Towers, England's worst-ever home defeat. Then in 1967, a year after England had won the World Cup, Scotland triumphed 3-2 at Wembley, leading the 'Tartan Army' to hail their team as the unofficial world champions.

• In 2010 Rangers defender David Weir became Scotland's oldest international when he played against Lithuania, aged 40 and 117 days.

WORLD CUP RECORD
1930-38 Did not enter
1950 Withdrew
1954 Round 1
1958 Round 1
1962-70 Did not qualify
1974 Round 1
1978 Round 1
1982 Round 1
1986 Round 1
1990 Round 1
1994 Did not qualify
1998 Round 1
2002 Did not qualify
2006 Did not qualify
2010 Did not qualify

SCOTTISH CUP

The Scottish Cup was first played for in 1873/74, shortly after the formation of the Scottish FA. Queen's Park, who the previous year had competed in the English FA Cup, were the first winners, beating Clydesdale 2-0 in the final in front of a crowd of 3,000 at the original Hampden Park.

• Queen's Park were the dominant force in the early years of the competition, winning 10 of the first 20 finals, including one in 1884 when their opponents, Vale of Leven, failed to turn up! Since then, Celtic (35 wins) and Rangers (33 wins) have ruled the

TOP 10

HIGHEST CAPPED SCOTLAND PLAYERS
1. Kenny Dalglish (1971-86) 102 caps
2. Jim Leighton (1982-98) 91 caps
3. Alex McLeish (1980-93) 77 caps
4. Paul McStay (1983-97) 76 caps
5. Tom Boyd (1990-2001) 72 caps
6. David Weir (1997-2010) 69 caps
7. Christian Dailly (1997-2008) 67 caps
8. Willie Miller (1975-89) 65 caps
9. Danny McGrain (1973-82) 62 caps
10. Richard Gough (1983-93) 61 caps
    Ally McCoist (1985-98) 61 caps

roost, although Queen's Park (10 wins) remain third in the list of all-time winners ahead of Hearts (eight wins).

• The only second-tier club to win the trophy are East Fife, who beat Kilmarnock 4-1 in a replay in 1938.

• Incredibly, the biggest-ever victories in the history of British football took place in the Scottish Cup on the same day, 12th September 1885. Dundee Harp beat Aberdeen Rovers 35-0 and were confident that they had set a new record. Yet, no doubt to their utter amazement, they soon discovered that Arbroath had thrashed Bon Accord, a cricket club who had been invited to take part in the competition by mistake, 36-0!

• Minted in 1885, the Scottish Cup trophy is the oldest national trophy in the world.

SCUNTHORPE UNITED

Year founded: 1899
Ground: Glanford Park (9,088)
Previous name: Scunthorpe & Lindsey United
Nickname: The Iron
Biggest win: 9-0 v Boston United (1953)
Heaviest defeat: 0-8 v Carlisle United (1952)

The club was founded in 1899 when Brumby Hall linked up with some other local teams. Between 1910 and 1958

they were known as Scunthorpe and Lindsey United after amalgamating with the latter team.

• Elected to the Third Division (North) when the league expanded in 1950, Scunthorpe won the division eight years later. Their only other honour came in 2007 when The Iron were crowned League One champions under former physio Nigel Adkins. Scunny fans celebrated that triumph by singing, "Who needs Mourinho, we've got our physio!"

• Among the famous names to play for Scunthorpe are England and Liverpool legends Kevin Keegan and Ray Clemence and, somewhat bizarrely, former England cricket captain Ian Botham, who made 11 appearances as a striker for Scunthorpe in the early 1980s.

• Nobody has worn Scunthorpe's claret shirt more often than loyal defender Jack Brownsword. Between 1950 and 1965 he turned out in 595 league games for The Iron, making his last appearance at the age of 41 to become the club's oldest-ever player.

• The club's record signing is defender Rob Jones, who joined Scunthorpe from Hibs for £700,000 in 2009. A year later The Iron sold striker Gary Hooper to Celtic for a club record £2.4 million.

• In 1988 Scunthorpe became the first club in the modern era to move to a new purpose-built stadium when they left their former ground, the Old Showground, for Glanford Park.

HONOURS
Division 3 (North) champions 1958
League One champions 2007

BILL SHANKLY

Born: Glenbuck, 2nd September 1913
Died: 29th September 1981
Managerial career:
1949-51 Carlisle United
1951-54 Grimsby Town
1954-55 Workington
1956-59 Huddersfield Town
1959-74 Liverpool

Liverpool legend Bill Shankly turned the Reds from a mediocre Second Division outfit into the most formidable side in England and laid the foundations for the Merseysiders' domination of Europe under his successor, Bob Paisley.

• Shankly arrived at Anfield in 1959 and led the Reds to the Second Division title in 1962. His slick-passing, hard-working team won the league title just two years later before winning the FA Cup for the first time in the club's history in 1965. By the time he retired in 1974, the always quotable Scot had added two more League Championships, another FA Cup and Liverpool's first European trophy, the UEFA Cup in 1973.

• Most of his playing days were spent with Preston, with whom he won the FA Cup in 1938. A tenacious right half, he also won five caps for Scotland before his career was interrupted by the Second World War.

• Although he died in 1981 Shankly remains a revered figure at Anfield, where his memory is preserved both by a huge statue and the Shankly Gates entrance.

• Much like ordinary Liverpool fans, Shankly hugely enjoyed winding up the Reds' city rivals and near neighbours.

TOP 10

PREMIER LEAGUE SCORERS

1.	Alan Shearer (1992-2006)	260
2.	Andy Cole (1993-2008)	187
3.	Thierry Henry (1999-2012)	176
4.	Robbie Fowler (1993-2008)	163
5.	Frank Lampard (1995-)	150
6.	Les Ferdinand (1992-2005)	149
7.	Michael Owen (1996-)	149
8.	Teddy Sheringham (1992-2007)	147
9.	Wayne Rooney (2002-)	144
10.	Jimmy Floyd Hasselbaink (1997-2007)	127

"If Everton were playing at the bottom of the garden, I'd pull the curtains," he once told a reporter.

ALAN SHEARER

Born: Newcastle, 13th August 1970
Position: Striker
Club career:
1988-92 Southampton 118 (23)
1992-96 Blackburn Rovers 138 (112)
1996-2006 Newcastle United 303 (148)
International record:
1992-2000 England 63 (30)

Alan Shearer's incredible total of 260 Premiership goals (including a record 11 hat-tricks) for Blackburn and Newcastle is easily a record for the league, none of his rivals having passed the double-century mark. No fewer than 20 of his goals came against Leeds United, a Premier League record for one player against the same opponents.

• Shearer began his career with Southampton, marking his full debut for the Saints in 1988 by scoring three goals in a 4-2 victory over Arsenal. Aged just 17 years and 240 days, he was the youngest-ever player to score a top-flight hat-trick.

• In 1992 Shearer moved to Blackburn for a then British record £3.3 million. He helped Rovers win the Premiership title in 1994/95, his impressive tally of 34 goals that campaign earning him one of his three Golden Boots.

• A then world record £15 million move to Newcastle followed in 1996,

Alan Shearer's 'raised arm salute' goal celebration – one of the iconic images of football in the 1990s

to the delight of the Geordie faithful. An instant hit at St James' Park, Shearer eventually became the club's all-time record goalscorer, his total of 206 goals in all competitions for the Magpies eclipsing the 49-year-old record of another Toon legend, Jackie Milburn.

• Strong, good in the air and possessing a powerful shot with both feet, Shearer proved a real handful for international defences, too. His five goals at Euro '96 powered England to the semi-finals of the tournament and won him the competition's Golden Boot. By the time he quit international football after Euro 2000 he had scored 30 goals for his country, a figure only surpassed by four other England players.

• Shearer became a pundit for the BBC after hanging up his boots in 2006, but three years later he sensationally returned to his beloved St James' Park as Newcastle caretaker manager. However, in his eight matches in charge he was unable to prevent the Geordies from dropping out of the Premier League for the first time.

SHEFFIELD UNITED

Year founded: 1889
Ground: Bramall Lane (32,702)
Nickname: The Blades
Biggest win: 10-0 v Port Vale (1892) and v Burnley (1929)
Heaviest defeat: 0-13 v Bolton (1890)

The club was founded at a meeting at the city's Adelphi Hotel in 1899 by the members of the Sheffield United Cricket Club, partly to make greater use of the facilities at Bramall Lane.

• The Blades enjoyed their heyday in the late Victorian era, winning the title in 1898, and lifting the FA Cup in both 1899 and 1902. The club won the FA Cup again in 1915, in what was to be the last final to be played before the First World War brought a halt to the sporting calendar. They chalked up another victory in 1925.

• The club's leading scorer is Harry Johnson, who bagged 201 league goals between 1919 and 1930. His successor at centre forward, Jimmy Dunne, scored

Losing the 2011/12 Play-Off final was a kick up the backside for Sheffield United

a record 41 goals in the 1930/31 season, helped by a purple patch when he found the net in 12 consecutive matches (another club record).

• The Blades' home, Bramall Lane, is one of the oldest sporting arenas in the world. It first hosted cricket in 1855, before football was introduced to the ground in 1862. Sixteen years later, in 1878, the world's first-ever floodlit match was played at the stadium between two sides picked from the Sheffield Football Association, the lights being provided by two generators.

• During an 18-year career with the club between 1948 and 1966, Joe Shaw made a record 631 appearances for the Blades.

• In 2006 Sheffield United became the first foreign club to take over a Chinese team when they purchased Chengdu Wuniu (now known as Chengdu Blades).

• The following year United broke their transfer record when they bought James Beattie from Everton for £4 million. In

2009 the Blades received a club record £8 million when they sold full backs Kyle Naughton and Kyle Walker to Tottenham.

HONOURS
Division 1 champions 1898
Division 2 champions 1953
Division 4 champions 1982
FA Cup 1899, 1902, 1915, 1925

IS THAT A FACT?
Sheffield United's total of 90 points in League One in 2011/12 was the highest ever by a team not gaining automatic promotion from the third tier. The Blades missed out in the play-offs, too, losing the final on penalties to Yorkshire rivals Huddersfield.

Despite their nickname, The Owls are just as happy playing during the day as at night

SHEFFIELD WEDNESDAY

Year founded: 1867
Ground: Hillsborough (39,732)
Previous name: The Wednesday
Nickname: The Owls
Biggest win: 12-0 v Halliwell (1891)
Heaviest defeat: 0-10 v Aston Villa (1912)

The club was formed as The Wednesday in 1867 at the Adelphi Hotel in Sheffield by members of the Wednesday Cricket Club, who originally met on that particular day of the week. In 1929 the club added 'Sheffield' to their name, but are still often referred to simply as 'Wednesday'.

• **In 1904 the Owls became the first club in the 20th century to win consecutive league championships. They did so again in 1929/30, but have not won the league since.**

• In 1935 Wednesday won the FA Cup for the third and last time, striker Ellis Rimmer scoring in every round of the competition.

• **Promoted to the Championship in 2012, Sheffield Wednesday have won** the second tier of English football five times (a total only surpassed by Manchester City and Leicester City). Their last triumph came in 1959 when they banged in a club record 106 goals on their way to the title.

• Andrew Wilson holds two significant records for the club. Between 1900 and 1920 he played in 501 league matches, scoring 199 goals. No Wednesday player, before or since, can match these figures.

• **In 1991, while residing in the old Second Division, the Owls won the League Cup for the first and only time in their history, beating Manchester United 1-0 at Wembley. It was the last time that a club from outside the top flight has lifted a major domestic cup.**

• On the opening day of the 2000/01 season Wednesday goalkeeper Kevin Pressman was sent off after just 13 seconds at Molineux for handling a Wolves shot outside the penalty area... the fastest dismissal ever in British football.

HONOURS
Division 1 champions 1903, 1904, 1929, 1930
Division 2 champions 1900, 1926, 1952, 1956, 1959
FA Cup 1896, 1907, 1935
League Cup 1991

PETER SHILTON

Born: Leicester, 18th September 1949
Position: Goalkeeper
Club career:
1966-75 Leicester City 286 (1)
1975-78 Stoke City 110
1978-82 Nottingham Forest 202
1982-87 Southampton 188
1987-92 Derby County 175
1995-96 Bolton Wanderers 1
1997 Leyton Orient 9
International record:
1970-90 England 125

Peter Shilton is the only player in the history of English football to have played 1,000 league games. He reached the landmark, aged 47, while keeping a clean sheet for Leyton Orient in their 2-0 win over Brighton on 22nd December 1996.

• **Shilton is England's highest-capped player with 125 appearances to his name. In his 20-year international career he played at three World Cups, where he kept 10 clean sheets – a goalkeeping record shared with France's Fabien Barthez.**

• A losing FA Cup finalist with Leicester City in 1969 at the age of 19, Shilton had to wait almost 10 years before he collected his first honour, the league championship with Nottingham Forest in 1978. He went on to win two European Cups with Forest before moving on to Southampton in 1982.

• Shilton is the last goalkeeper to be voted PFA Player of the Year, collecting the award in 1978. The only other 'keeper to be so honoured was Tottenham's Pat Jennings, two years earlier.

SHREWSBURY TOWN

Year founded: 1886
Ground: New Meadow (9,875)
Nickname: The Shrews
Biggest win: 11-2 v Marine (1995)
Heaviest defeat: 1-8 v Norwich City (1952) and v Coventry City (1963)

Founded at the Lion Hotel in Shrewsbury in 1886, the club played in regional football for many years until being elected to the Football League in 1950.

• Prolific striker Arthur Rowley is the club's record scorer, hitting 152 goals between 1958 and 1965 to complete his all-time league record of 434 goals (he also turned out for West Bromwich Albion, Fulham and Leicester City). His best season for the Shrews was in 1958/59 when he banged in a club best 38 goals.

• 'Sir' Mickey Brown is the club's leading appearance maker, playing in 418 league games in three spells at the club between 1986 and 2001. He was 'knighted' by the fans after scoring the winning goal against Exeter on the last day of the 1999/2000 season, thus preserving the club's league status and sending down local rivals Chester City instead.

• Shewsbury pulled off one of the biggest ever shocks in the FA Cup when they beat Premier League Everton 2-1 in 2003. However, at the end of the season they were relegated to the Conference (happily, the Shrews bounced back the next year).

• Promoted to League One in 2012, Shrewsbury have won the Welsh Cup six times – a record for an English club.

HONOURS
Division 3 champions 1979
Third Division champions 1994
Welsh Cup 1891, 1938, 1977, 1979, 1984, 1985

SILVA

DAVID SILVA

Born: Las Palmas, 8th January 1986
Position: Winger
Club career:
2003-04 Valencia B 14 (1)
2004-10 Valencia 119 (21)
2004-05 Eibar (loan) 35 (5)
2005-06 Celta Vigo 34 (4)
2010- Manchester City 71 (10)
International record:
2006- Spain 64 (18)

Tricky Manchester City winger David Silva joined the club from Valencia for £24 million in the summer of 2010 and in his first season in England helped the Eastlands outfit win the FA Cup. The following year he starred for City as the club won their first Premier League title.

• During the 2011/12 campaign Silva provided more assists (15) and produced more passes in the final third (800) than any other Premier League player. He also committed the most fouls (25) without once being shown a yellow card.

• One of the stars of the Valencia side that regularly managed to upset the twin powers of Barcelona and Real Madrid, Silva enjoyed his best moment with the Spanish side when they won the Copa del Rey in 2008, beating Getafe 3-1 in the final.

After a hard 90 minutes, David Silva always enjoys being carried home by Joe Hart

TOP 10

HIGHEST CAPPED SPAIN PLAYERS

1. Iker Casillas (2000-)   138 caps
2. Andoni Zubizarreta
   (1985-98)   126 caps
3. Xavi (2000-)   115 caps
4. Xabi Alonso (2003-)   103 caps
5. Raul (1996-2006)   102 caps
6. Carles Puyol (2000-)   99 caps
   Fernando Torres (2003-)
                                99 caps
8. Sergio Ramos (2005-)   93 caps
9. Fernando Hierro
   (1989-2002)   89 caps
10. David Villa (2005-)   82 caps

• A clever player who can dribble past opponents with apparent ease, Silva was first capped by Spain in 2006. He was a mainstay of the Spain side that won the Euro 2008 title, but was restricted to just two appearances as the Spanish topped that triumph by lifting the World Cup in 2010. However, he returned to the team at Euro 2012, heading the first goal in the final as Spain crushed Italy 4-0.

SIZE

The heaviest player in the history of the professional game was Willie 'Fatty' Foulke, who played in goal for Sheffield United, Chelsea and Bradford City. By the end of his career, the tubby custodian weighed in at an incredible 24 stone.

• At just five feet tall, Fred Le May is the shortest player ever to have appeared in the Football League. He played for Thames, Clapton Orient and Watford between 1930 and 1933.

• No prizes for guessing who the tallest ever England international is. It is, of course, giraffe-like striker Peter Crouch, who stands six feet seven inches in his socks. Crouch, though, is half an inch shorter than ex-Wolves striker Stefan Maierhofer and Birmingham's Serbian striker Nikola Zigic, who jointly claim the record as the tallest ever Premier League players.

• The shortest England international ever was Frederick 'Fanny' Walden, a five feet two inch winger with Tottenham who won the first of two caps in 1914.

SOUTHAMPTON

Year founded: 1885
Ground: St Mary's (32, 690)
Previous name: Southampton St Mary's
Nickname: The Saints
Biggest win: 14-0 v Newbury (1894)
Heaviest defeat: 0-8 v Tottenham (1936) and v Everton (1971)

Founded as Southampton St Mary's by members of St Mary's Church Young Men's Association in 1885, the club joined the Southern League in 1894 and became simply 'Southampton' the following year.

• The Saints won the Southern League six times in the decade up to 1904 and also appeared in two FA Cup finals during that period, losing to Bury in 1900 and to Sheffield United two years later.

• The club finally won the cup in 1976. Manchester United were hot favourites to beat the Saints, then in the Second Division, but the south coast side claimed the trophy thanks to Bobby Stokes's late strike. As scorer of the first (and only) goal in the final Stokes was rewarded with a free car... unfortunately, he still hadn't passed the driving test!

• Mick Channon, a member of that cup-winning team and now a successful racehorse trainer, is the Saints' leading scorer with a total of 185 goals in two spells at The Dell, the club's old ground. Derek Reeves holds the record for most goals in a season, notching 39 when the Saints won the Division Three title in 1959/60.

• Legendary winger Terry Paine, a member of England's 1966 World Cup-winning squad, is Southampton's longest serving player. Between 1956 and 1974 he wore the club's colours in no fewer than 713 league games before moving to Hereford United. Paine's amazing total of 824 league games puts him third in the all-time list, behind Peter Shilton and Tony Ford.

• England goalkeeper Shilton is the club's most-capped player, winning 49 of his record 125 caps while at The Dell.

• In August 2012 the Saints forked out a record £12 million to buy Uruguayan striker Gaston Ramirez from Bologna. A year earlier the club received a record cash injection reported to be around £12 million when teenage winger Alex Oxlade-Chamberlain signed for Arsenal.

• Southampton legend Matt Le Tissier was the first midfielder in the history of the Premiership to score a century of goals. His total of 101 strikes included 24 penalties, a figure only exceeded by Alan Shearer and Frank Lampard in the Premier League era.

• Helped by a superb run of 21 consecutive home league wins in 2011 – equalling the post-war record set by Liverpool in 1971/72 – Southampton returned to the Premier League after a seven-year absence in 2012.

HONOURS
Division 3 (South) champions 1922
Division 3 champions 1960
FA Cup 1976
Football League Trophy 2010

After two successive promotions, Southampton are back in the Premier League

The Spanish squad at Euro 2012 were all great friends, but they didn't care too much for Gerard Pique

SOUTHEND UNITED

Year founded: 1906
Ground: Roots Hall (12,392)
Nickname: The Shrimpers
Biggest win: 10-1 v Golders Green (1934), v Brentwood (1968) and v Aldershot (1990)
Heaviest defeat: 1-9 v Brighton and Hove Albion (1965)

Southend United were founded in 1906 at the Blue Boar pub, just 50 yards away from the club's home, Roots Hall.
• **After joining the Football League in 1920 the Shrimpers remained in the third tier for a record 46 years, before dropping into the Fourth Division in 1966.**
• The club's top appearance maker is Sandy Anderson, who turned out in 452 league games between 1950 and 1962. His team-mate Roger Hollis is Southend's leading marksman, rifling in 120 league goals in just six years at the club between 1954 and 1960.
• **A number of famous names have managed the club, including England World Cup-winning captain Bobby Moore and fellow England internationals Alvin Martin and Peter Taylor.**

• None of that illustrious trio, however, brought as much success to Roots Hall as former boss Steve Tilson. He guided the Shrimpers to consecutive promotions from the fourth tier to the Championship in 2005/06 and also presided over the club's greatest-ever victory, a 1-0 League Cup win against holders Manchester United in 2006.
• **A record six goals were disallowed for offside in Southend's 2-1 defeat at Swindon in 1948.**

> HONOURS
> *League One champions 2006*
> *Division 4 champions 1981*

SPAIN

First international: Spain 1 Denmark 0, 1920
Most capped player: Iker Casillas, 138 caps (2000-)
Leading goalscorer: David Villa, 51 goals (2005-)
First World Cup appearance: Spain 3 Brazil 1, 1934
Biggest win: Spain 13 Bulgaria 0, 1933
Heaviest defeat: Italy 7 Spain 1, 1928 and England 7 Spain 1, 1931

Considered by many the best and most attractive international side in the world, Spain are the first country in football history to win three major international titles on the trot following their successes at Euro 2008, the 2010 World Cup in South Africa and Euro 2012 in Poland and Ukraine.
• **Spain secured their first ever World Cup triumph with a 1-0 victory over Holland at the Soccer City stadium in Johannesburg, midfielder Andres Iniesta drilling home the all-important goal four minutes from the end of extra time. Despite their entertaining close passing style of play, Spain only managed to score eight goals in the tournament – the lowest total ever by the winning nation at a World Cup.**
• Along with Germany, Spain are the only country to have won the European Championships three times. Their first success came in 1964 when they had the advantage of playing the semi-final and final, against holders the Soviet Union, on home soil at Real Madrid's Bernabeu stadium. Then, in 2008, a single Fernando Torres goal was enough to see off Germany in the final in Vienna. Finally, in 2012, Spain made it a hat-trick of victories after annihilating Italy 4-0 in the final in Kiev.
• **Between 2007 and 2009 Spain went 35 matches without defeat (winning 32 and drawing just three) to equal the world record set by Brazil in the**

SPONSORSHIP

1990s. The run came to an end when Spain lost 2-0 to USA at the 2009 Confederations Cup, but the Spanish were soon back on form, going into the 2010 World Cup on the back of 18 consecutive victories before they surprisingly lost their opening match at the finals against Switzerland. That setback, though, was soon forgotten as Vicente del Bosque's men went on to lift the trophy, sparking jubilant scenes across Spain from Santander to Seville.

• Spain were the first non-UK team to beat England, defeating the Three Lions 4-3 in Madrid in 1929.

HONOURS

World Cup 2010
European championship 1964, 2008, 2012

World Cup record
1930 Did not enter
1934 Quarter-finals
1938 Did not enter
1950 Fourth place
1954 Did not qualify
1958 Did not qualify
1962 Round 1
1966 Round 1
1970 Did not qualify
1974 Did not qualify
1978 Round 1
1982 Round 2
1986 Quarter-finals
1990 Round 2
1994 Quarter-finals
1998 Round 1
2002 Quarter-finals
2006 Round 2
2010 Winners

SPONSORSHIP

The first competition in England to be sponsored was the Watney Cup in 1971, a pre-season tournament between the highest-scoring teams in the different divisions of the Football League.

IS THAT A FACT?
The longest shirt sponsorship deal in English football is between Tranmere Rovers and Wirral Borough Council, whose name first appeared on the club's kit in 1989.

• On 24th January 1976 Kettering Town became the first senior football club in the UK to feature a sponsor's logo on their shirts, Kettering Tyres, for their Southern League Premier Division match against Bath City. The Football Association ordered the removal of the logo, but finally accepted shirt sponsorship in June 1977. Two years later Liverpool became the first top-flight club to sport a sponsor's logo after signing a deal with Hitachi.

• The biggest sponsorship deal in world football was agreed between Manchester City and Etihad Airways in August 2011. The 10-year partnership, which includes stadium naming rights and shirt sponsorship, will boost City's coffers by a staggering £400 million.

• **A kit mix-up in the Tottenham dressing-room meant that half the Spurs team wore plain, unsponsored shirts for the 1987 FA Cup final against Coventry City. Needless to say, the Londoners' shirt sponsors, lager manufacturers Holsten, were distinctly unamused.**

• The League Cup was the first major English competition to be sponsored, being renamed the Milk Cup after receiving backing from the Milk Marketing Board in 1982. It has since been rebranded as the Littlewoods Cup, the Rumbelows Cup, the Littlewoods Cup, the Coca-Cola Cup, the Worthington Cup, the Carling Cup and the Capital One Cup. Since 1994 the FA Cup has been sponsored by Littlewoods, AXA, E.ON and Budweiser, but the competition is still known by its original name.

• **Stoke City have been sponsored by Britannia since 1997, making theirs the longest shirt sponsorship deal in the Premier League.**

JOCK STEIN

Born: Burnbank, 5th October 1922
Died: 10th September 1985
Managerial career:
1960-64 Dunfermline Athletic
1964-65 Hibernian
1965/66 Scotland
1965-78 Celtic
1978 Leeds United
1978-85 Scotland

Legendary Celtic boss Jock Stein was the first British manager to win the European Cup, guiding the Glasgow club to victory over Inter Milan in the 1967 final in Lisbon. During that same season, Stein's Celtic won every competition they entered – European Cup, Scottish League, Scottish Cup and Scottish League Cup.

• **Stein turned Celtic into the**

Etihad Airways' sponsorship deal with Manchester City is worth a record £400 million

dominant force in Scottish football, leading his side to an incredible nine consecutive league title triumphs between 1966 and 1974 after arriving from Hibs in 1965. He added a 10th title in 1977 before leaving the club the following year.

• As a centre half with Celtic, Stein had previously helped The Bhoys win the league and Scottish Cup in 1954... their first Double since 1914.

• Stein began his managerial career at Dunfermline, with whom he won the Scottish Cup in 1961. After leaving Celtic he managed Leeds for just 45 days before taking over as Scotland manager, a job he had previously held on a part-time basis in the mid-1960s.

• He led Scotland to the 1982 World Cup finals and had just seen his side qualify for the 1986 tournament when he died from a heart attack after the end of the 1985 qualifier against Wales at Ninian Park. His sudden death was mourned by the whole of Scotland.

• **He is remembered, though, primarily, for his great achievements at Celtic. Summing up what it meant to play for one of Britain's greatest clubs, Stein once said: "Celtic jerseys are not for second best... they don't fit inferior players."**

STEVENAGE

Year founded: 1976
Ground: Broadhall Way (6,722)
Previous name: Stevenage Borough
Nickname: The Boro
Biggest win: 7-0 v Merthyr (2006)
Heaviest defeat: 1-6 v Farnborough (2002)

The club was founded in 1976 as Stevenage Borough, following the bankruptcy of the town's former club, Stevenage Athletic. In 2010 the club decided to become simply 'Stevenage'.

• **Stevenage rose through the football pyramid to gain promotion to the Conference in 1994. Two years later they won the title but were denied promotion to the Football League as their tiny Broadhall Way stadium did not meet the league's standards.**

• Stevenage finally made it into the league in 2010 after topping the Conference table with an impressive 99 points. If the club's two victories against Chester City, who were expelled from the league during the season, had not been expunged then Stevenage would have set a new Conference record of 105 points.

• **Incredibly, the following season Stevenage were promoted again, after beating Torquay United 1-0 in the League Two play-off final at Old Trafford. Earlier in the year the club recorded their best ever one-off result, walloping Premier League bigshots Newcastle 3-1 in the FA Cup third round at Broadhall.**

• In 2007 Stevenage became the first club to lift a trophy at the new Wembley, beating Kidderminster Harriers 3-2 in the final of the FA Trophy watched by a competition record crowd of 53,262.

STOKE CITY

Year founded: 1863
Ground: Britannia Stadium (27,740)
Previous name: Stoke Ramblers, Stoke
Nickname: The Potters
Biggest win: 11-0 v Stourbridge (1914)
Heaviest defeat: 0-10 v Preston (1889)

Founded in 1863 by employees of the North Staffordshire Railway Company, Stoke are the second oldest league club in the country. Between 1868-70 the club was known as Stoke Ramblers, before simply becoming Stoke and then adding the suffix 'City' in 1925.

• **Stoke were founder members of the Football League in 1888 but finished bottom of the table at the end of the season. After another wooden spoon in 1890 the club dropped out of the league, but returned to the big time after just one season.**

• The club's greatest moment came in 1972 when they won the League Cup, beating favourites Chelsea 2-1 in the final at Wembley, thanks to a late winner by George Eastham. Aged 35 and 161 days at the time, Eastham is the oldest player ever to win the League Cup. The Potters had a great chance to add to their meagre haul of silverware

in 2011 when they reached the FA Cup final for the first time, but they lost 1-0 to Manchester City. At least their fans enjoyed the semi-final, when Stoke thrashed Bolton 5-0 in the biggest win yet by a club side at the new Wembley.

• **While playing in his second spell at Stoke, the great Stanley Matthews became the oldest player ever to appear in the top flight. On 6th February 1965 Matthews played his last game for the club against Fulham just five days after celebrating his 50th birthday.**

• The legendary Gordon Banks is Stoke's most-capped player. The brilliant goalkeeper, a World Cup winner in 1966, won 37 of his 73 England caps while with the Staffordshire outfit.

• **Freddie Steele is Stoke's leading scorer with 140 league goals between 1934 and 1949, including a club record 33 in the 1936/37 season. Stalwart defender Eric Skeels played in a record 507 league games for the Potters between 1960 and 1976.**

• On 23rd February 1957 Stoke thrashed Lincoln City 8-0 in a Second Division match. Incredibly, Neville Coleman bagged seven of the goals to set a club record which has never been matched since.

• **In August 2011 Stoke splashed out a club record £12 million to bring lanky Tottenham striker Peter Crouch to the Britannia Stadium. Earlier that year the Potters made their record sale when Turkish international Tuncay moved to German club Wolfsburg in a £4.5 million deal.**

• On 27th January 1974 Stoke became the first top-flight club to host Sunday football when they played Chelsea at their former home, The Victoria Ground. Ignoring the complaints of religious groups, a crowd of nearly 32,000 turned up to see Stoke win 1-0.

• **Stoke's most famous fan is former** *They Think It's All Over* **TV presenter Nick Hancock. In 2001 Hancock forked out £20,000 at an auction to buy Stanley Matthews's 1953 FA Cup-winners' medal, even though the wing wizard won the trophy with Blackpool!**

LUIS SUAREZ

Born: Salto, Uruguay, 24th January 1987
Position: Striker
Club career:
2005-06 Nacional 27 (10)
2006-07 Groningen 29 (10)
2007-11 Ajax 110 (81)
2011- Liverpool 44 (15)
International record:
2007- Uruguay 54 (28)

A quick-witted striker who is famed for his ability to score from the tightest of angles, Luis Suarez became Liverpool's most expensive signing when he joined the Merseysiders from Ajax for £22.8 million in January 2011. Later that same day, though, Suarez lost his record when Andy Carroll moved to the club from Newcastle for £35 million.

• **Suarez's first full season with the Reds was certainly eventful, as he helped Liverpool win the Carling Cup but, less impressively, was given an eight-match ban by the FA and fined £40,000 for racially abusing Manchester United defender Patrice Evra. When the two teams met later in the season Suarez hit the headlines again by refusing to shake Evra's hand before kick-off.**

• After spells with Nacional, in his native Uruguay, and Dutch outfit Groningen, Suarez made his name at Ajax, where he averaged three goals in four games during a three-year spell at the club. His most prolific season was in 2009/10 when he scored 35 goals in 33 games, a fantastic return which saw him named as Dutch Footballer of the Year.

• **His time in Amsterdam, though, ended on a sour note when he was banned for seven games after biting an opponent on the shoulder, an incident which earned him the unflattering nickname 'The Cannibal of Ajax'.**

• Just months earlier, he had been involved in another highly controversial incident at the 2010 World Cup. After starring for Uruguay in earlier rounds, Suarez became a villain for many fans outside South America when he saved a certain goal in the last-minute of the quarter-final against Ghana by punching the ball off the line. The

Africans missed the penalty and lost the subsequent shoot-out, although the red card Suarez received meant he was suspended for Uruguay's semi-final defeat by Holland. The following year, though, he was named Player of the Tournament as Uruguay won the Copa America.

You probably won't find this pic on Patrice Evra's wall!

SUBSTITUTES

Substitutes were first allowed in the Football League in the 1965/66 season. The first player to come off the bench was Charlton's Keith Peacock, who replaced injured goalkeeper Mike Rose after 11 minutes of the Addicks' match away to Bolton on 21st August 1965. On the same afternoon Barrow's Bobby Knox became the first substitute to score a goal when he notched against Wrexham.

• **The fastest-ever goal scored by a substitute was by Arsenal's Nicklas Bendtner, who headed in a corner against Tottenham at the Emirates on 22nd December 2007, just 1.8 seconds after replacing Emmanuel Eboue.**

• The most goals ever scored in a game by a substitute is four by Ole Gunnar Solskjaer in Manchester United's 8-1 win at Nottingham Forest in 1999. Incredibly, the Norwegian striker was only on the pitch for 19 minutes. During his United career Solskjaer scored a record 28 goals off the bench.

• **Substitutes were first allowed at the World Cup in 1970. The most goals scored by a sub at the tournament is three by Hungary's Lazlo Kiss against El Salvador in 1982. At France '98 Denmark's Ebbe Sand scored the fastest goal by a sub, netting against Nigeria just 16 seconds after coming off the bench.**

• The first substitute to score in the FA Cup final was Arsenal's Eddie Kelly, who notched his side's equaliser in their 2-1 win over Liverpool in 1971.

• **Newcastle goalkeeper Steve Harper has sat on the bench a record 315 times in Premier League fixtures, while Portsmouth striker Kanu has made a record 118 sub appearances.**

TOP 10

PREMIER LEAGUE SUBSTITUTE APPEARANCES

1.	Kanu	118
2.	Jermain Defoe	109
3.	Shoala Ameobi	107
4.	Ryan Giggs	94
5.	Louis Saha	90
6.	Joe Cole	90
7.	Peter Crouch	88
8.	Paul Scholes	87
9.	James Beattie	85
10.	Carlton Cole	84

SUNDERLAND

Year founded: 1879
Ground: Stadium of Light (49,000)
Previous name: Sunderland and District Teachers' AFC
Nickname: The Black Cats
Biggest win: 11-1 v Fairfield (1895)
Heaviest defeat: 0-8 v Sheffield Wednesday (1911), v West Ham (1968) and v Watford (1982)

The club was founded as the Sunderland and District Teachers' AFC in 1879 but soon opened its ranks to other professions and became simply 'Sunderland' the following year.

• **Sunderland were the first 'new' club to join the Football League, replacing Stoke in 1890. Just two years later they won their first league championship and they retained the title the** following year, in the process becoming the first club to score 100 goals in a league season. In 1895 Sunderland became the first club ever to win three championships, and their status was further enhanced when they beat Scottish champions Hearts 5-3 in a one-off 'world championship' match.

• In 1958 Sunderland were relegated after a then record 57 consecutive seasons in the top flight. Arsenal passed this particular landmark in 1983/84 and can now boast an impressive run of 86 successive seasons at the top level.

• **Sunderland were the first Second Division team in the post Second World War era to win the FA Cup, beating Leeds 1-0 at Wembley in 1973 in one of the biggest upsets of all time thanks to a goal by the late Ian Porterfield. Incredibly, their line-up featured not one international player.**

• Goalkeeper Jim Montgomery, a hero of that cup-winning side, is the Black Cats' record appearance maker, turning out in 537 league games between 1960 and 1977.

Stephane Sessegnon in action for Sunderland

• Sunderland's record victory was an 11-1 thrashing of Fairfield in the FA Cup in 1895. However, the club's best-ever league win, a 9-1 demolition of eventual champions and arch rivals Newcastle at St James' Park in 1908, probably gave their fans more pleasure. To this day, it remains the biggest-ever victory by an away side in the top flight.

• Sunderland last won the league championship in 1935/36, the last time, incidentally, that a team wearing stripes has topped the pile. The Wearsiders' success, though, certainly wasn't based on a solid defence... the 74 goals they conceded that season is more than any other top-flight champions before or since.

• In 1990 Sunderland became the only team to lose a play-off final yet still gain promotion, the Wearsiders going up to the old First Division in place of Swindon after the Robins were punished for financial irregularities.

• Inside forward Charlie Buchan is Sunderland's record scorer with 209 league goals between 1911 and 1925. Dave Halliday holds the record for a single season, hitting the target 43 times in 1928/29.

• Famed for their spending power in the late 1940s and early 1950s, when they were dubbed 'The Bank of England' club, Sunderland coughed up a record £14 million in August 2012 when they signed striker Steven Fletcher from Wolves. The year before the Black Cats sold their previous most expensive signing, Darren Bent, to Aston Villa for a club record £24 million.

• When Sunderland reached the League Cup final in 1985 they were captained by Barry Venison who, aged 20 years and seven months, was the youngest ever skipper in a major English cup final.

> **HONOURS**
> *Division 1 champions 1892, 1983, 1895, 1902, 1913, 1936*
> *Division 2 champions 1976*
> *Championship champions 2005, 2007*
> *Division 3 champions 1988*
> *FA Cup 1937, 1973*

SUPERSTITIONS

Many footballers, including some of the great names of the game, are highly superstitious and believe that performing the same personal routines before every

After an incident in the 1927 FA Cup final, Arsenal always wash a new goalkeepers' shirt before it is played in

game will bring them good luck. Republic of Ireland goalkeeper Shay Given, for instance, has a 'lucky' vial of Holy Water which he places in the back of his net before kick-off.

• Former England striker Gary Lineker never used to shoot at goal during the warm up, believing that if he hit the back of the net it would be a 'waste' of a goal. Then, if he didn't score in the first half he would always change his shirt at half-time.

• Kolo Toure's superstition almost cost his then club Arsenal dear in their 2009 Champions League clash with Roma. Believing that it would be bad luck to leave the dressing room before team-mate William Gallas, who was receiving treatment, Toure failed to appear for the start of the second half, leaving the Gunners to restart the match with just nine players!

• France developed a number of superstitions around Fabien Barthez at the 1998 World Cup, one of which demanded that skipper Laurent Blanc had to kiss the goalkeeper's bald head just before kick-off. It may all have been mumbo-jumbo, but the routine worked for the French who won the competition for the first time in their history.

• Some superstitions are not entirely irrational. For example, Arsenal always make sure that a new goalkeeper's jersey is washed before it is used for the first time. The policy stems from the 1927 FA Cup final, which the Gunners lost when goalkeeper Dan Lewis let in a soft goal against Cardiff. He later blamed his mistake on the ball slipping from his grasp and over the line as it brushed against the shiny surface of his new jumper.

- In October 2008 the coach of Zimbabwean side Midlands Portland Cement sent his 17-member squad into the crocodile-infested Zambezi river in a ritual cleansing ceremony ahead of an important match. Unfortunately, only 16 players emerged from the water a few minutes later and, unsurprisingly given the bad omens, the team went on to lose their next game.
- In a 2011 match between Ghana rivals Hearts of Oak and Asante Kotoko a cat that ran onto the pitch was killed by Hearts fans, who believed the animal had been sent on by their opponents to work its magic or 'juju' in their favour.

SWANSEA CITY

Year founded: 1912
Ground: Liberty Stadium (20,532)
Previous name: Swansea Town
Nickname: The Swans
Biggest win: 12-0 v Sliema Wanderers (1982)
Heaviest defeat: 0-8 v Liverpool (1990) and v Monaco (1991)

The club was founded as Swansea Town in 1912 and entered the Football League eight years later. The present name was adopted in 1970.
- Under former Liverpool striker **John Toshack the Swans climbed from the old Fourth Division to the top flight in just four seasons between 1978 and 1981, the fastest ever ascent through the Football League. The glory days soon faded, though, and by 1986 Swansea were back in the basement division.**

IS THAT A FACT?
During the 2011/12 season Swansea's Ashley Williams attempted more long balls, 464, than any other Premier League player.

- In 2011, though, Swansea beat Reading 4-2 in the Championship play-off final at Wembley to become the first Welsh club to reach the Premier League. Again, their rise was a rapid one as they had been in the basement tier just six years earlier. They performed well in the top flight, too, coming 11th – the club's second-highest ever finish.
- **Ivor Allchurch is the Swans' leading scorer, banging in 166 goals in two spells at the club between 1949 and 1968. Allchurch is also the club's most-decorated international, winning 42 caps for Wales while with Swansea. One-club man Wilfred Milne is the Swans' leading appearance maker, turning out in 586 league games between 1920 and 1937.**
- In 1961 the club became the first from Wales to compete in Europe, but were knocked out of the Cup Winners' Cup in the first round by East German side Carl Zeiss Jena. In the same competition the Swans recorded their biggest ever win, thrashing Maltese minnows Sliema Wanderers 12-0 in 1982.
- **Some of the club's most famous victories have come in the FA Cup. In 1926 Swansea knocked out Arsenal before losing in the semi-finals to Bolton and in 1964 the Swans again reached the last four after sensationally beating Liverpool at Anfield. Then, in 1999, the Welshmen became the first club from the bottom tier to knock out a Premier League club when they beat West Ham 1-0 in a third-round replay.**
- The Swans made their record signing in August 2012 when South Korean midfielder Ki Sung-Yueng moved from Celtic for £5 million. In the same month the Welsh outfit sold midfielder Joe Allen to Liverpool for a club record £15 million.
- **In 1936 Swansea set a Football League record for the longest distance travelled for consecutive matches when they visited Newcastle on Easter Sunday just a day after going to Plymouth.**

HONOURS
Division 3 (South) champions 1925, 1949
League One champions 2008
Third Division champions 2000
Football League Trophy 1994, 2006
Welsh Cup 1913, 1932, 1950, 1961, 1966, 1981, 1982, 1983, 1989, 1991

SWINDON TOWN

Year founded: 1879
Ground: The County Ground (14,700)
Previous name: Swindon Spartans
Nickname: The Robins
Biggest win: 10-1 v Farnham United Breweries (1925)
Heaviest defeat: 1-10 v Manchester City (1930)

The club was founded by the Reverend William Pitt in 1879, becoming Swindon Spartans two years later before adopting the name Swindon Town in 1883. In 1920 Swindon were founder members of the Third Division, kicking off their league career with a 9-1 thrashing of Luton.
- **The Robins' finest moment came in 1969 when, as a Third Division club, they beat mighty Arsenal 3-1 in the League Cup final on a mud-clogged Wembley pitch. Legendary winger Don Rogers was the star of the show, scoring two of Swindon's goals.**
- In 1993, three years after being denied promotion to the top flight for the first time because of a financial scandal, Swindon earned promotion to the Premiership via the play-offs. The following campaign, though, proved to be a miserable one as the Robins finished bottom of the pile and conceded 100 goals... a record for the Premier League.
- **Swindon won the Fourth Division title in 1985/86 with a then Football League best 102 points, a total which remains a record for the bottom tier. In 2012, under charismatic manager Paolo di Canio, they topped the fourth tier for a second time to earn promotion to League One.**
- John Trollope is Swindon's longest-serving player, appearing in 770 league games for the club between 1960 and 1980 – a record for a single club.
- **The first set of twins to score for the same team in the same Football League match were Swindon's Bill and Alf Stephens in a 2-0 win against Exeter in 1946.**

HONOURS
Second Division champions 1996
Division 4 champions 1986
League Two champions 2012
League Cup 1969

TERRY

JOHN TERRY

Born: Barking, 7th December 1980
Position: Defender
Club career:
1998- Chelsea 373 (28)
2000 Nottingham Forest (loan) 6 (0)
International record:
2003- England 77 (6)

Chelsea captain since 2004, Terry is the most successful skipper in the club's history, winning three Premier League titles, five FA Cups and two League Cups. In 2012, despite being suspended for the final against Bayern Munich, he added the Champions League to that list, making up for his disappointment four years earlier when he slipped and put his penalty wide in the shoot-out against Manchester United in the final in Moscow.

• A superb tackler who reads the game extremely well, Terry was voted PFA Player of the Year in 2005 after leading the Blues to the first of their back-to-back Premiership titles. With a total of 49 goals for the club in all competitions, he is the highest-scoring defender in Chelsea history.

• After making his England debut against Serbia & Montenegro in 2003, Terry went on to represent his country at Euro 2004 and the 2006 World Cup, where he was the only England player to be selected for the all-star FIFA squad at the end of the tournament. In May 2007 he became the first player to score in a full international at the new Wembley when he netted with a header in his side's 1-1 draw with Brazil.

• He was first appointed England captain by Steve McClaren in 2006 and retained the role under Fabio Capello. However, in February 2010 Terry was sensationally stripped of the armband following newspaper revelations about his private life. The following year, though, he reclaimed the captaincy only for the FA to take it off him again in February 2012 after he was charged by the police with racially abusing QPR defender Anton Ferdinand earlier in the season.

John Terry is Chelsea's most successful ever skipper

CARLOS TEVEZ

Born: Buenos Aires, Argentina, 5th February 1984
Position: Striker
Club career:
2001-04 Boca Juniors 75 (26)
2004-06 Corinthians 47 (31)
2006-07 West Ham United 26 (7)
2007-09 Manchester United 63 (19)
2009- Manchester City 79 (48)
International record:
2004- Argentina 59 (13)

Carlos Tevez has enjoyed mixed fortunes at Manchester City in his three years at the Etihad. In 2010/11 he was joint winner of the Golden Boot with Dimitar Berbatov and was a key figure as the club won the FA Cup for the first time since 1969. However, he missed much of the following season after being suspended by City for refusing to come on as a sub in City's Champions League match at Bayern Munich. He did, though, return to the side after six months absence to help City win their first ever Premier League title.

• Tevez began his career with Boca Juniors with whom he won the Copa Libertadores in 2003. He moved on to Brazilian side Corinthians the following year, and in 2005 became the first non-Brazilian for nearly 30 years to be named as the league's best player.

• He joined West Ham in 2006, but his first season in England was dogged by his controversial association with Media Sports Investments, a company that 'owned' Tevez and his fellow Argentine Javier Mascherano in breach of Premier League regulations.

• After scoring the goal that saved West Ham from relegation on the last day of the 2006/07 season, Tevez moved to Manchester United on a two-year deal. Despite winning two league titles and the Champions League during his time at Old Trafford, United boss Sir Alex Ferguson chose not to retain Tevez's services, and in the summer of 2009 he crossed the Manchester divide in a deal worth £25.5 million to MSI.

• A lively striker who never gives defenders a moment's peace, Tevez made his debut for Argentina in a World Cup qualifier against Ecuador in March 2004. Later that year he won a gold medal and the Golden Boot at the Athens Olympics, and he has since represented his country at two World Cups.

THROW-INS

Danny Brooks, a 28-year-old PE teacher from Halifax, holds the world record for the longest-ever throw. Taking advantage of his training as a gymnast, he used a forward hand spring technique to hurl the ball 49.78 metres in December 2009.

• Perhaps the most famous of all long-throw specialists is Stoke's Rory Delap. Since the Potters gained promotion to the Premier League in 2008 his enormous throws, fired in with a flat trajectory, have caused huge problems for Stoke's opponents and led to a number of vital goals for the team.

Carlos Tevez fends off Chelsea's David Luiz

• The most bizarre goal from a throw-in came in a derby between Birmingham City and Aston Villa in 2002. Villa defender Olaf Mellberg threw the ball back to goalkeeper Peter Enckelman and it dribbled under his foot and into the net. Despite Villa's protests, referee David Elleray ruled that the goal should stand because Enckelman had made contact with the ball.

• Throw-ins were replaced by kick ins from the touchline in the Diadora League (now the Ryman League) during the 1994/95 season, but the experiment was abandoned at the end of the campaign.

IS THAT A FACT?

Back in his native Argentina, Carlos Tevez performs with a band called Piola Vago which also includes his brother Diego. The group's biggest hit to date was a song entitled 'Lose Your Control'.

TORQUAY UNITED

Year founded: 1898
Ground: Plainmoor (6,104)
Previous name: Torquay, Torquay Town
Nickname: The Gulls
Biggest win: 9-0 v Swindon (1952)
Heaviest defeat: 2-10 v Fulham (1931) and v Luton (1933)

Founded as Torquay in 1898 by old boys of two local colleges, the club merged with Ellacombe FC to become Torquay Town in 1910. After a further merger, with Babbacombe FC in 1921, the club adopted their present name.

• **The Gulls returned to the Football League after a two-year absence in 2009 following a 2-0 defeat of** Cambridge United in the Conference play-off final at Wembley. The club had spent the previous 80 years in the bottom two divisions of the league, narrowly missing out on promotion to the old Second Division on goal average in both 1957 and 1968.

• Torquay's leading scorer is Sammy Collins who banged in 204 league goals, including a club record eight hat-tricks, between 1948 and 1958. His best season was in 1955/56 when he found the net 40 times to set another record for the Devon outfit.

• **On 3rd January 1977 Torquay defender Pat Kruse scored the fastest-ever own goal in English football history, netting at the wrong end against Cambridge United after just six seconds!**

• Torquay's youngest player is David Byng, who had only been 16 for 36 days when he played at Walsall on the opening day of the 1993/94 season. He scored, too, in the Gulls' 2-1 win.

FERNANDO TORRES

Born: Madrid, 20th March 1984
Position: Striker
Club career:
2001-07 Atletico Madrid 214 (82)
2007-11 Liverpool 102 (65)
2011- Chelsea 46 (7)
International record:
2003- Spain 99 (31)

When Fernando Torres moved from Liverpool to Chelsea for £50 million in January 2011 he became the most expensive player in British football history. The following year he helped the Blues win the FA Cup and Champions League, despite spending much of the campaign on the bench and struggling to find his best form when he did get on the pitch.

• **Torres began his career with local club Atletico Madrid, where his goalscoring**

The most expensive player in British football history, Chelsea's Fernando Torres

feats earned him the nickname 'El Niño' (The Kid) and the skipper's armband. Aged just 19 at the time, he was the youngest captain in Atletico's history.

• In 2007 Torres signed for Liverpool for a club record £20 million (plus Luis Garcia, who moved in the opposite direction). He was an instant hit at Anfield, becoming the first Liverpool player since 1948 to hit hat-tricks in consecutive home matches when he notched trebles against Middlesbrough and West Ham and, later in the season, scoring in eight successive home games to equal a record set by Reds legend Roger Hunt way back in 1962. His total of 24 league goals also set a new record for a foreign player in a debut season in English football.

• **Torres carried on his goalscoring form into Euro 2008, hitting the winning goal in the final in Vienna as Spain beat Germany to claim their first trophy for 44 years. To cap a truly memorable year he was named third in the World Footballer of the Year poll behind Cristiano Ronaldo and Lionel Messi.**

• Despite playing well below par and failing to score a single goal, Torres ended the 2010 World Cup in South Africa by picking up a winners' medal. He fared better at Euro 2012, claiming the Golden Boot after scoring three goals, including one in the final against Italy to help Spain win an unprecedented three consecutive trophies.

TOTTENHAM HOTSPUR

Year founded: 1882
Ground: White Hart Lane (36,310)
Previous name: Hotspur FC
Nickname: Spurs
Biggest win: 13-2 v Crewe (1960)
Heaviest defeat: 0-8 v Cologne (1995)

The club was founded as Hotspur FC in 1882 by a group of local cricketers, most of whom were former pupils of Tottenham Grammar School. Three years

IS THAT A FACT?
In 2012 Fernando Torres and his Chelsea and Spain team-mate Juan Mata became the first players for 24 years to win the Champions League and the European Championships in the same season.

later the club decided to add the prefix 'Tottenham'.

• **Tottenham were members of the Southern League when they won the FA Cup for the first time in 1901, defeating Sheffield United 3-1 in a replay at Burnden Park. Spurs' victory meant they were the first (and, so far, only) non-league club to win the cup since the formation of the Football League in 1888.**

• In 1961 Tottenham created history when they became the first club in the 20th century to win the fabled League and Cup Double. Their title success was based on a storming start to the season, Bill Nicholson's side winning their first 11 games to set a top-flight record which has not been matched since. By the end of the campaign, the north Londoners had won 31 of their 42 league matches to create another record for the top tier.

• **As Arsenal fans like to point out, Tottenham have failed to win the League since those 'Glory, Glory' days of skipper Danny Blanchflower, Dave Mackay and Cliff Jones. Spurs, though, have continued to enjoy cup success, and their total of eight victories in the FA Cup is only surpassed by the Gunners and Manchester United. Remarkably, five of those triumphs came in years ending in a '1', giving rise to the legend that these seasons were particularly lucky for Spurs.**

• Tottenham have also enjoyed much success in the League Cup, winning the competition four times – a record which puts them joint third on the all-time honours list behind Liverpool and Aston Villa. The last of these triumphs, in 2008 following a 2-1 defeat of holders Chelsea in the final, saw Tottenham became the first club to win the League Cup at the new Wembley.

• **Spurs have a decent record in Europe, too. In 1963 they thrashed Atletico Madrid 5-1 in the final of the European Cup Winners' Cup, the legendary Jimmy Greaves grabbing a brace, to become the first British club to win a European trophy. Then, in 1972, Tottenham defeated Wolves 3-2 on aggregate in the first-ever UEFA Cup final and the first European final to feature two English clubs. A third**

European triumph followed in 1984 when Tottenham beat Anderlecht in the first UEFA Cup final to be settled by penalties.

• Ace marksman Jimmy Greaves holds two goalscoring records for Tottenham. His total of 220 league goals between 1961 and 1970 is a club best, as is his impressive tally of 37 league goals in 1962/63. Clive Allen, though, struck an incredible total of 49 goals in all competitions in 1986/87, including a record 12 in the League Cup.

• **Stalwart defender Steve Perryman is the club's longest-serving player, pulling on the famous white shirt in 655 league games between 1969 and 1986, including 613 in the old First Division – a top-flight record for a player at a single club.**

• Tottenham's record buy is skilful Croatian midfielder Luka Modric, who cost £16.5 million when he moved to White Hart Lane from Dynamo Zagreb in 2008. In the same year Spurs received a club record £30.75 million from Manchester United for Bulgarian striker Dimitar Berbatov.

• **Tottenham's first title success was in 1950/51 when Arthur Rowe's stylish 'Push and Run' team topped the table just one year after winning the Second Division championship. In the years since, only Ipswich Town (in 1961 and 1962) have managed to claim the top two titles in consecutive seasons.**

• In 2000 Spurs' Ledley King scored the fastest ever goal in Premiership history, netting after just 9.7 seconds against Bradford City at Valley Parade.

• **Spurs' incredible 9-1 trouncing of Wigan on 22nd November 2009 was only the second time a club had scored nine goals in a Premier League game. Jermain Defoe's five-goal haul in the same match also equalled the Premiership individual scoring record.**

• Among the many famous faces who follow Spurs are 'Harry Potter' star Rupert Grint, actor Jude Law and veteran TV presenter Bruce Forsyth.

HONOURS
Division 1 champions 1951, 1961
Division 2 champions 1920, 1950
FA Cup 1901, 1921, 1961, 1962, 1967, 1981, 1982, 1991
League Cup 1971, 1973, 1999, 2008
Double 1961
European Cup Winners' Cup 1963
UEFA Cup 1972, 1984

YAYA TOURE

Born: Bouake, Ivory Coast, 13th May 1983
Position: Midfielder
Club career:
2001-03 Beveren 70 (3)
2003-05 Matalurh Donetsk 33 (3)
2005-06 Olympiacos 26 (3)
2006-07 Monaco 27 (5)
2007-10 Barcelona 74 (4)
2010- Manchester City 67 (12)
International record:
2004- Ivory Coast 67 (10)

Yaya Toure wrote himself into Manchester City folklore when he scored the winning goals in both the FA Cup semi-final and final in 2011, ending the club's 35-year quest for a major trophy. The following season he was a key part of the City side which won the Premier League for the first time, his dynamic displays earning him a place in the PFA Team of the Year.
• **A powerful midfielder who likes to switch from a defensive to an attacking role during games, Toure began his professional career in Belgium with Beveren. He later had spells in the Ukraine, Greece (where he won the double with Olympiacos in 2006) and France, before moving to Barcelona in 2007.**
• Toure was part of the Barcelona team which won an incredible six trophies in 2009, showing his versatility to good effect when he played at centre-back in the Champions League final against Manchester United. The following year he moved to Manchester City for £24

million, teaming up with his older brother, Kolo Toure.
• **A member of the Ivory Coast team that competed at the 2006 and 2010 World Cups, Toure was voted African Footballer of the Year in 2011 – the first non-striker to receive the award.**

TRANMERE ROVERS

Year founded: 1884
Ground: Prenton Park (16,567)
Previous name: Belmont FC
Nickname: Rovers
Biggest win: 13-0 v Oswestry United (1914)
Heaviest defeat: 1-9 v Tottenham (1953)

The club was founded as Belmont FC in 1884 by members of two local cricket clubs, changing its name to Tranmere Rovers the following year. In 1921 Rovers joined the Football League for the first time as members of the newly created Third Division (North).
• **The club enjoyed their greatest-ever moment in 2000 when they played Leicester City in the League Cup final at Wembley. Despite performing well on the day, Rovers lost 2-1.**
• Rovers' best-ever league victory, 13-4 against Oldham on Boxing Day 1935, set a record for the highest-scoring Football League match which remains to this day. Robert 'Bunny' Bell scored nine goals in the match, a record for the old Third

Division (North).
• **Between 1946 and 1955 Tranmere's Harold Bell appeared in 375 consecutive league games, a run unmatched by any other Football League player. Bell went on to make a club record 595 appearances before hanging up his boots in 1964.**
• In 1964 Tranmere conceded the fastest ever goal in Football League history, Bradford Park Avenue's Jim Fryatt netting against them after just four seconds. Understandably perhaps, Rovers never recovered from that early shock, going down to a 4-2 defeat.

HONOURS
Division 3 (North) champions 1938
Football League Trophy 1990
Welsh Cup 1935

TRANSFERS

The world's most expensive player is Portuguese winger Cristiano Ronaldo, who moved from Manchester United to Real Madrid in the summer of 2009 for a staggering £80 million. This beat the £56 million Real had paid AC Milan for Brazilian playmaker Kaka just a few weeks earlier. Prior to these two deals, the transfer record had not been broken since 2001, when Zinedine Zidane moved from Juventus to Real Madrid for £46 million.
• **The biggest transfer deal in the British game took place in January 2011 when Chelsea paid Liverpool £50 million for Spanish striker Fernando Torres.**
• The first player to be transferred for a four-figure fee in England was Alf

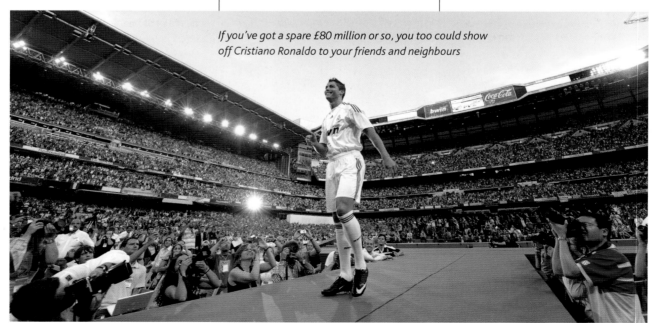

If you've got a spare £80 million or so, you too could show off Cristiano Ronaldo to your friends and neighbours

Common, who moved from Sunderland to Middlesbrough in 1905. In 1966 World Cup winner Alan Ball became the first six-figure footballer when he joined Everton from Blackpool, while Trevor Francis broke the £1 million barrier when he moved to Nottingham Forest from Birmingham City for £1,150,000 in 1979.

• In May 2012 Fleetwood Town striker James Vardy became the first non-league player to fetch a £1 million transfer fee when he joined Leicester City.

GIOVANNI TRAPATTONI

Born: Milan, 17th March 1939
Managerial record:
1976 AC Milan
1976-86 Juventus
1986-91 Inter Milan
1991-94 Juventus
1994-95 Bayern Munich
1995-96 Cagliari
1996-98 Bayern Munich
1998-2000 Fiorentina
2000-04 Italy
2004-05 Benfica
2005-06 Stuttgart
2006-08 Red Bull Salzburg
2008- Republic of Ireland

Republic of Ireland manager Giovanni Trapattoni is one of the most successful coaches in the history of the game, being one of just two managers to have won league titles in four countries (Italy, Germany, Portugal and Austria).

• Formerly a tough-tackling defender with AC Milan and Italy, Trapattoni became manager of Juventus in 1976 and, over the next 10 years, led the Old Lady to no fewer than six Serie A titles. He also guided Juve to triumphs in all three major European trophies, and remains the only manager to have achieved this feat with the same club.

• In 2000 Trapattoni was appointed manager of Italy, but his four-year spell in charge of the Azzurri was a disappointing one. He returned to club football, winning league titles with Benfica, Bayern Munich and Red Bull Salzburg, before becoming manager of the Republic of Ireland in 2008.

• The following year his dream of taking the Irish to the World Cup finals in South Africa was dashed by a hugely controversial goal by France's William Gallas in a play-off in Paris. He did, though, guide the Republic to the finals of Euro 2012 to become, at 73, the oldest ever coach at the European Championships.

TV AND RADIO

The first-ever live radio broadcast of a football match was on 22nd January 1927 when the BBC covered the First Division encounter between Arsenal and Sheffield United at Highbury. The Radio Times printed a pitch marked into numbered squares, which the commentators used to describe where the ball was at any given moment (which some suggest gave rise to the phrase 'back to square one').

• The 1937 FA Cup final between Sunderland and Preston was the first to be televised, although only parts of the match were shown by the BBC. The following year's final between Preston and Huddersfield was the first to be screened live and in full, although the audience was only around 10,000 as so few people had TV sets at the time.

• The biggest British TV audience ever for a football match (and, indeed, the biggest ever for any TV broadcast in this country) was 32.3 million for the 1966 World Cup final between England and West Germany. The viewing figures for the match, which was shown live by both BBC and ITV, were all the more remarkable as only 15 million households in the UK had TV sets. The biggest TV audience for an FA Cup final was in 1970 when 28.49 million people watched Chelsea beat Leeds 2-1 in a midweek replay at Old Trafford.

• A record cumulative TV audience of 26.4 billion watched the 2002 World Cup finals, including a record 1.3 billion for the final between Brazil and Germany.

• The latest TV deal between Sky, BT and the Premier League which starts in 2013 is the biggest in the history of the game. Under the terms of the deal the two companies will pay £3 billion over three years to show 154 live games per season – a 71% increase on the previous three-year agreement.

TWITTER

Cristiano Ronaldo has more followers on Twitter than any other footballer in the world, with around 12.6 million at the last count. During 2012 Ronaldo finally passed his Real Madrid team-mate Kaka on the Twitter leaderboard, the Brazilian›s popularity being boosted by his well-known devotion to Christianity. Neither player, though, can compete with the world›s most popular Twitter celebrity, the singer Lady Gaga, who has nearly 29 million followers.

• Former Liverpool winger Ryan Babbel was fined £10,000 by the FA after posting a picture of referee Howard Webb in a Manchester United shirt on his Twitter page, following his side's controversial 1-0 FA Cup defeat at Old Trafford in January 2011. The following year, after moving to German club Hoffenheim, he was in trouble again for tweeting 'I think the ref was on drugs' about being sent off against Hertha Berlin.

• In March 2011 West Ham striker Carlton Cole jokingly tweeted that Ghana fans at Wembley for the 2011 international with England would be surrounded by immigration officers after the match. The FA failed to see the funny side, and fined Cole £20,000.

• In May 2011 over 70,000 Twitter users identified Manchester United star Ryan Giggs as the previously unnamed Premier League footballer who had allegedly taken out a court injunction preventing former Big Brother contestant Imogen Thomas from revealing details of their relationship.

TOP 10

FOOTBALLERS WITH MOST FOLLOWERS ON TWITTER

1.	Cristiano Ronaldo (Real Madrid)	12.6 million
2.	Kaka (Real Madrid)	12.4 million
3.	Neymar (Santos)	5.1 million
4.	Wayne Rooney (Manchester United)	4.8 million
5.	Ronaldinho (Atletico Mineiro)	4.5 million
6.	Andres Iniesta (Barcelona)	4.2 million
7.	Cesc Fabregas (Barcelona)	4 million
8.	Gerard Pique (Barcelona)	3.9 million
9.	Carles Puyol (Barcelona)	3.5 million
10.	Rio Ferdinand (Manchester United)	3.2 million

Uruguay's attempt to build a human pyramid needed a bit of fine tuning…

Cup for a second time, defeating hosts Brazil 2-1 in 'the final' (it was actually the last and decisive match in a four-team final group). The match was watched by a massive crowd of 199,589 in the Maracana stadium in Rio de Janeiro, the largest ever to attend a football match anywhere in the world.

• At the 2010 World Cup in South Africa Uruguay finished fourth, their best showing since Mexico in 1970. However, the South Americans' campaign will mostly be remembered for a blatant handball on the line by striker Luis Suarez, which denied their opponents Ghana a certain winning goal in the teams' quarter-final clash.

• **In terms of population, Uruguay is easily the smallest nation ever to win the World Cup.**

• Uruguay and Argentina have played more international matches against each other than any other pair of countries in the world, a total of 176 games since 1901.

• **Uruguay are the most successful team in the history of the Copa America. Winners of the inaugural tournament in 1916, Uruguay have won the competition a total of 15 times, most recently lifting the trophy in 2011 after beating Paraguay 3-0 in the final.**

UEFA

UEFA, the Union of European Football Associations, was founded in 1954 at a meeting in Basel during the Swiss World Cup. Holding power over all the national FAs in Europe, it is the largest and most influential of the six continental confederations of FIFA.

• **UEFA competitions include the Champions League (first won as the European Cup by Real Madrid), the Europa League (formerly the UEFA Cup) and the UEFA Super Cup.**

• UEFA President Michel Platini, a former captain of France, is the sixth man to fill the role. The longest-serving UEFA President was Sweden's Lennart Johansson, who did the job for 17 years between 1990 and 2007.

• **Controversial UEFA decisions in the past include the introduction of penalty kicks to decide drawn European ties (from 1970) and the ban on English clubs competing in European competitions for five years from 1985 after the Heysel tragedy.**

URUGUAY

First international: Uruguay 2 Argentina 3, 1901
Most capped player: Diego Forlan, 88 caps (2002-)
Leading goalscorer: Diego Forlan, 33 goals (2002-)
First World Cup appearance: Uruguay 1 Peru 0, 1930
Biggest win: Uruguay 9 Bolivia 0, 1927
Heaviest defeat: Uruguay 0 Argentina 6, 1902

In 1930 Uruguay became the first winners of the World Cup, beating arch-rivals Argentina 4-2 in the final on home soil in Montevideo. The match was a repeat of the Olympic final of 1928, which Uruguay had also won.

• **In 1950 Uruguay won the World**

ROBIN VAN PERSIE

Born: Rotterdam, Holland, 6th August 1983
Position: Striker
Club career:
2001-04 Feyenoord 59 (15)
2004-12 Arsenal 194 (96)
20012- Manchester United
International record:
2005- Holland 68 (29)

Robin van Persie enjoyed his most prolific season to date with Arsenal in 2011/12, hitting 30 goals to win the Premier League Golden Boot and both Footballer of the Year awards. In August 2012, though, he dismayed Gunners fans by moving to Manchester United in a £24 million deal.

• **The son of two artists, Robin van Persie began his career with his local side, Feyenoord, making his first-team debut aged 17 in 2001 and winning the Dutch league's Best Young Talent award at the end of his first season. A UEFA Cup winner the following year, he moved to north London in 2004 for a £2.75 million fee.**

• In his first season with the Gunners, Van Persie fired his new club to the FA Cup final with two goals in the semi-final defeat of Blackburn Rovers. A month later he collected his first, and so far only, medal in English football when Arsenal defeated Manchester United on penalties in the final.

• **A clean striker of the ball, especially on his preferred left side, Van Persie made his international debut for Holland in a World Cup qualifier against Romania in 2005 and has since gone on to play nearly 70 times for his country.**

IS THAT A FACT?

During the 2011/12 season Robin van Persie scored against 17 of the 19 other Premier League teams, equalling a record first established by another Arsenal striker, Ian Wright, in 1996/97. The only teams that managed to stop the Dutchman scoring were Fulham and Manchester City.

Rafael Van Der Vaart

RAFAEL VAN DER VAART

Born: Heemskerk, Holland, 11th February 1983
Position: Midfielder
Club career:
2000-05 Ajax 117 (52)
2005-08 Hamburg 74 (29)
2008-10 Real Madrid 58 (11)
2010-12 Tottenham Hotspur 61 (24)
2012- Hamburg
International record:
2001- Holland 100 (19)

During the 2011/12 season attacking midfielder Rafael Van Der Vaart became only the third Tottenham player – after club legends Teddy Sheringham and Robbie Keane – to score in five consecutive Premier League matches.

• **Brought up in a caravan park, Van der Vaart joined the famed Ajax Academy as a child and made his debut for the Amsterdam club aged just 17. He went on to win two Dutch titles with Ajax before making a surprise move to German outfit Hamburg in 2005.**

• After three years in the Bundesliga Van der Vaart joined Real Madrid for £10 million in 2008. He experienced mixed fortunes at the Bernabeu, and was something of a bit-part player by the time of his £8 million transfer to Tottenham in August 2010. At White Hart Lane, though, he has been a revitalised figure, his outstanding form earning him a nomination for the PFA Player of the Year award in 2011 eventually won by team-mate Gareth Bale. In August 2012 Van der Vaart returned to Hamburg after signing a three-year deal with the Bundesliga club.

• Van der Vaart made his debut for Holland against Andorra way back in 2001. Now on 100 caps for his country, he helped the Dutch reach the 2010 World Cup final but had to settle for a runners-up medal after the Oranje were narrowly beaten by Spain.

• Van der Vaart is married to Dutch TV personality and model Sylvie Meis, who in 2008 hosted the FIFA World Player of the Year award.

NEMANJA VIDIC

Born: Uzice, Serbia, 21st October 1981
Position: Defender
Club career:
2000-04 Red Star Belgrade 67 (12)
2000-01 Spartak Subotica (loan) 27 (6)
2004-06 Spartak Moscow 39 (4)
2006- Manchester United 167 (14)
International record:
2003-11 Serbia 56 (2)

An aggressive, no-nonsense defender who is particularly powerful in the air, Nemanja Vidic has enjoyed huge success since joining Manchester United from Spartak Moscow in January 2006, winning four Premier League medals and the Champions League in 2008.

• **Vidic's consistent displays saw him voted into the PFA Team of the Year in three consecutive seasons between 2007 and 2009. His defensive partnership with Rio Ferdinand is rated by many as the best in the league, although the pair's injury woes mean that they have not been able to play in tandem as often as Sir Alex Ferguson would like.**

• Between 2008 and 2009 Vidic was sent off in three consecutive fixtures against United's big rivals Liverpool, the first player in Premier League history to suffer this fate.

• **First capped by Serbia in 2003, Vidic was a part of his country's 'Famous Four' back line which only conceded one goal in qualification for the 2006 World Cup. Unfortunately, suspension and injury prevented him from playing in the finals in Germany, but he did figure at the 2010 tournament in South Africa. The following year he announced his retirement from international football following criticism of his performances by fans.**

New Spurs boss AVB quickly introduced his fave 5-3-0 formation

ANDRE VILLAS-BOAS

Born: Porto, 17th October 1977
Managerial career:
2000-01 British Virgin Islands
2009-10 Academica de Coimbra
2010-11 Porto
2011-12 Chelsea
2012- Tottenham Hotspur

The youngest manager in the Premier League at the start of the 2012/13 season, Tottenham boss Andre Villas-Boas filled the vacancy left by the surprise departure of Harry Redknapp from White Hart Lane in June 2012.

• **The previous campaign was a difficult one for Villas-Boas, who was sacked by Chelsea after just eight months in charge at Stamford Bridge despite the west Londoners paying Porto a staggering £13.3 million to release him from his contract – a record 'transfer fee' for a manager.**

• In just a single season with Porto in 2010/11, Villas-Boas enjoyed enormous success. He led his team to a 'treble' of Portuguese league (with a record 21-point margin over the runners up, Benfica), Portuguese Cup and the Europa League following victory over fellow countrymen Braga in the final to become the youngest manager ever to win a European trophy.

• Villas-Boas had previously had short stints in charge of Academica de Coimbra and, as a 22-year-old, the British Virgin Islands, with whom he became the youngest-ever manager to coach a team in a World Cup qualifier.

• His big break, though, came when he was just a teenager when then Porto boss Bobby Robson recommended him for a prestigious coaching course in England. Villas-Boas returned to Porto to work as a youth coach and then, under manager Jose Mourinho, as a scout charged with assessing the strength and weaknesses of future opponents – a role Villas-Boas also filled for 'The Special One' between 2004 and 2009 after Mourinho moved to Chelsea and then Inter Milan.

THEO WALCOTT

Born: Stanmore, 16th March 1989
Position: Winger
Club career:
2005-06 Southampton 21 (4)
2006- Arsenal 149 (26)
International record:
2006- England 28 (4)

Arsenal winger Theo Walcott is the youngest player ever to represent England, coming off the bench to make his debut against Hungary at Old Trafford in 2006 when he was aged just 17 years and 75 days.

• **He has continued to set records for England, becoming the youngest player to score a hat-trick for the Three Lions when he notched three goals against Croatia in a World Cup qualifier in Zagreb in 2008, and finishing on the winning side in his first 14 internationals – the best ever such run by an England player. Despite his status as a 'lucky mascot', he was a shock omission from Fabio Capello's squad for the World Cup in South Africa, although the Italian later admitted leaving Walcott out was 'a mistake'. He did, though, play at Euro 2012, scoring a goal against Sweden before setting up Danny Welbeck's winner in**

England's 3-2 victory.

• Walcott began his career at Southampton and is the youngest player ever to appear for the Saints, making his debut as a sub against Wolves in 2005 when he was aged 16 years and 143 days.

• **After attracting huge media attention for his dynamic performances for the south coast outfit, Walcott moved to Arsenal for an eventual fee of £9.1 million, making him the most expensive 16-year-old in the history of the British game. He scored his first goal for the Gunners a year later in the Carling Cup final against Chelsea to become the second youngest scorer in the final of the competition.**

The youngest player to score a hat-trick for England, Arsenal's Theo Walcott

WALES

First international: Scotland 4 Wales 0, 1876
Most capped player: Neville Southall, 92 caps (1982-98)
Leading goalscorer: Ian Rush, 28 goals (1980-96)
First World Cup appearance: Wales 1 Hungary 1, 1958
Biggest win: Wales 11 Ireland 0, 1888
Heaviest defeat: Scotland 9 Wales 0, 1878

Wales are the least successful of the four British national sides, having qualified for just two major international tournaments in their history.

• Their finest hour came in 1958 when a Welsh side including such great names as John Charles, Ivor Allchurch and Jack Kelsey qualified for the World Cup finals in Sweden after beating Israel in a two-legged play-off. After drawing all three of their group matches, Wales then beat Hungary in a play-off to reach the quarter-finals where they lost 1-0 to eventual winners Brazil.

• In 1976 Wales made their best ever showing in the European Championships, reaching the quarter-finals before going down 3-1 on aggregate to Yugoslavia. Since then Wales supporters have had little to cheer, despite the efforts of the likes of Craig Bellamy, Ryan Giggs and all-time leading scorer Ian Rush.

• Wales winger Billy Meredith is the oldest international in the history of British football. He was aged 45 years

TOP 10

WALES GOALSCORERS

1.	Ian Rush (1980-96)	28 goals
2.	Trevor Ford (1946-57)	23 goals
	Ivor Allchurch (1950-66)	23 goals
4.	Dean Saunders (1986-2001)	22 goals
5.	Craig Bellamy (1998-2012)	19 goals
6.	Cliff Jones (1954-69)	16 goals
	Mark Hughes (1984-99)	16 goals
	Robert Earnshaw (2002-)	16 goals
9.	John Charles (1950-65)	15 goals
10.	John Hartson (1995-2005)	14 goals

and 229 days when he won the last of his 48 caps against England in 1920, a quarter of a century after making his international debut.

• Wales have the third best record in the British Home Championships with seven outright wins and five shared victories. Their best decade was the 1930s when they won the championship three times.

KYLE WALKER

Born: Sheffield, 28th May 1990
Position: Defender
Club career:
2008-09 Sheffield United 2 (0)
2008 Northampton Town (loan) 9 (0)
2009- Tottenham Hotspur 39 (2)
2009-10 Sheffield United (loan) 26 (0)
2010-11 QPR (loan) 20 (0)
2011 Aston Villa (loan) 15 (1)
International record:
2011- England 3 (0)

PFA Young Player of the Year in 2012, Kyle Walker is only the second Tottenham player to receive this prestigious award – after Glenn Hoddle in 1980.

• Walker came through the Sheffield United youth system, making his debut towards the end of the 2008/09 season. He played in the 2009 Championship play-off final against Burnley to become the youngest ever Blades player to appear at Wembley stadium.

• Along with fellow Blade Kyle Naughton, he joined Tottenham that summer, the combined fee of £8 million being the highest Sheffield United have ever achieved. Walker was immediately loaned back to Sheffield United, and then had further loan spells at QPR and Aston Villa, ironically scoring his first ever senior goal for Villa against the Blades in the FA Cup in January 2011.

• A former England Under-19 and Under-21 international, Walker was called up into the senior squad after establishing himself in the Spurs team at right-back during the 2011/12 season. He impressed on his first full start for England, earning the Man of the Match award after a dynamic display against Sweden in November

2011, but was ruled out of Euro 2012 through injury.

WALSALL

Year founded: 1888
Ground: Banks' Stadium (11,300)
Previous name: Walsall Town Swifts
Nickname: The Saddlers
Biggest win: 10-0 v Darwen (1899)
Heaviest defeat: 0-12 v Small Heath (1892) and v Darwen (1896)

The club was founded in 1888 as Walsall Town Swifts, following an amalgamation of Walsall Swifts and Walsall Town. Founder members of the Second Division in 1892, the club changed to its present name three years later.

• Walsall have never played in the top flight, but they have a history of producing cup shocks, the most famous coming back in 1933 when they sensationally beat eventual league champions Arsenal 2-0 in the FA Cup. The Saddlers' best run in the League Cup, meanwhile, came in 1984 when they reached the semi-finals before losing 4-2 on aggregate to eventual winners Liverpool.

• Two players share the distinction of being Walsall's all-time leading scorer: Tony Richards, who notched 184 league goals for the club between 1954 and 1963, and his strike partner Colin Taylor, who banged in exactly the same number in three spells with the Saddlers between 1958 and 1973.

• Colin Harrison is the club's longest-serving player, making 467 league appearances between 1964 and 1982.

• Striker Alan Buckley, who went on to manage the club, is Walsall's record signing, costing £175,000 when he joined the Saddlers from Midlands neighbours Birmingham City in June 1979. No other Football League club's most expensive purchase goes back as many years, and with the credit crunch biting there's every chance that it's a record Walsall won't be breaking any time soon.

WATFORD

WATFORD

Year founded: 1881
Ground: Vicarage Road (17,477)
Previous name: Watford Rovers, West Herts
Nickname: The Hornets
Biggest win: 10-1 v Lowestoft Town (1926)
Heaviest defeat: 0-10 v Wolves (1912)

Founded as Watford Rovers in 1881, the club changed its name to West Herts in 1893. Five years later, following a merger with Watford St Mary's, the club became Watford FC.

• The club's history was fairly nondescript until pop star Elton John became chairman in 1976 and invested a large part of his personal wealth in the team. With future England manager Graham Taylor at the helm, the Hornets rose from the Fourth to the First Division in just five years and reaching the FA Cup final in 1984. In the late 1990s Taylor returned to the club and worked his magic again, guiding the Hornets to two successive promotions and a brief taste of life in the Premiership.

• After finishing second in the old First Division in 1983, Watford made their one foray into Europe, reaching the third round of the UEFA Cup before losing to Sparta Prague.

• Luther Blissett, one of the star players of that period, is the club's record appearance maker. In three spells at Vicarage Road the energetic striker notched up 415 league appearances and scored 148 league goals (also a club record).

• In January 2007 Watford received a club record £9.65 million when they sold dynamic winger Ashley Young to Aston Villa. A few months later the Hornets splashed £3.25 million of this cash on West Brom's Nathan Ellington, their most expensive signing ever.

• Watford are the only non-Premier League club to have had two Italian managers: Gianluca Vialli (2001-02) and Gianfranco Zola.

HONOURS
Division 3 champions 1969
Second Division champions 1998
Division 4 champions 1978

Danny Welbeck's audition for Strictly Come Dancing was coming along nicely

DANNY WELBECK

Born: Manchester, 26th November 1990
Position: Striker
Club career:
2008- Manchester United 38 (10)
2009-10 Preston North End (loan) 8 (2)
2010-11 Sunderland (loan) 26 (6)
International record:
2011- England 9 (2)

An energetic and quick-thinking striker, Danny Welbeck played in all four of England's games at Euro 2012, making himself something of a national hero when he scored a late winner against Sweden in the group stage with an audacious backheel.

• A Manchester United youth product, Welbeck came to the fore in the 2008/09 season, scoring on his Premier League debut against Stoke City and helping the Red Devils win the Carling Cup. After loan spells at Preston and Sunderland, he returned to Old Trafford to establish himself as Wayne Rooney's main strike partner during the 2011/12 season.

• Welbeck's impressive displays saw him shortlisted for the 2012 PFA Young Player of the Year award, but he just missed out to Tottenham's Kyle Walker.

• The son of Ghanaian parents, Welbeck ironically made his full England debut against Ghana in a 1-1 draw at Wembley in March 2011. The following year he scored his first goal for his country, netting the winner against Belgium in a pre-Euro 2012 friendly with a clever lob.

WEMBLEY STADIUM

Built at a cost of £798 million, the new Wembley Stadium is the most expensive sporting venue ever. With a capacity of 90,000, it is also the second largest in Europe and the largest in the world to have every seat under cover.

• The stadium's most spectacular feature is a 315m-wide arch, the world's longest unsupported roof structure. Wembley also boasts a staggering 2,618 toilets, more than any other venue in the world.

• Originally scheduled to open in 2003, the stadium was not completed until 2007 due to a variety of financial and legal difficulties. The first professional match was played at the new venue on 17th March 2007 when England Under-21s met their Italian counterparts, with the first goal arriving after just 28 seconds when Giampaolo Pazzini struck for the visitors. Half an hour later, David Bentley became the first Englishman to score at the new stadium.

• The Wembley pitch has been relaid 11 times since the stadium opened in 2007 and has attracted a lot of criticism during that time, Chelsea captain John Terry declaring it "the worst we've played on all year" after

IS THAT A FACT?
Chelsea and Manchester United have both played at the new Wembley a record 11 times. Meanwhile, six Premier League clubs (Fulham, Newcastle, Norwich, QPR, Sunderland and Wigan) have still to make their debut at the stadium.

the Blues beat Portsmouth in the 2010 FA Cup final. Nonetheless, his former team-mate Didier Drogba seemed very much at home at Wembley, scoring a record eight goals in club games at the new stadium, including strikes in four FA Cup finals.

• The first Wembley Stadium was opened in 1923, having been constructed in just 300 days at a cost of £750,000. The first match played at the venue was the 1923 FA Cup final between Bolton and West Ham, although the kick-off was delayed for nearly an hour when thousands of fans spilled onto the pitch because of overcrowding in the stands.

• The last game played at the old Wembley was the World Cup qualifier between England and Germany on 7th October 2000. It proved to be a sad send off to the original 'home of English football' as Germany won 1-0, Dietmar Hamman scoring the last-ever goal under the Twin Towers.

• Arsenal and England defender Tony Adams played a record 60 games at Wembley between 1987 and 2000, a total boosted by the fact that the Gunners used the stadium for their home games in the Champions League in the 1990s.

• Wembley has hosted the European Cup/Champions League final on a record six occasions, and will also be the venue for the 2013 final.

ARSÈNE WENGER

Born: Strasbourg, France, 22nd October 1949
Managerial career:
1984-87 Nancy
1987-94 Monaco
1995-96 Nagoya Grampus Eight
1996- Arsenal

Arsenal boss Arsène Wenger is the most successful manager in the Gunners' history, having won the Premier League title three times and the FA Cup on four occasions – although it's now seven years since he last held a trophy aloft.

• After a modest playing career which included a stint with his local club Strasbourg, Wenger cut his managerial teeth with Nancy before moving to Monaco in 1987. He won the league title in his first season there, with a team including English stars Glenn Hoddle and Mark Hateley, and the

French Cup in 1991.

• Following a year in Japan with Nagoya Grampus Eight, Wenger arrived in north London in September 1996. In his first full season at Highbury he became the first non-British manager to win the league and cup Double, and he repeated this accomplishment in 2002.

• His greatest achievement, though, came in 2004 when his Arsenal side won the title after going through the entire Premiership season undefeated. Wenger's 'Invincibles', as they were dubbed, were hailed as the greatest team in English football history, not only for their record 49-game unbeaten run but also for their fluid attacking style of play which made the most of exceptional talents like Thierry Henry, Dennis Bergkamp and Patrick Vieira.

• Despite all his domestic triumphs, Wenger has found success in Europe elusive. In 2000 his Gunners side lost on penalties to Galatasaray in the UEFA Cup final and, even more painfully, his team narrowly lost to Barcelona in the 2006 Champions League final in Paris.

WEST BROMWICH ALBION

Year founded: 1878
Ground: The Hawthorns (26,272)
Previous name: West Bromwich Strollers
Nickname: The Baggies
Biggest win: 12-0 v Darwen (1892)
Heaviest defeat: 3-10 v Stoke City (1937)

Founded as West Bromwich Strollers in 1878 by workers at the local Salter's Spring Works, the club adopted the suffix 'Albion' two years later and were founder members of the Football League in 1888.

• The Baggies were the first club to lose two consecutive FA Cup finals, going down to Blackburn Rovers in 1886 and Aston Villa the following year. In 1888, though, West Brom recorded the first of their five triumphs in the cup, beating favourites Preston 2-1 in the final.

Arsenal's seven-year trophyless run has made Arsène Wenger rather tetchy...

• In 1931 West Brom became the first and only club to win promotion and the FA Cup in the same season. The Baggies came close to repeating this particular double in 2008, when they topped the Championship but were beaten in the FA Cup semi-finals by eventual winners Portsmouth.

• **West Brom claimed their only league title in 1920, in the first post-First World War season. The 60 points they amassed that season and the 104 goals they scored were both records at the time.**

• In 1966 West Brom won the last League Cup final to be played over two legs, overcoming West Ham 5-3 on aggregate. The next year they appeared in the first one-off final at Wembley, but surprisingly lost 3-2 to Third Division QPR after leading 2-0 at half-time.

• **The Baggies, though, returned to Wembley the following season and beat Everton 1-0 in the FA Cup final. West Brom's winning goal was scored in extra-time by club legend Jeff Astle, who in the process became one of just 12 players to have scored in every round of the competition. Astle also found the target in his side's 2-1 defeat by Manchester City in the 1970 League Cup final to become the first player to score in both domestic cup finals at Wembley.**

• In 1892 West Brom thrashed Darwen 12-0 to record their biggest-ever win. The score set a record for the top flight which has never been beaten, although Nottingham Forest equalled it in 1909. The Baggies' worst ever defeat came in 1937 when they suffered a 10-3 thrashing at the hands of Stoke City.

• **Cult hero Tony 'Bomber' Brown is West Brom's record scorer with 218 league goals to his name. The attacking midfielder is also the club's longest-serving player, turning out in 574**

IS THAT A FACT?

Manager of West Brom from 1902 to 1948, Fred Everiss holds the record for the longest time in charge of a Football League club. Highlights of his long reign included leading the Baggies to the league title in 1920 and the FA Cup in 1931.

league games between 1963 and 1980.

• In the 2004/05 season West Brom became the first club to avoid relegation from the Premiership after propping up the table at Christmas. However, the Baggies went down the following season and have since become something of a yo-yo club, making their most recent return to the top flight in 2010.

• **The club's record purchase is Republic of Ireland striker Shane Long, who joined the Baggies from Reading for £6.5 million in August 2011. The club's bank balance was boosted by a record £8.5 million when gangly defender Curtis Davies joined local rivals Aston Villa in 2008.**

• Among the famous faces who regularly attend matches at the Hawthorns are comedians Lenny Henry and Frank Skinner, and ITV football presenter Adrian Chiles.

HONOURS
Division 1 champions 1920
Division 2 champions 1902, 1911
Championship champions 2008
FA Cup 1888, 1892, 1931, 1954, 1968
League Cup 1966

WEST HAM UNITED

Year founded: 1895
Ground: Upton Park (35,016)
Previous name: Thames Ironworks
Nickname: The Hammers
Biggest win: 10-0 v Bury (1983)
Heaviest defeat: 2-8 v Blackburn (1963)

The club was founded in 1895 as Thames Ironworks by shipyard workers employed by a company of the same name. In 1900 the club was disbanded but immediately reformed under its present name.

• **The biggest and best supported club in east London, West Ham have a proud tradition in the FA Cup. In 1923 they reached the first final to be played at the original Wembley stadium, losing 2-0 to Bolton Wanderers.**

• The Hammers experienced a more enjoyable Wembley 'first' in 1965 when they became the first English side to win a European trophy on home soil, defeating Munich 1860 2-0 in the final

of the Cup Winners' Cup.

• **The following year West Ham were the only club to provide three members – Bobby Moore, Geoff Hurst and Martin Peters – of England's World Cup-winning team. Between them Hurst and Peters scored all four of England's goals in the final against West Germany while Moore, as captain, collected the trophy. The Hammers trio's remarkable contribution to the victory is commemorated by a statue near Upton Park.**

• Striker Vic Watson holds three significant goalscoring records for the club. He is West Ham's leading scorer, with an impressive 298 goals league between 1920 and 1935, including a record 42 goals in the 1929/30 season. In the same campaign Watson hit a record six goals in a match, a feat later equalled by Geoff Hurst in an 8-0 drubbing of Sunderland at Upton Park in 1968.

• **No West Ham player has turned out more often for the club than former manager Billy Bonds. Between 1967 and 1988 'Bonzo', as he was dubbed by fans and team-mates alike, appeared in 663 league games.**

• In 1980 West Ham became the last club from outside the top flight to win the FA Cup. The Hammers, then residing in the old Second Division, beat favourites Arsenal 1-0 thanks to a rare headed goal by Trevor Brooking. The east Londoners also won the cup in 1975, beating Fulham 2-0 – the last time that the winners have fielded an all-English line-up.

• **The legendary Bobby Moore is the club's most-capped international. He played 108 times for England to set a record that has since only been passed by Peter Shilton and David Beckham.**

• In their long and distinguished history West Ham have had just 14 managers, fewer than any other major English club. The longest serving of the lot was Syd King, who held the reins for 31 years from 1901 to 1932.

• **On Boxing Day 2006 Teddy Sheringham became the oldest player ever to score in the Premier League when he netted for West Ham against Portsmouth aged 40 years and 266 days. Four days later he made his last appearance for the Hammers at Manchester City, stretching his own record as the oldest outfield player in the league's history.**

• In March 2011 West Ham's bid to take over the Olympic Stadium in Stratford after the London games was approved by the Olympic Park Legacy Committee. The proposed move later ran into difficulties, but the club remain the favourites to move into the stadium after the games.

• Famous fans of the Hammers include comedians James Corden and Russell Brand, and *Bend It Like Beckham* actress Keira Knightly.

WIGAN ATHLETIC

Year founded: 1932
Ground: DW Stadium (25,138)
Nickname: The Latics
Biggest win: 7-1 v Scarborough (1997)
Heaviest defeat: 1-9 v Tottenham Hotspur (2009)

The club was founded at a public meeting at the Queen's Hotel in 1932 as successors to Wigan Borough, who the previous year had become the first ever club to resign from the Football League.

• After 34 failed attempts, including a bizarre application to join the Scottish Second Division in 1972, Wigan were finally elected to the old Fourth Division in 1978 in place of Southport. The Latics' fortunes, though, only really changed for the better in 1995 when local millionaire and owner of JJB Sports Dave Whelan bought the club and announced his intention to bring Premier League football to the rugby-mad town within 10 years.

• Remarkably, Whelan's dream was fulfilled exactly a decade later when Wigan clinched promotion to the

IS THAT A FACT?
During the 2011/12 season Wigan committed more fouls than any other Premier League team: 485, or an average of 12.76 per match.

Premiership with a 3-1 home win over Reading. Since then, the Latics have confounded the sceptics by retaining their Premier League status, despite regularly being among the pre-season favourites for the drop, and they are the only English club that has played in the top flight and never been relegated from it.

• **In 2006 Wigan played in a major cup final for the first time in their history when they took on Manchester United in the Carling Cup final at the Millennium Stadium in Cardiff. However, the Latics went home empty-handed after losing 4-0.**

• In November 2009 Wigan were hammered 9-1 at Tottenham, only the second time in Premier League history that a side had conceded nine goals. The eight goals the Latics let in after the break was a record for a Premiership half.

• **The club's record goalscorer is Andy Liddell, who hit 70 league goals between 1998 and 2003. Graeme Jones scored a season's best 31 goals in 1996/97 when Wigan were crowned champions of the Third Division (now League Two).**

• No player has pulled on Wigan's blue-and-white stripes more often than Kevin Langley, who made 317 league appearances in two spells at the club between 1981 and 1994.

• **Wigan's longest-serving manager is Paul Jewell, who was in charge at the DW Stadium for six years between 2001 and 2007.**

• In June 2009 Wigan received a club record £16 million when they sold Ecuadorian winger Antonio Valencia to Manchester United. The following year they spent £6.5 million on their most expensive purchase, Estudiantes striker Mauro Boselli.

JACK WILSHERE

Born: Stevenage, 1st January 1992
Position: Midfielder
Club career:
2008- Arsenal 37 (1)
2009-10 Bolton Wanderers (loan) 14 (1)
International record:
2010- England 5 (0)

Arsenal starlet Jack Wilshire

Tipped as a possible future England captain, Jack Wilshere is one of the emerging stars of the English game. His brilliant performances for Arsenal during the 2010/11 season were rewarded when he was voted PFA Young Player of the Year and named in the PFA Team of the Year.

• **The youngest player to appear for Arsenal in the league, Jack Wilshere was aged 16 and 256 days when he made his Premier League debut for the Gunners against Blackburn in September 2008. Two months later he became only the fifth 16-year-old in history to play in the Champions League when he came on as a sub against Dynamo Kiev.**

• In January 2010 Wilshere went on loan to Bolton, where his dribbling and passing skills impressed both Wanderers fans and neutrals alike. Bolton manager Owen Coyle was keen to keep him at the Reebok, but Arsène Wenger was confident that Wilshere could hold down a place in Arsenal's first team and called him back to the Emirates.

• **Then England manager Fabio Capello proved to be another admirer of Wilshere's talents, giving the youngster an England debut as a sub against Hungary at Wembley in August 2010. The following year he made his first start for his country, starring in a 3-1 friendly win away to Denmark. However, he missed out on Euro 2012 after injury sidelined him for the whole of the 2011/12 campaign.**

WOLVERHAMPTON WANDERERS

Year founded: 1877
Ground: Molineux (31,500)
Previous name: St Luke's
Nickname: Wolves
Biggest win: 14-0 v Cresswell's Brewery
Heaviest defeat: 1-10 v Newton Heath

Founded as St Luke's by pupils at a local school of that name in 1877, the club adopted its present name after merging with Blakenhall Wanderers two years later. Wolves were founder members of the Football League in 1888, finishing the first season in third place behind champions Preston and Aston Villa.

• The Black Country club enjoyed their heyday in the 1950s under manager Stan Cullis, a pioneer of long ball 'kick and rush' tactics. After a number of near misses, Wolves were crowned league champions for the first time in their history in 1954 and won two more titles later in the decade to cement their reputation as the top English club of the era.

• When Wolves won a number of high-profile friendlies against foreign opposition in the 1950s in some of the first-ever televised matches they were hailed as 'champions of the world' by the national press, a claim which helped inspire the creation of the European Cup. In 1958 Wolves became only the second English team to compete in the competition, following in the footsteps of trailblazers Manchester United.

• The skipper of that great Wolves team, centre half Billy Wright, is the club's most-capped international. Between 1946 and 1959 he won a then record 105 caps for England, captaining his country in 90 of those games.

• Steve Bull is Wolves' record scorer with an incredible haul of 250 league goals between 1986 and 1999. His impressive total of 306 goals in all competitions included a record 18 hat-tricks for the club.

• Stalwart defender Derek Parkin has pulled on the famous gold shirt more often than any other player, making 501 appearances in the league between 1967 and 1982.

• In 1972 Wolves reached the final of the UEFA Cup, losing 3-2 on aggregate to Tottenham in the first-ever European final between two English clubs. Two years later the club won the League Cup for the first time, beating Manchester City 2-1 in the final, and in 1980 they repeated that success thanks to a single goal by Andy Gray in the final against Nottingham Forest.

• Wolves were the first team in the country to win all four divisions of the Football League, completing the 'full house' in 1989 when they won the old Third Division title a year after claiming the Fourth Division championship.

• In June 2009 newly-promoted Wolves spent a club record £6.5 million on Reading striker Kevin Doyle, and they splashed out the same amount a year later on Burnley's Steven Fletcher. In August 2012 Fletcher moved on to Sunderland for a club record £14 million.

• In December 2006 Wolves became the first club to score 7,000 league goals, although they have since fallen behind Manchester United in the all-time goalscoring stakes.

• Wolves' most famous fan is veteran singer Robert Plant, formerly the front man of rock legends Led Zeppelin.

HONOURS
Division 1 champions 1954, 1958, 1959
Division 2 champions 1932, 1977
Championship champions 2009
Division 3 (North) champions 1924
Division 3 champions 1989
Division 4 champions 1988
FA Cup 1893, 1908, 1949, 1960
League Cup 1974, 1980
Football League Trophy 1988

Girl Power! Record crowds for women's football turned up to watch Team GB at the 2012 Olympics

WOMEN'S FOOTBALL

The first recorded women's football match took place between the north and south of England at Crouch End, London in 1895. The north won the game 7-1.

• The Women's FA was founded in 1969 and the first Women's FA Cup final took place two years later, Southampton beating Stewart and Thistle 4-1. The Saints went on to win the cup another seven times in the next 10 years, but the most successful side in the competition are Arsenal with 11 victories.

• The Women's Premier League (WPL) was formed in 1992. Again Arsenal have the best record in the competition with a total of 12 league titles to their name including seven on the trot from 2004-10. In a bid to attract more fans to games the top flight was reorganised in 2011 as a semi-professional summer league consisting of eight clubs, the FA Women's Super League, with the WPL becoming the second tier. Sunderland won the first Super League title and retained the trophy in 2012.

• The first British international women's match took place in 1972 when England beat Scotland 3-2. In 2005 England recorded their biggest ever win, thrashing Hungary 13-0. Their worst defeat was in 2000 when Norway won 8-0. Well-known players in the England team include captain Casey Stoney, winger Rachel Yankey and striker Kelly Smith.

• Since it was first competed for in China in 1991 there have been six Women's World Cup tournaments. The USA were the first winners and also lifted the trophy in 1999, while Germany are the only other country to have won the tournament twice (in 2003 and 2007). The holders are Japan who beat the United States on penalties in the 2011 final in Germany.

• The joint top scorers in the World Cup are Birgit Prinz (Germany) and Marta (Brazil) with 14 goals. In 2003 Prinz was offered the chance to join Italian men's side Perugia, but declined the chance to become the first ever woman to play in a professional men's league.

• Germany also hold the record for the biggest win in the tournament, thrashing Argentina 11-0 in 2007.

WORLD CUP

The most successful country in the history of the World Cup are Brazil, who have won the competition a record five times. Italy are Europe's leading nation with four wins, closely followed by three-time winners Germany. South American neighbours Argentina and Uruguay have both won the competition twice, the Uruguayans emerging victorious when the pair met in the first ever World Cup final in Montevideo in 1930. The only other countries to claim the trophy are England, France and Spain, the first two countries taking advantage of their host nation status to win the competition in 1966 and 1998 respectively, while the Spanish triumphed in South Africa in 2010 thanks to a 1-0 win over Holland in the final.

• Including both Japan and South Korea, who were joint hosts for the 2002 edition, the World Cup has been held in 15 different countries. The first nation to stage the tournament twice was Mexico (in 1970 and 1986), while Italy (1934 and 1990), France (1938 and 1998) and Germany (1974 and 2006) have also welcomed the world to the planet's biggest football festival on two occasions each. Brazil will host the tournament for a second time in 2014, while Russia (2018) and Qatar (2022) will get their first opportunity in the near future.

• As well as their unique quintet of World Cup victories, Brazil hold a host of lesser records in the competition. The South Americans are the only country to have played at all 19 tournaments, and along with Germany have played in a record seven finals. Brazil, though, are out in front when it comes to total wins (67) and total goals scored (210, including more than a few 25-yard screamers into the top corner from the likes of Rivelino, Zico and Kaka!).

It's easy to fall in love with the World Cup trophy but beware, kiss it and you turn orange!

this day that his shot bounced on the line after striking the crossbar, rather than over it. Naturally, England fans generally agree with the eagle-eyed Russian linesman, Tofik Bahramov, who awarded the goal...

• Just two players have appeared at a record five World Cups: Germany's midfield playmaker Lothar Matthaus (1982-98) and Mexican goalkeeper Antonio Carbajal (1950-66). Matthaus, though, holds the record for games played, making 25 appearances for his country.

• **Germany are the most successful side in World Cup shoot-outs, winning all four of their penalty duels including one in 1990 when they beat Bobby Robson's plucky England side in the semi-finals before going on to lift the trophy.**

• England may have endured some bitter disappointments at the tournament (including two more shoot-out defeats against Argentina in 1998 and Portugal in 2006) but the most unfortunate country in World Cup history are arch rivals Scotland, who have made eight appearances at the finals without once advancing to the knock-out stages.

• **The youngest player to appear at the finals is Norman Whiteside, who was just 17 years and 41 days when he made his World Cup debut for Northern Ireland against Yugoslavia at the 1982 tournament in Spain. The competition's oldest player, meanwhile, is Cameroon's Roger Milla, who was aged 42 years and 39 days when he played against Russia in 1994.** It was hardly a day to remember for the swivel-hipped striker, though, as Russia won 6-1 with a record five goals coming from the boot of Oleg Salenko.

• Just two men have won the competition as both a player and a coach: Brazil's Mario Zagallo (in 1958, 1962 and 1970) and Germany's Franz Beckenbauer (in 1974 and 1990).

• **Switzerland went a record 551 minutes without conceding a goal at the 2006 and 2010 World Cups, their fortress-like defence finally being breached by Chile's Mark Gonzalez in a 1-0 defeat in Port Elizabeth, South Africa.**

• In their opening game at the 2010 World Cup Spain went down 1-0 to Switzerland. However, the Spanish recovered to win their group and went on to claim the trophy, to become the first country to lift the World Cup after losing their first match. Spain also set a

• However, Hungary hold the record for the most goals scored in a single tournament, banging in 27 in just five games at the 1954 finals in Switzerland. Even this incredible tally, though, was not quite sufficient for the 'Magical Magyars' to lift the trophy as they went down to a 3-2 defeat in the final against West Germany, a team they had beaten 8-3 earlier in the tournament.

• Hungary also hold the record for the biggest ever victory at the finals, demolishing El Salvador 10-1 in 1982. That, though, was a desperately close encounter compared to the biggest win in qualifying, Australia's 31-0 annihilation of American Samoa in 2001, a game in which Aussie striker Archie Thompson helped himself to a record 13 goals.

• **The legendary Pele is the only player in World Cup history to have been presented with three winners' medals.** The Brazilian superstar enjoyed his first

success in 1958 when he scored twice in a 5-2 rout of hosts Sweden in the final, and was a winner again four years later in Chile despite hobbling out of the tournament with a torn leg muscle in the second match. He then made it a hat-trick in 1970, setting a sparkling Brazil side on the road to an emphatic 4-1 victory against Italy in the final with a trademark bullet header.

• The leading overall scorer in the World Cup is another famous Brazilian, Ronaldo, who notched 15 goals in total at three tournaments between 1998 and 2006, including both goals in his side's 2-0 defeat of Germany in the 2002 final.

• **England's Geoff Hurst had previously gone one better in 1966, scoring a hat-trick as the hosts beat West Germany 4-2 in the final at Wembley. His second goal, which gave England a decisive 3-2 lead in extra-time, was the most controversial in World Cup history and German fans still argue to

new record for the fewest goals scored by the tournament winner after finding the net just eight times in their seven games in South Africa.

WORLD CUP FINALS
1930 Uruguay 4 Argentina 2 (Uruguay)
1934 Italy 2 Czechoslovakia 1 (Italy)
1938 Italy 4 Hungary 2 (France)
1950 Uruguay 2 Brazil 1 (Brazil)
1954 West Germany 3 Hungary 2 (Switzerland)
1958 Brazil 5 Sweden 2 (Sweden)
1962 Brazil 3 Czechoslovakia 1 (Chile)
1966 England 4 West Germany 2 (England)
1970 Brazil 4 Italy 1 (Mexico)
1974 West Germany 2 Holland 1 (West Germany)
1978 Argentina 3 Holland 1 (Argentina)
1982 Italy 3 West Germany 1 (Spain)
1986 Argentina 3 West Germany 2 (Mexico)
1990 West Germany 1 Argentina 0 (Italy)
1994 Brazil 0 Italy 0 (USA)*
1998 France 3 Brazil 0 (France)
2002 Brazil 2 Germany 0 (Japan/South Korea)
2006 Italy 1 France 1 (Germany)*
2010 Spain 1 Holland 0 (South Africa)
* Won on penalties

WORLD CUP GOLDEN BALL

The Golden Ball is awarded to the best player at the World Cup following a poll of members of the global media. The first winner was Italian striker Paolo Rossi, whose six goals at the 1982 World Cup helped the Azzurri win that year's tournament in Spain.

• **Rossi was followed in 1986 by another World Cup winner, Argentina captain Diego Maradona, but since then only one player has claimed the**

IS THAT A FACT?
Only two players have won the World Cup Golden Ball and Golden Boot at the same tournament, Italian strikers Paolo Rossi (1982) and Salvatore Schillaci (1990).

Golden Ball and a winners' medal at the same tournament, Brazilian striker Romario in 1994.

• The only goalkeeper to win the award to date is Germany's Oliver Kahn in 2002. The most controversial winner, meanwhile, was France's mercurial midfielder Zinedine Zidane, who was named as the outstanding performer at the 2006 World Cup before the final – a game which ended in disgrace for Zidane after he was sent off for headbutting Italian defender Marco Materazzi.

WORLD CUP GOLDEN BALL WINNERS
1982 Paolo Rossi (Italy)
1986 Diego Maradona (Argentina)
1990 Salvatore Schillaci (Italy)
1994 Romario (Brazil)
1998 Ronaldo (Brazil)
2002 Oliver Kahn (Germany)
2006 Zinedine Zidane (France)
2010 Diego Forlan (Uruguay)

WORLD CUP GOLDEN BOOT

Now officially known as the 'Adidas Golden Shoe', the Golden Boot is awarded to the player who scores most goals in a World Cup finals tournament. The first winner was Guillermo Stabile, whose eight goals helped Argentina reach the final in 1930.

• French striker Just Fontaine scored a record 13 goals at the 1958 tournament in Sweden. At the other end of the scale, nobody managed

more than four goals at the 1962 World Cup in Chile, so the award was shared between six players.

• Surprisingly, it wasn't until 1978 that the Golden Boot was won outright by a player, Argentina's Mario Kempes, whose country also won the tournament. Since then only Italy's Paolo Rossi in 1982 and Brazil's Ronaldo in 2002 have won both the Golden Boot and a World Cup-winners' medal in the same year.

• **The only English player to win the Golden Boot is Gary Lineker, whose six goals in 1986 helped the Three Lions reach the quarter-finals in Mexico.**

• At the 2010 World Cup in South Africa Germany's Thomas Muller was one of four players to top the scoring charts with five goals, but FIFA's new rules gave him the Golden Boot because he had more assists than his three rivals for the award, David Villa, Wesley Sneijder and Diego Forlan.

WORLD FOOTBALLER OF THE YEAR

Now merged with the European Footballer of the Year award as the FIFA Ballon d'Or, the FIFA World Footballer of the Year was awarded between 1991 and 2009. The first winner was Lothar Matthaus of Germany, who topped a poll of international team coaches.

• **Two players, Brazilian striker Ronaldo and France's midfield maestro Zinedine Zidane, won the award a record three times. Ronaldo picked up the award in 1996, 1997 and 2002,**

Lionel Messi holds aloft the Ballon d'Or trophy

while Zidane was honoured in 1998, 2000 and 2003. Argetina's Lionel Messi was named World Footballer of the Year in 2009 and claimed the first two FIFA Ballon d'Or awards in 2010 and 2011 to give him three in total.

• Brazilian players won the award a record eight times. No English player ever won the award, although David Beckham was a runner-up in both 1999 and 2001 and Frank Lampard came second in 2005.

• The oldest winner of the World Footballer of the Year award was 33-year-old Fabio Cannavaro in 2006. The youngest winner was Ronaldo, who was just 20 when he first won the award in 1996.

• Readers of *World Soccer* magazine have voted for their own World Footballer of the Year since 1982, when Italy's Paolo Rossi topped the poll. The only player to win the award three times is Ronaldo (in 1996, 1997 and 2002), while the only English player to head the list was Michael Owen in 2001.

WYCOMBE WANDERERS

Year founded: 1887
Ground: Adams Park (10,284)
Nickname: The Chairboys
Biggest win: 15-1 v Witney Town (1955)
Heaviest defeat: 0-8 v Reading (1899)

Wycombe Wanderers were founded in 1887 by a group of young furniture-makers (hence the club's nickname, The Chairboys) but had to wait until 1993 before earning promotion to the Football League.

• **Under then manager Martin O'Neill the club went up to the Second Division (now League One) in their first season, beating Preston in the play-off final.**

• In 2001 The Chairboys caused a sensation by reaching the semi-finals of the FA Cup where they lost 2-1 to eventual winners Liverpool at Villa Park.

• **Wycombe also reached the semi-finals of the Carling Cup in 2007, but were beaten 5-1 on aggregate by eventual winners Chelsea.**

• Combative midfielder Steve Brown made a club record 371 league appearances for Wycombe between 1994 and 2004.

HONOURS
Conference champions 1993
FA Amateur Cup 1931

XAVI

Born: Barcelona, 25th January 1980
Position: Midfielder
Club career:
1997-2000 Barcelona B 61 (4)
1998- Barcelona 414 (48)
International record:
2000- Spain 115 (11)

The creative heartbeat of Barcelona's hypnotic tiki-taka passing game, Xavi has come through the club's fabled youth system to head the list of the Catalans' appearance makers, having played in 629 games in all competitions (including 126 Champions League matches, another club record).

• **Since making his debut for Barca in 1998, Xavi has won an Aladdin's Cave of silverware, including five La Liga titles and three Champions League winners' medals. His outstanding individual contribution to his team's success was recognised in 2010 when he was voted the third-best player in the world, behind club-mates Lionel Messi and Andres Iniesta, for the inaugural FIFA Ballon d'Or award. In the same year he was voted World Player of the Year by the readers of *World Soccer* magazine.**

• Xavi first played for Spain in 2000 and is now one of just five players to have won a century of caps for his country. In 2008 he was voted Player of the Tournament when Spain won the European Championships and, two years later, he was a key member of the Spanish side that won the World Cup for the first time after beating Holland in the final in South Africa.

• **To nobody's surprise he was a vastly**

influential figure at Euro 2012, making more passes than any other player at the tournament and setting up two goals in the final as Spain ran riot, thrashing Italy 4-0 to win a third successive international trophy.

YEOVIL TOWN

Year founded: 1890
Ground: Huish Park (9,665)
Previous names: Yeovil, Yeovil Casuals
Nickname: The Glovers
Biggest win: 12-1 v Westbury United (1923)
Heaviest defeat: 0-8 v Manchester United (1949)

Founded in 1890, initially as Yeovil and then as Yeovil Casuals (1895-1907), the club had to wait until 2003 before finally entering the Football League when they were promoted as Conference champions by a record 17 points margin.

Spanish pass-master Xavi

• Before they made it into League Two, Yeovil were famed FA Cup giant-killers, knocking out no fewer than 20 league clubs – a record for a non-league outfit. Their most notable scalp came in 1949 when they beat Sunderland 2-1 in the fourth round on their famously sloping Huish Park pitch.

• That legendary match was watched by a club record crowd of 17,123, around twice the capacity of the new Huish Park. Sadly for their loyal fans, the Glovers fell to an 8-0 defeat against reigning cup holders Manchester United in the next round, still the club's record loss.

• Stalwart striker Dave Taylor scored a club record 285 goals for Yeovil during their non-league days, including an impressive 59 in 1960/61 – another club record.

HONOURS
League Two champions 2005
Conference champions 2003

YORK CITY

Year founded: 1922
Ground: Bootham Crescent (7,872)
Nickname: The Minstermen
Biggest win: 9-1 v Southport (1957)
Heaviest defeat: 0-12 v Chester City (1936)

Founded in 1922 by former members of an amateur club of the same name, York City joined the Football League in 1929 and rose as high as the old Division Two in the mid-1970s. The Minstermen lost their league status in 2004 but bounced back in 2012 after beating Luton Town 2-1 in the Conference play-off final at Wembley.

• York have a proud tradition in the FA Cup, reaching the semi-final in 1955 before losing to eventual winners Newcastle in a replay. In 1985, a year after becoming the first club to amass 100 points in a season while topping Division Four, the Minstermen performed more FA Cup heroics by beating mighty Arsenal 1-0 in the fourth round.

• Perhaps, though, the club's most famous victory came in 1995 when they sensationally beat Manchester United 3-0

Ashley Young sets off on another dribble

at Old Trafford in a League Cup tie – one of the most humiliating defeats suffered by the Red Devils in their long history.

• In 2009 York City and their opponents Kidderminster Harriers set a new record for a penalty shoot-out in England by successfully converting the first 25 of their spot-kicks in an FA Trophy tie. York eventually won the epic penalty duel 13-12.

HONOURS
Division 4 champions 1984

ASHLEY YOUNG

Born: Stevenage, 9th July 1985
Position: Winger
Club career:
2002-07 Watford 98 (19)
2007-11 Aston Villa 156 (30)
2011- Manchester United 24 (6)
International record:
2007- England 26 (6)

During the 2011/12 season nippy Manchester United winger Ashley Young became the first England player to score in four straight international appearances since Wayne Rooney three years earlier, finding the net against Wales, Montenegro, Holland and Norway. Less happily, he missed his penalty in the quarter-final shoot-out against Italy at Euro 2012, a tournament at which he failed to shine.

• Young began his career at Watford, scoring on his debut for the Hornets against Millwall in 2003. He was voted Watford's Young Player of the Year in 2005 and the following season his 15 goals helped the club reach the Premiership after beating Leeds 3-0 in the play-off final.

• In January 2007 Young joined Aston Villa for a then club record £9.75 million and later that month he scored on his Villa debut in a 3-1 defeat at Newcastle. His dashing displays for the Birmingham club earned him three FA Premiership Player of the Month awards in 2008,